Course:
**Ways of Knowing**
**HCom 301**

**Dr. John Berteaux**

California State University Monterey
Bay
Philosophy, Pre Law, and Peace Studies

## McGraw-Hill

*A Division of The* **McGraw·Hill** *Companies*

**McGraw–Hill Primis**
ISBN–10: 0–39–015078–9
ISBN–13: 978–0–39–015078–3

Text:

Discourses
**Abel**

Modern Epistemology: A New Introduction
**Everitt–Fisher**

The Feminist Philosophy Reader
**Bailey–Cuomo**

Copernican Questions: A Concise Invitation
to the Philosophy of Science
**Parsons**

and others . . .

111   NULLGEN   ISBN–10: 0–39–015078–9   ISBN–13: 978–0–39–015078–3

# Contents

# The Problems of Philosophy

Bertrand Russell

Bertrand Russell was born in Trelleck, Wales, in 1872. Both his parents died when he was young, and he and his older brother were raised by their paternal grandmother. Bertrand received his initial education from governesses and tutors. In 1890 he enrolled in Cambridge University, where he studied mathematics and then philosophy, receiving his degree in 1894. Russell was a fellow at Cambridge from 1895 to 1901 and a lecturer in philosophy from 1910 to 1916. In 1908 he became a member of the Royal Society. After his lectureship at Cambridge, Russell supported himself by writing and giving public lectures. On the death of his brother in 1931, he became Earl Russell. He moved to the United States in 1938, teaching first at the University of Chicago and then at the University of California at Los Angeles. He lectured at the Barnes Foundation in Philadelphia from 1941 to 1943. The following year he returned to England, having been invited to become a fellow again at Cambridge. In 1949 he became an honorary member of the British Academy and received the Order of Merit. The following year he was awarded the Nobel Prize for Literature. Russell died in 1970 near Penryndeudraeth, Wales, at the age of ninety-seven.

Russell's numerous works include *The Principles of Mathematics* (1903), *Principia Mathematica* (coauthored with Alfred North Whitehead; 3 volumes, 1910, 1912, 1913), *The Problems of Philosophy* (1912), *Our Knowledge of the External World* (1914), *The Conquest of Happiness* (1930), *An Inquiry into Meaning and Truth* (1940), and *A History of Western Philosophy* (1945).

Our reading is from the final chapter of *The Problems of Philosophy*, "The Value of Philosophy." Russell argues that, although philosophy does not enhance our physical well-being, it greatly enriches our mental lives. This enrichment does not come from providing definitive answers to philosophical questions, for practically all philosophical questions remain undecided. For example, no one has ever proved—or is likely ever to prove—that the universe has or does not have a purpose. For Russell, the uncertainty in philosophy is an asset rather than a liability: By teaching us to inquire about the universe and to question our ordinary beliefs, philosophy liberates us from the prejudices of common sense, culture, and custom. Although philosophy does not provide definite answers about how things *are*, it broadens our mind by showing us many different ways that they *might* be.

A further value of philosophy, according to Russell, is its ability to free us from our instinctive tendency to interpret everything in terms of self. By attempting to see the universe as it is, rather than simply how it affects us, we enlarge our self by leaving behind (as much as is possible) our hopes and fears, our preconceptions and prejudices. And when we enlarge our self, we also enlarge the sphere of our actions and affections.

▼

## Chapter 15: The Value of Philosophy

Having now come to the end of our brief and very incomplete review of the problems of philosophy, it will be well to consider, in conclusion, what is the value of philosophy and why it ought to be studied. It is the more necessary to consider this question, in view of the fact that many men, under the influence of science or of practical affairs, are inclined to doubt whether philosophy is anything better than innocent but useless trifling,

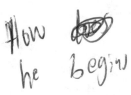
How did he begin

hair-splitting distinctions, and controversies on matters concerning which knowledge is impossible.

This view of philosophy appears to result, partly from a wrong conception of the ends of life, partly from a wrong conception of the kind of goods which philosophy strives to achieve. Physical science, through the medium of inventions, is useful to innumerable people who are wholly ignorant of it; thus the study of physical science is to be recommended, not only, or primarily, because of the effect on the student, but rather because of the effect on mankind in general. This utility does not belong to philosophy. If the study of philosophy has any value at all for others than students of philosophy, it must be only indirectly, through its effects upon the lives of those who study it. It is in these effects, therefore, if anywhere, that the value of philosophy must be primarily sought.

But further, if we are not to fail in our endeavour to determine the value of philosophy, we must first free our minds from the prejudices of what are wrongly called "practical" men. The "practical" man, as this word is often used, is one who recognises only material needs, who realises that men must have food for the body, but is oblivious of the necessity of providing food for the mind. If all men were well off, if poverty and disease had been reduced to their lowest possible point, there would still remain much to be done to produce a valuable society; and even in the existing world the goods of the mind are at least as important as the goods of the body. It is exclusively among the goods of the mind that the value of philosophy is to be found; and only those who are not indifferent to these goods can be persuaded that the study of philosophy is not a waste of time.

Philosophy, like all other studies, aims primarily at knowledge. The knowledge it aims at is the kind of knowledge which gives unity and system to the body of the sciences, and the kind which results from a critical examination of the grounds of our convictions, prejudices, and beliefs. But it cannot be maintained that philosophy has had any very great measure of success in its attempts to provide definite answers to its questions. If you ask a mathematician, a mineralogist, a historian, or any other man of learning, what definite body of truths has been ascertained by his science, his answer will last as long as you are willing to listen. But if you put the same question to a philosopher, he will, if he is candid, have to confess that his study has not achieved positive results such as have been achieved by other sciences. It is true that this is partly accounted for by the fact that, as soon as definite knowledge concerning any subject becomes possible, this subject ceases to be called philosophy, and becomes a separate science. The whole study of the heavens, which now belongs to astronomy, was once included in philosophy; Newton's great work was called "the mathematical principles of natural philosophy." Similarly, the study of the human mind, which was, until very lately, a part of philosophy, has now been separated from philosophy and has become the science of psychology. Thus, to a great extent, the uncertainty of philosophy is more apparent than real:

those questions which are already capable of definite answers are placed in the sciences, while those only to which, at present, no definite answer can be given, remain to form the residue which is called philosophy.

This is, however, only a part of the truth concerning the uncertainty of philosophy. There are many questions—and among them those that are of the profoundest interest to our spiritual life—which, so far as we can see, must remain insoluble to the human intellect unless its powers become of quite a different order from what they are now. Has the universe any unity of plan or purpose, or is it a fortuitous concourse of atoms? Is consciousness a permanent part of the universe, giving hope of indefinite growth in wisdom, or is it a transitory accident on a small planet on which life must ultimately become impossible? Are good and evil of importance to the universe or only to man? Such questions are asked by philosophy, and variously answered by various philosophers. But it would seem that, whether answers be otherwise discoverable or not, the answers suggested by philosophy are none of them demonstrably true. Yet, however slight may be the hope of discovering an answer, it is part of the business of philosophy to continue the consideration of such questions, to make us aware of their importance, to examine all the approaches to them, and to keep alive that speculative interest in the universe which is apt to be killed by confining ourselves to definitely ascertainable knowledge.

Many philosophers, it is true, have held that philosophy could establish the truth of certain answers to such fundamental questions. They have supposed that what is of most importance in religious beliefs could be proved by strict demonstration to be true. In order to judge of such attempts, it is necessary to take a survey of human knowledge, and to form an opinion as to its methods and its limitations. On such a subject it would be unwise to pronounce dogmatically; but if the investigations of our previous chapters have not led us astray, we shall be compelled to renounce the hope of finding philosophical proofs of religious beliefs. We cannot, therefore, include as part of the value of philosophy any definite set of answers to such questions. Hence, once more, the value of philosophy must not depend upon any supposed body of definitely ascertainable knowledge to be acquired by those who study it.

The value of philosophy is, in fact, to be sought largely in its very uncertainty. The man who has no tincture of philosophy goes through life imprisoned in the prejudices derived from common sense, from the habitual beliefs of his age or his nation, and from convictions which have grown up in his mind without the cooperation or consent of his deliberate reason. To such a man the world tends to become definite, finite, obvious; common objects rouse no questions, and unfamiliar possibilities are contemptuously rejected. As soon as we begin to philosophize, on the contrary, we find . . . that even the most everyday things lead to problems to which only very incomplete answers can be given. Philosophy, though unable to tell us with certainty what is the true answer to the doubts which it raises, is able to suggest many possibilities which enlarge our thoughts and free them from the tyranny of custom. Thus, while diminishing our feeling of certainty as to what things are, it greatly increases our knowledge as to what they may be; it removes the somewhat arrogant dogmatism of those who have never travelled into the region of liberating doubt, and it keeps alive our sense of wonder by showing familiar things in an unfamiliar aspect.

Apart from its utility in showing unsuspected possibilities, philosophy has a value—perhaps its chief value—through the greatness of the objects which it contemplates, and the freedom from narrow and personal aims resulting from this contemplation. The life of the instinctive man is shut up within the circle of his private interests: family and friends may be included, but the outer world is not regarded except as it may help or hinder what comes within the circle of instinctive wishes. In such a life there is something feverish and confined, in comparison with which the philosophic life is calm and free. The private world of instinctive interests is a small one, set in the midst of a great and powerful world which must, sooner or later, lay our private world in ruins. Unless we can so enlarge our interests as to include the whole outer world, we remain like a garrison in a beleaguered fortress, knowing that the enemy prevents escape and that ultimate surrender is inevitable. In such a life there is no peace, but a constant strife between the insistence of desire and the powerlessness of will. In one way or another, if our life is to be great and free, we must escape this prison and this strife.

One way of escape is by philosophic contemplation. Philosophic contemplation does not, in its widest survey, divide the universe into two hostile camps—friends and foes, helpful and hostile, good and bad—it views the whole impartially. Philosophic contemplation, when it is unalloyed, does not aim at proving that the rest of the universe is akin to man. All acquisition of knowledge is an enlargement of the Self, but this enlargement is best attained when it is not directly sought. It is obtained when the desire for knowledge is alone operative, by a study which does not wish in advance that its objects should have this or that character, but adapts the Self to the characters which it finds in its objects. This enlargement of Self is not obtained when, taking the Self as it is, we try to show that the world is so similar to this Self that knowledge of it is possible without any admission of what seems alien. The desire to prove this is a form of self-assertion, and like all self-assertion, it is an obstacle to the growth of Self which it desires, and of which the Self knows that it is capable. Self-assertion, in philosophic speculation as elsewhere, views the world as a means to its own ends; thus it makes the world of less account than Self, and the Self sets bounds to the greatness of its goods. In contemplation, on the contrary, we start from the not-Self, and through its greatness the boundaries of Self are enlarged; through the infinity of the universe the mind which contemplates it achieves some share in infinity.

For this reason greatness of soul is not fostered by those philosophies which assimilate the universe to Man. Knowledge is a form of union of Self and not-Self; like all union, it is impaired by dominion, and therefore by any attempt to force the universe into conformity with what we find in ourselves. There is a widespread philosophical tendency towards the view which tells us that man is the measure of all things, that truth is man-made, that space and time and the world of universals[1] are properties of the mind, and that, if there be anything not created by the mind, it is unknowable and of no account for us. This view . . . is untrue; but in addition to being untrue, it has the effect of robbing philosophic contemplation of all that gives it value, since it fetters contemplation to Self. What it calls knowledge is not a union with the not-Self, but a set of prejudices, habits, and desires, making an impenetrable veil between us and the world beyond. The man who finds pleasure in such a theory of knowledge is like the man who never leaves the domestic circle for fear his word might not be law.

The true philosophic contemplation, on the contrary, finds its satisfaction in every enlargement of the not-Self, in everything that magnifies the objects contemplated, and thereby the subject contemplating. Everything, in contemplation, that is personal or private, everything that depends upon habit, self-interest, or desire, distorts the object, and hence impairs the union which the intellect seeks. By thus making a barrier between subject and object, such personal and private things become a prison to the intellect. The free intellect will see as God might see, without a *here* and *now,* without hopes and fears, without the trammels of customary beliefs and traditional prejudices, calmly, dispassionately, in the sole and exclusive desire of knowledge—knowledge as impersonal, as purely contemplative, as it is possible for man to attain. Hence also the free intellect will value more the abstract and universal knowledge into which the accidents of private history do not enter, than the knowledge brought by the senses, and dependent, as such knowledge must be, upon an exclusive and personal point of view and a body whose sense-organs distort as much as they reveal.

The mind which has become accustomed to the freedom and impartiality of philosophic contemplation will preserve something of the same freedom and impartiality in the world of action and emotion. It will view its purposes and desires as parts of the whole, with the absence of insistence that results from seeing them as infinitesimal fragments in a world of which all the rest is unaffected by any one man's deeds. The impartiality which, in contemplation, is the unalloyed desire for truth, is the very same quality of mind which, in action, is justice, and in emotion is that universal love which can be given to all, and not only to those who are judged useful or admirable. Thus contemplation enlarges not only the objects of our thoughts, but also the objects of our actions and our affections: it makes us citizens of the universe, not only of one walled city at war with all the rest. In this citizenship of the universe consists man's true freedom, and his liberation from the thraldom of narrow hopes and fears.

Thus, to sum up our discussion of the value of philosophy: Philosophy is to be studied, not for the sake of any definite answers to its questions, since no definite answers can, as a rule, be known to be true, but rather for the sake of the questions themselves; because these questions enlarge our conception of what is possible, enrich our intellectual imagination, and diminish the dogmatic assurance which closes the mind against speculation; but above all because, through the greatness of the universe which philosophy contemplates, the mind also is rendered great, and becomes capable of that union with the universe which constitutes its highest good.

▶ NOTE

1. *universals:* realities corresponding to general concepts or terms [D.C.A., ed.]

# The Problems of Philosophy

Bertrand Russell

**Reading Questions**

*According to Russell:*

1. How do the goods that philosophy seeks to achieve differ from those that physical science seeks to achieve?

2. What kind of knowledge does philosophy seek to obtain?

3. How does philosophy free us from "the tyranny of custom"?

4. How does philosophical contemplation, by beginning with the not-self, enlarge the self?

5. How does the impartiality of philosophical contemplation carry over into the world of action and emotion?

**Discussion Questions**

*In your own view:*

1. Is it a waste of time to seek the answers to philosophical questions for which we are unlikely ever to find the correct answer? What is your criterion for determining whether something is a waste of time?

2. Is it always good to question our beliefs and customs, or should we simply accept some of them without questioning them?

3. If we are searching for the meaning of life, is it better to turn to religion than to philosophy?

4. Is it beneficial to the self to enlarge the self? Does philosophy help us do this?

5. Does philosophy increase our freedom of thought? of action? of emotion?

# The Problems of Philosophy

Bertrand Russell

Bertrand Russell was born in Trelleck, Wales, in 1872. Both his parents died when he was young, and he and his older brother were raised by their paternal grandmother. Bertrand received his initial education from governesses and tutors. In 1890 he enrolled in Cambridge University, where he studied mathematics and then philosophy, receiving his degree in 1894. Russell was a fellow at Cambridge from 1895 to 1901 and a lecturer in philosophy from 1910 to 1916. In 1908 he became a member of the Royal Society. After his lectureship at Cambridge, Russell supported himself by writing and giving public lectures. On the death of his brother in 1931, he became Earl Russell. He moved to the United States in 1938, teaching first at the University of Chicago and then at the University of California at Los Angeles. He lectured at the Barnes Foundation in Philadelphia from 1941 to 1943. The following year he returned to England, having been invited to become a fellow again at Cambridge. In 1949 he became an honorary member of the British Academy and received the Order of Merit. The following year he was awarded the Nobel Prize for Literature. Russell died in 1970 near Penrhyndeudraeth, Wales, at the age of ninety-seven.

Russell's numerous works include *The Principles of Mathematics* (1903), *Principia Mathematica* (coauthored with Alfred North Whitehead; 3 volumes, 1910, 1912, 1913), *The Problems of Philosophy* (1912), *Our Knowledge of the External World* (1914), *The Conquest of Happiness* (1930), *An Inquiry into Meaning and Truth* (1940), and *A History of Western Philosophy* (1945).

Our reading is from the first two chapters of *The Problems of Philosophy*. In Chapter 1, "Appearance and Reality," Russell describes the paradoxes that arise when we assume that the way physical objects appear to us is the way they really are. For example, a table appears different under different conditions: Its brown color seems lighter under bright light, its smooth texture seems rougher under a microscope. How can I say that the table *really* has one of these colors or textures rather than another? Russell argues that when I perceive a physical object, what I know directly is not the object itself, but my *sense-data* (my perceptions of the object); any statement about the properties of the object is an *inference* and could be mistaken. Moreover, it is theoretically possible that no physical objects exist at all—that the world consists entirely of minds and their ideas. It is even conceivable the world consists entirely of *my* mind and *my* ideas.

In Chapter 2, "The Existence of Matter," Russell argues that although it is theoretically possible that no physical objects exist, it is more reasonable to suppose that they do than that they do not.

▼

## Chapter 1: Appearance and Reality

. . . In daily life, we assume as certain many things which, on a closer scrutiny, are found to be so full of apparent contradictions that only a great amount of thought enables us to know what it is that we really may believe. In the search for certainty, it is natural to begin with our present experiences; and in some sense, no doubt, knowledge is to be derived from them. But any statement as to what it is that our immediate experiences make us know is very likely to be wrong. It seems to me that I am now sitting in a chair, at a table of a certain shape, on which I see sheets of paper with writ-

*Russell's thesis*

ing or print. By turning my head I see out of the window buildings and clouds and the sun. I believe that the sun is about ninety-three million miles from the earth; that it is a hot globe many times bigger than the earth; that, owing to the earth's rotation, it rises every morning, and will continue to do so for an indefinite time in the future. I believe that, if any other normal person comes into my room, he will see the same chairs and tables and books and papers as I see, and that the table which I see is the same as the table which I feel pressing against my arm. All this seems to be so evident as to be hardly worth stating, except in answer to a man who doubts whether I know anything. Yet all this may be reasonably doubted, and all of it requires much careful discussion before we can be sure that we have stated it in a form that is wholly true.

To make our difficulties plain, let us concentrate attention on the table. To the eye it is oblong, brown and shiny, to the touch it is smooth and cool and hard; when I tap it, it gives out a wooden sound. Anyone else who sees and feels and hears the table will agree with this description, so that it might seem as if no difficulty would arise; but as soon as we try to be more precise our troubles begin. Although I believe that the table is "really" of the same colour all over, the parts that reflect the light look much brighter than the other parts, and some parts look white because of reflected light. I know that, if I move, the parts that reflect the light will be different, so that the apparent distribution of colours on the table will change. It follows that if several people are looking at the table at the same moment, no two of them will see exactly the same distribution of colours, because no two can see it from exactly the same point of view, and any change in the point of view makes some change in the way the light is reflected.

For most practical purposes these differences are unimportant, but to the painter they are all-important: the painter has to unlearn the habit of thinking that things seem to have the colour which common sense says they "really" have, and to learn the habit of seeing things as they appear. Here we have already the beginning of one of the distinctions that cause most trouble in philosophy—the distinction between "appearance" and "reality," between what things seem to be and what they are. The painter wants to know what things seem to be, the practical man and the philosopher want to know what they are; but the philosopher's wish to know this is stronger than the practical man's, and is more troubled by knowledge as to the difficulties of answering the question.

To return to the table. It is evident from what we have found, that there is no colour which pre-eminently appears to be *the* colour of the table, or even of any one particular part of the table—it appears to be of different colours from different points of view, and there is no reason for regarding some of these as more really its colour than others. And we know that even from a given point of view the colour will seem different by artificial light, or to a colour-blind man, or to a man wearing blue spectacles, while in the dark there will be no colour at all, though to touch and hearing the table will be unchanged. Thus colour is not something which is inherent in the table, but something depending upon the table and the spectator and the way the light falls on the table. When, in ordinary life, we speak of *the* colour of the table, we only mean the sort of colour which it will seem to have to a normal spectator from an ordinary point of view under usual conditions of light. But the other colours which appear under other conditions have just as good a right to be considered real; and therefore, to avoid favouritism, we are compelled to deny that, in itself, the table has any one particular colour.

The same thing applies to the texture. With the naked eye one can see the grain, but otherwise the table looks smooth and even. If we looked at it through a microscope, we should see roughnesses and hills and valleys, and all sorts of differences that are imperceptible to the naked eye. Which of these is the "real" table? We are naturally tempted to say that what we see through the microscope is more real, but that in turn would be changed by a still more powerful microscope. If, then, we cannot trust what we see with the naked eye, why should we trust what we see through a microscope? Thus, again, the confidence in our senses with which we began deserts us.

The *shape* of the table is no better. We are all in the habit of judging as to the "real" shapes of things, and we do this so unreflectingly that we come to think we actually see the real shapes. But, in fact, as we all have to learn if we try to draw, a given thing looks different in shape from every different point of view. If our table is "really" rectangular, it will look, from almost all points of view, as if it had two acute angles and two obtuse angles. if opposite sides are parallel, they will look as if they converged to a point away from the spectator; if they are of equal length, they will look as if the nearer side were longer. All these things are not commonly noticed in looking at a table, because experience has taught us to construct the "real" shape from the apparent shape, and the "real" shape is what interests us as practical men. But the "real" shape is not what we see; it is something inferred from what we see. And what we see is constantly changing in shape as we move about the room; so that here again the senses seem not to give us the truth about the table itself, but only about the appearance of the table.

Similar difficulties arise when we consider the sense of touch. It is true that the table always gives us a sensation of hardness, and we feel that it resists pressure. But the sensation we obtain depends upon how hard we press the table and also upon what part of the body we press with; thus the various sensations due to various pressures or various parts of the body cannot be supposed to reveal *directly* any definite property of the table, but at most to be *signs* of some property which perhaps *causes* all the sensations, but is not actually apparent in any of them. And the same applies still more obviously to the sounds which can be elicited by rapping the table.

Thus it becomes evident that the real table, if there is one, is not the same as what we immediately experience by sight or touch or hearing. The real table, if there is one, is not *immediately* known to us at all, but must be an inference from what is immediately known. Hence, two very difficult questions at once arise; namely, (1) Is there a real table at all? (2) If so, what sort of object can it be?

It will help us in considering these questions to have a few simple terms of which the meaning is definite and clear. Let us give the name of "sense-data" to the things that are immediately known in sensation: such things as colours, sounds, smells, hardnesses, roughnesses, and so on. We shall give the name "sensation" to the experience of being immediately aware of these things. Thus, whenever we see a colour, we have a sensation *of* the colour, but the colour itself is a sense-datum, not a sensation. The colour is that *of* which we are immediately aware, and the awareness itself is the sensation. It is plain that if we are to know anything about the table, it must be by means of the sense-data—brown colour, oblong shape, smoothness, etc.—which we associate with the table; but for the reasons which have been given, we cannot say that the table *is* the sense-data, or even that the sense-data are directly properties of the table. Thus a problem arises as to the relation of the sense-data to the real table, supposing there is such a thing.

The real table, if it exists, we will call a "physical object." Thus we have to consider the relation of sense-data to physical objects. The collection of all physical objects is called "matter." Thus our two questions may be restated as follows: (1) Is there any such thing as matter? (2) If so, what is its nature?

The philosopher who first brought prominently forward the reasons for regarding the immediate objects of our senses as not existing independently of us was Bishop Berkeley (1685–1753).[1] His *Three Dialogues between Hylas and Philonous, in Opposition to Sceptics and Atheists,* undertake to prove that there is no such thing as matter at all, and that the world consists of nothing but minds and their ideas. Hylas has hitherto believed in matter, but he is no match for Philonous, who mercilessly drives him into contradictions and paradoxes, and makes his own denial of matter seem, in the end, as if it were almost common sense. The arguments employed are of very different value: some are important and sound, others are confused or quibbling. But Berkeley retains the merit of having shown that the existence of matter is capable of being denied without absurdity, and that if there are any things that exist independently of us they cannot be the immediate objects of our sensations.

There are two different questions involved when we ask whether matter exists, and it is important to keep them clear. We commonly mean by "matter" something which is opposed to "mind," something which we think of as occupying space and as radically incapable of any sort of thought or consciousness. It is chiefly in this sense that Berkeley denies matter; that is to say, he does not deny that the sense-data which we commonly take as signs of the existence of the table are really signs of the existence of *something* independent of us, but he does deny that this something is nonmental, that it is neither mind nor ideas entertained by some mind. He admits that there must be something which continues to exist when we go out of the room or shut our eyes, and that what we call seeing the table does really give us reason for believing in something which persists even when we are not seeing it. But he thinks that this something cannot be radically different in nature from what we see, and cannot be independent of seeing altogether, though it must be independent of *our* seeing. He is thus led to regard the "real" table as an idea in the mind of God. Such an idea has the required permanence and independence of ourselves, without being—as matter would otherwise be—something quite unknowable, in the sense that we can only infer it, and can never be directly and immediately aware of it.

Other philosophers since Berkeley have also held that, although the table does not depend for its existence upon being seen by me, it does depend upon being seen (or otherwise apprehended in sensation) by *some* mind—not necessarily the mind of God, but more often the whole collective mind of the universe. This they hold, as Berkeley does, chiefly because they think there can be nothing real—or at any rate nothing known to be real—except minds and their thoughts and feelings. We might state the argument by which they support their view in some such way as this: "Whatever can be thought of is an idea in the mind of the person thinking of it; therefore nothing can be thought of except ideas in minds; therefore anything else is inconceivable, and what is inconceivable cannot exist."

Such an argument, in my opinion, is fallacious; and of course those who advance it do not put it so shortly or so crudely. But whether valid or not, the argument has been very widely advanced in one form or another; and very many philosophers, perhaps a majority, have held that there is nothing real except minds and their ideas. Such philosophers are called "idealists." When they come to explaining matter, they either say, like Berkeley, that matter is really nothing but a collection of ideas, or they say, like Leibniz (1646–1716),[2] that what appears as matter is really a collection of more or less rudimentary minds.

But these philosophers, though they deny matter as opposed to mind, nevertheless, in another sense, admit matter. It will be remembered that we asked two questions; namely, (1) Is there a real table at all? (2) If so, what sort of object can it be? Now both Berkeley and Leibniz admit that there is a real table, but Berkeley says it is certain ideas in the mind of God, and Leibniz says it is a colony of souls. Thus both of them answer our first question in the affirmative, and only diverge from the views of ordinary mortals in their answer to our second question. In fact, almost all philosophers seem to be agreed that there is a real table: they almost all agree that, however much our sense-data—colour, shape, smoothness, etc.—may depend upon us, yet their occurrence is a sign of something existing independently of us, something differing, perhaps, completely from our sense-data, and yet to be regarded as causing those sense-data whenever we are in a suitable relation to the real table.

Now obviously this point in which the philosophers are agreed—the view that there *is* a real table, whatever its nature may be—is vitally important, and it will be worth while to consider what reasons there are for accepting this view before we go on to the further question as to the nature of the real table. Our next chapter, therefore, will be concerned with the reasons for supposing that there is a real table at all. . . .

## Chapter 2: The Existence of Matter

In this chapter we have to ask ourselves whether, in any sense at all, there is such a thing as matter. Is there a table which has a certain intrinsic nature, and continues to exist when I am not looking, or is the table merely a product of my imagination, a dreamtable in a very prolonged dream? This question is of the greatest importance. For if we cannot be sure of the independent existence of objects, we cannot be sure of the independent existence of other people's bodies, and therefore still less of other people's minds, since we have no grounds for believing in their minds except such as are derived from observing their bodies. Thus if we cannot be sure of the independent existence of objects, we shall be left alone in a desert—it may be that the whole outer world is nothing but a dream, and that we alone exist. This is an uncomfortable possibility; but although it cannot be strictly *proved* to be false, there is not the slightest reason to suppose that it is true. In this chapter we have to see why this is the case.

Before we embark upon doubtful matters, let us try to find some more or less fixed point from which to start. Although we are doubting the physical existence of the table, we are not doubting the existence of the sense-data which made us think there was a table; we are not doubting that, while we look, a certain colour and shape appear to us, and while we press, a certain sensation of hardness is experienced by us. All this, which is psychological, we are not calling in question. In fact, whatever else may be doubtful, some at least of our immediate experiences seem absolutely certain. . . .

Thus it is our particular thoughts and feelings that have primitive certainty. And this applies to dreams and hallucinations as well as to normal perceptions: when we dream or see a ghost, we certainly do have the sensations we think we have, but for various reasons it is held that no physical object corresponds to these sensations. Thus the certainty of our knowledge of our own experiences does not have to be limited in any way to allow for exceptional cases. Here, therefore, we have, for what it is worth, a solid basis from which to begin our pursuit of knowledge.

The problem we have to consider is this: Granted that we are certain of our own sense-data, have we any reason for regarding them as signs of the existence of something else, which we can call the physical object? When we have enumerated all the sense-data which we should naturally regard as connected with the table, have we said all there is to say about the table, or is there still something else—something not a sense-datum, something which persists when we go out of the room? Common sense unhesitatingly answers that there is. What can be bought and sold and pushed about and have a cloth laid on it, and so on, cannot be a *mere* collection of sense-data. If the cloth completely hides the table, we shall derive no sense-data from the table, and therefore, if the table were merely sense-data, it would have ceased to exist, and the cloth would be suspended in empty air, resting, by a miracle, in the place where the table formerly was. This seems plainly absurd; but whoever wishes to become a philosopher must learn not to be frightened by absurdities.

One great reason why it is felt that we must secure a physical object in addition to the sense-data, is that we want the *same* object for different people. When ten people are sitting round a dinner table, it seems preposterous to maintain that they are not seeing the same tablecloth, the same knives and forks and spoons and glasses. But the sense-data are private to each separate person; what is immediately present to the sight of one is not immediately present to the sight of another: they all see things from slightly different points of view, and therefore see them slightly differently. Thus, if there are to be public neutral objects, which can be in some sense known to many different people, there must be something over and above the private and particular sense-data which appear to various people. What reason, then, have we for believing that there are such public neutral objects?

The first answer that naturally occurs to one is that, although different people may see the table slightly differently, still they all see more or less similar things when they look at the table, and the variations in what they see follow the laws of perspective and reflection of light, so that it is easy to arrive at a permanent object underlying all the different people's sense-data. I bought my table from the former occupant of my room; I could not buy *his* sense-data, which died when he went away, but I could and did buy the confident expectation of more or less similar sense-data. Thus it is the fact that different people have similar sense-data, and that one person in a given place at different times has similar sense-data, which makes us suppose that over and above the sense-data there is a permanent public object which underlies or causes the sense-data of various people and various times.

Now insofar as the above considerations depend upon supposing that there are other people besides ourselves, they beg the very question at issue. Other people are represented to me by certain sense-data, such as the sight of them or the sound of their voices, and if I had no reason to believe that there were physical objects independent of my sense-data, I should have no reason to believe that other people exist except as part of my dream. Thus, when we are trying to show that there must be objects independent of our own sense-data, we cannot appeal to the testimony of other people, since this testimony itself consists of sense-data, and does not reveal other people's experiences unless our own sense-data are signs of things existing independently of us. We must therefore, if possible, find, in our own purely private experiences, characteristics which show, or tend to show, that there are in the world things other than ourselves and our private experiences.

In one sense it must be admitted that we can never *prove* the existence of things other than ourselves and our experiences. No logical absurdity results from the hypothesis that the world consists of myself and my thoughts and feelings and sensations, and that everything else is mere fancy. In dreams a very complicated world may seem to be present, and yet on waking we find it was a delusion; that is to say, we find that the sense-data in the dream do not appear to have corresponded with such physical objects as we should naturally infer from our sense-data. . . . There is no logical impossibility in the supposition that the whole of life is a dream, in which we ourselves create all the objects that come before us. But although this is not logically impossible, there is no reason whatever to suppose that it is true; and it is, in fact, a less simple hypothesis, viewed as a means of accounting for the facts of our own life, than the commonsense hypothesis that there really are objects independent of us, whose action on us causes our sensations.

The way in which simplicity comes in from supposing that there really are physical objects is easily seen. If the cat appears at one moment in one part of the room, and at another in another part, it is natural to suppose that it has moved from the one to the other, passing over a series of intermediate positions. But if it is merely a set of sense-data, it cannot have ever been in any place where I did not see it; thus we shall have to suppose that it did not exist at all while I was not looking, but suddenly sprang into being in a new place. If the cat exists whether I see it or not, we can understand from our own experience how it gets hungry between one meal and the next; but if it does not exist when I am not seeing it, it seems odd that appetite should grow during nonexistence as fast as during existence. And if the cat consists only of sense-data, it cannot be *hungry*, since no hunger but my own can be a sense-datum to me. Thus the behaviour of the sense-data which represent the cat to me, though it seems quite natural when regarded as an expression of hunger, becomes utterly inexplicable when regarded as mere movements and changes of patches of colour, which are as incapable of hunger as a triangle is of playing football.

But the difficulty in the case of the cat is nothing compared to the difficulty in the case of human beings. When human beings speak—that is, when we hear certain noises which we associate with ideas, and simultaneously see certain motions of lips and expressions of face—it is very difficult to suppose that what we hear is not the expression of a thought, as we know it would be if we emitted the same sounds. Of course similar things happen in dreams, where we are mistaken as to the existence of other people. But dreams are more or less suggested by what we call waking life, and are capable of being more or less accounted for on scientific principles if

we assume that there really is a physical world. Thus every principle of simplicity urges us to adopt the natural view, that there really are objects other
than our selves and our sense-data which have an existence not dependent
upon our perceiving them.

Of course it is not by argument that we originally come by our belief in
an independent external world. We find this belief ready in ourselves as
soon as we begin to reflect: it is what may be called an *instinctive* belief. We
should never have been led to question this belief but for the fact that, at any
rate in the case of sight, it seems as if the sense-datum itself were instinctively
believed to be the independent object, whereas argument shows that the object cannot be identical with the sense-datum. This discovery, however—
which is not at all paradoxical in the case of taste and smell and sound, and
only slightly so in the case of touch—leaves undiminished our instinctive belief that there *are* objects *corresponding* to our sense-data. Since this belief
does not lead to any difficulties, but on the contrary tends to simplify and
systematise our account of our experiences, there seems no good reason for
rejecting it. We may therefore admit—though with a slight doubt derived
from dreams—that the external world does really exist, and is not wholly dependent for its existence upon our continuing to perceive it.

The argument which has led us to this conclusion is doubtless less
strong than we could wish, but it is typical of many philosophical arguments, and it is therefore worthwhile to consider briefly its general character and validity. All knowledge, we find, must be built up upon our instinctive beliefs, and if these are rejected, nothing is left. But among our
instinctive beliefs some are much stronger than others, while many have,
by habit and association, become entangled with other beliefs, not really
instinctive, but falsely supposed to be part of what is believed instinctively.

Philosophy should show us the hierarchy of our instinctive beliefs, beginning with those we hold most strongly, and presenting each as much isolated and as free from irrelevant additions as possible. It should take care
to show that, in the form in which they are finally set forth, our instinctive
beliefs do not clash, but form a harmonious system. There can never be
any reason for rejecting one instinctive belief except that it clashes with
others; thus, if they are found to harmonise, the whole system becomes
worthy of acceptance.

It is of course *possible* that all or any of our beliefs may be mistaken, and
therefore all ought to be held with at least some slight element of doubt.
But we cannot have *reason* to reject a belief except on the ground of some
other belief. Hence, by organising our instinctive beliefs and their consequences, by considering which among them it is most possible, if necessary,
to modify or abandon, we can arrive, on the basis of accepting as our sole
data what we instinctively believe, at an orderly systematic organisation of
our knowledge, in which, though the *possibility* of error remains, its likeli-
hood is diminished by the interrelation of the parts and by the critical
scrutiny which has preceded acquiescence.

▶ NOTES

1. George Berkeley was an Irish philosopher and the Anglican bishop of Cloyne, Ireland, from 1734 to 1752. [D.C.A., ed.]
2. Gottfried Wilhelm Leibniz was a German philosopher and mathematician. [D.C.A.]

# The Problems of Philosophy (selection 2)

Bertrand Russell

### Reading Questions

*According to Russell:*

1.  When we seem to experience a table, why is the real table not the same as what we immediately experience through our senses?

2.  For Berkeley, what is the real nature of what we call matter? For Leibniz, what is its real nature?

3.  What is the solid basis from which the pursuit of knowledge can begin?

4.  When one is trying to prove that there are objects independent of one's own sense-data, why is it illegitimate to appeal to the testimony of other people?

5.  Why is it more reasonable to believe that objects exist independently of oneself than to believe that what seem to be objects are only one's own sense-data?

### Discussion Questions

*In your own view:*

1.  Is color an intrinsic quality of a physical object, or simply something we attribute to it?

2.  Are sense-data the only things we directly know?

3.  Is the existence of the physical world an inference from sense-data?

4.  Can science tell us how physical objects are in themselves, independent of subjective interpretation?

5.  When should we trust an instinctive belief?

CHAPTER 1

# What Is Epistemology?

## 1.1 What Sort of Theory Is a Theory of Knowledge?

The term "epistemology" derives from the two Greek words, "episteme," meaning "knowledge," and "logos," meaning "logic" or "rationale." So in modern English, epistemology has come to mean the theory of knowledge. But what is a theory of knowledge? We are accustomed to scientists formulating theories and testing them, theories for example about the cause of earthquakes or the structure of the atom, and even if we do not know enough science to understand the details of these theories, we can understand what sort of thing a theory about the cause of earthquakes might be. But how could there be a theory of knowledge? What would be the data which the theory was trying to explain? What would be the test of the correctness of the theory? Why should we need such a theory anyway? Our answers to these and related questions will become clearer as the book proceeds. However, let us begin by explaining eight problems which epistemology would traditionally tackle.

## 1.2 Eight Problems of Traditional Epistemology

### (i) What is knowledge?

First of all, epistemologists have tried to offer an account of what knowledge is. We will find that in modern epistemology, this task has typically taken the form of trying to provide a definition of the word "know" (or more accurately of sentences containing the word). It might seem surprising that an inquiry into the nature of knowledge should focus on the word rather than the thing or state which the word denotes. After all, scientists developing a theory about the cause of earthquakes do not spend a great deal of time talking about the word "earthquake." Why philosophy has taken this linguistic turn is a large

**2**

question. But part of the reason is that modern philosophers have come to feel that the way in which the old question "What is knowledge?" could best be answered was by focusing on the *concept* of knowledge; they then interpreted talk of concepts as being a shorthand way of referring to certain facts about language. Hence the old question "What is knowledge?," which seems to be about a phenomenon in the world, becomes transformed at least partly into a linguistic question, a question about the definition of the word "know." As we will see in Chapter 2, the definition sought is of a rather peculiar kind, and not at all the sort of thing which you might find in a dictionary.

## (ii) What kinds of knowledge are there?

Secondly, epistemologies have historically tried to tell us something about the kinds of knowledge that there are. Most epistemologists, for example, have drawn a major distinction between empirical knowledge and a priori knowledge. Exactly what these terms mean is something that will occupy us later (see Chapter 5, section 2), but for the moment we can take it that empirical knowledge is knowledge derivable only from experience, and a priori knowledge is knowledge gained by reason alone. Are there really these two kinds of knowledge? It is easy to produce examples which seem to show that there must be. If I come to know that a particular flower is red by looking at it, surely that is knowledge that I have gained by experience, in this case by my visual experience. And if I know that if $A$ is greater than $B$ and $B$ is greater than $C$, then $A$ is greater than $C$, or that no statement can be both wholly true and wholly false at the same time, surely that is something that my reason tells me when I simply reflect on what it is that the statement is saying. Yet some philosophers have wanted to deny that experience by itself can be a source of knowledge, and others have denied that reason alone can be.

Descartes (1596–1650), the French thinker who is generally regarded as the founder of modern philosophy, is an example of someone who denies that the senses alone can be a source of knowledge. In a famous passage in his *Meditations*, he considers the knowledge that we have of a piece of a wax, and writes:

> . . . the perception I have of it is a case not of vision or touch or imagination. . . . but of purely mental scrutiny. (Descartes, Vol. 2, 21)

Here we have a contrast between the senses of vision and touch on the one hand, which, according to Descartes, do not by themselves give us knowledge of the wax, and "purely mental scrutiny" on the other. What he means by this phrase is not made explicit, but what is clear is that he thinks that our knowledge of the wax comes from the mind and not from the senses alone. No doubt Descartes would also have said in connection with the flower mentioned previously that my knowledge that it is red comes not from the senses but from "purely mental scrutiny." At the end of his discussion of the wax example, Descartes generalizes what he has been saying about the wax to cover our knowledge of all physical things:

Everitt–Fisher: Modern
Epistemology: A New
Introduction

1. What Is Epistemology?

Text

© The McGraw–Hill
Companies, 1995

21

> I now know that even bodies are not strictly perceived by the senses or the
> faculty of imagination but by the intellect alone, and that this perception
> derives not from their being touched or seen but from their being understood.
> (Descartes, Vol. 2, 22)

Again, we have an explicit contrast between the senses, which are declared not
to be a source of knowledge, and something else (in this case, the intellect or
understanding), which is a source of knowledge. So Descartes would be one
philosopher who would deny that there is any empirical knowledge, if that
term is understood as knowledge derivable only from experience.

By contrast, John Stuart Mill (1806–1873), the leading British philosopher
of his day, took the opposite line. He thought that *all* knowledge was empirical, and hence denied the existence of any a priori knowledge. Speaking, for
example, of the law of noncontradiction (which we quoted previously as saying that no statement can be both wholly true and wholly false), he had this
to say:

> I consider it to be, like other axioms, one of our first and most familiar gen-
> eralisations from experience. The original foundation of it I take to be, that
> Belief and Disbelief are two different mental states, excluding one another.
> This we know by the simplest observation of our own minds. (Mill, Bk. II,
> ch. 7, sec. 5, 183)

So Mill thinks that even the principle of noncontradiction is known empirically. And he goes on to make clear that he thinks, *contra* Descartes, that all of
our knowledge is derived from experience. So that is a second task for our epistemology: what are the arguments for and against claiming that there are two
kinds of knowledge, and what are the implications of accepting either view?

## (iii) What are the sources of knowledge?

A related task, though one that is worth listing separately, is to consider what
the sources of knowledge are. It is natural when we first start reflecting on
where our knowledge comes from to pick on sense experience as the main and
perhaps the only source of knowledge. We know about the things around us
because we can use our senses to see them, touch, hear them, and so on. So,
again in spite of what Descartes was saying, it looks as if sense experience has
a good claim to be a source of knowledge. But how many senses are there?
Common thought recognizes five, but some thinkers have suggested that we
ought to recognize more, such as a sense of balance, or the sense which enables
us to know without looking where our limbs are (usually called propriocep-
tion). And if we are recognizing new senses, where (if at all) does a moral sense
fit in? But even if we recognize the existence of a number of other senses, there
are still many things which we know about ourselves without having senses
of any kind. To know what I am thinking, for example, or what emotions I am
feeling, I do not have to use any of my senses; some philosophers have consequently postulated a faculty of introspection as a source of knowledge about
the contents of our own minds.

© The McGraw-Hill
Companies, 1995

Everitt–Fisher: Modern
Epistemology: A New
Introduction

1. What Is Epistemology?

Text

22

**4**

Another favored source of knowledge has been reason or the intellect or the understanding. We saw how Descartes claimed, rather surprisingly, that our knowledge of a piece of wax was attributable not to our senses but to our intellect. More commonly, philosophers have argued that it is our intellect that tells us of the truths of logic and mathematics. We just "see" (in a nonvisual sense of the term) that certain things are true, or that one thing follows from another.

Should memory be counted as a source of knowledge? It seems in some ways to be like one. In answer to the question "How do you know?," we might reply "I can remember it," just as we might reply "I can see it," suggesting that memory functions like the sense of sight in supplying us with knowledge. But on the other hand, it seems unlike other sources of knowledge, in that it does not enable us to know anything new: memory is simply the retention of knowledge which is provided by some other source.

Testimony (and its more specific variety, authority) are other possible sources of knowledge. It seems that the great majority of the things we know about, we know because we have been told of them by other people, or because we have read what other people have said about them. If we focus on the idea of authority, we find that at different times in our intellectual history, different degrees of emphasis have been placed on the deliverances of persons and texts in special positions of authority. Sometimes authority has been contrasted with what our own senses tell us, and regarded as a superior source of knowledge. At other times, the pendulum has swung the other way, and the deliverances of authority have been treated as one branch of our sensory knowledge.

Beyond testimony come other alleged sources of knowledge, such as revelation, or parapsychological powers, such as telepathy, clairvoyance, and precognition. In mentioning these, we are not of course endorsing at all the claim that they do give us knowledge. Rather, we are saying that one of the tasks which has occupied epistemologists at different times in the past is trying to adjudicate between the claims made on behalf of *all* of these alleged sources of knowledge: what makes something a source of knowledge, what makes two sources of knowledge two rather than one, and so on? (Some of these questions will be taken up again in Chapter 13.)

### (iv) What is the structure of our body of knowledge?

A fourth task concerns the structure of our total body of knowledge. We are familiar with the thought that one piece of knowledge can presuppose another. For example, I could not know that John's wife is a doctor unless I also know that John has a wife. But epistemologists are interested in a more general kind of dependence than this. For example, it is clear that in general our knowledge of the future depends on our knowledge of the past and present. Or, to give another example, if we have any knowledge of what other people are thinking and feeling, this must depend on our knowledge of their behavior. Some

Everitt–Fisher: Modern
Epistemology: A New
Introduction

1. What Is Epistemology?

Text

© The McGraw–Hill
Companies, 1995

23

What Is Epistemology?                                                                              **5**

philosophers, in thinking about these dependencies, have thought that our knowledge is like a building, in that it rests ultimately on some "foundational" knowledge. If so, what would this foundational knowledge be like? Other philosophers, however, have argued that our knowledge is more like a spider's web where each strand in the web plays a part in supporting all the other strands, which in turn play a part in supporting it. There have been advocates for both of these views and also for other ways of seeing the structure of our knowledge; and we shall spend a good deal of time discussing this issue.

## (v)  What are the limits of what can be known?

A fifth task which has concerned epistemologists is to demarcate the limits of the knowable. Putting the matter like this may make it sound rather abstract, but the idea of the distinction is familiar in ordinary conversation and is often appealed to by people with no philosophical training. Here are three examples of it in action.

Suppose that there is an argument between a pacifist and someone who takes the more common view that killing, though in general wrong, is sometimes morally justified. Let us call this second person the traditionalist. We can easily imagine in some detail how a debate between these two might go. The pacifist will say that in her view, it is human life that has supreme value; that killing someone is an irreversible process, so that one can never undo the harm one does to one's victim; that no one is morally perfect, and that therefore no one is morally entitled to deprive another person of her life; that killing brutalizes the killer; that violence breeds only further violence; and so on. The traditionalist, however, is likely to say that killing is sometimes necessary to avoid a greater evil, that one has to weigh the life of the victim against the lives and welfare of many other people, that what is important is not mere life itself, but the quality of life, and so on. After some argument along these lines, they may reach an impasse, when one of them says "Well, that's just your opinion" or "You cannot prove it" or "It's only a subjective judgment anyway," or some such similarly dismissive phrase. Someone who says this is implicitly assuming the truth of a particular theory of knowledge. They are assuming the existence of a distinction between what is knowable and what is not knowable, and placing in the category of what is not knowable the class of moral judgments.

A second example concerns disputes about the existence of God. Throughout Western intellectual history, there have been many attempts to prove that God exists. Some of these arguments can seem very convincing, but to each of them there is a counterargument which seems to have roughly equal force. Thus we find Descartes defending the ontological argument, and Kant (1724–1804) attacking it, Butler (1692–1752) defending the argument to design and Hume (1711–1776) attacking it, and so on. This sort of seemingly irresolvable conflict has led some people to say that no one can really know whether or not God exists. They often mean by this not just that no one has

Everitt–Fisher: Modern
Epistemology: A New
Introduction

1. What Is Epistemology?

Text

© The McGraw–Hill
Companies, 1995

**6**

up to now succeeded in proving the matter one way or the other, but rather
that in principle the issue cannot be conclusively settled. And if they do take
this view, they are again tacitly adopting a particular theory of knowledge.
They are drawing a line between the knowable and the unknowable, and
putting assertions about God into the unknowable category.

A final example concerns the sensations of other people. Can I know
exactly what your sensations are? Or, a more difficult case, perhaps, can I
know exactly what a dog's sensations feel like to the dog? Of course, I might
have a more-or-less reliable guess at what you or the dog feel. If the dog's leg
has just been broken by a passing car, and it is whining and whimpering, and
resists all attempts to touch its leg, then *very* probably it is in pain. But would
it be possible to *know* that this was so? And would it be possible to know
exactly what kind of pain it felt? Many people have thought that the answer
to these questions is "no." This means that once again, they are operating with
a tacit distinction between the knowable and unknowable. As epistemologists,
we would want to investigate this distinction. Is it the same distinction which
is being appealed to in each of these types of cases? What is it that determines
which category a given type of assertion should be placed in? This, then, is a
fifth task which falls within the field of traditional epistemology.

It is worth emphasizing that the contrast here is between what is knowable in principle and what is not knowable in principle. There are many things
which we do not currently know. But these do not count as unknowable in
the sense in which we are here using the term. For science advances, our
instruments of detection improve, and what today is in practice unknowable,
tomorrow is known. When people say, however, that moral judgments are a
matter of opinion not knowledge or that the existence of God is a matter of
faith not knowledge, what is meant is not just that we do not now have enough
evidence to achieve knowledge. The thought rather is that no conceivable evidence which we might hope to acquire in the future will enable us to gain
knowledge in these areas.

## (vi) What are the mechanisms by which we gain knowledge?

A sixth aim can be summarized as the task of finding mechanisms for knowledge, or at least making sure that such mechanisms are possible. What this
means can best be shown with an example. Take the case that we mentioned
earlier of seeing a red flower, and thereby coming to know that it is red. We
know that there is a causal link between the flower and the knower. Light
waves are reflected from the flower and enter the eye of the observer. They
there produce chemical changes in the cones of the retina of the observer, and
these changes in turn cause electrical impulses to flow up the optic nerve to
the visual cortex in the brain. The end result is that the observer gains some
knowledge about the flower. The details of this causal chain are not important
for the philosopher, although obviously they are important for the physiolo-

Everitt–Fisher: Modern
Epistemology: A New
Introduction

1. What Is Epistemology?

Text

© The McGraw–Hill
Companies, 1995

25

gist. What is important for the philosopher is that the existence of some such causal chain as this, linking the flower to the observer, helps to make intelligible how an observer can come to have knowledge of an object that may, for example, be at a considerable distance from her. If we take the common sense view that looking at a flower can sometimes give you knowledge of what color it is, then we know that there is a causal mechanism which could explain *how* the knowledge is gained.

Contrast this with a different case. Some people believe that they have precognitive powers. They believe that they can see into the future, where this does not mean that on the basis of evidence from the past and present, they can infer more-or-less reliably some facts about the future, as the meteorologist tries to infer what tomorrow's weather will be like. The idea of precognition is rather that without the need for any evidence, they just know what the future will be like. There are several puzzling features to precognition, and one in particular that is relevant here is that there does not seem to be any mechanism which could explain how what is going to happen tomorrow could bring it about that today I know about tomorrow's events. If we reject the possibility that the future might cause the past and present, then it seems impossible that today's knowledge can be based on tomorrow's events. In other words, if someone claims to know things in a particular way, but there is no mechanism to explain how such knowledge is possible, then we would doubt their claim to have knowledge in this case.

So, a sixth task for traditional epistemology is to ensure that for each kind of knowledge admitted by our epistemology, there is some mechanism that makes it intelligible how there could be knowledge of that kind. As mentioned previously, the full details of the mechanism need not concern the philosopher. But what she must take care to avoid is countenancing a kind of knowledge, while having no idea at all of how knowledge of that sort is possible.

## (vii) How is knowledge related to belief and justification?

So far in our listing of the tasks of epistemology, we have concentrated on the concept of knowledge. But epistemology is concerned with other related concepts as well, and in particular with the two concepts of belief and justification. As we will see shortly, on virtually every traditional account of knowledge, belief and justification are components of knowledge, and that is one reason for an epistemologist to be interested in those concepts. A second reason is that there are certain areas where knowledge is difficult to come by, and yet where some well-founded or justified belief is possible. In such areas, justified belief takes on for us the action-guiding role that knowledge can play for us in other areas. Indeed, some philosophers, such as Bertrand Russell (1872–1969), who are in general doubtful about the possibility of many kinds of knowledge, would maintain that the idea of justified belief is of more importance and interest than the idea of knowledge itself. Subsequent chapters will deal extensively with these issues.

## (viii) How ought we to proceed in order to acquire knowledge?

A number of epistemologists in the past have not merely wanted to describe what knowledge is, what its limits are, and so on, they have wanted to *improve* the ways in which people think and reason. Thus, there has sometimes been a normative element in epistemological writings: the author has told us how we *ought* to conduct our search after knowledge, and what would be *right* for us to accept, and hence what we would be *justified* in believing. This task clearly requires some grasp of what knowledge is, what its limits are, what its sources are and hence is intimately related to the epistemological concerns we have previously outlined.

A good example of this is provided by Descartes. As we saw in section 1.2 (ii), he was firmly opposed to a reliance on the senses alone as a source of knowledge and regarded such a reliance as a major obstacle to intellectual progress. Accordingly, a number of his epistemological writings have a strongly normative content, an element of his thinking which is reflected in the titles of some of his works, such as *Discourse on the Method of Rightly Conducting One's Reason and Seeking Truth in the Sciences.*

This concern with how we *ought* to think can be found in many later epistemologists, including those writing in our own day. The contemporary philosopher of science Karl Popper (1902–1994), for example, has sought to change the ways in which (some) scientists formulate their theories and interpret the results of tests of those theories. As we shall see in section 10.5, Popper thinks that scientists ought to take seriously only those theories which are in principle falsifiable. He accordingly dismisses some allegedly scientific theories (such as Marxism and psychoanalysis) not because they have, as it were, got their facts wrong, but because they are unfalsifiable and hence are the wrong *sort* of theory to embody scientific understanding. One of the most recent examples in this tradition can be found in the work of the modern philosopher Stephen Stich, especially in his book *The Fragmentation of Reason.*

## 1.3 Epistemology and What There Is

Those, then, are the main tasks which epistemology has been concerned with in the past. But it will be helpful for later study to mention two other areas which are adjacent to epistemology and to which we will occasionally refer. These are metaphysics and ontology.

### (i) The terms "metaphysics" and "ontology" explained

The term "metaphysics" originates in Greek philosophy with the writings of Aristotle (384 B.C.–322 B.C.). Aristotle produced a work dealing with the nature of the physical world, entitled the *Physics*. When his work was being collected and edited, included in the same volume as the *Physics* were a number of unti-

Everitt–Fisher: Modern
Epistemology: A New
Introduction

1. What Is Epistemology?

Text

© The McGraw–Hill
Companies, 1995

27

What Is Epistemology?                                                        **9**

tled writings. These came to be known as the *Meta-physics*, from the Greek
"meta ta physika" (after the things of nature). Later commentators took the
term to refer not just to the relative position of the writings, but rather to their
content; in their hands, "metaphysics" came to mean something that was
beyond or above the physical world, or existing apart from the world of nature.
This is a sense (though not the only sense) which the term has retained into
the twentieth century. In the contemporary usage which we shall be concerned
with, metaphysics covers the realm of ontology.

   "Ontology" comes from the Greek "ontos," meaning "being," and "logos,"
meaning (as we said earlier) "logic" or "rationale," and means literally "the
study of being" or "the study of existence." But that by itself is not a very helpful definition. Surely, it might be objected, many other subjects are concerned
with existence. Astronomers study the being or existence of heavenly bodies,
biologists study the being or existence of living things, chemists study the
being of chemical substances, and so on. What, then, is peculiar to the philosopher's concern with existence? The answer is that the philosophers have been
concerned to list and describe the most basic kinds of things that exist.

## (ii) Material objects

Let us illustrate this idea further. We know that the world contains both suit-
cases and telephones, and that they are very different kinds of objects. But
nevertheless from one point of view, they are the same kind of thing, since
they are both material objects. They are both composed of the same sorts of
stuff (subatomic particles, etc.) differently arranged. Similarly with other
objects that in ordinary life we think of as being very different from each other,
such as pins and mountains, airplanes, and baseballs. Given that all these
things do exist, it seems that we have to admit to our ontology the category
of material thing. But do we have to admit anything else? Does the universe
consist exclusively of material things?

## (iii) Minds

Many philosophers have thought that the answer to this cannot be "yes," and
have sought to show that our ontology must include other fundamental kinds
of things. Let us consider briefly some favored additions. First, many philosophers (and many nonphilosophers too) have claimed that minds are a kind of
entity irreducibly different from anything physical. They have argued that
although minds may be causally dependent on bits of material stuff, like brains
or central nervous systems, they are not actually identical with those physical
entities. They have claimed that a mind is not itself a physical or a material
thing, but has to be classified as nonphysical or nonmaterial. Part of what is
meant by this claim is that minds do not have any spatial properties: they do
not have a size or a shape or a location in space. So if this line of thought is
right, we have to accept a fundamental dualism in our ontology: the world
consists of the collection of all physical things and of nonphysical minds as well.

**10**                                                           Modern Epistemology

## (iv) Abstract objects

Some thinkers have claimed, however, that we need to recognize the existence of a third kind of object, irreducibly different both from material things and from minds. Think, for example, of the number 1. Is that a material thing? If so, where is it, and what are its physical properties? Certainly the *numeral* "1" is a physical thing—or at least particular inscriptions of the numeral are. It makes sense to ask where a particular inscription of the numeral is located, how big it is, what its chemical composition is (i.e., in terms of the ink used), and so on. But of course the number 1 is not the same as the numeral which we can write or print. The number is what is denoted by the numeral, and once we have distinguished numbers and numerals, it seems clear that the number cannot itself be a physical thing. Are numbers then mental things? Some people have thought so. But if they are, they must be mental in a very different way from the way in which, for example, a feeling of anger is mental. The feeling of anger comes into someone's mind at a particular time, lasts for a certain length of time, and then ceases. If that particular person had never existed, that particular feeling of anger would never have existed either. By contrast, the number 1 does not come into existence at a particular moment when someone has a thought and then cease to exist when she starts to think about something else. We could not sensibly ask "Did the number 1 exist yesterday?" as we could ask "Was anyone angry yesterday?" The existence of the number 1 does not depend upon the existence of any particular person, in the way in which that person's feelings depend on that person: the number would still have existed even if the person had never been born. Indeed, even if nobody had ever been born, and hence there had never been any minds, it seems that it would still have been true that 1 + 1 = 2. So it looks as if numbers cannot be mental items after all. And if they are not mental things at all, then we shall have to admit to our ontology a third kind of entity that is neither physical nor mental but abstract. Abstract entities will differ from both physical and mental ones, in that they will exist and yet not be in space or time.

## (v) Space and time

Mention of space and time brings up a further puzzling item. Is space a material thing or a mental thing or an abstract thing, or does it belong to a fourth category of existence? Some thinkers have thought that space was a sort of unique nonmaterial stuff, independent of matter (this was roughly the view of the great physicist Isaac Newton [1642–1727]), while others have held that it does not exist in its own right at all, but is simply a set of relations holding between material things (this was roughly the view of the German philosopher Leibniz [1646–1716]). Similar conflicts persist over the nature of time. Should we think of it as a kind of thing in its own right, or is it just a set of relations holding between events? And if we say that space and time are just

Everitt–Fisher: Modern
Epistemology: A New
Introduction

1. What Is Epistemology?

Text

© The McGraw–Hill
Companies, 1995

29

sets of relations, what sort of entity is a relation? Presumably it is not itself a material or a mental thing. So is it another abstract thing, and if so, is it the same kind of abstract thing as a number?

We do not need to answer these questions here. We raise them in order to illustrate the sorts of issues which concern an ontologist. But there are also links here with epistemology. Recall, for instance, what we said a moment ago about the sixth task for our epistemology, the issue of a causal mechanism for knowledge. Suppose that in reflecting on the nature of numbers, we took the view that they are indeed mind-independent objects that have a nonspatial and nontemporal existence. This is a view which can seem very plausible. It seems to account for the objectivity which arithmetic has, and for the fact that we discover arithmetical truths, we do not arbitrarily make them up as we go along. But if we take that view, we have a great problem in explaining how we could ever come to know about numbers. For if numbers are not in space or time, they presumably cannot interact with us causally in the way that physical objects can. How then can we ever get to know about them? It seems that our epistemology and our ontology are in conflict here. What this shows is that although epistemology and ontology are two separate concerns, when we undertake one, we will be well advised to keep an eye on the other.

### Exercises

1. Without rereading the chapter, explain in half a page the traditional tasks of epistemology.
2. Without rereading the chapter, check how carefully you read it by *briefly* answering the following questions:
   a. what is the difference between empirical and a priori knowledge? (give an example of each)
   b. describe *two* structures which our body of knowledge might be thought to have
   c. give two examples of things which might be thought to be unknowable
   d. what are metaphysics and ontology?
   e. list three basic categories of object which philosophers have countenanced
3. Before reading Chapter 2, write in no more than one page your own account of what knowledge is. To help you do this, ask yourself the following questions:
   a. can you know something to be true if in fact it is false?
   b. if you know something, can you also believe it? do you *have to* believe it if you know it?
   c. if you claim to know something, do you have to be able to justify that claim?
   d. if you know something do you have to be *certain* of it?
   e. what would you have to know to know that Smith was the murderer?

# The Republic

Plato

Plato was born in Athens in about 428 B.C.E. As a youth he associated with Socrates, a philosopher who constantly challenged fellow Athenians to think about virtue and to improve their souls. Plato's initial interest was in politics, but he soon became disillusioned, especially when, under the democracy that was restored after the rule of the "Thirty Tyrants," Socrates was arrested on false charges of impiety and the corruption of youth, convicted, and condemned to die. After the execution of Socrates, Plato moved to nearby Megara for a time and may have traveled to Egypt. In 388 he visited Italy and the city of Syracuse in Sicily. Returning to Athens, he founded the Academy, a school devoted both to philosophical inquiry and to the philosophically based education of politicians. Plato spent most of his life teaching at the Academy (Aristotle was his most famous student) and writing philosophical works. He made two more trips to Syracuse, in 368 and 361, apparently with the intention of turning the city's ruler, Dionysius the Younger, into a "philosopher-king." (If this was indeed his purpose, he failed.) Plato died in Athens in 347 at the age of eighty-one.

Most of Plato's works are written as conversations between Socrates and one or more interlocutors on some topic concerning morality. His best-known "dialogues" (the name by which his surviving works are known) are the *Euthyphro, Apology, Crito, Phaedo, Meno, Symposium,* and *Republic.*

Our selection is from the *Republic,* a work cast as a report by Socrates of a conversation he had the previous day with several people, including Glaucon and Adeimantus (Plato's older brothers). In the dialogue Socrates presents his views on a number of topics, but scholars agree these views are Plato's own, not those of the historical Socrates. Our readings are taken from exchanges between Socrates and Glaucon in Books V, VI, and VII.

In Book V Glaucon asks Socrates who the true philosophers are. Socrates, alluding to the etymology of the word ("lovers of wisdom"), says that they are "lovers of the vision of truth." Expanding on this notion, Socrates explains that philosophers are those who love the One rather than the Many. For example, a philosopher goes beyond the love of individual beautiful things to love absolute beauty (beauty itself, the form of beauty). The forms are fully real and are the objects of genuine knowledge, whereas the Many lie between being and not-being and are the objects of mere opinion.

In Book VI Socrates explains that the Many belong to the visible world, which is seen by the eye, while the forms reside in the intelligible world, which is grasped by the mind. He illustrates the two worlds by describing a line divided into two main parts, with each of these parts subdivided into two parts. Each of the resulting four segments of the line represents a type of object of knowledge. Corresponding to each of the four types of object of cognition is a distinct condition in the soul.

Socrates further illustrates this theory of knowledge in Book VII through the famous allegory of the cave. We are like prisoners who live their entire lives inside a cave. Just as such prisoners would think that shadows on the cave wall were real and would be unaware of the real world outside the cave, so we think that the visible world of the Many is real, ignorant of the intelligible world of forms.

▼

Reprinted from *The Dialogues of Plato,* trans. Benjamin Jowett. 3rd ed., vol. 3. New York: Macmillan, 1892.

## Book V

. . . [Glaucon asked:] Who are the true philosophers?

Those, I [Socrates] replied, who are lovers of the vision of truth.

That is right, he said; but I would like to know what you mean.

I might have difficulty explaining it to someone else, I replied; but I am sure that you will admit a proposition that I am about to make.

What is the proposition?

That since beauty is the opposite of ugliness, they are two.

Certainly.

And inasmuch as they are two, each of them is one.

True again.

And of the just and the unjust, good and evil, and of every other class, the same remark holds; taken singly, each of them is one; but from the various combinations of them with actions and things and with one another, they are seen in all sorts of lights and appear many?

Very true.

And this is the distinction that I draw between the sight-loving, art-loving, practical class of people, and those of whom I am speaking, who are alone worthy of the name of philosophers.

How do you distinguish them? he asked.

The lovers of sounds and sights are, as I conceive, fond of fine tones and colors and shapes and all the artificial products made out of them, but their mind is incapable of seeing or loving absolute beauty.

True, he replied.

Few people are able to attain the sight of this.

Very true.

And he who, having a sense of beautiful things, has no sense of absolute beauty, or who, if another leads him to a knowledge of that beauty, is unable to follow—is such a one awake or in a dream? Reflect: Is not the dreamer, whether asleep or awake, one who likens dissimilar things, putting the copy in the place of the real object?

I would certainly say that such a one was dreaming.

But take the other case, one who recognizes the existence of absolute beauty and is able to distinguish absolute beauty from the objects that participate in it, neither putting the objects in the place of absolute beauty nor absolute beauty in the place of the objects—is he dreaming or is he awake?

He is wide awake.

And may we not say that the mind of the one who knows has knowledge, and that the mind of the other, who opines only, has opinion?

Certainly. . . .

I would ask the person who is of opinion that there is no beautiful in itself or no unchangeable form of beauty itself, but who believes in many beautiful things—the lover of beautiful sights, who cannot bear to be told that the beautiful is one, that the just is one, or that anything is one—I would ask him this question: Will you be so very kind, sir, as to tell us whether, of all these beautiful things, there is one that will not also appear ugly; or of the just, one that will not also appear unjust; or of the holy, one that will not also appear unholy?

No, he replied; the beautiful will in some way appear ugly; and the same is true of the rest.

And may not the many that are doubles be also halves—that is, doubles of one thing, and halves of another?

Quite true.

And things great and small, heavy and light, as they are termed, will not be denoted by these names any more than by the opposite names?

True; both these and the opposite names will always attach to all of them.

And can any one of those many things that are called by particular names be said to be this rather than not to be this?

He replied: They are like the punning riddles asked at feasts, or the children's puzzle about the eunuch aiming at the bat, with what he hit him, and upon what the bat was sitting.[1] The individual objects of which I am speaking are also a riddle, and have a double sense, and you cannot fix them in your mind either as being or not-being, or both, or neither.

Then what will you do with them? I asked. Can they have a better place than between being and not-being? For they are clearly not in greater darkness or negation than not-being, or more full of light and existence than being.

That is quite true, he said.

We seem, then, to have discovered that the many conventions that the multitude entertain about the beautiful and about all other things are tossing about in some region that is half-way between pure being and pure not-being?

We have.

Yes, and we had agreed earlier that anything of this kind that we might find was to be described as matter of opinion, and not as matter of knowledge—the intermediate flux that is caught and detained by the intermediate faculty.

Quite true.

Then those who see many beautiful things, but who do not see absolute beauty and cannot follow any guide who points the way there; who see many just things, and not absolute justice, and the like—such persons may be said to have opinion but not knowledge.

That is certain.

But those who see the things themselves, which are always the same and unchangeable, may be said to know, and not to have opinion only?

Neither can that be denied.

These persons love and embrace the subjects of knowledge, the others those of opinion? The latter are the same persons, you will remember, who listened to sweet sounds and gazed upon fair colors, but would not tolerate the existence of absolute beauty

Yes, I remember.

Shall we then be guilty of any impropriety in calling them lovers of opinion rather than lovers of wisdom? Will they be very angry at us for describing them in this way?

I shall tell them not to be angry; no man should be angry at what is true.

But those who love the truth in each thing are to be called lovers of wisdom and not lovers of opinion.

Assuredly.

## Book VI

. . . There are many beautiful things and many good things, and so also for other things that we describe and define; to all of them the term "many" is applied.

True, he said.

And there is an absolute beauty and an absolute good, and there is an absolute for all the other things to which the term "many" is applied; for they may be brought under a single form, which is called the essence[2] of each.

Very true.

The many, as we say, are seen but not known, and the forms are known but not seen.

Exactly. . . .

May I suppose that you have this distinction of the visible and intelligible fixed in your mind?

Yes.

Now take a line that has been cut into two unequal parts, and divide each of them again in the same proportion. Suppose that the two main divisions correspond to the visible and to the intelligible. Then compare the subdivisions with respect to their clearness and lack of clearness, and you will find that the first section in the sphere of the visible consists of images. And by images I mean, first shadows, then reflections in water and in solid, smooth, and polished bodies, and everything of that kind. Do you understand?

Yes, I understand.

Imagine now that the other section, of which this is only an image, includes the animals that we see, and everything that grows or is made.

Very good.

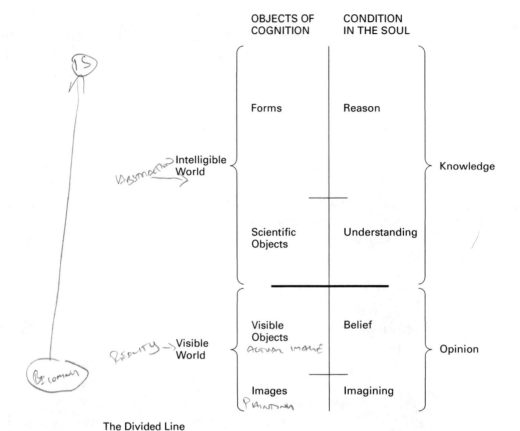

| OBJECTS OF COGNITION | CONDITION IN THE SOUL | |
|---|---|---|
| Forms | Reason | |
| Intelligible World | | Knowledge |
| Scientific Objects | Understanding | |
| Visible Objects | Belief | |
| Visible World | | Opinion |
| Images | Imagining | |

The Divided Line

Would you not admit that both the sections of this division have different degrees of truth, and that the copy is related to the original as the sphere of opinion is related to the sphere of knowledge?

Most undoubtedly.

Next proceed to consider how the sphere of the intelligible is to be divided.

How?

In this way: There are two subdivisions. In the lower one, the soul uses the figures given by the former division as images. This inquiry can only be hypothetical, and instead of going upward to a principle, it descends down to a conclusion. In the higher subdivision, the soul passes out of hypotheses and goes up to a principle that is above hypotheses, making no use of images as in the former case, but proceeding only in and through the forms themselves.

I do not quite understand your meaning, he said.

Then I will try again; you will understand me better when I have made some preliminary remarks. You are aware that students of geometry, arithmetic, and related sciences assume the odd and the even, the various figures, the three kinds of angles, and things related to these in each branch of science. These are their hypotheses, which they and everybody are supposed to know. Therefore they do not think it necessary to give any account of them either to themselves or others; but they begin with them, and go on until they arrive at last, and in a consistent manner, at their conclusion.

Yes, he said, I know.

And do you not also know that, although they make use of the visible forms and reason about them, they are thinking not of these, but of things that they resemble; not of the figures that they draw, but of the absolute square and the absolute diameter, and so on. The things that they draw or make, which have shadows and reflections in water of their own, they use as images; but they are really seeking to see the things themselves, which can be seen only with the eye of the mind.

That is true.

This is the kind of thing I spoke of as intelligible, although in the search for it the soul is compelled to use hypotheses, not ascending to a first principle, because the soul is unable to rise above the region of hypothesis, but employing the objects of which the shadows below are images, and which have a greater distinctness than their images, and therefore have a higher value.

I understand, he said, that you are speaking of the province of geometry and related sciences.

And when I speak of the other division of the intelligible, you will understand me to speak of that other sort of knowledge, which reason itself attains by the power of dialectic,[3] using the hypotheses not as first principles, but only as hypotheses—that is to say, as steps and points of departure into a world that is above hypotheses—in order that it may soar beyond them to the first principle of the whole. Clinging to this first principle and then to that which depends on it, by successive steps reason descends again, without the aid of any sensible[4] object, moving from forms and through forms, and ending in forms.

I understand you, he replied; but not perfectly, for you seem to me to be describing a task that is really tremendous. At any rate, I understand you to say that knowledge and being, which the science of dialectic contemplates, are clearer than the notions of the sciences, as they are called, which proceed from hypotheses only. These notions are contemplated by the understanding, and not by the senses; yet, because they start from hypotheses and do not ascend to a principle, those who contemplate them appear to you not to exercise higher reason upon them, although, when a first principle is added to them, they are intelligible. And I suppose that you would call the mental habit concerned with geometry and related sciences understanding and not reason, because it is intermediate between opinion and reason.

You have quite sufficiently grasped my meaning, I said; and now, corresponding to these four divisions, let there be four conditions in the soul—reason corresponding to the highest, understanding to the second, belief to the third, and imagining to the last. Let us arrange them in proportion and consider that they have clearness in the same degree that their objects have truth.

I understand, he replied, and give my assent and accept your arrangement.

### Book VII

Next, I said, let me use a comparison to show how far our nature is enlightened or unenlightened. Imagine human beings living in an underground cave that has an entrance open to the light and reaching all along the cave. They have been here since childhood, with their legs and necks chained so that they cannot move and can look forward only, being prevented by the chains from turning their heads. Above and behind them a fire is blazing at a distance, and between the fire and the prisoners there is a roadway. You will see, if you look, a low wall built along the roadway, like the screen that puppeteers have in front of them, over which they show their puppets.

I see.

And do you see, I said, men passing along the wall carrying all sorts of implements, and statues and figures of animals made of wood and stone and various materials, which appear over the wall? Some of them are talking, others silent.

You have shown me a strange image, and they are strange prisoners.

Like ourselves, I replied; and would see they anything of themselves or of one another except the shadows that the fire casts on the opposite wall of the cave?

How could they, he said, if they were never allowed to move their heads?

And of the objects being carried, they would, in like manner, see only the shadows?

Yes, he said.

And if they were able to converse with one another, would they not suppose that they were naming what was actually before them?

Very true.

And suppose further that the prison had an echo that came from the other side. Would they not presume that, when one of those persons carrying the objects spoke, the voice that they heard came from the passing shadow?

No question, he replied.

To them, I said, the truth would be literally nothing but the shadows of the images.

That is certain.

Now look again, and see what will naturally follow if the prisoners are released from their bonds and from their error. At first, when any of them is freed and compelled to stand up suddenly and turn his neck around and walk and look toward the light, he will suffer sharp pains. The glare will distress him, and he will be unable to see the realities of which in his former state he had seen the shadows. And then imagine someone saying to him that what he saw before was an illusion, but that now, when he is approaching nearer to being and his eye is turned toward more real existence, he has a clearer vision. What will be his reply? And you may further imagine that his instructor is pointing to the objects as they pass and requiring him to name them—will he not be perplexed? Will he not consider the shadows that he formerly saw to be truer than the objects now being shown to him?

Far truer.

And if he is compelled to look straight at the light, will he not have a pain in his eyes that will make him turn away to take refuge in the objects of vision that he can see, which he will consider to be in reality clearer than the things now being shown to him?

True, he said.

And suppose that he is reluctantly dragged up a steep and rough ascent, and held fast until he is forced into the presence of the sun itself—is he not likely to be pained and irritated? When he approaches the light, his eyes will be dazzled. And will he be able to see anything at all of what are now called realities?

No, not immediately, he said.

He will need to grow accustomed to the sight of the upper world. First he will see the shadows best, next the reflections of men and other objects in the water, and then the objects themselves. Then he will gaze upon the light of the moon and the stars and the spangled heaven; and he will see the sky and the stars by night better than the sun or the light of the sun by day.

Certainly.

Finally he will be able to see the sun—not mere reflections of it in the water, but in its own proper place and not in another—and he will contemplate it as it is.

Certainly.

He will then proceed to conclude that this is what gives the season and the years, and is the guardian of everything in the visible world, and in a certain way the cause of all things that he and his companions have been accustomed to see.

Clearly, he said, he would do that next.

And when he remembered his old habitation and the wisdom of the cave and his fellow prisoners, do you not suppose that he would count himself happy because of the change, and pity them?

Certainly he would.

And if they were in the habit of conferring honors among themselves on those who were quickest to observe the passing shadows and to remark which of them went before, and which followed after, and which were together, and who were therefore best able to draw conclusions as to the future—do you think he would care for such honors and glories, or envy those who received them? Would he not say with Homer,

Better to be the poor servant of a poor master,[5]

and to endure anything, rather than think as they do and live as they do?

Yes, he said, I think he would rather suffer anything than entertain these false notions and live in this miserable manner.

Imagine also, I said, this man coming suddenly down into the cave and returning to his old place. Would he not be certain to have his eyes full of darkness?

To be sure, he said.

And if there were a contest, and he had to compete in measuring the shadows with those permanent prisoners while his sight was still weak and before his eyes had become steady (and the time needed to acquire this new habit of sight might be very considerable), would he not appear ridiculous? Men would say that up he went and then came down without his eyes, and that it would be better not even to think of ascending. And if anyone tried to free another and lead him up to the light, would they not kill if they could lay their hands on him?[6]

No question, he said.

This entire allegory, I said, you may now append, dear Glaucon, to what we said before. The prison house is the world of sight, the light of the fire is the sun, and if you interpret the journey upward to be the ascent of the soul into the intelligible world, you will not miss what I hope to convey, since that is what you wanted to hear. Only God knows whether it is true. But, whether true or false, my opinion is that in the world of knowledge the form of the good appears last of all, and is seen only with an effort. When seen, it is also inferred to be the cause of all things beautiful and right, parent of light and of the lord of light in this visible world, and the immediate source of reason and truth in the intelligible world. And he who would act wisely either in public or private life must have his eye fixed on it.

I agree, he said, insofar as I am able to understand you.

Moreover, I said, you must not wonder that those who reached this height are unwilling to descend to human affairs; for their souls are ever hastening to the upper world, where they desire to dwell. And this desire is very natural, if our allegory may be trusted.

Yes, very natural.

And is it surprising that one who, passing from divine contemplations to the evils of human life, would behave inappropriately and in a ridiculous manner—who, while his eyes are blinking and before he has become accustomed to the surrounding darkness, is compelled to fight in courts of law, or in other places, about the images or the shadows of images of justice, and compelled to contend with the conceptions of those who have never yet seen absolute justice?

Anything but surprising, he replied.

Anyone with common sense will remember that bewilderment of the eyes is of two kinds and arises from two causes, either from coming out of the light or from going into the light, and he will believe that this is also true of the soul. When one who remembers this sees anyone whose vision is perplexed and weak, he will not be too ready to laugh; he will first ask whether the soul has come out of the brighter life and is unable to see because it is unaccustomed to the dark, or, having turned from darkness to the day, is dazzled by excess of light. And he will count the former soul happy in its condition and state of being, and he will pity the latter one. And if he has a mind to laugh at the soul that comes from below into the light, there would be more reason to laugh at this than to laugh at a soul that has returned from the light above into the cave.

That, he said, is a very just distinction.

But then, if I am right, certain professional educators must be wrong when they say that they can put knowledge into the soul that lacks it, as if putting sight into blind eyes.

They undoubtedly say this, he replied.

But our argument shows that the power and capacity of learning exists in the soul already; and that just as the eye was unable to turn from darkness to light without the whole body, so too the instrument of knowledge can only by the movement of the whole soul be turned from the world of becoming into that of being, and learn by degrees to endure the sight of being, and of the brightest and best of being—namely, the good.

Very true.

*[handwritten margin note: PLATO'S THEORY OF EDUCATION]*

---

► NOTES

1. The children's puzzle illustrates Socrates' point about the same thing having opposite qualities: A eunuch is a man and not a man, a bat is a bird and not a bird, the pumice stone thrown by the eunuch is a stone and not a stone, and the reed the bat was sitting on is a branch and not a branch. [D. C. ABEL, EDITOR]

2. *essence:* the "what it is" of a thing; its being [D. C. ABEL]

3. *dialectic:* a process of question-and-answer in which one person, by asking a series of probing questions on a topic, stimulates the other person to reflect more deeply on the topic and understand it more fully [D. C. ABEL]

4. *sensible:* able to be sensed [D. C. ABEL]

5. Homer, *Odyssey,* Book XI, lines 489–490. The words are spoken by the ghost of Achilles, the greatest Greek warrior of the Trojan War. Homer (ninth or eighth century B.C.E.) was a Greek epic poet. [D. C. ABEL]

6. Plato alludes to the death of Socrates, whom the Athenians convicted of corrupting the youth and executed. [D. C. ABEL]

# The Republic (selection 1)

Plato

### Reading Questions

*According to Socrates in his conversation with Glaucon:*

1. How do philosophers differ from other people with respect to what they love?

2. In what sense are things in the visible world "between being and not-being"?

3. What objects of cognition are represented by each of the four segments of the divided line? What are the four corresponding conditions of the soul?

4. How does the allegory of the cave illustrate the kinds of knowledge presented in the divided line?

5. What does the allegory of the cave illustrate about the nature of education?

### Discussion Questions

*In your own view:*

1. Do a beautiful dog, a beautiful tree, and a beautiful song have something in common that makes them beautiful? If so, is it something physical?

2. Is there a sense in which things in the visible world are between being and not-being?

3. Does all scientific knowledge depend on hypotheses? If so, is there any kind of knowledge that does not?

4. Is the process of education similar to the ascent from a cave into the daylight?

5. Do human beings have the innate power to see the highest truths?

# Meno

Plato

Plato was born in Athens in about 428 B.C.E. As a youth he associated with Socrates, a philosopher who constantly challenged fellow Athenians to think about virtue and to improve their souls. Plato's initial interest was in politics, but he soon became disillusioned, especially when, under the democracy that was restored after the rule of the "Thirty Tyrants," Socrates was arrested on false charges of impiety and the corruption of youth, convicted, and condemned to die. After the execution of Socrates, Plato moved to nearby Megara for a time and may have traveled to Egypt. In 388 he visited Italy and the city of Syracuse in Sicily. Returning to Athens, he founded the Academy, a school devoted both to philosophical inquiry and to the philosophically based education of politicians. Plato spent most of his life teaching at the Academy (Aristotle was his most famous student) and writing philosophical works. He made two more trips to Syracuse, in 368 and 361, apparently with the intention of turning the city's ruler, Dionysius the Younger, into a "philosopher-king." (If this was indeed his purpose, he failed.) Plato died in Athens in 347 at the age of eighty-one.

Most of Plato's works are written as conversations between Socrates and one or more interlocutors on some topic concerning morality. His best-known "dialogues" (the name by which his surviving works are known) are the *Euthyphro, Apology, Crito, Phaedo, Meno, Symposium,* and *Republic.*

Our reading is a selection from the *Meno,* a dialogue that addresses the question of how we acquire virtue. Meno, a wealthy young man from Thessaly, asks Socrates how virtue is acquired—by teaching, by practice, or in some other way. Socrates tells Meno he cannot answer any questions about the *qualities* of virtue (what *sort of* a thing it is) because he does not yet know the *nature* of virtue (*what* it is). He then invites Meno to join him in an inquiry into the nature of virtue. Meno responds by trying to force Socrates into a dilemma: If he doesn't know what he is looking for (the nature of virtue), then how can he look for it, or know when he has found it? And if he *does* know what he is looking for, there is no point in searching for it. Socrates thinks this is a false dilemma, and to show why, he recounts to Meno what he heard "from certain wise men and women who spoke of things divine." These wise persons said that the human soul lives on after death, and is reincarnated many times. Before it reenters the world, the soul has knowledge of all that is. After being reincarnated, we do learn, but this learning is really *recollection*—a process of remembering what we knew clearly before we were reborn. Meno's dilemma is false because in a sense we *do* know what we are looking for (we knew it before rebirth), and in a sense we do *not* know, because we have not yet recollected what we previously knew. To demonstrate to Meno that knowledge is recollection, Socrates asks to speak to his slave-boy. By a series of questions, Socrates leads this uneducated boy to remember something that he was unaware of knowing: what geometrical figure has an area exactly twice that of a given square.

▼

*The Dialogues of Plato,* trans. Benjamin Jowett. 3rd ed. vol. 2. New York: Macmillan, 1892 (updated stylistically).

*Meno.* Can you tell me, Socrates, whether virtue is acquired by teaching or by practice? Or, if neither by teaching nor by practice, then whether it comes to man by nature or in [some] other way?

*Socrates.* Meno, there was a time when the Thessalians were famous among the other Hellenes only for their riches and their riding. But now, if I am not mistaken, they are equally famous for their wisdom, especially at Larisa, which is the native city of your friend Aristippus. And this is Gorgias'[1] doing. For when he came there, the flower of the Aleuadae—among them your admirer Aristippus—and the other chiefs of the Thessalians fell in love with his wisdom. And he has taught you the habit of answering questions in a grand and bold style, which [benefits] those who know, and is the style in which he himself answers all comers. And any Hellene who likes may ask him anything. How different is our lot, my dear Meno! Here at Athens there is a dearth of the commodity, and all wisdom seems to have emigrated from us to you. I am certain that if you were to ask any Athenian whether virtue was natural or acquired, he would laugh in your face, and say: "Stranger, you have far too good an opinion of me, if you think that I can answer your question. For I literally do not know what virtue is, and much less whether it is acquired by teaching or not." And I myself, Meno, living as I do in this region of poverty, am as poor as the rest of the world. And I confess with shame that I know literally nothing about virtue—and when I do not know the [nature] of anything, how can I know [its qualities]? How, if I knew nothing at all of Meno, could I tell if he was fair or the opposite of fair, rich and noble or the reverse of rich and noble? Do you think that I could?

*Men.* No, indeed. But are you in earnest, Socrates, in saying that you do not know what virtue is? And am I to carry back this report of you to Thessaly?

*Soc.* Not only that, my dear boy, but you may say further that I have never known of anyone else who did, in my judgment.

*Men.* Then you have never met Gorgias when he was at Athens?

*Soc.* Yes, I have.

*Men.* And did you not think that he knew? . . .

*Soc.* What, according to you and your friend Gorgias, is the definition of virtue?

*Men.* Socrates, I used to be told, before I knew you, that you were always doubting yourself and making others doubt. And now you are casting your spells over me, and I am simply getting bewitched and enchanted, and am at my wits' end. And if I may venture to make a jest upon you, you seem to me both in your appearance and in your power over others to be very like the flat torpedo fish, who [numbs] those who come near him and touch him, as you have now [numbed] me, I think. For my soul and my tongue are really torpid, and I do not know how to answer you. And though I have been delivered of an infinite variety of speeches about virtue before now, and to many persons—and very good ones they were, as I thought—at this moment I cannot even say what virtue is. And I think that you are very wise in not voyaging and going away from home, for if you did in other places as you do in Athens, you would be cast into prison as a magician.

*Soc.* You are a rogue, Meno, and had all but caught me.

*Men.* What do you mean, Socrates?

*Soc.* I can tell why you made a simile about me.

*Men.* Why?

*Soc.* In order that I might make another simile about you. For I know that all [handsome] young gentlemen like to have [handsome] similes made about them—as well they may—but I shall not return the compliment. As to my being a torpedo, if the torpedo is torpid as well as the cause of torpidity in others, then indeed I am a torpedo, but not otherwise. For I perplex others not because I am clear, but because I am utterly perplexed myself. And now I know not what virtue is, and you seem to be in the same case, although you did once perhaps know before you touched me. However, I have no objection to join with you in the inquiry.

*Men.* And how will you inquire, Socrates, into that which you do not know? What will you put forth as the subject of inquiry? And if you find what you want, how will you ever know that this is the thing which you did not know?

*Soc.* I know, Meno, what you mean. But just see what a tiresome dispute you are introducing. You argue that a man cannot inquire either about that which he knows, or about that which he does not know. For if he knows, he has no need to inquire; and if not, he cannot, for he does not know the very subject about which he is to inquire.

*Men.* Well, Socrates, and is not the argument sound?

*Soc.* I think not.

*Men.* Why not?

*Soc.* I will tell you why: I have heard from certain wise men and women who spoke of things divine that—

*Men.* What did they say?

*Soc.* They spoke of a glorious truth, as I conceive.

*Men.* What was it? And who were they?

*Soc.* Some of them were priests and priestesses, who had studied how they might be able to give [an account] of their profession. There have been poets also who spoke of these things by inspiration, like Pindar[2] and many others who were inspired. And they say—mark, now, and see whether their words are true—they say that the soul of man is immortal, and at one time has an end, which is termed dying, and at another time is born again, but is never destroyed. And the moral is that a man ought to live always in perfect holiness.

For in the ninth year Persephone[3] sends the souls of those from whom she has received the penalty of ancient crime back again from beneath into the light of the sun above, and these are they who become noble kings and mighty men and great in wisdom and are called saintly heroes in [later] ages.[4]

The soul then, as being immortal, and having been born again many times and having seen all things that exist, whether in this world or in the world below, has knowledge of them all. And it is no wonder that it should be able to call to remembrance all that it ever knew about virtue, and about everything. For as all nature is akin and the soul has learned all things, there is no difficulty in its eliciting (or, as men say, *learning*) out of a single recollection all the rest, if a man is strenuous and does not faint. For all inquiry and all learning is but recollection. And therefore we ought not to listen to this sophistical argument about the impossibility of inquiry, for it will make us idle, and is sweet only to the sluggard. But the other saying will make us active and inquisitive. Confiding in that, I will gladly inquire with you into the nature of virtue.

*Men.* Yes, Socrates. But what do you mean by saying that we do not learn, and that what we call learning is only a process of recollection? Can you teach me how this is?

*Soc.* I told you, Meno, just now that you were a rogue. And now you ask whether I can teach you, when I am saying that there is no teaching, but only recollection—and thus you imagine that you will involve me in a contradiction.

*Men.* Indeed, Socrates, I protest that I had no such intention. I only asked the question from habit. But if you can prove to me that what you say is true, I wish that you would.

*Soc.* It will be no easy matter, but I will try to please you to the utmost of my power. Suppose that you call one of your numerous attendants, that I may demonstrate on him.

*Men.* Certainly. Come hither, boy.

*Soc.* He is Greek, and speaks Greek, does he not?

*Men.* Yes, indeed; he was born in the house.

*Soc.* Attend now to the questions which I ask him, and observe whether he learns from me or only remembers.

*Men.* I will.

*Soc.* Tell me, boy, do you know that a figure like this is a square?[5]

*Boy.* I do.

*Soc.* And you know that a square figure has these four lines equal?

*Boy.* Certainly.

*Soc.* And these lines which I have drawn through the middle of the square[6] are also equal?

*Boy.* Yes.

*Soc.* A square may be of any size?

*Boy.* Certainly.

*Soc.* And if one side of the figure be of two feet, and the other side be of two feet, how much will the whole be? Let me explain: if in one direction the space was of two feet, and in the other direction of one foot, the whole would be of two feet taken once?[7]

*Boy.* Yes.

*Soc.* But since this side is also of two feet, there are twice two feet?

*Boy.* There are.

*Soc.* Then the square is of twice two feet?

*Boy.* Yes.

*Soc.* And how many are twice two feet? Count and tell me.[8]

*Boy.* Four, Socrates.

*Soc.* And might there not be another square twice as large [in area] as this, and having like this the lines equal?

*Boy.* Yes.

*Soc.* And how many [square] feet will that be?

*Boy.* Eight feet.

*Soc.* And now try and tell me the length of the line which forms the side of that double square. [The side of the original square] is two feet. What will [the side of the double-area square] be?

*Boy.* Clearly, Socrates, it will be double.

*Soc.* Do you observe, Meno, that I am not teaching the boy anything, but only asking him questions. And now he fancies that he knows how long a line is necessary in order to produce a figure of eight square feet, does he not?

*Men.* Yes.

*Soc.* And does he really know?

*Men.* Certainly not.

*Soc.* He only guesses that because the square is double, the line is double.

*Men.* True.

*Soc.* Observe him while he recalls the steps in regular order.

*[To the boy:]* Tell me, boy, do you assert that a double area comes from a double line? Remember that I am not speaking of an oblong, but of a figure equal every way, and twice the size of this—that is to say, of eight feet. And I want to know whether you still say that a double square comes from a double line.

*Boy.* Yes.

*Soc.* But does not this line become doubled if we add another such line here?[9]

*Boy.* Certainly.

*Soc.* And four such lines will make a space containing eight feet?

*Boy.* Yes.

*Soc.* Let us [draw] such a figure. Would you not say that this is the figure of eight feet?

*Boy.* Yes.

*Soc.* And are there not these four divisions[10] in the figure, each of which is equal to the figure of four feet?

*Boy.* True.

*Soc.* And is not that four times four?

*Boy.* Certainly.

*Soc.* And four times is not double?

*Boy.* No, indeed.

*Soc.* But how much?

*Boy.* Four times as much.

*Soc.* Therefore the double line, boy, has given an area not twice, but *four* times as much.

*Boy.* True.

*Soc.* Four times four is sixteen, is it not?

*Boy.* Yes.

*Soc.* What line would give you an area of eight feet? This gave one of sixteen feet, did it not?

*Boy.* Yes.

*Soc.* And the space of four feet is made from this half line?

*Boy.* Yes.

*Soc.* Good. And is not an area of eight feet twice the size of this, and half the size of the other?

*Boy.* Certainly.

*Soc.* Such an area, then, will be made out of a line greater than this one, and less than that one?

*Boy.* Yes, I think so.

*Soc.* Very good; I like to hear you say what you think. And now tell me, is not this a line of two feet and that of four?

*Boy.* Yes.

*Soc.* Then the line which forms the side of eight feet ought to be more than this line of two feet, and less than the other of four feet?

*Boy.* It ought.

*Soc.* Try and see if you can tell me how much it will be.

*Boy.* Three feet.

*Soc.* Then if we add a half to this line of two, that will be the line of three. Here are two and there is one; and on the other side, here are two also and there is one: and that makes the figure of which you speak?

*Boy.* Yes.

*Soc.* But if there are three feet this way and three feet that way, the whole space will be three times three feet?

*Boy.* That is evident.

*Soc.* And how much are three times three feet?

*Boy.* Nine.

*Soc.* And how much is the double of four?

*Boy.* Eight.

*Soc.* Then the figure of eight is not made out of a line of three?

*Boy.* No.

*Soc.* But from what line? Tell me exactly—and if you would rather not [calculate it], try and *show* me the line.

*Boy.* Indeed, Socrates, I do not know.

*Soc.* Do you see, Meno, what advances he has made in his power of recollection? He did not know at first, and he does not know now, what is the side of a figure of eight feet. But *then* he thought that he knew, and answered confidently as if he knew, and had no difficulty. Now he has a difficulty, and neither knows nor fancies that he knows.

*Men.* True.

*Soc.* Is he not better off in knowing his ignorance?

*Men.* I think that he is.

*Soc.* If we have made him doubt and given him the torpedo's shock, have we done him any harm?

*Men.* I think not.

*Soc.* We have certainly, as would seem, assisted him in some degree to the discovery of the truth. And now he will wish to remedy his ignorance, but then he would have been ready to tell all the world again and again that the double area should have a double side.

*Men.* True.

*Soc.* But do you suppose that he would ever have inquired into or learned what he fancied that he knew—though he was really ignorant of it—until he had fallen into perplexity, [realizing] that he did not know and [then feeling a desire] to know?

*Men.* I think not, Socrates.

*Soc.* Then he was the better for the torpedo's touch?

*Men.* I think so.

*Soc.* Mark now the farther development. I shall only ask him, and not teach him—and he shall share the inquiry with me. And do you watch and see if you find me telling or explaining anything to him, instead of eliciting his opinion.

Tell me, boy, is not this a square of four [square] feet which I have drawn?

*Boy.* Yes.

*Soc.* And now I add another square equal to the former one?

*Boy.* Yes.

*Soc.* And a third, which is equal to either of them?

*Boy.* Yes.

*Soc.* Suppose that we fill up the vacant corner?

*Boy.* Very good.

*Soc.* Here, then, there are four equal areas?[11]

*Boy.* Yes.

*Soc.* And how many times larger is this area than [the original area]?

*Boy.* Four times.

*Soc.* But it ought to have been twice as large only, as you will remember.

*Boy.* True.

*Soc.* And does not this line, reaching from corner to corner, bisect each of these [smaller squares]?[12]

*Boy.* Yes.

*Soc.* And are there not here four equal lines which contain this area?

*Boy.* There are.

*Soc.* Look and see how large this area is.

*Boy.* I do not understand.

*Soc.* Has not each interior line cut off half of the four [smaller squares]?

*Boy.* Yes.

*Soc.* And how many such [halves] are there in this section?[13]

*Boy.* Four.

*Soc.* And how many in this?[14]

*Boy.* Two.

*Soc.* And four is how many times two?

*Boy.* Twice.

*Soc.* And this area is how many [square] feet?

*Boy.* Eight.

*Soc.* And from what line do you get this figure?

*Boy.* From this.

*Soc.* That is, from the line which extends from corner to corner of the figure of four feet?

*Boy.* Yes.

*Soc.* And that is the line which the learned call the "diagonal." And if this is the proper name, then you, Meno's slave, are prepared to affirm that the double area is the square of the diagonal?

*Boy.* Certainly, Socrates.

*Soc.* What do you say of him, Meno? Were not all these answers given out of his own head?

*Men.* Yes, they were all his own.

*Soc.* And yet, as we were just now saying, he did not know?

*Men.* True.

*Soc.* But still he had in him those notions of his—had he not?

*Men.* Yes.

*Soc.* Then he who does not know may still have true notions of that which he does not know?

*Men.* He has.

*Soc.* And at present these notions have just been stirred up in him, as in a dream. But if he were frequently asked the same questions, in different forms, he would know [these things] as well as anyone?

*Men.* I dare say.

*Soc.* Without anyone teaching him, he will recover his knowledge for himself, if he is only asked questions?

*Men.* Yes.

*Soc.* And this spontaneous recovery of knowledge in him is recollection?

*Men.* True.

*Soc.* And this knowledge which he now has, must he not either have acquired or always possessed?

*Men.* Yes.

► NOTES

1. Gorgias (about 483–376 B.C.E.) was one of the professional Greek educators known as the Sophists. [D.C.A., ed.]

2. Pindar (about 522–438 B.C.E.) was a Greek lyric poet. [D.C.A.]

3. In Greek mythology, Persephone, with Pluto, ruled over the underworld. [D.C.A.]

4. Pindar, fragment 98 in the Greek edition of August Boeckh; fragment 133 in the Greek edition of Theodor Bergk. [D.C.A.]

5. Socrates here draws a square in the sand. [D.C.A.]

6. Socrates draws a vertical line through the middle (the midpoints) of the top and bottom lines of the square, and a horizontal line through the middle (the midpoints) of the left and right sides of the square. This creates four equal, smaller squares inside the original square. [D.C.A.]

7. *two feet taken once:* that is, two square feet. [D.C.A.]

8. The boy counts the total number of smaller squares drawn inside the larger square. [D.C.A.]

9. Socrates, drawing in the sand, extends one side of the original square to twice its length. [D.C.A.]

10. Socrates has drawn three additional lines, each twice the length of the side of the original square, so that the original square is inside (in a corner of) the new, larger square. He then draws a vertical line connecting the midpoints of the top and bottom sides of the new square, and a horizonal line connecting the midpoints of the left and right sides. This creates in the larger squares four smaller squares, each the size of the original square. [D.C.A.]

11. The resulting figure is one large square composed of four equal, smaller squares. The sides of the smaller squares have a length of two; the sides of the larger square have a length of four. [D.C.A.]

12. Socrates draws a diagonal inside each of the four smaller squares. He draws them so that they form a diamond inside the larger square. [D.C.A.]

13. *this section:* the interior, diamond-shaped square. [D.C.A.]

14. *this:* the original square, from which the larger square was constructed. [D.C.A.]

# Meno

Plato

**Reading Questions**

*According to Socrates in his dialogue with Meno:*

1. How does he (Socrates) differ from Gorgias?

2. Why does he (Socrates) perplex others with his questions?

3. Why is the following a false dilemma? "Inquiry is pointless because, if one knows, there is no need to inquire; and if one does not know, one will not recognize the correct answer."

4. What benefit can result from falling into perplexity?

5. Why is the slave-boy able to answer his questions correctly?

**Discussion Questions**

*In your own view:*

1. Must we know what virtue is before we can fruitfully inquire about its qualities?

2. Is it possible to know what virtue is without being able to define it?

3. Did Meno's slave-boy in some sense know how to double the area of a square before his conversation with Socrates? If so, in what sense did he know it?

4. Does the fact that we can recognize the correct answer to a question mean that, in some way, we already know the answer? If so, in what way?

5. Would Socrates' method of eliciting knowledge about mathematics be effective for eliciting knowledge about virtue?

# Discourse on Method

René Descartes

René Descartes was born in La Haye (now called Descartes), France, in 1596. As a youth he was educated by the Jesuits at their college in La Flèche. In about 1614 he began studying at the University of Poitiers, receiving his degree in 1616. Deciding to travel rather than practice law, he went to Holland in 1618 to serve in the army of Dutch Prince Maurice Nassau as a gentleman volunteer. One day in November 1619, while on a military tour of Germany, Descartes sat alone in a room reflecting on a new philosophical system that would unify all branches of knowledge and give them the certainty of mathematics. That night he had three dreams, which he interpreted as a divine commission to construct this new system of knowledge. He left the army shortly afterward and traveled for several years. In 1628 he settled in Holland, where he lived for more than twenty years. There he did research in science and in mathematics (laying the foundations for analytic geometry) and developed his philosophy. In 1649, after much hesitation, Descartes acceded to the request of Queen Christina of Sweden to come to Stockholm to tutor her in philosophy. The harsh winter and the rigorous schedule imposed on him by the queen (philosophy lessons at five o'clock in the morning, for example) took their toll on his health: He died of pneumonia in 1650.

Descartes's major works are *Rules for the Direction of the Mind* (written in 1628, published posthumously), *Discourse on Method* (1637), *Meditations on First Philosophy* (1641), *Principles of Philosophy* (1644), and *The Passions of the Soul* (1649).

Our reading is from the *Discourse on Method* (the customary, shortened title for *Discourse on the Method of Rightly Conducting the Reason and Seeking Truth in the Sciences*). In this work, Descartes discusses his education, his discovery of his method for attaining truth in the sciences, and his application of this method to various sciences, including philosophy. In Part One, Descartes explains that as a youth he pursued his education with the great hope of "gaining all that is useful in life," but was disappointed that so little of what he learned had a solid foundation. So he ended his formal education and spent the rest of his youth traveling, "resolving to seek no other science than what I could find in myself, or at least in the great book of the world."

In Part Two, Descartes narrates that one day when he was in Germany he resolved to build his knowledge on a firm foundation by removing from his mind all opinions that he had previously accepted as true, and replacing them with solidly grounded truths. His chief concern was to devise a method that would guarantee the truth of the conclusions of his reasonings and provide a sure basis for extending his knowledge. Reflecting on certain useful things he had learned in logic, geometry, and algebra, he formulated four rules of inquiry and began to follow them conscientiously. After applying his method with great success to problems in mathematics, he decided to apply it to philosophy, which was the foundation of the other sciences.

Descartes describes in Part Four the fruits of his meditations devoted to establishing philosophy on an absolutely firm basis. When he began doubting everything that could possibly be doubted, including the existence of his body and of the external world, he discovered one thing that could not possibly be false—the fact that he existed. In his own memorable phrase, "I think, therefore I am." Reflecting that his existence was certain because his idea of his existence was "clear and distinct," Descartes concluded that every clarity and distinctness guarantee the truth of an idea. He then reasoned that

God must exist, because only an infinite being could be the source of his (Descartes's) idea of an infinite being. Moreover, God has all perfections, and God must exist because existence is a perfection and is therefore part of the essence of God.

### Part One

Good sense is the best distributed thing in the world, for everyone thinks himself so well provided with it, that even those most difficult to please in all other things do not usually desire more of it than they have. It is unlikely that everyone is mistaken about this. Rather, it seems to indicate that the power of forming a good judgment and distinguishing the true from the false, which is properly called "good sense" or "reason," is by nature equal in all men. It also seems to indicate that the diversity of our opinions does not result from some men being more rational than others, but only from the fact that we lead our thoughts along different paths and do not all consider the same things. It is not enough to have a good mind; the main thing is to apply it well. The greatest souls are capable of the greatest vices as well as the greatest virtues; and those who proceed very slowly, if they always follow the straight path, can advance much faster than those who run but leave the path.

For myself, I have never ventured to presume that my mind was in any way more perfect than that of the ordinary man. I have often wished to have a wit as quick, an imagination as clear and distinct, or a memory as ample or ready, as some others have. Besides these qualities I do not know any others that perfect the human mind. As for reason or sense, since it is the only thing that constitutes us as men and distinguishes us from beasts, I believe that it is complete in each individual. In this I follow the common opinion of philosophers, who say that the question of more or less occurs only in the sphere of the incidental qualities and does not affect the forms, or natures, of individuals of the same species.

I will not hesitate to say that I think that I have been very fortunate that in my youth I happened upon certain paths that led me to considerations and maxims from which I have formed a method that, it seems to me, has enabled me to gradually increase my knowledge and gradually raise it to the highest possible point that the mediocrity of my talents and the brief duration of my life allows me to reach. I always try, when making judgments about myself, to err on the side of diffidence rather than presumption; and when I look with the eye of a philosopher on the various actions and enterprises of all mankind, practically all of them seem vain and useless. But I have already reaped so much fruit from my method that I do not cease to get extreme satisfaction from the progress that I seem to have already made in the search for truth, and I have such hopes for the future as to venture to believe that, if among the occupations of men, simply as men, there is one in particular that is solidly good and important, it is the one that I have chosen.

It is always possible that I may be deceiving myself, and that what I take to be gold and diamonds is no more than copper and glass. I know how much we are we subject to delusion in matters concerning ourselves, and also how much we should distrust judgments in our favor made by our friends. But in this discourse I will be very happy to show the paths I have followed, and to set forth my life as in a picture, so that everyone may judge it for himself. Then, learning from public opinions what people think of it, I will have a new means of instructing myself, which I will add to those that I have been using.

My aim here is not to teach the method that everyone should follow in order to conduct his reason well, but only to show how I have tried to conduct my own. Those who give precepts should consider themselves more skillful than those to whom they give them, and if they are in the smallest matter they must of course take the blame for it. I view this work simply as a history—or a fable, if you prefer—in which, among certain things that could be imitated, there are possibly many others that it would not be reasonable to follow. I hope that this work will be useful to some without being hurtful to any, and that all will thank me for my frankness.

I have been nourished on literary studies since my childhood. Because I was persuaded that through these studies I could gain all that is useful in life, I had an extreme desire to acquire instruction. But so soon as I had completed the entire course of study (when one is usually received into the ranks of the learned), I entirely changed my opinion. For I found myself embarrassed with so many doubts and errors that it seemed to me that my effort to instruct myself only increased the discovery of my own ignorance. And yet I was studying at one of the most celebrated schools in Europe, where I thought that there must be men of learning, if such men existed anywhere in the world. There I learned everything that the others learned; and because I was not satisfied with the sciences that were taught, I read all the books that came into my hands that discussed matters considered most unusual and rare. I knew how others judged me, and I did not think that I was seen as inferior to my fellow students, although among them were persons destined to fill the places of our teachers. Finally, our century seemed to me to be as flourishing and as fertile in great minds as any that had preceded it. This made me take the liberty of judging all others by myself and of concluding that there was no learning in the world such as I had been led to believe it to be.

I never failed to value the exercises done in the schools. I knew that the languages one learns there are essential for understanding ancient literature; that fables with their charm stimulate the mind; that histories of memorable deeds exalt the mind; and that, if read with discretion, these books help us make sound judgments. I knew that reading good books is like a conversing with the honorable men of past centuries who wrote them—in fact, a studied conversation in which they reveal to us the best of their thoughts. I knew that eloquence has a power and beauty beyond compare;

that poetry has most ravishing delicacy and sweetness; and that mathematics contains subtle discoveries and inventions that can not only satisfy the curious, but also further all the arts and decrease human labor. I knew that the writings dealing with morals contain many useful teachings and many useful exhortations to virtue; that theology points the way to heaven; and that philosophy teaches us to speak apparent truth on all things and causes us to be admired by the less learned. I knew that jurisprudence, medicine, and all other sciences bring honor and riches to those who cultivate them. Finally, I knew that it is good to have examined all things, even those most full of superstition and falsehood, in order to know their true value and avoid being deceived by them.

I believed that I had already given sufficient time to languages and even to reading the histories and fables of ancient literature. To converse with those of other centuries is almost the same thing as to travel. It is good to know something about the customs of different peoples in order to judge our own more sanely, and not to think that everything unlike our own ways is absurd and contrary to reason, as do those who have seen nothing. But when one spends too much time traveling, one becomes a stranger in one's own country; and when one is too curious about things practiced in past centuries, one is usually very ignorant about those practiced in one's own time. Besides, fables make one imagine as possible many events that are impossible. And even the most accurate histories, if they do not exactly misrepresent or exaggerate the value of things in order to maker them more worthy to be read, at least omit all the basest and least illustrious things. From this it follows that what is retained is not portrayed as it really is, and that those who regulate their conduct by examples derived from such sources are liable to fall into the excesses of the knights-errant of the literature of chivalry and undertake projects beyond their abilities.

I highly valued eloquence and I loved poetry. But I thought that both were gifts of the mind rather than fruits of study. Those who have the strongest power of reasoning, and who most skillfully arrange their thoughts to make them clear and intelligible, have the best power of persuasion even if they can speak only the language of lower Brittany and have never learned rhetoric. Those who have the most delightful original ideas and know how to express them with the greatest style and sweetness would be the best poets even if they did not know the art of poetry.

I was especially delighted with mathematics because of the certainty and self-evidence of its reasoning. But I did not yet understand its true use. Believing that mathematics was useful only in the mechanical arts, I was astonished that a higher edifice had not been built upon its firm and solid foundation. On the other hand, I compared the writings on morals by the ancient pagans to superb and magnificent palaces built only on sand and mud. They highly praise the virtues and show that they should be prized more than anything else in the world, but they do not sufficiently teach us to become acquainted with the virtues, and often what they call by a fine name is nothing but insensibility, pride, despair, or parricide.

I respected our theology and desired as much as anyone to attain heaven. But after learning as a highly assured fact that the road is open just as much to the most ignorant as to the most learned, and that the revealed truths that lead us to heaven are beyond our understanding, I did not dare submit them to the feebleness of my reasonings. I thought that, in order to undertake to examine them and succeed in doing so, I would need to receive extraordinary assistance from above, and to be more than a mere man.

I will not say anything about philosophy except that, seeing that it has been cultivated for many centuries by the best minds that have ever lived, and that nevertheless no single thing in it is not subject to dispute and is therefore not doubtful, I did not presume to believe that I could fare better there than others had done. And considering that there could be many conflicting opinions on the same matter, all supported by learned people, but never be more than one that is true, I judged as nearly false all opinions that were simply probable.

As to the other sciences, because they derive their principles from philosophy, I judged that nothing solid could be built on foundations so far from firm. Neither the honor nor the promised gain was sufficient to persuade me to pursue these sciences, for, thanks be to God, I did not find myself in a situation that required me to pursue an occupation in science as a way to increase my fortune. Although I did not pretend to scorn all glory, as the Cynics[1] did, I yet had very small esteem for what I could acquire only through false titles. Finally, as to bad doctrines, I thought that I already knew their worth well enough not to be deceived to by the promises of an alchemist, the predictions of an astrologer, the tricks of a magician, or the artifices or empty boastings of any who profess to know what they do not know.

This is why, as soon as I was old enough to emerge from the control of my tutors, I left literary studies entirely. Resolving to seek no other science than what I could find in myself, or at least in the great book of the world, I spent the rest of my youth traveling, seeing courts and armies, engaging with men of different temperaments and positions, collecting varied experiences, and testing myself in the various situations where fortune place me. In all circumstances I brought my mind to bear on the things that came before it, so that I could profit from my experience. For it seemed to me that I could find much more truth in the reasonings that each man makes on matters that specially concern him, and the outcome of which would soon punish him if he made a wrong judgment, than in reasonings made in his study by a man of letters, when these reasonings have no result and do not affect him, unless perhaps they make him more vain, the farther they are from common sense—because then he was required to use more ingenuity and skill to try to make them seem probable. I always had an extreme desire to learn to distinguish the true from the false, in order to see clearly in my actions and to walk with confidence in this life.

It is true that when I considered only the customs of other men, I found in them nothing to give me settled convictions. I observed in them almost as much diversity as I had previously seen in the opinions of philosophers. This was so much the case that the greatest profit I derived from studying them was this: In observing many things that seem very extravagant and ridiculous to us, but were commonly accepted and approved by other great nations, I learned not to believe too certainly the things of which I had persuaded only by example and custom. Thus little by little I was delivered from many errors that might have obscured our natural vision and made us less able to listen to reason. After I had spent several years studying the book of the world in this way and trying to acquire some experience, one day I resolved to make myself an object of study and to use the entire strength of my mind to choose which path to follow. This succeeded much better, I believe, than if I had never left either my country or my books.

**Part Two**

At that time I was in Germany, where I had been called by the wars that are still going on there. As I was returning to the army from the coronation of the emperor, the winter weather detained me in quarters where I had no conversations to divert me and, fortunately, no cares or passions to trouble me. The whole day I stayed alone inside a stove-heated room, where I had complete leisure to occupy myself with my own thoughts. One of the first of the considerations to occur to me was that very often there is less perfection in works composed of several parts and made by the hands of various masters, than in those on which a single person has worked. Thus we see that buildings planned and carried out by one architect alone are usually more beautiful and better proportioned than those that many have tried to put in order and improve, using old walls built with other purposes in mind. In the same way, those ancient cities that were originally villages and over time became great towns are usually badly constructed compared to those laid out on level ground by engineers following their own ideas. . . . I came to think that similarly the sciences found in books—in those at least with only probable reasonings and no demonstrations, composed of the gradually accumulated opinions of many different individuals—do not approach the truth as nearly as the simple reasoning that a man of common sense can quite naturally carry out regarding things immediately before him. I thought that since we all were children before becoming men, and since for we were governed for long time by our appetites and by our teachers (who often contradicted each another, and none of whom perhaps always gave the best advice), it is almost impossible for our judgments to be as excellent or as solid as they would have been if we had had complete use of our reason since our birth and had been guided by it alone.

It is true that we do not see all the houses in a town being razed to the ground for the sole purpose of rebuilding the town in another fashion and making the streets more beautiful. Nevertheless, we see that many people have their own houses knocked down in order to rebuild them, and that sometimes they are forced so to do when there is a danger that the house will fall down by itself, and when the foundation is not firm. From such examples I argued to myself that it made no sense for a private individual to plan to reform a state by altering everything, and to overturn a state in order to set it right again. Nor did it make sense to reform the whole body of the sciences, or the order of teaching established by the schools. But with regard to all the opinions I had accepted up until this time, I thought I could do no better than to try once and for all to remove them completely, in order to replace them later with better ones, or with the same ones if I adjusted them to the level of reason. I firmly believed that by this means I would succeed in directing my life much better than if I had built only on old foundations and relied on principles that I accepted in my youth without examining their truth. . . .

My plan has never gone beyond trying to reform my own opinions and build on a foundation entirely my own. If my work has given me a certain satisfaction, so that I here present to you a draft of it, I do not so do because I wish to suggest that anyone imitate it. Those to whom God has been most generous in bestowing his graces will perhaps have more exalted plans. But I fear that, for many, even my plan will seem too bold. The simple resolve to strip oneself of all opinions and beliefs formerly accepted is not an example that everyone should follow. The world is, so to speak composed of two kinds of minds that should not follow my plan. Some minds, believing themselves to be cleverer than they are, cannot refrain from making impulsive judgments and do not have sufficient patience to arrange their thoughts in proper order. If they take the liberty of doubting the principles they formerly accepted and stray from the common path, they will never be able to keep to the path that they must follow to reach the goal more quickly, and they will be always be wandering. Second, there are those minds that have enough reason or modesty to judge that they are less able to distinguish truth from falsehood than some others are who might instruct them. They are right to be content to follow the opinions of these others, rather than search for better opinions themselves.

For myself, I would undoubtedly have been in the second group if I had never had more than one teacher, or if had I never known the differences that have always existed among the opinions of men of the greatest learning. But I had been taught, even in my college days, that there is nothing imaginable that is so strange or so incredible that it has not been stated by some philosopher. I further recognized in the course of my travels that those whose sentiments are very contrary to ours are not necessarily barbarians or savages, but may be as rational or even more rational than we are. I also considered how the same person, with the same mind, brought up from childhood among the French or Germans, would become different if he had lived his whole life among the Chinese or cannibals. I likewise noticed how, even in fashions of clothing, the same thing that pleased us ten years ago, and that will perhaps please us again before ten years have passed, seems at the present time extravagant and ridiculous. I thus concluded that it is much more custom and example that persuade us than any certain knowledge. The voice of the majority is not a proof of any value regarding truths that are somewhat difficult to discover, because such truths are much more likely to be discovered by one man than by a whole people. I could not, however, choose anyone whose opinions seemed preferable to those of others, and I found that I was, so to speak, forced to be my own leader.

Like a person who walks alone in the dark, I resolved to go so slowly, and to use so much circumspection in all things, that even if I progressed very little, I would at least prevent myself from falling. I did not wish to completely reject any single opinion that might formerly have crept into my beliefs without having been introduced there by reason, until I had first spent sufficient time planning out the project that I had undertaken, and seeking the true method of arriving at a knowledge of everything that my mind could know.

When I was younger, within the discipline of philosophy I studied some logic, and within mathematics I studied some geometrical analysis and algebra. These three arts or sciences seemed able to make a contribution to my plan. But when I examined them, I observed that, with respect to logic, syllogisms and most of its other doctrines were better suited to explain to others what one already knows . . . than to learning new things. And although logic does contain many very true and very good precepts, so many other harmful and superfluous precepts are mixed in with them that it is almost as difficult to separate the two as to sculpt a Diana or a Minerva out of block of marble that is not yet hewn. And as to the [geometrical] analysis of the ancients and the algebra of the moderns, they include only the most abstract things, which seem to have no actual use. In addition, the former is always so restricted to considering symbols that it cannot exercise the understanding without greatly tiring the imagination; and the latter is so subjected to certain rules and formulas that it produces a confused and obscure art that embarrasses the mind, instead of producing a science that cultivates it. This made me think that I must find some other method—one that included the advantages of these three, but lacked their faults. And just as a large number of laws often gives excuses for evildoing, and a state is therefore much better ruled when it has very few laws and they are strictly observed; in the same way, instead of the great number of precepts that constitute logic, I believed that I would find quite sufficient the following four, provided that I adhered to a firm and constant resolve never to fail to observe them.

The first of these was never to accept anything as true that I did not clearly recognize to be true; that is to say, to carefully avoid precipitous and biased judgments, and to include in my judgments only what was presented to my mind so clearly and distinctly that I could have no occasion to doubt it.

The second was to divide up each of the difficulties that I examined into as many parts as possible, and as were required to resolve the difficulties better.

The third was to carry on my reflections in due order, beginning with objects that were simplest and easiest to understand, in order to rise gradually, by degrees, to knowledge of the most complex objects, assuming an order even among objects that are not naturally ordered among themselves.

The last was in all cases to make enumerations so complete, and reviews so general, that I would be certain that I omitted nothing.

Those long chains of reasoning, simple and easy as they are, that geometers use to arrive at the most difficult demonstrations, led me to imagine that everything that falls under human knowledge might very likely be mutually related in the same fashion; and that, provided only that we refrain from accepting as true anything that is not so, and always retain the order necessary to deduce one conclusion from the other, there can be nothing so distant that we cannot reach to it, or so hidden that we cannot discover it. I had little trouble discovering which objects it was necessary to begin with, for I already knew that it was with those that are the simplest and easiest to know. And considering that, of all those who have sought truth in the sciences, mathematicians alone were able to make demonstrations—in other words, to produce evident and certain reasons—I did not doubt that I should begin my investigations with the same objects. I did not hope for any practical result in doing so, except that my mind would become accustomed to the nourishment of truth and would not content itself with false reasons. But I had no intention of trying to master all those particular sciences that share the name "mathematics";[2] and observing that, although their objects are different, they do not fail to agree about considering only the various relations or proportions present in these objects, I thought that it would be better if I examined these proportions only in general, without viewing them otherwise than in the objects that would best help me know them. I would not in any way restrict the proportions to these objects; afterwards I could better apply them to all other objects to which they were applicable. Then, having carefully noted that in order to know the proportions, I would sometimes need to consider each one in particular, and sometimes merely keep them in mind or take them in groups, I thought that, in order the better to consider them in detail, I should picture them in the form of lines, because I could find no method that was simpler or that I could represent more distinctly to my imagination and my senses. I considered, however, that in order to keep them in my memory or to take several at once, it would be necessary for me to explain them by certain symbols, as short as possible. And for this purpose it would I would borrow all that is best from geometrical analysis and algebra, and correct the errors of the one by means of the other.

As a matter of fact, I can say that, by exactly following the few precepts that I had chosen, I gained so much facility in sifting out all the questions included in these two sciences, that in the two or three months that I spent examining them—having begun the simplest and most general, and with each truth that I discovered becoming a rule for helping discover other truths—not only did I arrive at the solution of many questions that, until then, I had considered very difficult, but it seemed to me, towards the end, that I was able to determine, for the unsolved cases, by what means and how far it was possible to solve them. . . .

Since I had not restricted this method to any particular topic, I promised myself to apply it as usefully to the difficulties of other sciences as I had done to those of algebra. Not that I would have dared undertake to examine right away all the difficulties that might present themselves—that would itself have been contrary to the order that the method prescribes. But having noticed that the principles of these sciences must all derive from philosophy, in which still had not found anything certain, I thought that it was necessary above all to try to establish certainty in philosophy. Since I considered this task the most important thing in the world, and the place where precipitous and biased judgments were most to be feared, I decided not to try to undertake it until I reached an age more mature than twenty-three (my age at the time) and until I had spent a great deal of time beforehand preparing myself by eradicating from my mind all the bad opinions that I had previously accepted, by accumulating a variety of experiences as material for my reasonings, and by always exercising myself in the method I had prescribed, in order to strengthen myself in it more and more. . . .

**Part Four**

I do not know whether I should tell you about the first meditations I made [after settling in Holland], for they are so metaphysical[3] and so unusual that they will perhaps not suit everyone's taste. Nevertheless, in order that one may judge whether the foundations that I have laid are sufficiently firm, I find myself forced to refer to them in some way. For a long time I had noted that it is sometimes necessary in ordinary activities to follow opinions that one knows are very uncertain, just as if they were indisputable, as I said above.[4] But because I wished to give myself entirely to the search for truth, I thought that it was necessary for me to do the opposite, and to reject as absolutely false everything in which I could imagine the least doubt, in order to see if afterwards any of my beliefs remained absolutely indubitable. Thus, because our senses sometimes deceive us, I wished to suppose that nothing is just as they cause us to imagine it. And because there are men who deceive themselves in their reasoning and fall into fallacious arguments, even in the simplest matters of geometry, and because I judged that I was as liable to err as anyone else, I rejected as false all the reasons that I had previously accepted as demonstrations. And finally, since all the same thoughts that we have while awake may also come to us while we sleep, without any of them being at that time true, I resolved to assume that everything that ever entered into my mind was no more true than the illusions of my dreams. But immediately afterwards I noticed that while I thus wished to think all things false, it was necessary that the "I" who thought this was something. And seeing that this truth, "I think, therefore I am," was so certain and so assured that all the most extravagant suppositions of the skeptics were unable to shake it, I concluded that I could accept it without scruple as the first principle of the philosophy I was seeking.

Then, examining attentively that what I was, I saw that I could pretend that I had no body, and that there was no world and no place where I was. Yet I could not pretend that I did not exist. On the contrary, I saw from the very fact that I thought of doubting the truth of other things, it followed very evidently and certainly that I existed. On the other hand, if I had only ceased to think, even if everything else that I had ever imagined was true, I would have no reason to think that I had existed. From this I knew that I was a substance whose whole essence, or nature, is to think; and that for its existence it does not need any place and does not depend on any material thing. Consequently this "I"—in other words, the soul—through which I am what I am, is entirely distinct from body and is more easily known than it. Even if the body did not exist, the "I" would not cease to be what it is.

After this I considered in general what is required for a proposition to be true and certain; for since I had just discovered one that I knew was such, I thought that I ought also to know what this certainty consisted in. And having noticed that there was nothing at all in the statement "I think, therefore I am" that assures me that I am saying the truth, except that I see very clearly that in order to think it is necessary to exist, I concluded that I could take as a general rule that the things that we conceive very clearly and distinctly are all true—remembering, however, that there is some difficulty what those things are that we conceive distinctly.

After this, reflecting on the fact that I doubted, and that consequently my existence was not entirely perfect (for I saw clearly that it was a greater perfection to know than to doubt), I resolved to seek the source of my thought of something more perfect than I was. I recognized very clearly that the source must be some nature that was in fact more perfect. As to the thoughts that I had of many other things outside of me, such as the heavens, the earth, light, heat, and a thousand others, I had little difficulty knowing their source because, noticing that nothing in them that seemed to make them superior to me, I could believe that, if they were true, they depended on my nature, insofar as my nature possessed some perfection. And I could believe that if they were not true, I regarded them as nothing—in other words, that they were in me because I had some defect. But this could not apply to the idea of a being more perfect than my own, for to regard it as nothing would be manifestly impossible. And because it is no less contradictory to say that the more perfect results from and depends on the less perfect, than to say that something proceeds from nothing, I could not regard it as coming from myself. Hence it followed that it had been placed in me by a nature that was truly more perfect than I was, and that even had within itself all the perfections of which I could form any idea—that is to say, to explain myself in one word, it was God. To this I added the following: Since I knew some perfections that I did not possess, I was not the only being in existence (I will here use freely, if you permit, the terminology of the school); but that there was necessarily some other more perfect being on which I depended, and from which I acquired all that I had. For if I had existed alone and independent of any others, so that I had from myself all that perfection of being in which I participated to however small an extent, I would have been able, for the same reason, to have had all the remainder of perfection that I knew I lacked. Thus I myself would be infinite, eternal, immutable, all-knowing, all-powerful, and, finally, would have all the perfections that I could discern in God. For, following reasonings that I just made, in order to know the nature of God as far as my nature is capable of knowing it, I had only to consider, with regard to all these things that I found some idea of in myself, whether it was a perfection to possess them or not. And I was assured that none of those that indicated an imperfection was in God, but that all the others were in God. I saw that doubt, inconstancy, sadness, and similar things could not be in him, since I myself would be glad not to have them. In addition to this, I had ideas of many things that could be sensed and were corporeal; for, although I might suppose that I was dreaming, and that everything I saw or imagined was false, I could not at the same time deny that the ideas were truly in my thoughts. I had already recognized very clearly in myself that the nature of the intelligent is distinct from that of the corporeal. And observing that all composition gives evidence of dependence, and that dependence is manifestly an imperfection, I concluded that it could not be a perfection in God to be composed of these two natures, and that consequently he was not so composed. I judged, however, that if there were any bodies in the world, or even any intelligences or other natures that were not wholly perfect, their existence must depend on his power in such a way that they could not subsist without him for a single moment.

After this I desired to seek other truths, and I put before myself the object studied by geometers, which I conceived as continuous body, or a space indefinitely extended in length, breadth, height or depth, which can be divided various parts, have various figures and sizes, and be moved or transposed in all sorts of ways—for geometers suppose all this to be the object of their study. I went through some of their simplest demonstrations, and after noticing that the great certainty that everyone attributes to these demonstrations is founded solely on the fact that they are conceived with clearness, in accordance with the rule I have just laid down, I also noticed that there was nothing at all in them to assure me of the existence of their object. For example, I saw very well that, if we suppose that a triangle exists, its three angles must certainly equal two right angles; but I did not see anything that assured me that any triangle exists in the world. But when I reexamined the idea I had of a perfect being, I found that in this case existence was included in it in the same way that the equality of its three angles to two right angles is included in the idea of a triangle, or that the equidistance to the center of all points on the surface is included in the idea of sphere—indeed, in the case of a perfect being, it was even more evident. Consequently it is at least as certain that God, who is this perfect being, is, or exists, as any demonstration in geometry could be. . . .

If there are any persons not sufficiently persuaded of the existence of God and of their soul by the reasons that I have brought forward, I wish that they knew that all other things of which they perhaps think they are more assured (for example, that they have a body, that there are stars and an earth, and so on) are less certain. For although we have a moral certainty[5] of these things, which would seem to make it extravagant of us to doubt them, with regard to metaphysical certainty, no one (unless he is unreasonable) can deny that there is sufficient cause for not having complete assurance. For we realize that when we are asleep we may imagine in the same way that we have another body, and that we see other stars and another earth, without there being anything of the kind. How do we know that the thoughts that come in dreams are more false than those that we have when we are awake, since often the former are not less lively and vivid than the latter? Even if the wisest minds study the matter as much as they wish, I do not believe that they will be able to give any sufficient reason for removing this doubt, unless they presuppose the existence of God. For to begin with, that which I have just taken as a rule—namely, that all the things that we conceive very clearly and very distinctly are true—is certain only because God is, or exists, and because he is a Perfect Being, and because everything in us comes from him. From this it follows that our ideas or notions, which are real things that come from God, must be true to the extent that they are clear and distinct. If we somewhat often have ideas that contain some falsity, this must be because they have something confused or obscure. The reason for this is that they participate in negation—that is, they exist in us as confused only because we are not wholly perfect. And it is evident that it is no less contradictory that error or imperfection (to extent that it is error or imperfection) proceeds from God, than that truth or perfection proceeds from nothing. But if we did not know that everything is real and true in us proceeds from a perfect and infinite Being, then, no matter how clear and distinct our ideas, were, we would have no reason to assure ourselves that they had the perfection of being true.

After the knowledge of God and the soul has thus made us certain of this rule, it is very easy to understand that the dreams we imagine in our sleep should not make us in any way doubt the truth of the thoughts we have when awake. For even if in sleep one had some very distinct idea (for example, geometer discovering some new demonstration), one's sleep would not prevent the idea from being true. As to the most ordinary error in our dreams, which consists in their representing to us various objects in the same way that our external senses do, it does not matter that this gives us occasion to suspect the truth of such ideas, because they can often enough deceive us when we are not sleeping, just as when those who have jaundice see everything as yellow, or when stars or other bodies that are very remote appear much smaller than they really are. Finally, whether we are awake or asleep, we should never allow ourselves to be persuaded except by the evidence of our reason.

► N O T E S

1. *Cynics:* a school of ancient Greek philosophy that held the ideal of self-sufficiency through the mastery of one's desires and needs  [D. C. ABEL, EDITOR]

2. In Descartes' time, sciences such as astronomy and music were considered branches of mathematics [D. C. ABEL]

3. *metaphysical:* relating to *metaphysics,* the study of the nature and kinds of reality [D. C. ABEL]

4. *above:* in Part Three, which is not included in this selection [D. C. ABEL]

5. *moral certainty:* a very high degree of probability, but not absolute, metaphysical certainty [D. C. ABEL]

# Discourse on Method

René Descartes

### Reading Questions

*According to Descartes:*

1. What are the advantages of studying ancient literature? What are the dangers?

2. What two kinds of persons should not undertake the project of doubting all the opinions that they formerly accepted as true?

3. When trying to build a firm foundation for knowledge, what opinions should one accept as true? What kind of objects should one begin reflecting on?

4. When one attempts to doubt all things, what is the one thing that cannot be doubted?

5. Why is it more certain that God exists than that there are stars and an earth?

### Discussion Questions

*In your own view:*

1. Is Descartes's four-step method the best way to attain certain knowledge?

2. What does it mean for an idea to be "clear and distinct"? Are all such ideas necessarily true?

3. If you cannot doubt the existence of your mind, but can doubt the existence of your body, does it follow that you *are* a mind?

4. Can the idea of an infinite being be caused only by an infinite being?

5. Is existence part of the nature of a perfect being? If so, would it be a contradiction for a perfect being not to exist?

# Meditations on First Philosophy

René Descartes

René Descartes was born in La Haye (now called Descartes), France, in 1596. As a youth he was educated by the Jesuits at their college in La Flèche. In about 1614 he began studying at the University of Poitiers, receiving his degree in 1616. Deciding to travel rather than practice law, he went to Holland in 1618 to serve in the army of the Dutch Prince Maurice of Nassau as a gentleman volunteer. One day in November 1619, while on a military tour of Germany, Descartes sat alone in a room reflecting on a new philosophical system that would unify all branches of knowledge and give them the certainty of mathematics. That night he had three dreams, which he interpreted as a divine commission to construct this new system of knowledge. He left the army shortly afterward and traveled for several years. In 1628 he settled in Holland, where he lived for more than twenty years. There he did research in science and in mathematics (laying the foundations for analytic geometry) and developed his philosophy. In 1649, after much hesitation, Descartes acceded to the request of Queen Christina of Sweden to come to Stockholm to tutor her in philosophy. The harsh winter and the rigorous schedule imposed on him by the queen (philosophy lessons at five o'clock in the morning, for example) took their toll on his health: He died of pneumonia in 1650.

Descartes' major works are *Rules for the Direction of the Mind* (written in 1628, published posthumously), *Discourse on Method* (1637), *Meditations on First Philosophy* (1641), *Principles of Philosophy* (1644), and *The Passions of the Soul* (1649).

Our reading is from *Meditations on First Philosophy*. (By "first philosophy" Descartes means truths about the basic topics of philosophy, which for him are God, the soul [mind], and the external world.) In Meditation I, Descartes explains his "method of doubt": He will not accept as true anything of which he cannot be absolutely certain. But practically everything seems open to doubt; Descartes reflects that he might even be deceived in his belief that there is an external world. For how can he be sure that there is not some powerful "evil demon" who tricks him into thinking there is an external world by placing images directly in his mind?

In Meditation II, Descartes realizes that he can be absolutely certain of at least one thing—that he exists, for even if he is deceived about the existence of the external world, he could not be deceived unless he existed. As he formulates this argument elsewhere, "I think, therefore I am." This "I" that exists is "a thing that thinks." Descartes goes on to argue that if there are material things, their essential nature would be extension (three-dimensionality), and that extension is grasped by the mind, not by the senses.

In our selection from Meditation III, Descartes reflects on the certitude of his own existence and formulates a general criterion for truth: "All things that I perceive very clearly and very distinctly are true." He then presents a proof for the existence of God. He finds that his mind contains an idea of an infinite being, and reasons that he himself—who is merely a *finite* being—could not have invented such an idea. Descartes concludes that the idea of an infinite being must have been placed in his mind by the infinite being itself. Therefore this infinite being (God) exists.

▼

Reprinted from *The Philosophical Works of Descartes*, trans. Elizabeth M. Haldane and G. R. T. Ross, Vol. 1. Cambridge, England: Cambridge University Press, 1911 (updated stylistically).

### Meditation I. Of the Things That May Be Doubted

Some years ago I realized how many false beliefs I had from my earliest youth admitted as true, and how doubtful everything was that I had constructed on this basis. From that time I was convinced that I must, once and for all, seriously undertake to rid myself of all the opinions I had previously accepted and start again from the foundation, if I wanted to establish any firm and permanent structure in the sciences. But since this enterprise appeared to be very great, I waited until I had reached an age mature enough so that I could not hope at any later date to be better fitted to carry out my plan. This caused me to delay so long that I feel that I would be wrong to spend in deliberation the time still remaining for me to act. Today, then, since—very opportunely for the plan I have in view—I have freed my mind from every care, and have secured for myself sufficient leisure time in quiet retirement, I will at last seriously and freely address myself to the general destruction of all my former opinions.

Now for this goal it is not necessary for me to show that all of these opinions are false—I could perhaps never be able to do that. But since reason already persuades me that I ought no less carefully to withhold my assent from matters that are not entirely certain and indubitable than from those that appear to me to be obviously false, if I am able to find in each one some reason to doubt, this will be enough to justify rejecting it. And for that goal I will not need to examine each opinion in particular, which would be an endless undertaking. The destruction of the foundations necessarily brings with it the downfall of the rest of the building, so I will only attack those principles upon which all my former opinions rested.

Everything that up to the present time I have accepted as most true and certain, I have learned either from the senses or through the senses. But it is sometimes proved to me that these senses are deceptive, and it is wiser not to trust entirely to anything by which we have once been deceived.

But although the senses sometimes deceive us concerning objects that are hardly perceptible or are far away, there are yet many other things that we cannot reasonably doubt, although we recognize them by means of the senses. For example, there is the fact that I am here, seated by the fire, wearing a dressing gown, holding this piece of paper in my hands, and other similar matters. And how could I deny that these hands and this body are mine—unless I compare myself to certain insane persons, whose brains are so troubled and clouded by the violent vapors of black bile that they constantly assure us that they think they are kings when they are really quite poor, or that they are clothed in purple when they are really without clothing, or who imagine that they have an earthenware head or are nothing but pumpkins or are made of glass. But they are insane, and I would not be any less insane if I took them as a model.

At the same time I must remember that I am a man, and that consequently I am in the habit of sleeping, and that in my dreams I represent to myself the same things or sometimes even less probable ones, than insane persons do in their waking moments. How often has it happened to me that in the night I dreamed that I found myself in this particular place, that I was dressed and seated near the fire, while in reality I was lying undressed in bed! At this moment it does indeed seem to me that I am looking at this piece of paper with my eyes awake, that this head that I move is not asleep, and that I extend my hand deliberately and intentionally and perceive it. What happens in sleep does not appear as clear or distinct as this. But in thinking this over, I remind myself that on many occasions I have in sleep been deceived by similar illusions, and in dwelling carefully on this reflection I see that there are no certain indications by which wakefulness may be clearly distinguished from sleep. I am lost in astonishment, and my astonishment is so great that can almost persuade me that I am now dreaming.

Now let us assume that we are asleep and that all these particulars—for example, that we open our eyes, shake our head, extend our hands, and so on—are false delusions; and let us reflect that possibly neither our hands nor our whole body are what they appear to us to be. At the same time we must at least admit that the things represented to us in sleep are like painted representations that must have been formed as counterparts of something real and true, and that in this way those general things at least (eyes, head, hands, the whole body) are not imaginary things, but things really existing. As a matter of fact even when painters try with the greatest skill to represent sirens and satyrs[1] by strange and extraordinary forms, they cannot give them natures that are entirely new, but merely make a composite of the parts of different animals. Or if their imagination is fertile enough to invent something so novel that nothing similar has ever before been seen, and their work represents a thing that is purely fictitious and absolutely false, it is certain at least that the colors of which the thing is composed are necessarily real. And for the same reason, although these general things—namely, eyes, head, hands, and so on—may be imaginary, we are bound at the same time to admit that there are at least some other objects simpler and more universal, which are real and true. And from these, as from certain real colors, all these images of things that occur in our thoughts (whether true and real or false and imaginary) are formed.

This class of things includes corporeal nature in general and its extension, the shape of extended things, their quantity or magnitude and number, the place in which they are, the time that measures their duration, and so on.

That is possibly why it seems reasonable to conclude from this that physics, astronomy, medicine, and all other sciences that consider composite things, are very doubtful and uncertain; and that arithmetic, geometry, and other sciences of this kind, which deal only with very simple and very general things, without taking great trouble to determine whether they actually exist or not, contain some measure of certainty and an element of the indubitable. For whether I am awake or asleep, two and three together always make five, and a square can never have more than four sides; and it does not seem possible that truths so clear and apparent can be suspected of any falsity.

Nevertheless, I have long had fixed in my mind the belief that an all-powerful God exists, who created me such as I am. But how do I know that he has not brought it about that there is no earth, no heaven, no extended object, no magnitude, no place, and that nevertheless they seem to me to exist just exactly as I now see them? And besides, as I sometimes imagine that others deceive themselves in the things that they think they know best, how do I know that I am not deceived every time that I add two and three, or count the sides of a square, or make judgments about even simpler things, if simpler things can be imagined? But possibly God has not desired that I should be so deceived, for he is said to be supremely good. If, however, it is contrary to his goodness to have made me such that I *constantly* deceive myself, it would also appear to be contrary to his goodness to permit me to be *sometimes* deceived, and nevertheless I cannot doubt that he does permit this.

There may indeed be those who would prefer to deny the existence of a God so powerful, rather than believe that all other things are uncertain. Let us not oppose them for the present, and grant that all that is here said of a God is a fiction. Nevertheless, in whatever way they suppose that I have arrived at the state of being that I have reached—whether they attribute it to fate, to accident, to a continual succession of events, or to something else—since to err and deceive oneself is a defect, it is clear that the less powerful the author to whom they assign my origin, the greater the probability that I am so imperfect as to deceive myself always. To these reasons I have certainly nothing to reply, but at the end I feel forced to admit that there is nothing in all that I formerly believed to be true, of which I cannot in some measure doubt—and this is not through lack of thought or through frivolity, but for reasons that are very powerful and maturely considered. Therefore, in the future I should not less carefully refrain from assenting to these opinions than to what is obviously false, if I desire to arrive at any certainty.

But it is not sufficient to have made these remarks; I must also be careful to keep them in mind. For former and commonly held opinions still return frequently to my mind, since long and familiar custom has given them the right to occupy my mind against my inclination and has rendered them almost masters of my belief. Nor will I ever lose the habit of deferring to them or of placing my confidence in them, so long as I consider them as they really are—that is, opinions in some measure doubtful (as I have just shown), and at the same time highly probable, so that there is much more reason to believe in than to deny them. That is why I think that I will not be acting wrongly if, deliberately taking a contrary belief, I allow myself to be deceived, and for a certain time pretend that all these opinions are entirely false and imaginary, until at last, having in this way balanced my former prejudices with my latter ones, my judgment will no longer be dominated by bad usage or turned away from the right knowledge of the truth. I am assured that there can be neither peril nor error in this course, and that I cannot now yield too much to distrust, since I am not considering the question of action, but only of knowledge.

I will then suppose that not God (who is supremely good and the fountain of truth) but some evil demon, no less powerful than deceitful, has employed his whole energies in deceiving me. I will think that the heavens, the earth, colors, shapes, sound, and all other external things are nothing but the illusions and dreams of which this demon has availed himself in order to lay traps for my credulity. I will consider myself as having no hands, no eyes, no flesh, no blood, no senses, yet falsely believing myself to possess all these things. I will remain obstinately attached to this idea, and if it is not in my power by this means to arrive at the knowledge of any truth, I may at least do what is in my power and, with firm purpose, avoid assenting to any false thing or being imposed upon by this deceiver, however powerful and deceptive he may be. But this task is a toilsome one, and imperceptibly a certain laziness leads me back to the course of my ordinary life. And just as a prisoner enjoys an imaginary liberty while asleep, but fears to awaken when he begins to suspect that his liberty is merely a dream and goes along with these agreeable illusions in order to prolong the deception—so I, imperceptibly of my own accord, fall back into my former opinions and dread awakening from this slumber, lest the waking toil that would follow the tranquility of this slumber would have to be spent not in daylight, but in the excessive darkness of the difficulties that have just been discussed.

### Meditation II. Of the Nature of the Human Mind, and That It Is More Easily Known Than the Body

Yesterday's meditation filled my mind with so many doubts that it is no longer in my power to forget them. And yet I do not see how I can resolve them. Just as if I had suddenly fallen into very deep water, I am so disconcerted that I can neither stand on the bottom, nor swim and bring myself to the surface. I will nevertheless make an effort and follow the same path that I did yesterday—that is, I will proceed by setting aside everything in which the least doubt could be supposed to exist, just as if I had discovered that it was absolutely false. And I will follow this road until I find something that is certain, or at least, if I can do nothing else, until I learn

72    Abel: Discourses        Theories of Knowledge        René Descartes,
                                                            "Meditations on first
                                                            Philosophy" (selection 1)
                                                            with Study Questions
                                                            © The McGraw–Hill
                                                            Companies, 2006

for certain that there is nothing in the world that is certain. Archimedes,[2] in order to shift earth from its place and move it elsewhere, demanded only one fixed and immovable point. In the same way, I will have the right to have high hopes if I am fortunate enough to discover just one thing that is certain and indubitable.

I will suppose, then, that all the things that I see are false; I will persuade myself that nothing has ever existed of all that my fallacious memory represents to me. I will consider that I possess no senses; I will imagine that body, shape, extension, movement, and place are mere fictions of my mind. What, then, can be judged as true? Perhaps nothing at all, except that nothing in the world is certain.

But how can I know there is not something other than those things that I have just considered, which does not allow of the slightest doubt? Is there not some God, or some other being by whatever name we call it, who puts these reflections into my mind? That is not necessary—for is it not possible that I can produce them myself? I myself, am I not at least something? But I have already denied that I have senses and a body. Yet I hesitate, for what follows from that? Am I so dependent on body and senses that I cannot exist without these? But I was persuaded that there was nothing in all the world, that there was no heaven, no earth, that there were no minds, and no bodies. Was I not then likewise persuaded that I did not exist? Not at all; surely I myself did exist, since I persuaded myself of something. But there is some deceiver or other, very powerful and very cunning, who employs his ingenuity in deceiving me. Then without doubt I exist also if he deceives me. And let him deceive me as much as he will, he can never cause me to be nothing so long as I think that I am something. So, after having reflected well and carefully examined all things, I must come to the definite conclusion that the proposition "I am, I exist" is necessarily true each time that I pronounce it, or that I mentally conceive it.

But I do not yet know clearly enough what I am, I who am certain that I am. So I must be careful not to imprudently take some other object to be this "I," and thus go astray in respect to this knowledge that I hold to be the most certain and most evident of all that I have formerly learned. That is why I will now consider anew what I believed myself to be before I began these reflections. I will withdraw all my former opinions that might even in a small degree be invalidated by the reasons that I have just brought forward, in order that nothing at all be left beyond that which is absolutely certain and indubitable.

What then did I formerly believe myself to be? Undoubtedly I believed myself to be a man. But what is a man? Shall I say "a rational animal"? Certainly not; for then I would have to inquire what an animal is, and what rationality is—and thus from a single question I would fall into an infinity of other and more difficult questions; and I do not wish to waste the little time and leisure remaining to me in trying to unravel subtleties like these. I will instead stop here to consider the thoughts that of themselves spring up in my mind, and that were not inspired by anything beyond my own nature alone when I thought about my being. In the first place, then, I considered myself as having a face, hands, arms, and that whole system of members composed of bones and flesh as seen in a corpse, which I called the body. In addition to this, I considered that I was nourished, that I walked, that I felt, and that I thought; and I referred all these actions to the soul. But I did not stop to consider what the soul was, or if I did stop, I imagined that it was something extremely subtle like a wind or a flame or an ether, spread throughout my more solid parts. As to body, I had no manner of doubt about its nature, but thought I had a very clear knowledge of it. And if I had desired to explain the body according to the notions I had then formed of it, I would have described it as follows: By the body I understand all that can be defined by a certain shape; something that can be confined in a certain place and can fill a given space in such a way that every other body will be excluded from it; something that can be perceived by touch, sight, hearing, taste, or smell; something that can be moved in many ways—not by itself, but by something that is foreign to it, by which it is touched. For to have the power of self-movement, as the power of sensing or thinking, I did not consider to pertain to the nature of body; on the contrary, I was rather astonished to find that faculties similar to them existed in some bodies.

But what am I, now that I suppose that there is a certain demon who is extremely powerful and, if I may say so, malicious, who employs all his powers in deceiving me? Can I affirm that I possess the least of all those things that I have just said pertain to the nature of body? I pause to consider, I revolve all these things in my mind, and I find none of which I can say that it pertains to me. It would be tedious to stop to enumerate them. Let us pass to the attributes of soul and see if there is any one that is in me. What about nutrition or walking? But if I have no body, it is also true that I can neither walk nor take nourishment. Another attribute is sensation. But one cannot have sensation without a body, and besides I have thought I perceived many things during sleep that, in my waking moments, I realized that I did not experience at all. What about thinking? I find here that thought is an attribute that belongs to me; it alone cannot be separated from me. I am, I exist; that is certain. But how often? Just when I think; for it might possibly be the case if I ceased entirely to think, that I would likewise cease entirely to exist. I do not now admit anything that is not necessarily true. To speak accurately, I am no more than a  thing that thinks—that is to say, a mind, or soul, or intellect, or reason,  which are terms whose significance was formerly unknown to me. I am, however, a real thing and really exist. But what thing? I have answered: a thing that thinks.

And what more? I will exercise my imagination. I am not a collection of members that we call the human body; I am not a subtle air distributed through these members; I am not a wind, a fire, a vapor, a breath, or anything at all that I can imagine or conceive—because I have assumed that all these were nothing. Without changing that supposition, I find myself certain only of the fact that I am something. But perhaps it is true that these same things that I supposed were nonexistent because they are unknown to me, are really not different from the self that I know. I am not sure about this, and I will not dispute about it now; I can only judge things that are known to me. I know that I exist, and I inquire what I am, I whom I know to exist. But it is very certain that the knowledge of my existence taken in its precise significance does not depend on things whose existence is not yet known to me; consequently it does not depend on those that I can invent in imagination. And indeed the very term "invent" proves to me my error, for I really do this if I imagine myself as something, since to imagine is nothing else than to contemplate the shape or image of a corporeal thing. But I already know for certain that I am, and that it may be that all these images, and, speaking generally, all things that relate to the nature of body, are nothing but dreams. For this reason I see clearly that I have as little reason to say, "I will stimulate my imagination in order to know more distinctly what I am," than if I were to say, "I am now awake, and I perceive something that is real and true; but because I do not yet perceive it distinctly enough, I will deliberately go to sleep so that my dreams may represent the perception with the greatest truth and evidence." And thus I know for certain that nothing of all that I can understand by means of my imagination belongs to this knowledge that I have of myself, and that it is necessary to recall the mind from this mode of thought with the utmost diligence in order that it may be able to know its own nature with perfect distinctness.

But what then am I? A thing that thinks. What is a thing that thinks? A thing that doubts, understands, affirms, denies, wills, refuses, and also imagines and has sensations. . . .

[Consider] the things that we most commonly believe to be the most distinctly comprehended, namely, the bodies that we touch and see—not bodies in general, for these general ideas are usually a little more confused, but one body in particular. Let us take, for example, this piece of wax: It has just been taken from the hive, and it has not yet lost the sweetness of the honey it contains; it still retains some of the odor of the flowers from which it has been collected; its color, shape, and size are apparent; it is hard, cold, easily handled; and if you strike it with your knuckle, it will emit a sound. Finally, all the things necessary to cause us to distinctly recognize a body are present in it. But notice that while I speak and approach the fire, what remained of the taste is eliminated, the smell evaporates, the color alters, the shape is destroyed, the size increases, it becomes liquid and hot and one can hardly handle it, and when it is struck, no sound is emitted. Does the same wax remain after this change? We must admit that it remains; no one would judge otherwise. What then did I know so distinctly in this piece of wax? It could certainly be none of the things that the senses brought to my notice, since everything that falls under taste, smell, sight, touch, and hearing, is found to be changed, and yet the same wax remains.

Perhaps it was what I now think, namely, that this wax was not the sweetness of honey, or the agreeable scent of flowers, or the whiteness, or the shape, or the sound, but simply a body that a little while before appeared to me as perceptible under these forms, and that is now perceptible under others. But what, precisely, is it that I imagine when I form such conceptions? Let us attentively consider this, and, taking away all that does not belong to the wax, let us see what remains. Certainly nothing remains except a certain extended thing that is flexible and movable. But what is the meaning of "flexible" and "movable"? Is it not that I imagine that this round piece of wax is able to become square and to pass from a square to a triangular shape? No, certainly it is not that, since I imagine it admits of an infinity of similar changes, and I nevertheless do not know how to encompass this infinity by my imagination, and consequently this conception I have of the wax is not brought about by the faculty of imagination. What now is this extension? Is it not also unknown? For it becomes greater when the wax is melted, greater when it is boiled, and still greater when the heat increases. And I would not conceive rightly what wax is, if I did not think that even this piece that we are considering is capable of receiving more variations in extension than I have ever imagined. We must then grant that I could not even understand through the imagination what this piece of wax is, and that it is my mind alone that perceives it. I am speaking of this piece of wax in particular, but for wax in general it is even clearer. But what is this piece of wax that cannot be understood except by the mind? It is certainly the same wax that I see, touch, imagine; in short, it is the same wax that I have always believed it to be from the beginning. But what must particularly be observed is that its perception is not an act of vision, touch, or imagination (and has never been such, although it may have previously appeared to be so), but only an intuition of the mind, which may be imperfect and confused as it was formerly, or clear and distinct as it is at present, according to the degree of attention I pay to the elements that are found in it, and of which it is composed.

Yet in the meantime I am greatly astonished when I consider the how feeble the mind is and how prone to error. Although I consider all this in my own mind without giving external expression to my thoughts, words often impede me and I am almost deceived by the terms of ordinary language. For we say that we see the same wax, if it is present, and not that we simply judge that it is the same from its having the same color and shape.

From this I might conclude that I knew the wax by means of vision and not simply by the intuition of the mind—unless I happen to remember that, when looking from a window and saying that I see men passing in the street, I really do not see them, but *infer* that what I see is men, just as I say that I see wax. And yet what do I see from the window except hats and coats that may cover automatons? Yet I judge these to be men. And similarly, solely by the faculty of judgment that rests in my mind do I comprehend what I believed I saw with my eyes. . . .

## Meditation III. Of God, That He Exists

I will now close my eyes, stop my ears, and divert all my senses. I will eliminate even from my thoughts all the images of corporeal things, or (since that is hardly possible) at least I will judge them as empty and false. And thus conversing only with myself and considering my own nature, I will try little by little to reach a better knowledge of and acquaintance with myself. I am a thing that thinks—that is, a thing that doubts, affirms, denies, knows a few things and is ignorant of many things, wills, desires, and also imagines and perceives. For, as I remarked before, although the things that I perceive and imagine are perhaps nothing at all apart from me and in themselves, I am nevertheless certain that these modes of thought that I call perceptions and imaginations, insofar as they are only modes of thought, certainly reside in me.

And in the little that I have just said, I think I have summed up all that I really know, or at least all that, so far, I have discovered that I know. In order to try to extend my knowledge further, I will now look around more carefully and see whether I cannot still discover in myself some other things that I have not previously perceived. I am certain that I am a thing that thinks. But do I not then likewise know what is necessary to make me certain of a truth? Certainly in this initial knowledge there is nothing that assures me of its truth, except the clear and distinct perception of what I affirm. And this would not suffice to assure me that what I say is true, if it could ever happen that a thing that I conceived so clearly and distinctly could be false. Accordingly, it seems to me that already I can establish as a general rule that all things that I perceive very clearly and very distinctly are true. . . .

Among my ideas, some appear to me to be innate, some adventitious,[3] and others formed by myself. My power of understanding what a thing is, or a truth is, or a thought is, appears to me to come from any source other than my own nature. But if I now hear some sound, see the sun, or feel heat, I have previously judged that these sensations proceeded from certain things existing outside of me. And finally it seems to me that sirens, hippogriffs,[4] and the like, are formed out of my own mind. But again I may possibly persuade myself that all these ideas are what I call adventitious, or else that they are all innate, or all fictitious—for I have not yet clearly discovered their true origin.

My principal task now is to consider, with respect to those ideas that appear to me to proceed from certain objects outside me, the reasons that cause me to think that these ideas are similar to the objects. It seems indeed, in the first place, that I am taught this lesson by nature; and, secondly, I experience in myself that these ideas do not depend on my will or therefore on myself—for they often present themselves to my mind in spite of my will. Just now, for instance, whether I will it or do not will it, I feel heat; and thus I persuade myself that this feeling or idea of heat is produced in me by something different from me, namely, the heat of the fire near which I sit. And nothing seems to me more obvious than the judgment that this object imprints its likeness rather than anything else upon me.

Now I must discover whether these proofs are sufficiently strong and convincing. When I say that I am taught by nature, I merely mean a certain spontaneous inclination that impels me to believe in this connection, and not a natural light that makes me recognize that it is true. These two things are very different; for I cannot doubt that which the natural light causes me to believe to be true—for example, that it follows from the fact that I doubt, that I exist; or other facts of this same kind. I possess no other faculty that is equally trustworthy for distinguishing truth from falsehood, which could teach me that what this natural light shows me to be true is not really true. But as far as natural impulses are concerned, I have frequently noticed that, when I had to actively choose between virtue and vice, they often enough led me to the worse choice; and this is why I do not see any reason for following them with regard to truth and error.

And as to the other reason—namely, that these ideas must proceed from objects outside me, since they do not depend on my will—I do not find it any more convincing. For just as these impulses of which I have spoken are found in me, even though they do not always concur with my will, so perhaps there is in me some faculty capable of producing these ideas without the assistance of any external things, even though it is not yet known by me—just as they apparently are produced in me during sleep, without the aid of any external objects.

And finally, though they did proceed from objects different from myself, it is not necessary that they should resemble these objects. On the contrary, I have noticed that in many cases there was a great difference between the object and its idea. I find, for example, two completely different ideas of the sun in my mind. One derives from the senses, and should be placed in the category of adventitious ideas; according to this idea, the sun seems to be extremely small. The other derives from astronomical reasoning,—that is, it derives from certain notions innate in me (or else it is formed by me in some other way)—and in accordance with this, the sun appears to be several times greater than the earth. These two ideas cannot, indeed, both resemble the same sun, and reason makes me believe that the one that seems to have originated directly from the sun itself is the one most dissimilar to the sun.

All this causes me to believe that, up until the present time, it has not been by a judgment that was certain but only by a sort of blind impulse that I believed that things exist outside of me and different from me and convey their ideas or images to me by the organs of my senses, or by some other method, whatever it might be. . . .

But among my ideas, in addition to the idea that represents me to myself, concerning which there can here be no difficulty, there is another that represents God, others that represent corporeal and inanimate things, angels, and animals, and others that represent men like myself.

With regard to the ideas that represent other men, or animals, or angels, I can however easily conceive that they might be formed by a mixture of the other ideas that I have of myself, of corporeal things, and of God—even if, apart from me, no men or animals or angels existed in all the world.

With regard to the ideas of corporeal objects, I do not recognize in them anything so great or so excellent that they might not have possibly proceeded from myself. . . .

There remains only the idea of God, concerning which we must consider whether it is something that cannot have proceeded from myself. By the word "God" I understand a substance that is infinite, independent, all-knowing, all-powerful, and that created me and everything else (if there is anything else). All these characteristics are such that the more diligently I attend to them, the less they appear capable of proceeding from me alone. Therefore, from what has been already said, we must conclude that God necessarily exists.

For although the idea of *substance* is in me because of the fact I am substance, nevertheless I would not have the idea of an *infinite* substance—since I am finite—if it had not proceeded from some substance that was truly infinite.

Nor should I imagine that I do not perceive the infinite by a true idea, but only by the negation of the finite, just as I perceive rest and darkness by the negation of movement and light. On the contrary, I see that there is clearly more reality in infinite substance than in finite substance, and therefore that in some way I have in me the notion of the infinite before the notion of the finite—that is to say, the notion of God before that of myself. For how would it be possible for me to know that I doubt and desire (that is, that I lack something) and that I am not wholly perfect, unless I had in me some idea of a being more perfect than myself, in comparison with which I recognize the deficiencies of my nature? . . .

It only remains to me to examine how I have acquired this idea from God. For I have not received it through the senses, and it is never presented to me unexpectedly, as usually happens with ideas of things perceivable by the senses, when these things present themselves (or seem to present themselves) to my external sense organs. Nor is it a fiction of my mind, for it is not in my power to take from it or to add anything to it. Consequently the only alternative is that it is innate in me, just as the idea of myself is innate in me.

---

▶ NOTES

1. In Greek mythology, *sirens* are female and partly human creatures who lure sailors to their destruction with their beautiful singing; *satyrs* are woodland creatures with features of both a horse and a goat, fond of unrestrained revelry. [D. C. ABEL, EDITOR]

2. Archimedes (about 287–212 B.C.E.) was a Greek mathematician and inventor. [D. C. ABEL]

3. *adventitious:* coming from an external source [D. C. ABEL]

4. *hippogriffs:* mythical animals that are part horse and part griffin (a griffin is a mythical animal that is part eagle and part lion) [D. C. ABEL]

# Meditations on First Philosophy (selection 1)

René Descartes

### Reading Questions

*According to Descartes:*

1. What method will ensure that all one's knowledge has a firm foundation?

2. Why could not even a supremely powerful "evil demon" deceive one about the fact that one exists?

3. What is the nature of the "I" that exists? How does it differ from the nature of material things, such as wax?

4. What is the general criterion for determining whether a perception is true?

5. Why must God be the source of the idea that one has of God?

### Discussion Questions

*In your own view:*

1. Can you be absolutely certain that you are not dreaming right now?

2. If you cannot doubt the existence of your mind, but can doubt the existence of your body, does it follow that you *are* a mind?

3. Could the "I" that thinks be the physical brain?

4. What does it mean for an idea to be "clear and distinct"? Are all such ideas necessarily true?

5. Is our idea of God innate? If so, does this prove that God exists?

# An Essay Concerning Human Understanding

John Locke

John Locke was born in Wrington, England, in 1632. After attending Westminster School, he enrolled in Oxford University, receiving his bachelor's degree in 1656 and his master's degree two years later. He then taught Latin and Greek at Oxford. In 1661 he began the study of medicine, but never completed his degree. He was appointed censor of moral philosophy in 1664, but two years later he left Oxford to become the personal physician of the influential politician Anthony Ashley Cooper, Earl of Shaftesbury. Locke then spent four years in France (1675–1679), where he explored the philosophical ideas of René Descartes, Pierre Gassendi, and others. The England to which Locke returned was in political turmoil, and Shaftesbury fled to Holland in 1682. The next year, Locke, who was under suspicion because of his close association with Shaftesbury, also fled to Holland. He returned to England in 1689, and the next year published two major philosophical works that were the fruit of many years of thought: *An Essay Concerning Human Understanding* and *Two Treatises of Government.* Locke continued to write and publish, his final project (published posthumously) being a series of commentaries on the epistles of Paul. He died in Oates in 1704 at the age of seventy-two.

Locke's main works, in addition to the *Essay* and the *Two Treatises,* are *A Letter Concerning Toleration* (1689), *Some Thoughts Concerning Education* (1693), and *The Reasonableness of Christianity* (1695).

Our selection is from the *Essay Concerning Human Understanding.* Locke begins by rejecting the view, popular in his day, that the mind is endowed with innate principles, i.e., that the mind by its very nature, prior to any experience, knows such truths as "It is impossible for the same thing to be and not to be." He argues that such principles cannot be innate because some people ("children and idiots") have no knowledge of them. Locke then proceeds to present his own theory of how ideas enter the mind. The mind is originally blank, like a sheet of white paper; ideas are imprinted through experience. All ideas arise either through sensation (experience of external objects) or reflection (experience of the operations of our mind). According to Locke, "we have nothing in our minds which did not come about in one of these two ways." After experience has furnished the mind with simple ideas, the mind can go on to combine them into complex ideas that are not the direct objects of experience.

Locke then explains how ideas are related to qualities. By "quality" he means the power of an object to produce an idea in our mind. For example, to say that a snowball has the qualities of being round and white means that it can create these ideas in us. Locke proceeds to distinguish two kinds of qualities. *Primary qualities* are those that produce ideas that resemble the object and really exist in it; examples of these qualities are figure, extension, and motion or rest. *Secondary qualities,* by contrast, produce ideas that do *not* resemble the object and do not exist in it; examples of such qualities are color, sound, and taste. So although we experience a snowball as both round and white, it really is round but really is not white. Locke goes on to explain *how* qualities produce ideas in us.

▼

## Book I: Neither Principles nor Ideas Are Innate

**Chapter I: No Innate Speculative Principles**  1. It is an established opinion among some men that there are in the understanding certain *innate principles;* some primary notions, *koinai ennoiai,*[1] characters, as it were, stamped upon the mind of man, which the soul receives in its very first being and brings into the world with it. It would be sufficient to convince unprejudiced readers of the falseness of this supposition, if I should only show (as I hope I shall in the following parts of this discourse) how men, barely by the use of their natural faculties, may attain to all the knowledge they have, without the help of any innate impressions; and may arrive at certainty, without any such original notions or principles. For I imagine anyone will easily grant that it would be impertinent to suppose the ideas of colours innate in a creature to whom God has given sight and a power to receive them by the eyes from external objects: and no less unreasonable would it be to attribute several truths to the impressions of nature, and innate characters, when we may observe in ourselves faculties fit to attain as easy and certain knowledge of them as if they were originally imprinted on the mind.

But because a man is not permitted without censure to follow his own thoughts in the search of truth when they lead him ever so little out of the common road, I shall set down the reasons that made me doubt of the truth of that opinion, as an excuse for my mistake, if I be in one; which I leave to be considered by those who, with me, dispose themselves to embrace truth wherever they find it.

2. There is nothing more commonly taken for granted than that there are certain *principles,* both *speculative* and *practical* (for they speak of both), universally agreed upon by all mankind: which therefore, they argue, must needs be the constant impressions which the souls of men receive in their first beings, and which they bring into the world with them, as necessarily and really as they do any of their inherent faculties.

3. This argument, drawn from universal consent, has this misfortune in it, that if it were true in matter of fact, that there were certain truths wherein all mankind agreed, it would not prove them innate, if there can be any other way shown how men may come to that universal agreement in the things they do consent in, which I presume may be done.

4. But, which is worse, this argument of universal consent, which is made use of to prove innate principles, seems to me a demonstration that there are none such: because there are none to which all mankind give an universal assent. I shall begin with the speculative, and instance in those magnified principles of demonstration, "Whatsoever is, is" and "It is impossible for the same thing to be and not to be"; which, of all others, I think have the most allowed title to innate. These have so settled a reputation of maxims universally received, that it will no doubt be thought strange if anyone should seem to question it. But yet I take liberty to say that these propositions are so far from having an universal assent, that there are a great part of mankind to whom they are not so much as known.

5. For, first, it is evident that all children and idiots have not the least apprehension or thought of them. And the want of that is enough to destroy that universal assent which must needs be the necessary concomitant

of all innate truths: it seeming to me near a contradiction to say that there are truths imprinted on the soul, which it perceives or understands not: imprinting, if it signify anything, being nothing else but the making certain truths to be perceived. For to imprint anything on the mind without the mind's perceiving it, seems to me hardly intelligible. If therefore children and idiots have souls, have minds, with those impressions upon them, *they* must unavoidably perceive them, and necessarily know and assent to these truths; which since they do not, it is evident that there are no such impressions. For if they are not notions naturally imprinted, how can they be innate? And if they are notions imprinted, how can they be unknown? To say a notion is imprinted on the mind, and yet at the same time to say that the mind is ignorant of it and never yet took notice of it, is to make this impression nothing. No proposition can be said to be in the mind which it never yet knew, which it was never yet conscious of. For if any one [proposition] may, then, by the same reason, all propositions that are true and the mind is capable ever of assenting to, may be said to be in the mind, and to be imprinted: since, if any one can be said to be in the mind, which it never yet knew, it must be only because it is capable of knowing it; and so the mind is of all truths it ever shall know. Nay, thus truths may be imprinted on the mind which it never did, nor ever shall know; for a man may live long, and die at last in ignorance of many truths which his mind was capable of knowing, and that with certainty. So that if the capacity of knowing be the natural impression contended for, all the truths a man ever comes to know will, by this account, be every one of them innate; and this great point will amount to no more, but only to a very improper way of speaking; which, while it pretends to assert the contrary, says nothing different from those who deny innate principles. For nobody, I think, ever denied that the mind was capable of knowing several truths. The capacity, they say, is innate; the knowledge acquired. But then to what end such contest for certain innate maxims? If truths can be imprinted on the understanding without being perceived, I can see no difference there can be between any truths the mind is *capable* of knowing in respect of their original:[2] they must all be innate or all adventitious:[3] in vain shall a man go about to distinguish them. He therefore that talks of innate notions in the understanding cannot (if he intend thereby any distinct sort of truths) mean such truths to be in the understanding as it never perceived, and is yet wholly ignorant of. For if these words "to be in the understanding" have any propriety, they signify to be understood. So that to be in the understanding and not to be understood, to be in the mind and never to be perceived, is all one as to say anything is and is not in the mind or understanding. If therefore these two propositions, "Whatsoever is, is" and "It is impossible for the same thing to be and not to be," are by nature imprinted, children cannot be ignorant of them: infants, and all that have souls, must necessarily have them in their understandings, know the truth of them, and assent to [them]. . . .

## Book II: Of Ideas

### Chapter I: Of Ideas in General, and Their Original

1. Every man being conscious to himself that he thinks, and that which his mind is applied about while thinking being the *ideas* that are there, it is past doubt that men have in their minds several ideas—such as are those expressed by the words *whiteness, hardness, sweetness, thinking, motion, man, elephant, army, drunkenness,* and others. It is in the first place then to be inquired, *How he comes by them?*

I know it is a received doctrine that men have native ideas and original characters stamped upon their minds in their very first being. This opinion I have at large examined already; and, I suppose what I have said in the foregoing Book will be much more easily admitted, when I have shown whence the understanding may get all the ideas it has; and by what ways and degrees they may come into the mind—for which I shall appeal to everyone's own observation and experience.

2. Let us then suppose the mind to be, as we say, white paper, void of all characters, without any ideas. How comes it to be furnished? Whence comes it by that vast store which the busy and boundless fancy of man has painted on it with an almost endless variety? Whence has it all the *materials* of reason and knowledge? To this I answer, in one word, from EXPERIENCE. In that all our knowledge is founded; and from that it ultimately derives itself. Our observation, employed either about external sensible[4] objects or about the internal operations of our minds perceived and reflected on by ourselves, is that which supplies our understandings with all the *materials* of thinking. These two are the fountains of knowledge from whence all the ideas we have, or can naturally have, do spring.

3. First, our senses, conversant about particular sensible objects, do convey into the mind several distinct perceptions of things, according to those various ways wherein those objects do affect them. And thus we come by those *ideas* we have of *yellow, white, heat, cold, soft, hard, bitter, sweet,* and all those which we call sensible qualities; which when I say the senses convey into the mind, I mean, they from external objects convey into the mind what produces there those perceptions. This great source of most of the ideas we have, depending wholly upon our senses, and derived by them to the understanding, I call SENSATION.

4. Secondly, the other fountain from which experience furnishes the understanding with ideas is the perception of the operations of our own mind within us, as it is employed about the ideas it has got—which operations, when the soul comes to reflect on and consider, do furnish the understanding with another set of ideas, which could not be had from things without. And such are *perception, thinking, doubting, believing, reasoning, knowing, willing,* and all the different actings of our own minds—which we being conscious of, and observing in ourselves, do from these receive into our understandings as distinct ideas as we do from bodies affecting our senses. This source of ideas every man has wholly in himself; and though it be not

sense, as having nothing to do with external objects, yet it is very like it, and might properly enough be called *internal sense*. But as I call the other SENSATION, so I call this REFLECTION, the ideas it affords being such only as the mind gets by reflecting on its own operations within itself. By reflection, then, in the following part of this discourse, I would be understood to mean, that notice which the mind takes of its own operations, and the manner of them, by reason whereof there come to be ideas of these operations in the understanding. These two, I say, namely, external material things, as the objects of SENSATION, and the operations of our own minds within, as the objects of REFLECTION, are to me the only originals from whence all our ideas take their beginnings. The term *operations* here I use in a large sense, as comprehending not barely the actions of the mind about its ideas, but some sort of passions[5] arising sometimes from them, such as is the satisfaction or uneasiness arising from any thought.

5. The understanding seems to me not to have the least glimmering of any ideas which it does not receive from one of these two. *External objects* furnish the mind with the ideas of sensible qualities, which are all those different perceptions they produce in us; and the *mind* furnishes the understanding with ideas of its own operations.

These, when we have taken a full survey of them, and their several modes, combinations, and relations, we shall find to contain all our whole stock of ideas; and that we have nothing in our minds which did not come in one of these two ways. Let any one examine his own thoughts and thoroughly search into his understanding; and then let him tell me, whether all the original ideas he has there, are any other than of the objects of his senses, or of the operations of his mind, considered as objects of his reflection. And how great a mass of knowledge soever he imagines to be lodged there, he will, upon taking a strict view, see that he has not any idea in his mind but what one of these two have imprinted—though perhaps, with infinite variety compounded and enlarged by the understanding, as we shall see hereafter.

6. He that attentively considers the state of a child at his first coming into the world, will have little reason to think him stored with plenty of ideas that are to be the matter of his future knowledge. It is *by degrees* he comes to be furnished with them. And though the ideas of obvious and familiar qualities imprint themselves before the memory begins to keep a register of time or order, yet it is often so late before some unusual qualities come in the way, that there are few men that cannot recollect the beginning of their acquaintance with them. And if it were worthwhile, no doubt a child might be so ordered as to have but a very few, even of the ordinary ideas, till he were grown up to a man. But all that are born into the world, being surrounded with bodies that perpetually and diversely affect them, variety of ideas, whether care be taken of it or not, are imprinted on the minds of children. Light and colours are busy at hand everywhere, when the eye is but open; sounds and some tangible qualities fail not to so-

licit their proper senses, and force an entrance to the mind—but yet, I think, it will be granted easily that if a child were kept in a place where he never saw any other but black and white till he were a man, he would have no more ideas of scarlet or green, than he that from his childhood never tasted an oyster, or a pineapple, has of those particular relishes.

7. Men then come to be furnished with fewer or more simple ideas from without, according as the objects they converse with afford greater or less variety; and from the operations of their minds within, according as they more or less reflect on them. For, though he that contemplates the operations of his mind cannot but have plain and clear ideas of them; yet, unless he turn his thoughts that way and considers them *attentively,* he will no more have clear and distinct ideas of all the operations of his mind, and all that may be observed therein, than he will have all the particular ideas of any landscape, or of the parts and motions of a clock, who will not turn his eyes to it and with attention heed all the parts of it. The picture or clock may be so placed that they may come in his way every day; but yet he will have but a confused idea of all the parts they are made up of, till he applies himself with attention to consider them each in particular.

8. And hence we see the reason why it is pretty late before most children get ideas of the operations of their own minds; and some have not any very clear or perfect ideas of the greatest part of them all their lives. Because, though they pass there continually, yet, like floating visions, they make not deep impressions enough to leave in their mind clear, distinct, lasting ideas, till the understanding turns inward upon itself, reflects on its own operations, and makes them the objects of its own contemplation. Children, when they come first into it, are surrounded with a world of new things, which, by a constant solicitation of their senses, draw the mind constantly to them; forward to take notice of new, and apt to be delighted with the variety of changing objects. Thus the first years are usually employed and diverted in looking abroad. Men's business in them is to acquaint themselves with what is to be found without; and so growing up in a constant attention to outward sensations, seldom make any considerable reflection on what passes within them, till they come to be of riper years; and some scarce ever at all. . . .

**Chapter II: Of Simple Ideas** 1. The better to understand the nature, manner, and extent of our knowledge, one thing is carefully to be observed concerning the ideas we have; and that is, that some of them are *simple* and some *complex.*

Though the qualities that affect our senses are, in the things themselves, so united and blended that there is no separation, no distance between them; yet it is plain, the ideas they produce in the mind enter by the senses simple and unmixed. For, though the sight and touch often take in from the same object, at the same time, different ideas—as a man sees at once motion and colour; the hand feels softness and warmth in the same piece of wax: yet the simple ideas thus united in the same subject are as perfectly distinct as those that come in by different senses. The coldness and hardness which a man feels in a piece of ice [are] as distinct ideas in the mind as the smell and whiteness of a lily; or as the taste of sugar, and smell of a rose. And there is nothing can be plainer to a man than the clear and distinct perception he has of those simple ideas; which, being each in itself uncompounded, contains in it nothing but *one uniform appearance, or conception in the mind,* and is not distinguishable into different ideas.

2. These simple ideas, the materials of all our knowledge, are suggested and furnished to the mind only by those two ways above mentioned, namely, sensation and reflection. When the understanding is once stored with these simple ideas, it has the power to repeat, compare, and unite them, even to an almost infinite variety, and so can make at pleasure new complex ideas. But it is not in the power of the most exalted wit or enlarged understanding, by any quickness or variety of thought, to *invent* or *frame* one new simple idea in the mind, not taken in by the ways before mentioned: nor can any force of the understanding *destroy* those that are there. The dominion of man in this little world of his own understanding [is] much the same as it is in the great world of visible things; wherein his power, however managed by art and skill, reaches no farther than to compound and divide the materials that are made to his hand; but can do nothing towards the making the least particle of new matter, or destroying one atom of what is already in being. The same inability will every one find in himself, who shall go about to fashion in his understanding one simple idea, not received in by his senses from external objects, or by reflection from the operations of his own mind about them. I would have anyone try to fancy any taste which had never affected his palate; or frame the idea of a scent he had never smelled, and when he can do this, I will also conclude that a blind man has ideas of colours, and a deaf man true distinct notions of sounds. . . .

**Chapter VIII: Some Further Considerations Concerning Our Simple Ideas of Sensation** 1. Concerning the simple ideas of Sensation, it is to be considered—that whatsoever is so constituted in nature as to be able, by affecting our senses, to cause any perception in the mind, does thereby produce in the understanding a simple idea; which, whatever be the external cause of it, when it comes to be taken notice of by our discerning faculty, it is by the mind looked on and considered there to be a real positive idea in the understanding, as much as any other whatsoever; though, perhaps, the cause of it be but a privation of the subject.

2. Thus the ideas of heat and cold, light and darkness, white and black, motion and rest, are equally clear and positive ideas in the mind; though, perhaps, some of the causes which produce them are barely privations in those subjects from whence our senses derive those ideas. These the understanding, in its view of them, considers all as distinct positive

ideas, without taking notice of the causes that produce them: which is an inquiry not belonging to the idea, as it is in the understanding, but to the nature of the things existing without us. These are two very different things, and carefully to be distinguished; it being one thing to perceive and know the idea of white or black, and quite another to examine what kind of particles they must be, and how ranged in the superficies, to make any object appear white or black. . . .

7. To discover the nature of our ideas the better, and to discourse of them intelligibly, it will be convenient to distinguish them *as they are ideas or perceptions in our minds;* and *as they are modifications of matter in the bodies that cause such perceptions in us:* that so we may not think (as perhaps usually is done) that they are exactly the images and resemblances of something inherent in the subject; most of those of sensation being in the mind no more the likeness of something existing without us, than the names that stand for them are the likeness of our ideas, which yet upon hearing they are apt to excite in us.

8. Whatsoever the mind perceives *in itself,* or is the immediate object of perception, thought, or understanding, that I call *idea;* and the power to produce any idea in our mind, I call *quality* of the subject wherein that power is. Thus a snowball having the power to produce in us the ideas of white, cold, and round, the power to produce those ideas in us as they are in the snowball, I call qualities; and as they are sensations or perceptions in our understandings, I call them ideas; which *ideas,* if I speak of sometimes as in the things themselves, I would be understood to mean those qualities in the objects which produce them in us.

9. Qualities thus considered in bodies are:

*First,* such as are utterly inseparable from the body, in what state soever it be; and such as in all the alterations and changes it suffers, all the force can be used upon it, it constantly keeps; and such as sense constantly finds in every particle of matter which has bulk enough to be perceived; and the mind finds inseparable from every particle of matter, though less than to make itself singly be perceived by our senses. For example, take a grain of wheat, divide it into two parts; each part has still solidity, extension, figure, and mobility: divide it again, and it retains still the same qualities; and so divide it on, till the parts become insensible;[6] they must retain still each of them all those qualities. For division (which is all that a mill, or pestle, or any other body, does upon another, in reducing it to insensible parts) can never take away either solidity, extension, figure, or mobility from any body, but only makes two or more distinct separate masses of matter, of that which was but one before; all which distinct masses, reckoned as so many distinct bodies, after division, make a certain number.

These I call *original* or *primary qualities* of body, which I think we may observe to produce simple ideas in us, namely solidity, extension, figure, motion or rest, and number.

10. *Secondly,* such qualities which in truth are nothing in the objects themselves but powers to produce various sensations in us by their primary qualities, i.e., by the bulk, figure, texture, and motion of their insensible parts, as colours, sounds, tastes, etc. These I call *secondary qualities*. To these might be added a *third* sort, which are allowed to be barely powers; though they are as much real qualities in the subject as those which I, to comply with the common way of speaking, call qualities, but for distinction, secondary qualities. For the power in fire to produce a new colour, or consistency, in *wax* or *clay*—by its primary qualities, is as much a quality in fire as the power it has to produce in *me* a new idea or sensation of warmth or burning, which I felt not before—by the same primary qualities, namely, the bulk, texture, and motion of its insensible parts.

11. The next thing to be considered is how bodies produce ideas in us; and that is manifestly by impulse, the only way which we can conceive bodies to operate in.

12. If then external objects be not united to our minds when they produce ideas therein; and yet we perceive these *original* qualities in such of them as singly fall under our senses, it is evident that some motion must be thence continued by our nerves or animal spirits, by some parts of our bodies, to the brains or the seat of sensation, there to produce in our minds the particular ideas we have of them. And since the extension, figure, number, and motion of bodies of an observable bigness may be perceived at a distance by the sight, it is evident some singly imperceptible bodies must come from them to the eyes, and thereby convey to the brain some motion; which produces these ideas which we have of them in us.

13. After the same manner that the ideas of these original qualities are produced in us, we may conceive that the ideas of *secondary* qualities are also produced, namely, by the operation of insensible particles on our senses. For, it being manifest that there are bodies and good store of bodies, each [of which] are so small that we cannot by any of our senses discover either their bulk, figure, or motion—as is evident in the particles of the air and water, and others extremely smaller than those; perhaps as much smaller than the particles of air and water, as the particles of air and water are smaller than peas or hail-stones—let us suppose at present that the different motions and figures, bulk and number, of such particles, affecting the several organs of our senses, produce in us those different sensations which we have from the colours and smells of bodies; e.g., that a violet, by the impulse of such insensible particles of matter, of peculiar figures and bulks, and in different degrees and modifications of their motions, causes the ideas of the blue colour and sweet scent of that flower to be produced in our minds. It [is] no more impossible to conceive that God should annex such ideas to such motions, with which they have no similitude, than that he should annex the idea of pain to the motion of a piece of steel dividing our flesh, with which that idea has no resemblance.

14. What I have said concerning colours and smells may be understood also of tastes and sounds, and other the like sensible qualities; which, whatever reality we by mistake attribute to them, are in truth nothing in the objects themselves, but powers to produce various sensations in us; and depend on those primary qualities, namely, bulk, figure, texture, and motion of parts, as I have said.

15. From whence I think it easy to draw this observation—that the ideas of primary qualities of bodies are resemblances of them, and their patterns do really exist in the bodies themselves, but the ideas produced in us by these secondary qualities have no resemblance of them at all. There is nothing like our ideas, existing in the bodies themselves. They are, in the bodies we denominate from them, only a power to produce those sensations in us: and what is sweet, blue, or warm in idea, is but the certain bulk, figure, and motion of the insensible parts in the bodies themselves, which we call so.

16. Flame is denominated hot and light; snow, white and cold; and manna, white and sweet, from the ideas they produce in us. Which qualities are commonly thought to be the same in those bodies that those ideas are in us, the one the perfect resemblance of the other, as they are in a mirror, and it would by most men be judged very extravagant if one should say otherwise. And yet he that will consider that the same fire that at one distance produces in us the sensation of warmth, does, at a nearer approach, produce in us the far different sensation of pain, ought to bethink himself what reason he has to say—that this idea of warmth, which was produced in him by the fire, is *actually in the fire;* and his idea of pain, which the same fire produced in him the same way, is *not* in the fire. Why are whiteness and coldness in snow, and pain not, when it produces the one and the other idea in us; and can do neither, but by the bulk, figure, number, and motion of its solid parts?

17. The particular bulk, number, figure, and motion of the parts of fire or snow are really in them—whether anyone's senses perceive them or no: and therefore they may be called real qualities, because they really exist in those bodies. But light, heat, whiteness, or coldness are no more really in them than sickness or pain is in manna. Take away the sensation of them; let not the eyes see light or colours, nor the ears hear sounds; let the palate not taste, nor the nose smell, and all colours, tastes, odours, and sounds, *as they are such particular ideas,* vanish and cease and are reduced to their causes, i.e., bulk, figure, and motion of parts. . . .

26. To conclude. Beside those before-mentioned primary qualities in bodies, namely, bulk, figure, extension, number, and motion of their solid parts; all the rest, whereby we take notice of bodies and distinguish them one from another, are nothing else but several powers in them, depending on those primary qualities; whereby they are fitted, either by immediately operating on our bodies to produce several different ideas in us; or else, by operating on other bodies, so to change their primary qualities as to ren-

der them capable of producing ideas in us different from what before they did. The former of these, I think, may be called secondary qualities *immediately perceivable;* the latter, secondary qualities *mediately perceivable.*

---

▶ NOTES

1. *koinai ennoiai:* common conceptions (Greek) [D.C.A., ed.]
2. *original:* origin [D.C.A.]
3. *adventitious:* coming from an external source [D.C.A.]
4. *sensible:* able to be sensed [D.C.A.]
5. *passions:* states of being acted upon (being "passive"); contrasted to actions [D.C.A.]
6. *insensible:* not able to be sensed [D.C.A.]

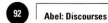
# An Essay Concerning Human Understanding (selection 1)

John Locke

### Reading Questions

*According to Locke:*

1. What disproves the claim that speculative principles such as "Whatever is, is" are innate?

2. What are the two "fountains of knowledge" that provide our minds with material for thinking? What kind of material does each one provide?

3. What is a simple idea? What are the two sources of simple ideas?

4. What power of an object is designated by the term "quality"?

5. What is the difference between a *primary quality* and a *secondary quality*? Why are only primary qualities appropriately called *real* qualities?

### Discussion Questions

*In your own view:*

1. Are we born with any knowledge encoded in our brains?

2. Can the mind perceive things other than physical objects and its own operations?

3. Does all knowledge derive ultimately from either sensation or reflection?

4. Do the secondary qualities of an object have any resemblance at all to the object?

5. Can we be certain that ideas produced by primary qualities resemble the object?

# An Enquiry Concerning Human Understanding

David Hume

David Hume was born in 1711 in Edinburgh, Scotland. His family wanted him to become a lawyer, but he found himself more interested in liberal arts than law. After three years at the University of Edinburgh (1723–1725), Hume withdrew to study literature, history, and philosophy privately at home. His intensive study took its toll on his health, and in 1729 he nearly had a nervous breakdown. In 1734 Hume went to Bristol, England, to take a job as a clerk for a sugar company. But he disliked the life of commerce and soon resigned his job. Hume then lived in France three years, studying philosophy. In 1744 he applied for a position in moral philosophy at the University of Edinburgh. Not chosen for the post, he spent the next several years in various occupations in England and abroad. Hume lived in Edinburgh from 1751 to 1763 and then went to Paris, where he served as secretary to the British Embassy for three years. Upon his return, he first lived in London but then moved back to Edinburgh, where he died in 1776.

Hume's major works are *A Treatise of Human Nature* (three volumes, 1739–1740), *An Enquiry Concerning Human Understanding* (1748; originally entitled *Philosophical Essays Concerning Human Understanding,* but renamed in the 1758 edition), *An Enquiry Concerning the Principles of Morals* (1751), *History of England* (six volumes, 1754–1762), and *Dialogues Concerning Natural Religion* (published posthumously, 1779).

Our reading is from the *Enquiry Concerning Human Understanding.* Hume begins by distinguishing two kinds of perceptions of the mind: impressions and ideas. *Impressions* consist of direct sense experiences of things outside us (sensations) or inside us (passions and emotions); *ideas* are copies of such impressions. Impressions are distinguished from ideas by their greater "force and vivacity"; hearing a sound is an impression, whereas recalling the sound is an idea. Some ideas (for example, a gold mountain) are not direct copies of a particular impression, but modifications or combinations of impressions (gold and a mountain). To clarify an idea, we need simply go back to the impression(s) from which it derives.

Hume next inquires about our knowledge of "matters of fact" (things that could be otherwise than they are). He observes that we rely on the notion of cause and effect when we go beyond the matters of fact provided by impressions and memories of impressions. But how do we *know* that one thing is caused by another? Judgments of causality are based on experience; when we see that event A is followed regularly by event B, we infer that A causes B and that if A occurs in the future, it will be followed by B. But what justifies this inference? It is not based on impressions—for while we do have impressions of A and B as successive events, we have no impression of a third entity, a "cause," which links A and B. Consequently, we can *never know* that there is such a thing as causality. Hume argues that our belief in causality results not from a reasoning process, but from the unavoidable human tendency to believe that two events we experience as constantly conjoined are related as cause and effect.

▼

### Section II: Of the Origin of Ideas

Everyone will readily allow that there is a considerable difference between the perceptions of the mind when a man feels the pain of excessive heat or the pleasure of moderate warmth, and when he afterwards recalls to his memory this sensation or anticipates it by his imagination. These faculties may mimic or copy the perceptions of the senses, but they never can entirely reach the force and vivacity of the original sentiment.[1] The utmost we say of them, even when they operate with greatest vigour, is that they represent their object in so lively a manner that we could *almost* say we feel or see it. But, except the mind be disordered by disease or madness, they never can arrive at such a pitch of vivacity as to render these perceptions altogether undistinguishable. All the colours of poetry, however splendid, can never paint natural objects in such a manner as to make the description be taken for a real landscape. The most lively thought is still inferior to the dullest sensation.

We may observe a like distinction to run through all the other perceptions of the mind. A man in a fit of anger is actuated in a very different manner from one who only thinks of that emotion. If you tell me that any person is in love, I easily understand your meaning and form a just conception of his situation, but never can mistake that conception for the real disorders and agitations of the passion. When we reflect on our past sentiments and affections, our thought is a faithful mirror and copies its objects truly, but the colours which it employs are faint and dull in comparison of those in which our original perceptions were clothed. It requires no nice discernment or metaphysical head to mark the distinction between them.

Here therefore we may divide all the perceptions of the mind into two classes or species, which are distinguished by their different degrees of force and vivacity. The less forcible and lively are commonly denominated *thoughts* or *ideas*. The other species want a name in our language, and in most others; I suppose, because it was not requisite for any but philosophical purposes, to rank them under a general term or appellation. Let us, therefore, use a little freedom and call them *impressions*, employing that word in a sense somewhat different from the usual. By the term *impression*, then, I mean all our more lively perceptions, when we hear, or see, or feel, or love, or hate, or desire, or will. And impressions are distinguished from ideas, which are the less lively perceptions, of which we are conscious when we reflect on any of those sensations or movements above mentioned.

Nothing, at first view, may seem more unbounded than the thought of man, which not only escapes all human power and authority, but is not even restrained within the limits of nature and reality. To form monsters and join incongruous shapes and appearances costs the imagination no more trouble than to conceive the most natural and familiar objects. And while the body is confined to one planet, along which it creeps with pain and difficulty; the thought can in an instant transport us into the most distant regions of the universe; or even beyond the universe, into the unbounded chaos, where nature is supposed to lie in total confusion. What never was seen, or heard of, may yet be conceived; nor is any thing beyond the power of thought, except what implies an absolute contradiction.

But though our thought seems to possess this unbounded liberty, we shall find, upon a nearer examination, that it is really confined within very narrow limits and that all this creative power of the mind amounts to no more than the faculty of compounding, transposing, augmenting, or diminishing the materials afforded us by the senses and experience. When we think of a golden mountain, we only join two consistent ideas, *gold* and *mountain,* with which we were formerly acquainted. A virtuous horse we can conceive because, from our own feeling, we can conceive virtue; and this we may unite to the figure and shape of a horse, which is an animal familiar to us. In short, all the materials of thinking are derived either from our outward or inward sentiment: the mixture and composition of these belongs alone to the mind and will. Or, to express myself in philosophical language, all our ideas or more feeble perceptions are copies of our impressions or more lively ones.

To prove this, the two following arguments will, I hope, be sufficient. First, when we analyze our thoughts or ideas, however compounded or sublime, we always find that they resolve themselves into such simple ideas as were copied from a precedent[2] feeling or sentiment. Even those ideas which, at first view, seem the most wide of this origin, are found, upon a nearer scrutiny, to be derived from it. The idea of God, as meaning an infinitely intelligent, wise, and good Being, arises from reflecting on the operations of our own mind and augmenting, without limit, those qualities of goodness and wisdom. We may prosecute[3] this enquiry to what length we please; where we shall always find that every idea which we examine is copied from a similar impression. Those who would assert that this position is not universally true nor without exception, have only one, and that an easy method of refuting it; by producing that idea, which, in their opinion, is not derived from this source. It will then be incumbent on us, if we would maintain our doctrine, to produce the impression, or lively perception, which corresponds to it.

Secondly, if it happen from a defect of the organ that a man is not susceptible of any species of sensation, we always find that he is as little susceptible of the correspondent ideas. A blind man can form no notion of colours; a deaf man of sounds. Restore either of them that sense in which he is deficient; by opening this new inlet for his sensations, you also open an inlet for the ideas; and he finds no difficulty in conceiving these objects. . . .

When we entertain, therefore, any suspicion that a philosophical term is employed without any meaning or idea (as is but too frequent), we need but enquire, *from what impression is that supposed idea derived?* And if it be impossible to assign any, this will serve to confirm our suspicion. By bringing ideas into so clear a light we may reasonably hope to remove all dispute which may arise concerning their nature and reality. . . .

### Section IV: Sceptical Doubts Concerning the Operations of the Understanding

**Part I** All the objects of human reason or enquiry may naturally be divided into two kinds, to wit, *relations of ideas* and *matters of fact.* Of the first kind are the sciences of geometry, algebra, and arithmetic; and in short, every affirmation which is either intuitively or demonstratively certain. *That the square of the hypothenuse is equal to the square of the two sides* is a proposition which expresses a relation between these figures. *That three times five is equal to the half of thirty* expresses a relation between these numbers. Propositions of this kind are discoverable by the mere operation of thought, without dependence on what is anywhere existent in the universe. Though there never were a circle or triangle in nature, the truths demonstrated by Euclid[4] would for ever retain their certainty and evidence.

Matters of fact, which are the second objects of human reason, are not ascertained in the same manner; nor is our evidence of their truth, however great, of a like nature with the foregoing. The contrary of every matter of fact is still possible; because it can never imply a contradiction and is conceived by the mind with the same facility and distinctness, as if ever so conformable to reality. *That the sun will not rise tomorrow* is no less intelligible a proposition and implies no more contradiction than the affirmation, *that it will rise.* We should in vain, therefore, attempt to demonstrate its falsehood. Were it demonstratively false, it would imply a contradiction and could never be distinctly conceived by the mind.

It may, therefore, be a subject worthy of curiosity, to enquire what is the nature of that evidence which assures us of any real existence and matter of fact, beyond the present testimony of our senses or the records of our memory. This part of philosophy, it is observable, has been little cultivated, either by the ancients or moderns; and therefore our doubts and errors, in the prosecution of so important an enquiry, may be the more excusable, while we march through such difficult paths without any guide or direction. They may even prove useful, by exciting curiosity and destroying that implicit faith and security which is the bane of all reasoning and free enquiry. The discovery of defects in the common philosophy, if any such there be, will not, I presume, be a discouragement, but rather an incitement, as is usual, to attempt something more full and satisfactory than has yet been proposed to the public.

All reasonings concerning matter of fact seem to be founded on the relation of *cause and effect.* By means of that relation alone we can go beyond the evidence of our memory and senses. If you were to ask a man why he believes any matter of fact, which is absent; for instance, that his friend is in the country, or in France; he would give you a reason; and this reason would be some other fact; as a letter received from him, or the knowledge of his former resolutions and promises. A man finding a watch or any other machine in a desert island would conclude that there had once been men in that island. All our reasonings concerning fact are of the same nature. And here it is constantly supposed that there is a connexion between the present fact and that which is inferred from it. Were there nothing to bind them together, the inference would be entirely precarious. The hearing of an articulate voice and rational discourse in the dark assures us of the presence of some person. Why? Because these are the effects of the human make and fabric, and closely connected with it. If we anatomize all the other reasonings of this nature, we shall find that they are founded on the relation of cause and effect, and that this relation is either near or remote, direct, or collateral. Heat and light are collateral effects of fire, and the one effect may justly be inferred from the other.

If we would satisfy ourselves, therefore, concerning the nature of that evidence which assures us of matters of fact, we must enquire how we arrive at the knowledge of cause and effect.

I shall venture to affirm, as a general proposition which admits of no exception, that the knowledge of this relation is not, in any instance, attained by reasonings a priori,[5] but arises entirely from experience, when we find that any particular objects are constantly conjoined with each other. Let an object be presented to a man of ever so strong natural reason and abilities; if that object be entirely new to him, he will not be able, by the most accurate examination of its sensible[6] qualities, to discover any of its causes or effects. Adam, though his rational faculties be supposed, at the very first, entirely perfect, could not have inferred from the fluidity and transparency of water that it would suffocate him, or from the light and warmth of fire that it would consume him. No object ever discovers, by the qualities which appear to the senses, either the causes which produced it, or the effects which will arise from it; nor can our reason, unassisted by experience, ever draw any inference concerning real existence and matter of fact.

This proposition *that causes and effects are discoverable, not by reason but by experience* will readily be admitted with regard to such objects as we remember to have once been altogether unknown to us; since we must be conscious of the utter inability, which we then lay under, of foretelling what would arise from them. Present two smooth pieces of marble to a man who has no tincture of natural philosophy;[7] he will never discover that they will adhere together in such a manner as to require great force to separate them in a direct line, while they make so small a resistance to a lateral pressure. Such events, as bear little analogy to the common course of nature, are also readily confessed to be known only by experience; nor does any man imagine that the explosion of gunpowder or the attraction of a loadstone could ever be discovered by arguments a priori. In like manner, when an effect is supposed to depend upon an intricate machinery or secret[8] structure of parts, we make no difficulty in attributing all our knowledge of it to experience. Who will assert that he can give the ultimate reason why milk or bread is proper nourishment for a man, not for a lion or a tiger?

But the same truth may not appear, at first sight, to have the same evidence with regard to events which have become familiar to us from our first appearance in the world, which bear a close analogy to the whole course of nature, and which are supposed to depend on the simple qualities of objects, without any secret structure of parts. We are apt to imagine that we could discover these effects by the mere operation of our reason, without experience. We fancy that were we brought on a sudden into this world, we could at first have inferred that one billiard ball would communicate motion to another upon impulse; and that we needed not to have waited for the event, in order to pronounce with certainty concerning it. Such is the influence of custom, that, where it is strongest, it not only covers our natural ignorance, but even conceals itself and seems not to take place, merely because it is found in the highest degree.

But to convince us that all the laws of nature, and all the operations of bodies without exception, are known only by experience, the following reflections may, perhaps, suffice. Were any object presented to us, and were we required to pronounce concerning the effect which will result from it, without consulting past observation; after what manner, I beseech you, must the mind proceed in this operation? It must invent or imagine some event which it ascribes to the object as its effect; and it is plain that this invention must be entirely arbitrary. The mind can never possibly find the effect in the supposed cause, by the most accurate scrutiny and examination. For the effect is totally different from the cause and consequently can never be discovered in it. Motion in the second billiard ball is a quite distinct event from motion in the first; nor is there anything in the one to suggest the smallest hint of the other. A stone or piece of metal raised into the air, and left without any support, immediately falls: but to consider the matter a priori, is there anything we discover in this situation which can beget the idea of a downward, rather than an upward, or any other motion, in the stone or metal?

And as the first imagination or invention of a particular effect, in all natural operations, is arbitrary, where we consult not experience; so must we also esteem the supposed tie or connexion between the cause and effect, which binds them together and renders it impossible that any other effect could result from the operation of that cause. When I see, for instance, a billiard ball moving in a straight line towards another; even suppose motion in the second ball should by accident be suggested to me, as the result of their contact or impulse; may I not conceive that a hundred different events might as well follow from that cause? May not both these balls remain at absolute rest? May not the first ball return in a straight line or leap off from the second in any line or direction? All these suppositions are consistent and conceivable. Why then should we give the preference to one, which is no more consistent or conceivable than the rest? All our reasonings a priori will never be able to show us any foundation for this preference.

In a word, then, every effect is a distinct event from its cause. It could not, therefore, be discovered in the cause, and the first invention or conception of it, a priori, must be entirely arbitrary. And even after it is suggested, the conjunction of it with the cause must appear equally arbitrary; since there are always many other effects, which to reason must seem fully as consistent and natural. In vain, therefore, should we pretend to determine any single event, or infer any cause or effect, without the assistance of observation and experience. . . .

**Part II**  But we have not yet attained any tolerable satisfaction with regard to the question first proposed. Each solution still gives rise to a new question as difficult as the foregoing, and leads us on to farther enquiries. When it is asked, *What is the nature of all our reasonings concerning matter of fact?* the proper answer seems to be that they are founded on the relation of cause and effect. When again it is asked, *What is the foundation of all our reasonings and conclusions concerning that relation?* it may be replied in one word, experience. But if we still carry on our sifting humour[9] and ask, *What is the foundation of all conclusions from experience?* this implies a new question, which may be of more difficult solution and explication. Philosophers that give themselves airs of superior wisdom and sufficiency have a hard task when they encounter persons of inquisitive dispositions who push them from every corner to which they retreat, and who are sure at last to bring them to some dangerous dilemma. The best expedient to prevent this confusion is to be modest in our pretensions, and even to discover the difficulty ourselves before it is objected to us. By this means, we may make a kind of merit of our very ignorance.

I shall content myself, in this section, with an easy task and shall pretend[10] only to give a negative answer to the question here proposed. I say then, that even after we have experience of the operations of cause and effect, our conclusions from that experience are *not* founded on reasoning or any process of the understanding. This answer we must endeavour both to explain and to defend.

It must certainly be allowed that nature has kept us at a great distance from all her secrets and has afforded us only the knowledge of a few superficial qualities of objects, while she conceals from us those powers and principles on which the influence of those objects entirely depends. . . . If a body of like colour and consistence with that bread, which we have formerly eaten, be presented to us, we make no scruple of repeating the experiment, and foresee, with certainty, like nourishment and support. Now this is a process of the mind or thought, of which I would willingly know the foundation. It is allowed on all hands that there is no known connexion between the sensible qualities and the secret powers; and consequently, that the mind is not led to form such a conclusion concerning their constant and regular conjunction, by anything which it knows of their nature. As to past *experience,* it can be allowed to give *direct* and *certain* information of those precise objects only, and that precise period of time, which fell under its cognizance: but why this experience should be extended to future times and to other objects which, for aught we know, may be only in appearance similar; this is the main question on which I would insist. The bread which I formerly ate nourished me; that is, a body of such sensible qualities was, at that time, endued with such secret powers. But does it follow that other bread must also nourish me at another time, and that like sensible qualities must always be attended with like secret powers? The consequence seems nowise necessary. At least it must be acknowledged that there is here a consequence drawn by the mind; that there is a certain step taken; a process of thought and an inference which wants to be explained. These two propositions are far from being the same, *I have found that such an object has always been attended with such an effect,* and *I foresee that other objects which are in appearance similar will be attended with similar effects.* I shall allow, if you please, that the one proposition may justly be inferred from the other; I know, in fact, that it always is inferred. But if you insist that the inference is made by a chain of reasoning, I desire you to produce that reasoning. The connexion between these propositions is not intuitive. There is required a medium[11] which may enable the mind to draw such an inference, if indeed it be drawn by reasoning and argument. What that medium is, I must confess, passes my comprehension; and it is incumbent on those to produce it, who assert that it really exists and is the origin of all our conclusions concerning matter of fact. . . .

When a new object, endowed with similar sensible qualities, is produced, we expect similar powers and forces and look for a like effect. From a body of like colour and consistence with bread we expect like nourishment and support. But this surely is a step or progress of the mind, which wants to be explained. When a man says, *I have found, in all past instances, such sensible qualities conjoined with such secret powers;* and when he says, *Similar sensible qualities will always be conjoined with similar secret powers,* he is not guilty of a tautology, nor are these propositions in any respect the same. You say that the one proposition is an inference from the other. But you must confess that the inference is not intuitive; neither is it demonstrative. Of what nature is it, then? To say it is experimental, is begging the question. For all inferences from experience suppose, as their foundation, that the future will resemble the past and that similar powers will be conjoined with similar sensible qualities. If there be any suspicion that the course of nature may change and that the past may be no rule for the future, all experience becomes useless and can give rise to no inference or conclusion. It is impossible, therefore, that any arguments from experience can prove this resemblance of the past to the future, since all these arguments are founded on the supposition of that resemblance. Let the course of things be allowed hitherto ever so regular; that alone, without some new argument or inference, proves not that, for the future, it will continue so. In vain do you pretend to have learned the nature of bodies from your past experience. Their secret nature, and consequently all their effects and influence, may change without any change in their sensible qualities. This happens sometimes and with regard to some objects: Why may it not happen always and with regard to all objects? What logic, what process of argument secures you against this supposition? My practice, you say, refutes my doubts. But you mistake the purport of my question. As an agent, I am quite satisfied in the point; but as a philosopher, who has some share of curiosity, I will not say scepticism, I want to learn the foundation of this inference. No reading, no enquiry has yet been able to remove my difficulty or give me satisfaction in a matter of such importance. Can I do better than propose the difficulty to the public, even though, perhaps, I have small hopes of obtaining a solution? We shall at least, by this means, be sensible[12] of our ignorance, if we do not augment our knowledge. . . .

### Section V: Sceptical Solution of These Doubts

**Part I** . . . Suppose a person, though endowed with the strongest faculties of reason and reflection, to be brought on a sudden into this world; he would, indeed, immediately observe a continual succession of objects, and one event following another; but he would not be able to discover anything farther. He would not, at first, by any reasoning, be able to reach the idea of cause and effect; since the particular powers by which all natural operations are performed never appear to the senses; nor is it reasonable to conclude, merely because one event, in one instance, precedes another, that therefore the one is the cause, the other the effect. Their conjunction may be arbitrary and casual. There may be no reason to infer the existence of one from the appearance of the other. And in a word, such a person, without more experience, could never employ his conjecture or reasoning concerning any matter of fact, or be assured of anything beyond what was immediately present to his memory and senses.

Suppose, again, that he has acquired more experience and has lived so long in the world as to have observed familiar objects or events to be constantly conjoined together; what is the consequence of this experience? He immediately infers the existence of one object from the appearance of the other. Yet he has not, by all his experience, acquired any idea or knowledge of the secret power by which the one object produces the other; nor is it by any process of reasoning [that] he is engaged to draw this inference. But still he finds himself determined to draw it: And though he should be convinced that his understanding has no part in the operation, he would nevertheless continue in the same course of thinking. There is some other principle which determines him to form such a conclusion.

This principle is custom or habit. For wherever the repetition of any particular act or operation produces a propensity to renew the same act or operation, without being impelled by any reasoning or process of the understanding, we always say that this propensity is the effect of *custom*. By employing that word, we pretend not to have given the ultimate reason of such a propensity. We only point out a principle of human nature which is universally acknowledged and which is well known by its effects. Perhaps we can push our enquiries no farther or pretend to give the cause of this cause, but must rest contented with it as the ultimate principle which we can assign of all our conclusions from experience. It is sufficient satisfaction that we can go so far, without repining at the narrowness of our faculties because they will carry us no farther. And it is certain we here advance a very intelligible proposition at least, if not a true one, when we assert that, after the constant conjunction of two objects—heat and flame, for instance, weight and solidity—we are determined by custom alone to expect the one from the appearance of the other. This hypothesis seems even the only one which explains the difficulty why we draw, from a thousand instances, an inference which we are not able to draw from one instance that is in no respect different from them. Reason is incapable of any such variation. The conclusions which it draws from considering one circle are the same which it would form upon surveying all the circles in the universe. But no man, having seen only one body move after being impelled by another, could infer that every other body will move after a like impulse. All inferences from experience, therefore, are effects of custom, not of reasoning.

Custom, then, is the great guide of human life. It is that principle alone which renders our experience useful to us and makes us expect, for the future, a similar train of events with those which have appeared in the past. Without the influence of custom, we should be entirely ignorant of every matter of fact beyond what is immediately present to the memory and senses. We should never know how to adjust means to ends, or to employ our natural powers in the production of any effect. There would be an end at once of all action, as well as of the chief part of speculation.

But here it may be proper to remark that though our conclusions from experience carry us beyond our memory and senses and assure us of matters of fact which happened in the most distant places and most remote ages, yet some fact must always be present to the senses or memory, from which we may first proceed in drawing these conclusions. A man who should find in a desert country the remains of pompous[13] buildings would conclude that the country had, in ancient times, been cultivated by civilized inhabitants; but did nothing of this nature occur to him, he could never form such an inference. We learn the events of former ages from history; but then we must peruse the volumes in which this instruction is contained, and thence carry up our inferences from one testimony to another, till we arrive at the eyewitnesses and spectators of these distant events. In a word, if we proceed not upon some fact present to the memory or senses, our reasonings would be merely hypothetical; and however the particular links might be connected with each other, the whole chain of inferences would have nothing to support it, nor could we ever, by its means, arrive at the knowledge of any real existence. If I ask why you believe any particular matter of fact which you relate, you must tell me some reason; and this reason will be some other fact, connected with it. But as you cannot proceed after this manner *in infinitum,*[14] you must at last terminate in some fact which is present to your memory or senses; or must allow that your belief is entirely without foundation.

What, then, is the conclusion of the whole matter? A simple one; though, it must be confessed, pretty remote from the common theories of philosophy. All belief of matter of fact or real existence is derived merely from some object present to the memory or senses, and a customary conjunction between that and some other object. Or in other words; having found, in many instances, that any two kinds of objects—flame and heat, snow and cold—have always been conjoined together; if flame or snow be presented anew to the senses, the mind is carried by custom to expect heat or cold and to *believe* that such a quality does exist and will discover itself upon a nearer approach. This belief is the necessary result of placing the mind in such circumstances. It is an operation of the soul, when we are so situated, as unavoidable as to feel the passion of love when we receive benefits, or hatred, when we meet with injuries. All these operations are a species of natural instincts, which no reasoning or process of the thought and understanding is able either to produce or to prevent.

---

▶ NOTES

1. *sentiment:* perception [D.C.A., ed.]
2. *precedent:* prior [D.C.A.]
3. *prosecute:* pursue [D.C.A.]
4. Euclid, who flourished in about 300 B.C.E., was a Greek geometer. [D.C.A.]
5. *a priori:* based on abstract reasoning, independent of experience (literally, in Latin, "from what comes earlier") [D.C.A.]
6. *sensible:* able to be sensed [D.C.A.]
7. *natural philosophy:* the philosophy of nature, i.e., natural science [D.C.A.]
8. *secret:* unseen [D.C.A.]
9. *sifting humour:* questioning frame of mind [D.C.A.]
10. *pretend:* undertake [D.C.A.]
11. *medium:* basis for an inference [D.C.A.]
12. *sensible:* aware [D.C.A.]
13. *pompous:* magnificent [D.C.A.]
14. *in infinitum:* to infinity (Latin) [D.C.A.]

# An Enquiry Concerning Human Understanding (selection 1)

David Hume

### Reading Questions

*According to Hume:*

1. What is the difference between an *impression* and an *idea* (a thought)?

2. What is the difference between *relations of ideas* and *matters of fact?*

3. How do we come to know the relation of cause and effect?

4. Why can no arguments from *experience* prove that the future will resemble the past?

5. What causes our conviction that one thing is caused by another? Why can no reasoning process produce or prevent this conviction?

### Discussion Questions

*In your own view:*

1. Do the contents of our mind consist entirely of impressions and ideas?

2. Does an idea have no meaning if it cannot be traced back to an impression?

3. Can we ever be certain that one thing caused another? that it had any cause at all?

4. Is it legitimate to appeal to past experience to argue that the future will probably resemble the past?

5. Is *custom* an adequate explanation for our belief in causality?

# Critique of Pure Reason

Immanuel Kant

Immanuel Kant was born in 1724 in Königsberg, Prussia, where he spent his entire life. As a boy he attended the Collegium Fridericanum, a school run by the Pietists (the Lutheran sect to which his family belonged). In 1740 he enrolled in the University of Königsberg, where he studied a wide variety of subjects, including theology, philosophy, mathematics, physics, and medicine. He withdrew from the university in 1747 to support himself by working as a private tutor for various families in eastern Prussia. He resumed his studies in 1754 and completed his degree the following year. He then became a lecturer at the University of Königsberg, teaching such diverse subjects as mathematics, geography, mineralogy, and philosophy. Fifteen years later he was appointed Professor of Logic and Metaphysics. His writings—especially his monumental *Critique of Pure Reason* (1781)—brought him increasing fame, and students came from afar to hear him lecture. In 1797 he stopped lecturing, but he continued to write. He died in Königsberg in 1804 at the age of seventy-nine.

Kant's principal works, in addition to the *Critique of Pure Reason*, are *Prolegomena to Any Future Metaphysics* (1783), *Fundamental Principles of the Metaphysics of Morals* (1785), *Critique of Practical Reason* (1788), and *Critique of Judgment* (1790).

Our reading is taken from Kant's second edition of the *Critique of Pure Reason*, published in 1787. Kant's project in this book is to investigate how much we can know by "pure reason" (reason itself, apart from any experience). In his Preface, Kant observes that we typically assume that our knowledge (cognition) must conform to objects—that when we know something, our mind must match the way the objects are. If this assumption is correct, it would be impossible to have any knowledge of objects a priori (prior to our experience of them). Kant rejects this assumption; he holds the converse, that *objects* must conform to our *knowledge*—that when we know something, objects must match the way our minds are. Objects conform to our way of receiving sense experience (intuition) and to our way of intellectually synthesizing this sense experience (thought). That is to say, our minds are constructed in such a way that we necessarily *sense* objects through the forms of "sensibility" (namely, space and time) and we necessarily *think* objects through certain "categories" (also called "concepts") of the understanding, such as causality and unity. This means that we can know certain things about objects a priori. For example, we know that we will experience them as existing in space and as being caused. But according to Kant, even though we know that objects will invariably *appear to us* in certain ways, we can never know how things are in *themselves*.

In his Introduction, Kant explains that a priori knowledge is characterized by necessity and universality. He then explains that some of our judgments (those in mathematics and metaphysics, for example) are not only a priori but synthetic. (A *synthetic* proposition adds something to a concept, while an *analytic* one does not.) Kant's doctrine about the structure of the mind is designed to explain how such synthetic a priori judgments are possible.

In the final two sections of our reading, Kant gives arguments to show that space and time (the forms of sensibility) are a priori, and explains that there are twelve categories of the understanding, corresponding to the twelve kinds of judgment.

▼

From Immanuel Kant, *Critique of Pure Reason*, trans. J. M. D. Meiklejohn. London, England: George Bell & Sons, 1878.

### Preface to the Second Edition

Whether the treatment of that portion of our knowledge that lies within the province of pure reason advances with that undeviating certainty that characterizes the progress of science, we shall be at no loss to determine. If we find those who are engaged in metaphysical[1] pursuits unable to come to an understanding of the method they ought to follow; if we find them, after the most elaborate preparations, invariably brought to a standstill before the goal is reached, and compelled to retrace their steps and strike into fresh paths, then we may then feel quite sure that they are far from having attained the certainty of scientific progress, and may rather be said to be merely groping about in the dark. In these circumstances we shall render an important service to reason if we succeed in simply indicating the path along which it must travel in order to arrive at any results—even if it should be found necessary to abandon many of those aims that, without reflection, have been proposed for its attainment. . . .

It has until now been assumed that our cognition must conform to the objects; but all attempts to ascertain anything about these objects a priori,[2] by means of concepts, and thus to extend the range of our knowledge, have been rendered abortive by this assumption. Let us then make the experiment whether we may not be more successful in metaphysics if we assume that . . . objects must conform to our cognition. This appears, at all events, to accord better with the *possibility* of our gaining the end we have in view—that is to say, arriving at the cognition of objects a priori, of determining something with respect to these objects before they are given to us. We here propose to do just what Copernicus[3] did in attempting to explain the celestial movements. When he found that he could make no progress by assuming that all the heavenly bodies revolved round the spectator, he reversed the process and tried the experiment of assuming that the spectator revolved, while the stars remained at rest. We may make the same experiment with regard to the intuition[4] of objects. If the intuition must conform to the nature of the objects, I do not see how we can know anything of them a priori. If, on the other hand, the object conforms to the nature of our faculty of intuition, I can then easily conceive the possibility of such an a priori knowledge. Now as I cannot rest in the mere intuitions, but—if they are to become cognitions—must refer them, as *representations,* to something, as *object,* and must determine the latter by means of the former, here again there are two courses open to me. *Either,* first, I may assume that the concepts by which I effect this determination conform to the object (and in this case I am reduced to the same perplexity as before); *or,* secondly, I may assume that the objects, or, which is the same thing, that *experience* (in which alone, as given objects, they are known) conforms to my concepts—and then I am at no loss how to proceed. For experience itself is a mode of cognition that requires understanding. Before objects are given to me (that is, a priori), I must presup-

Copernican Revolution

pose in myself laws of the understanding that are expressed in concepts a priori. To these concepts, then, all the objects of experience must necessarily conform. . . .

**Introduction to the Second Edition**

**I. On the Difference between Pure and Empirical Knowledge**

That all our knowledge begins with experience there can be no doubt. For how is it possible that the faculty of cognition should be awakened into exercise otherwise than by means of objects that affect our senses, and partly of themselves produce representations, partly rouse our powers of understanding into activity, to compare, to connect, or to separate these, and so to convert the raw material of our sense impressions into a knowledge of objects, which is called experience? With respect to time, therefore, no knowledge of ours is antecedent to experience, but begins with it.

But, though all our knowledge *begins with* experience, it by no means follows that all knowledge *arises out of* experience. For, on the contrary, it is quite possible that our empirical knowledge is a compound of that which we receive through impressions and that which the faculty of cognition supplies from itself (sense impressions giving merely the *occasion*), an addition that we cannot distinguish from the original element given by sense, until long practice has made us attentive to it and skillful in separating it. It is therefore a question that requires close investigation, and not to be answered at first sight, whether there exists a knowledge altogether independent of experience, and even of all sense impressions. Knowledge of this kind is called a priori, in distinction from empirical knowledge, which has its sources a posteriori (that is, in experience).

But the expression "a priori" is not as yet definite enough to indicate adequately the whole meaning of the question stated above. For in speaking of knowledge that has its sources in experience, it is customary to say that this or that may be known a priori, because we do not derive this knowledge immediately from experience, but from a general rule, which, however, we have itself borrowed from experience. Thus, if a man undermined the foundation of his house, we say "He might know a priori that it would have fallen"—that is, he needed not to have waited for the experience that it did actually fall. But still, a priori, he could not know even this much. For, that bodies are heavy, and, consequently that they fall when their supports are taken away, must have been known to him previously, by means of experience.

By the term "a priori knowledge," therefore, we shall understand, not such as is independent of this or that kind of experience, but such as is absolutely so of all experience. Opposed to this is empirical knowledge, or that which is possible only a posteriori (that is, through experience). A priori knowledge is either pure or impure. Pure a priori knowledge is that with which no empirical element is included. For example, the proposition "Every change has a cause" is an a priori proposition, but impure, because change is a concept that can only be derived from experience.

## II. The Human Intellect, Even in an Unphilosophical State, Is in Possession of Certain A Priori Cognitions

The question now is by what *criterion* we may securely distinguish a pure from an empirical cognition. Experience no doubt teaches us that this or that object is constituted in such and such a manner, but not that it could not possibly exist otherwise. Now in the first place, if we have a proposition that contains the idea of necessity in its very concept, it is an a priori judgment; if, moreover, it is not derived from any other proposition, unless from one equally involving the idea of necessity, it is absolutely a priori. Secondly, an empirical judgment never exhibits strict and absolute, but only assumed and comparative universality (by induction); therefore, the most we can say is that, as far as we have observed up until now, there is no exception to this or that rule. If, on the other hand, a judgment carries with it strict and absolute universality (that is, admits of no possible exception), it is not derived from experience, but is valid absolutely a priori.

Empirical universality is, therefore, only an arbitrary extension of validity from what may be predicated of a proposition valid in most cases, to what is asserted of a proposition that holds good in all cases—as, for example, in the affirmation "All bodies are heavy." When, on the contrary, strict universality characterizes a judgment, it necessarily indicates another peculiar source of knowledge—namely, a faculty of a priori cognition. Necessity and strict universality, therefore, are infallible tests for distinguishing pure from empirical knowledge, and are inseparably connected with each other. But as in the use of these criteria the empirical limitation is sometimes more easily detected than the contingency[5] of the judgment, or the unlimited universality that we attach to a judgment is often a more convincing proof than its necessity, it may be advisable to use the criteria separately, each being by itself infallible.

The fact that in the sphere of human cognition, we have judgments that are necessary, and in the strictest sense universal, consequently pure a priori, it will be an easy matter to show. If we desire an example from the sciences, we need only take any proposition in mathematics. If we cast our eyes upon the commonest operations of the understanding, the proposition "Every change must have a cause" will amply serve our purpose. In the latter case, indeed, the concept of a cause so plainly involves the concept of a necessity of connection with an effect, and of a strict universality of the law, that the very notion of a cause would entirely disappear, if were we to derive it, as Hume[6] did, from a frequent association of what happens with what precedes it, and from a habit, originating from

CATEGORIES ARE NECESSARY FOR EXPERIENCE

this, of connecting representations. The necessity inherent in the judgment would be merely subjective. Besides, without seeking for such examples of principles existing a priori in cognition, we might easily show that such principles are the indispensable basis of the possibility of experience itself, and consequently prove their existence a priori. For from where could our experience itself acquire certainty, if all the rules on which it depends were themselves empirical, and consequently fortuitous? No one, therefore, can admit the validity of the use of such rules as first principles. But, for the present, we may content ourselves with having established the fact that we do possess and exercise a faculty of pure a priori cognition; and, secondly, with having pointed out the proper tests of such cognition—namely, universality and necessity.

An a priori origin is manifest, however, not only in judgments, but even in concepts. For example, if we take away by degrees from our concepts of a body all that can be referred to mere sense experience—color, hardness or softness, weight, even impenetrability—the body will then vanish; but the space that it occupied still remains, and this it is utterly impossible to annihilate in thought. Again, if we take away, in like manner, from our empirical concept of any object, corporeal or incorporeal, all properties that mere experience has taught us to connect with it, still we cannot think away those through which we think it as substance, or adhering to substance, although our concept of substance is more determined than that of an object. Compelled, therefore, by that necessity with which the concept of substance forces itself upon us, we must confess that it has its seat in our faculty of a priori cognition. . . .

### IV. On the Difference between Analytic and Synthetic Judgments

In all judgments in which the relation of a subject to the predicate is thought (I mention affirmative judgments only here; the application to negative will be very easy), this relation is possible in two different ways. Either the predicate B belongs to the subject A, as something that is contained (though covertly) in the concept A; or the predicate B lies completely out of the concept A, although it stands in connection with it. In the first instance, I term the judgment *analytic;* in the second, *synthetic.* Analytic judgments (affirmative) are therefore those in which the connection of the predicate with the subject is thought through identity; those judgments in which this connection is thought without identity are called synthetic judgments. The former may be called *explicative,* the latter *augmentative* judgments; because the former add in the predicate nothing to the concept of the subject, but only analyze it into its constituent concepts, which were thought already in the subject, although in a confused manner; the latter add to our concepts of the subject a predicate that was not contained in it, and that no analysis could ever have discovered in it. For example, when I say "All bodies are extended," this is an analytic judgment. For I need not go beyond the concept of *body* in order to find extension connected with it, but merely analyze the concept— that is, become conscious of the manifold properties that I think in that concept—in order to discover this predicate in it: It is therefore an analytic judgment. On the other hand, when I say "All bodies are heavy," the predicate is something totally different from that which I think in the mere concept of a body. By the addition of such a predicate, therefore, it becomes a synthetic judgment.

Judgments of experience, as such, are always synthetic. For it would be absurd to think of grounding an analytic judgment on experience, because in forming such a judgment, I need not go out of the sphere of my concepts, and therefore recourse to the testimony of experience is quite unnecessary. That "bodies are extended" is not an empirical judgment, but a proposition that stands firm a priori. For before addressing myself to experience, I already have in my concept all the requisite conditions for the judgment, and I need only to extract the predicate from the concept, according to the principle of contradiction, and thereby at the same time become conscious of the necessity of the judgment—a necessity that I could never learn from experience. On the other hand, though at first I do not at all include the predicate of weight in my concept of body in general, that concept still indicates an object of experience, a part of the totality of experience, to which I can still add other parts; and this I do when I recognize by observation that bodies are heavy. I can know beforehand by analysis the concept of body through the characteristics of extension, impenetrability, shape, and so on, all which are thought in this concept. But now I extend my knowledge, and looking back on experience from which I had derived this concept of body, I find weight at all times connected with the above characteristics, and therefore I synthetically add to my concepts this as a predicate, and say "All bodies are heavy." Thus it is experience upon which rests the possibility of the synthesis of the predicate of weight with the concept of body, because both concepts, although the one is not contained in the other, still belong to one another (only contingently, however), as parts of a whole, namely, of experience, which is itself a synthesis of intuitions.

But to synthetic a priori judgments, such aid is entirely lacking. If I go out of and beyond the concept A, in order to recognize another B as connected with it, what foundation have I to rest on, whereby to render the synthesis possible? I have here no longer the advantage of looking out in the sphere of experience for what I want. Let us take, for example, the proposition "Everything that happens has a cause." In the concept of "something that happens," I indeed think an existence that is preceded by a certain time, and so on, and from this I can derive analytic judgments. But the concept of a cause lies quite out of the above concept and indicates something entirely different from "that which happens," and is consequently not contained in that concept. How then am I able to assert concerning the general concept "that which happens," something entirely different from that concept, and to recognize that the concept of cause, although not contained in it, yet belongs to it, and even necessarily? What is here the unknown = X, upon which the understanding rests when it believes it has found, out of the concept A, a foreign predicate B, which it nevertheless considers to be connected with it? It cannot be experience, because the principle adduced annexes the two representations, cause and effect, to [a third] representation, existence—not only with universality, which experience cannot give, but also with the expression of necessity—[something done] therefore completely a priori and from pure concepts. Upon such synthetic, that is, augmentative propositions, depends the whole aim of our speculative a priori knowledge; for although analytic judgments are indeed highly important and necessary, they are important and necessary only to arrive at that clearness of concepts that is requisite for a sure and extended synthesis, and this alone is a real acquisition.

### V. In All Theoretical Sciences of Reason, Synthetic A Priori Judgments Are Contained as Principles

1. Mathematical judgments are always synthetic. Up until now, this fact, though incontestably true and very important in its consequences, seems to have escaped the analysts of the human mind—in fact, to be in complete opposition to all their conjectures. For as it was found that mathematical conclusions all proceed according to the principle of contradiction (which the nature of every apodictic certainty[7] requires), people became persuaded that the fundamental principles of this science also were recognized and admitted in the same way. But the notion is fallacious; for although a synthetic proposition can certainly be discerned by means of the principle of contradiction, this is possible only when another synthetic proposition precedes, from which the latter is deduced, but never of itself.

Before all, it should be observed that proper mathematical propositions are always a priori judgments, and not empirical, because they carry along with them the concept of necessity, which cannot be given by experience. If this be objected, it does not matter; I will then limit my assertion to *pure* mathematics, the very concept of which implies that it consists of knowledge altogether nonempirical and a priori.

We might, indeed, at first suppose that the proposition 7 + 5 = 12 is a merely analytic proposition, following (according to the principle of contradiction) from the concept of a sum of seven and five. But if we regard it more narrowly, we find that our concept of the sum of seven and five contains nothing more than the uniting of both sums into one, whereby it cannot at all be thought what this single number is that embraces both. The concept of twelve is by no means obtained by merely thinking the union of seven and five; and we may analyze our concept of such a possible sum as long as we wish, still we shall never discover in it the notion of twelve. We must go beyond these concepts and have recourse to an intuition that corresponds to one of the two—our five fingers, for example, or, like Segner in his *Arithmetic*,[8] five points—and so by degrees, add the units contained in the five given in the intuition, to the concept of seven. For I first take the number 7, and for the concept of 5 I call in the aid of the fingers of my hand as objects of intuition. I then add to the number 7 the units that I before took together (by means of the material image my hand) to make up the number 5, and by this process, I see the number 12 arise. That 7 should be added to 5, I have certainly thought in my concept of a sum = 7 + 5, but not that this sum was equal to 12. Arithmetical propositions are therefore always synthetic, of which we may become more clearly convinced by trying large numbers. For it will thus become quite evident that, turn and twist our concepts as we may, it is impossible, without having recourse to intuition, to arrive at the sum total or product by means of the mere analysis of our concepts. Just as little is any principle of pure geometry analytic. "A straight line between two points is the shortest" is a synthetic proposition. For my concept of *straight* contains no notion of *quantity*, but is merely *qualitative*. The concept of the *shortest* is therefore wholly an addition, and by no analysis can it be extracted from our concept of a straight line. Intuition must therefore here lend its aid, by means of which and thus only, our synthesis is possible. . . .

2. The science of natural philosophy (physics) contains in itself synthetic a priori judgments, as principles. I shall adduce two propositions: "In all changes of the material world, the quantity of matter remains unchanged" and "In all communication of motion, action and reaction must always be equal." In both of these, not only is the necessity—and therefore their a priori origin—clear, but also that they are synthetic propositions. For in the concept of matter, I do not think its permanency, but merely its presence in space, which it fills. I therefore really go out of and beyond the concept of matter in order to add to it something a priori, which I did not think in it. The proposition is therefore not analytic but synthetic, and nevertheless conceived a priori; and so it is with regard to the other propositions of the pure part of natural philosophy.

3. As to metaphysics, even if we look upon it merely as an attempted science—yet, from the nature of human reason, an indispensable one—we find that it must contain synthetic a priori propositions. It is not merely the duty of metaphysics to dissect, and thereby analytically to illustrate the concepts that we form a priori of things; but we seek to widen the range of our a priori knowledge. For this purpose, we must avail ourselves of principles that add something to the original concept—something not identical with, nor contained in it—and by means of synthetic a priori judgments, leave far behind us the limits of experience; for example, in the proposition

"The world must have a beginning," and such like. Thus metaphysics, according to the proper aim of the science, consists merely of synthetic a priori propositions.

### VI. The Universal Problem of Pure Reason

It is extremely advantageous to be able to bring a number of investigations under the formula of a single problem. For in this manner, we not only facilitate our own labor, inasmuch as we define it clearly to ourselves, but also render it easier for others to decide whether we have done justice to our undertaking. The proper problem of pure reason, then, is contained in the question "How are synthetic a priori judgments possible?"

That metaphysical science has until now remained in so vacillating a state of uncertainty and contradiction is only to be attributed to the fact that this great problem, and perhaps even the difference between analytic and synthetic judgments, did not sooner suggest itself to philosophers. Upon the solution of this problem, or upon sufficient proof of the impossibility of synthetic a priori knowledge, depends the existence or downfall of the science of metaphysics. Among philosophers, David Hume came the nearest of all to this problem; yet it never acquired in his mind sufficient precision, nor did he regard the question in its universality. On the contrary, he stopped short at the synthetic proposition of the connection of an effect with its cause (*principium causalitatis*),[9] insisting that such an a priori proposition was impossible. According to his conclusions, then, all that we term metaphysical science is a mere delusion, arising from the fancied insight of reason into that which is in truth borrowed from experience, and to which habit has given the appearance of necessity. Against this assertion, destructive to all pure philosophy, he would have been guarded, had he had our problem before his eyes in its universality. For he would then have perceived that, according to his own argument, there likewise could not be any pure mathematical science, which assuredly cannot exist without synthetic a priori propositions—an absurdity from which his good understanding must have saved him.

In the solution of the above problem is at the same time comprehended the possibility of the use of pure reason in the foundation and construction of all sciences that contain theoretical a priori knowledge of objects—that is to say, the answer to the following questions:

How is pure mathematical science possible?
How is pure natural science possible?

With respect to these sciences, since they do certainly exist, it may with propriety be asked how they are possible; for that they must be possible, is shown by the fact that they really exist. But as to metaphysics, the miserable progress it has made so far, and the fact that of no one system yet brought forward can be said, with regard to its true aim, to exist—these facts leave anyone at liberty to doubt with reason the very possibility of its existence.

Yet, in a certain sense, this kind of knowledge must unquestionably be looked upon as *given;* in other words, metaphysics must be considered as really existing, if not as a science, nevertheless as a natural disposition of the human mind *(metaphysica naturalis)*.[10] For human reason, without any instigations imputable to the mere vanity of great knowledge, unceasingly progresses, urged on by its own feeling of need, towards such questions as cannot be answered by any empirical application of reason, or principles derived from it; and so there has always really existed in every man some system of metaphysics. It will always exist, so soon as reason awakes to the exercise of its power of speculation. And now the question arises: How is metaphysics, as a natural disposition, possible? In other words, how, from the nature of universal human reason, do those questions arise that pure reason proposes to itself and that it is impelled by its own feeling of need to answer as well as it can?

But since in all the attempts previously made to answer the questions that reason is prompted by its very nature to propose to itself—for example, whether the world had a beginning, or has existed from eternity— reason has always met with unavoidable contradictions, we must not rest satisfied with the mere natural disposition of the mind to metaphysics, that is, with the existence of the faculty of pure reason, from which, indeed, some sort of metaphysical system always arises. But it must be possible to arrive at certainty in regard to the question whether we know or do not know the things of which metaphysics treats. We must be able to arrive at a decision on the subjects of its questions, or on the ability or inability of reason to form any judgment respecting them; and therefore either to extend with confidence the bounds of our pure reason, or to set strictly defined and safe limits to its action. This last question that arises out of the above universal problem, would properly run thus: How is metaphysics possible as a science?

Thus, the critique of reason leads at last, naturally and necessarily, to science; and, on the other hand, the dogmatic use of reason without criticism leads to groundless assertions, against which others equally specious can always be set, thus ending unavoidably in skepticism.

Besides, this science cannot be of great and formidable prolixity, because it has not to do with objects of reason, the variety of which is inexhaustible, but merely with reason itself and its problems—problems that arise out of its own bosom, and are not proposed to it by the nature of outward things, but by its own nature. And when once reason has previously become able completely to understand its own power in regard to objects that it meets within experience, it will be easy to determine securely the extent and limits of its attempted application to objects beyond the confines of experience. . . .

**Transcendental Doctrine of Elements.[11] First Part: The Transcendental Aesthetic[12]**

In whatever mode or by whatever means our knowledge may relate to objects, it is at least quite clear that the only manner in which it immediately relates to them, is by means of an *intuition*. To this as the indispensable groundwork, all thought points. But an intuition can take place only insofar as the object is given to us. This is only possible, to man at least, on the condition that the object affects the mind in a certain manner. The capacity for receiving representations (receptivity) through the mode in which we are affected by objects, is called *sensibility*. By means of sensibility, therefore, objects are given to us, and it alone furnishes us with intuitions. By the understanding they are *thought*, and from the understanding arise *concepts*. But all thought must, directly or indirectly, by means of certain signs, relate ultimately to intuitions, and consequently, with us, to sensibility, because in no other way can an object be given to us. . . .

The science of all the principles of sensibility a priori, I call transcendental aesthetic. There must, then, be such a science, forming the first part of the transcendental doctrine of elements, in distinction to the part that contains the principles of pure thought, which is called transcendental logic. . . .

**Section I. On Space**

By means of the external sense (a property of the mind), we represent to ourselves objects as outside, and these all in space. In space alone are their shape, dimensions, and relations to each other determined or determinable. The internal sense, by means of which the mind contemplates itself or its internal state, gives, indeed, no intuition of the soul as an object; yet there is nevertheless a determinate form, under which alone the contemplation of our internal state is possible, so that all that which relates to the inward determinations of the mind is represented in relations of time. Of time we cannot have any external intuition, any more than we can have an internal intuition of space. What then are time and space? Are they real existences? Or are they merely relations or determinations of things, such, however, as would equally belong to these things in themselves, though they should never become objects of intuition? Or are they such as belong only to the form of intuition, and consequently to the subjective constitution of the mind, without which these predicates of time and space could not be attached to any object? In order to become informed on these points, we shall first give an exposition of the concept of space. By exposition, I mean the clear, though not detailed, representation of that which belongs to a concept; and an exposition is metaphysical when it contains that which represents the concept as given a priori.

1. Space is not a concept that has been derived from outward experiences. For, in order that certain sensations may relate to something outside me (that is, to something that occupies a different part of space from that in which I am), thus in order that I may represent them not merely as outside of and near to each other, but also in separate places, the representation of space must already exist as a foundation. Consequently, the representation of space cannot be borrowed from the relations of external phenomena through experience; but, on the contrary, this external experience is itself only possible through the antecedent representation.

2. Space then is a necessary representation a priori, which serves for the foundation of all external intuitions. We never can imagine or make a representation to ourselves of the nonexistence of space, though we may easily enough think that no objects are found in it. It must therefore be considered as the condition of the possibility of phenomena, and by no means as a determination dependent on them, and is a representation a priori, which necessarily supplies the basis for external phenomena. . . .

### Section II. On Time

1. Time is not an empirical concept. For neither coexistence nor succession would be perceived by us, if the representation of time did not exist as a foundation a priori. Without this presupposition we could not represent to ourselves that things exist together at one and the same time, or at different times—that is, contemporaneously, or in succession.

2. Time is a necessary representation, lying at the foundation of all our intuitions. With regard to phenomena in general, we cannot think away time from them, and represent them to ourselves as out of and unconnected with time, but we can quite well represent to ourselves time void of phenomena. Time is therefore given a priori. In it alone all reality of phenomena is possible. These may all be annihilated in thought, but time itself, as the universal condition of their possibility, cannot be so annulled. . . .

### Analytic of Concepts. Chapter 1: On the Transcendental Clue to the Discovery of All Pure Concepts of the Understanding

### Section II. Of the Logical Function of the Understanding in Judgments

If we abstract all the content of a judgment, and consider only the intellectual form of it, we find that the function of thought in a judgment can be brought under four heads, of which each contains three moments. These may be conveniently represented in the following table:

I.

*Quantity of Judgments*

Universal

Particular

Singular

II.

*Quality*

Affirmative

Negative

Infinite

III.

*Relation*

Categorical

Hypothetical

Disjunctive

IV.

*Modality*

Problematic

Assertoric

Apodictic . . .

### Section III. Of the Pure Concepts of the Understanding, or Categories

. . . There arise exactly so many pure concepts of the understanding, applying a priori to objects of intuition in general, as there are logical functions in all possible judgments. For there is no other function or faculty existing in the understanding besides those enumerated in that table. These concepts we shall, with Aristotle, call categories,[13] our purpose being originally identical with his, notwithstanding the great difference in the execution.

Table of Categories

I.

*Of Quantity*

Unity

Plurality

Totality

II.

*Of Quality*

Reality

Negation

Limitation

III.

*Of Relation*

Of Inherence and Subsistence

*(substantia et accidens)*[14]

Of Causality and Dependence

(cause and effect)

Of Community

(reciprocity between agent and patient)[15]

IV.

*Of Modality*

Prossibility—Impossibility

Existence—Nonexistence

Necessity—Contingency . . .

This, then, is a catalog of all the originally pure concepts of the synthesis that the understanding contains a priori, and these concepts alone entitle it to be called a pure understanding, inasmuch as only by them it can render the manifold of intuition conceivable—in other words, think an object of intuition. This division is made systematically from a common principle—namely, the faculty of judgment (which is just the same as the power of thought)—and has not arisen rhapsodically from a haphazard search for pure concepts, the full number of which we could never be certain, since we would employ induction alone and would not consider that, by this method, we could never understand why precisely these concepts, and no others, abide in the pure understanding.

▶ NOTES

1. *metaphysical:* relating to *metaphysics,* the branch of philosophy that studies the fundamental nature of reality [D. C. ABEL, EDITOR]

2. *a priori:* independent of experience (literally, in Latin, "from what comes earlier"); contrasted with *a posteriori,* dependent on experience ("from what comes later") [D. C. ABEL]

3. Nicolaus Copernicus (1473–1543) was a Polish astronomer. [D. C. ABEL]

4. *intuition:* sense experience [D. C. ABEL]

5. *contingency:* the state of being able to be or not to be; contrasted with *necessity* [D. C. ABEL]

6. David Hume (1711–1776) was a Scottish philosopher and historian. [D. C. ABEL]

7. *apodictic certainty:* absolute certainty [D. C. ABEL]

8. Johann Andreas von Segner, *Anfangsgründe der Arithmetic, Geometrie and der Geometrischen Berechnungen* (1756). Segner (1704–1777) was a German mathematician and naturalist. [D. C. ABEL]

9. *principium causalitatis:* (Latin) the principle of causality [D. C. ABEL]

10. *metaphysica naturalis:* (Latin) natural metaphysics [D. C. ABEL]

11. *Transcendental Doctrine of Elements: Elements* are the forms that our minds impose on objects; the doctrine Kant proposes is *transcendental* because the forms that our minds impose are a priori and thus transcend the objects themselves. [D. C. ABEL]

12. *Aesthetic:* something pertaining to sensation (*aisthēsis* in Greek) [D. C. ABEL]

13. The Greek philosopher Aristotle (384–322 B.C.E.) wrote a treatise called *Categories* (*Katēgoriai,* "predicates"), which postulates ten ways in which we think about things and in which things exist. [D. C. ABEL]

14. *substantia et accidens:* (Latin) substance [what subsists in itself] and accident [what inheres in a substance] [D. C. ABEL]

15. *agent and patient:* that which acts, and that which is acted upon [D. C. ABEL]

# Critique of Pure Reason

Immanuel Kant

**Reading Questions**

*According to Kant:*

1.  What new assumption about the relation of objects to our cognition of them might enable us to have a priori cognition of objects? How is this new assumption regarding knowledge similar to the new assumption that Copernicus made regarding celestial movements?

2.  How is it possible for knowledge to *begin with* experience but not entirely *arise out of* experience?

3.  Why is the proposition "Everything that happens has a cause" an *a priori* judgment rather than an *empirical* judgment? Why is it a *synthetic* judgment rather than an *analytic* judgment?

4.  Why is the representation of *space* a priori and not empirical? Why is the same true for the representation of *time?*

5.  Why is the number of *categories* (pure concepts of the understanding) the same as the number of the kinds of possible *judgments?*

**Discussion Questions**

*In your own view:*

1.  Do objects really exist in space and time, or is that simply how we experience them?

2.  Can we be certain that every change has a cause? If so, is this because every change really *does* have a cause, or because our minds experience reality through the a priori *category* of cause-and-effect?

3.  Does the fact that we experience objects through our mental framework mean that we can know only how things *appear* to us, and not know objects as they are *in themselves?*

4.  If we know only how things appear to us, can we be certain that things are anything more than appearances?

5.  Can the mind, by reflecting on itself, know its own structure?

# Objective Reality, Male Reality, and Social Construction

Sally Haslanger

Sally Haslanger was born in Norwalk, Connecticut, in 1955. She attended Reed College and graduated in 1977 with a bachelor's degree in philosophy and religion. After completing a master's degree in philosophy at the University of Virginia in 1980, she enrolled in the doctoral program in philosophy at the University of California-Berkeley, where she was awarded her degree in 1985. She was Assistant Professor of Philosophy at the University of California-Irvine (1985–1986), Princeton University (1986–1989), and the University of Pennsylvania (1989–1992). Haslanger then accepted an appointment as Associate Professor of Philosophy and Women's Studies at the University of Michigan. In 1998 she went to the Massachusetts Institute of Technology as Associate Professor of Philosophy, and was promoted to Professor in 2004. She has long been active in women's studies programs and is currently a member of the Women's Studies Steering Committee at the Massachusetts Institute of Technology. She served for four years as an associate editor of *Hypatia: A Journal of Feminist Philosophy* (2001–2005) and has been a consulting editor for the journal *Episteme: Epistemological Controversies in the Humanities and the Social Sciences* since 2002. Haslanger has been a National Humanities Fellow (1995–1996) and an American Council of Learned Societies Fellow (2002), and has received several awards for excellence in education, including the Distinguished Faculty Award of the Michigan Association of Governing Boards of State Universities (1997).

Haslanger's publications include journal articles and chapters in books published by Cornell University Press, Oxford University Press, and Cambridge University Press. She is coeditor (with Charlotte Witt) of *Adoption Matters: Philosophical and Feminist Essays* (2005).

Our reading is from "Objective Reality, Male Reality, and Social Construction," Haslanger's 1996 abridgement of her article "Ontology and Social Reconstruction," published in 1995. Haslanger examines to what extent "social construction" affects our theories of the nature of reality (metaphysics [ontology]) and the nature of our knowledge of reality (epistemology). In the broad sense, something is a social construction if it is "an intended or unintended product of a social practice." A thing is *discursively* constructed if what it is, or how it is, is determined—at least in part—by what is attributed to it (for example, an individual woman is discursively constructed). Discursive constructions depend on classifications, and a classification apparatus (a descriptive term, a conceptual distinction, or a detailed classification scheme) can itself be socially constructed. Haslanger calls the social construction of a classification apparatus a *pragmatic* construction. The pragmatic construction of a classification apparatus is *weak* if social factors only partly determine how we use it (for example, the distinction between men and women, taken as groups of individuals); the pragmatic construction is *strong* if social factors entirely determine how we use it (for example, the hypothesized ideal of "Woman's Nature"). A strongly pragmatic construction gives the illusion of capturing facts about objects, but it does not actually do so.

Turning to metaphysics, Haslanger points out that the distinction between what is real and unreal is pragmatically constructed in the weak sense. Some philosophers claim that reality is pragmatically constructed in the *strong* sense, and that therefore independent reality is a fiction. Haslanger rejects this claim, arguing that it rests on the false assumption that independent reality can be defined only in terms of objective knowledge.

▼

### Social Construction

... The notion of "social construction" is applied to a wide variety of items, and seemingly with rather different senses. At least initially, it is useful to think of social constructions on the model of artifacts. In the very broadest sense let's say:

> *Generic social construction:* Something is a social construction in the generic sense if it is an intended or unintended product of a social practice.

In addition to straightforward artifacts like washing machines and power drills, there is a clear sense in which, say, the Supreme Court of the U.S. and chess games are artifacts, as are languages, literature, and scientific inquiry. Because each of these depends for its existence on a complex social context, they are all social constructions in the broad sense in question. Granting that these various sorts of artifacts are very different sorts of things and are "constructed" in different ways (for example, some are purposefully designed, others not), at this point there is no reason whatsoever to think they are anything less than fully *real;* and their reality is perfectly concrete—that is, they don't exist just "in our heads."

But things get more complicated when we consider further the different ways that things can be "products" of a social context. At least in the case of human beings, the mere fact of how we are (even potentially) described or classified can have a direct impact on our self-understandings and our actions, because typically these descriptions and classifications bring with them normative expectations and evaluations. This works in several ways. Forms of description or classification provide for kinds of intention. For example, given the classification "cool," I can set about to become cool or avoid being cool, and so on. But also, such classifications can function in justifying behavior. For example, "We didn't invite him because he's not cool" and such justifications, in turn, can reinforce the distinction between those who are cool and those who are uncool.

The main point to note here is that our classificatory schemes, at least in social contexts, may do more than just map preexisting groups of individuals; rather, our attributions have the power to both establish and reinforce groupings that may eventually come to "fit" the classifications.

In such cases, classificatory schemes function more like a script than a map. This gives us a second and more narrow conception of social construction falling under the general idea of artifacts. On this narrower conception, something is socially constructed if what or how it is depends on a kind of feedback loop involving activities such as naming or classifying. Sometimes this form of construction is called "linguistic" or "discursive" construction, so I'll keep with this terminology:

> *Discursive construction:* A socially constructed object is the way it is, at least in part, because of what is attributed (and/or self-attributed) to it.

I'd say that there is no doubt that in this sense you and I are socially constructed: We are the individuals we are today at least partly as a result of what has been attributed (and self-attributed) to us. In other words, there is a sense in which adult human beings are a special kind of artifact.

Things get even more complicated, though, because there's still another wrinkle to consider. The idea of discursive construction depends on there being descriptions, distinctions, and classifications at hand whose attribution to things makes a difference—I am the way I am today because people have had the linguistic and conceptual resources to describe me as, for example, "smart" or "stupid," "attractive" or "ugly." There is a third sense of social construction on which it makes sense to say that *these classificatory schemes themselves*—our distinctions such as smart/stupid, attractive/ugly, rather than the things that respond to them—are socially constructed. Very roughly, to say that such a scheme is socially constructed is to say that its use is determined not by the "intrinsic" or "objective" features of the objects to which it is applied, but by social factors.

This characterization is purposely vague; so to help us explore some of the issues, let's go back to the example of "being cool": (At least initially) the distinction between those who are cool and those who are uncool is not capturing intrinsic differences between people; rather, it is a distinction marking certain social relations (that is, it distinguishes status in the in-group), and the fact that it is employed in any given context is a reflection of the importance of in-group/out-group relations. For example, suppose I need a way to establish a cohort; I do so by calling those I like "cool" and those I don't, "uncool." The distinction does not capture a difference in the individuals so called except insofar as they are related to me (based on my likes and dislikes), and its use in the context is determined not by the intrinsic coolness of the individuals but by the social task of establishing the cohort.

Noting the influence of social forces upon the distinctions we draw, let us define this third form of social construction, as follows:

> *Pragmatic[1] construction:* A classificatory apparatus (be it a full-blown classification scheme, or just a conceptual distinction or descriptive term) is socially constructed just in case its use is determined, at least in part, by social factors.

Construed in its weakest form, the point in claiming that a given distinction is pragmatically constructed is simply to say that our use of that distinction is as much due to contingent historical and cultural influences as to anything else: We inherit vocabularies and classificatory projects, and decide between alternatives based on utility, simplicity, and so on. This point is easy to grant; it would be hard to deny that the discursive resources we employ are socially conditioned in these ways and more. In a stronger form, however, the point is that such social factors *alone* determine our use of the distinction in question; in short, it is to emphasize that there's no "fact of the matter" that it captures. So let's distinguish two kinds of pragmatic construction:

> A distinction is *weakly* pragmatically constructed if social factors only partly determine our use of it.

> A distinction is *strongly* pragmatically constructed if social factors wholly determine our use of it, and it fails to represent accurately any "fact of the matter."

We'll come back to the weak form of pragmatic construction shortly; let me first unpack this strong form further, because there is an ambiguity in the suggestion that there's no fact of the matter that such a pragmatically constructed distinction captures. In the example of "cool," I use the term to establish my cohort, and in doing so my ascriptions are guided by my likes and dislikes. So there may be a real social distinction (admittedly parochial) that corresponds to my use—I call Mary and George "cool," Susan and John "uncool," and the application of the terms corresponds to whom I like and whom I don't. But note also that in attributing "coolness" to someone, I'm doing so with the background assumption in play that the "coolness" is an intrinsic feature of the individual and is not merely a matter of whom I like. In calling Mary and George "cool," I'm suggesting that there is something cool *about them* that has nothing to do with me—supposedly, it's *their coolness* that warrants my use of the term. It is here that the question of fact arises: Insofar as I am attributing intrinsic coolness to someone, my attribution misfires since no one (at least no one at this stage of the process) is, so to speak, cool *in themselves*. In such cases I want to say that my attributions of coolness are false—there is no fact about their coolness that I am accurately representing, even if my use of the terms corresponds to some other features of the individuals. So:

> Strong pragmatic constructions are, in an important sense, illusions projected onto the world; their use might nevertheless track—*without accurately representing*—a genuine distinction.

The main point is that in such cases there are no available facts (for example, about intrinsic coolness or uncoolness) that my attributions could be tracking; so instead, we might conclude, they must be functioning wholly as a means to a social goal.

On the face of it, there is a significant difference between weak and strong pragmatic construction. In cases of weak pragmatic construction, our choices of descriptive terms, classificatory schemes, and so on, are conditioned by social factors (such as values, interests, history), but of course this is compatible with those terms and classifications capturing real facts and distinctions. The world provides us with more facts and distinctions than we could ever know what to do with. Acknowledging that what ones we bother to notice or name is largely determined by our background and interests does not impugn in any general way the accuracy of our attributions. In cases of strong pragmatic construction, however, the attributions are, by hypothesis, not accurately capturing facts, though there is an illusion that they are.

It is important to note that because in the case of pragmatic construction, what's constructed is (at least primarily) a distinction or classificatory scheme, the thought that our classifications are socially constructed leads naturally to the idea that knowledge is socially constructed. Given the preceding discussion, we must allow that there are different ways to cash out the claim that knowledge is socially constructed, but we can cast two of them in terms of weak and strong pragmatic constructions. Roughly:

> Our *knowledge* is weakly/strongly socially constructed (in the relevant senses) if the distinctions and classifications we employ in making knowledge claims are weakly/strongly pragmatically constructed.

To see how these different kinds of social construction function, let's shift from the artificial example of "cool" I've been using to something more substantive and, for some, more familiar. I'll run briefly through the different kinds using an example of the social construction of gender. As usual, allow at least a provisional distinction between sex and gender. Gender is defined relationally: men and women are two groups defined by their social relations to each other. I've argued elsewhere,[2] drawing on the work of Catharine MacKinnon, that we can usefully model one process by which gender is constructed roughly as follows: The ideal of Woman is an externalization of men's desire (so-called Woman's Nature is what men find desirable). This ideal is projected onto individual females and is regarded as intrinsic and essential to them. Accepting these attributions of Womanhood, individual women then internalize the norms appropriate to the ideal and aim to conform their behavior to them. And in general, behavior toward women is "justified" by reference to this ideal. This, in turn, is responsible for significant empirical differences between men women.

In this example, individual women are *discursively constructed*—that is, we are the individuals we are because of the attribution (and self-attribution) of Womanhood to us; or, more simply, because we've been viewed (and so treated) as having a Woman's Nature. This ideal of Woman's Nature, however, is *strongly pragmatically constructed;* it is an illusion projected onto women whose basis lies in complex social/sexual relations, not in the intrinsic or essential features of women. And further it is plausible that the distinctions between both man and woman, and male and female (taken as groups of individuals) are *weakly pragmatically constructed:* The fact that we draw these distinctions as we do is to be at least partly explained by social factors, though there are also very real differences between both men and women, male and female.

To summarize, the following would be plausible examples of each kind of construction:

> *Discursively constructed:* individual women; cool dudes.

> *Strongly pragmatically constructed:* Woman's Nature; intrinsic coolness.

> *Weakly pragmatically constructed:* the distinction between men and women, between male and female; the distinction between those who wear black T-shirts more than once a week and those who don't.

### The Social Construction of Reality

Given the different kinds of social construction just sketched, there are a variety of different senses we might give to the claim that *reality* is socially constructed. For example, the claim might be that the reality is an artifact—that human beings are in some significant way involved in bringing about or constituting everything there is; or it might be that reality is discursively constructed—that our linguistic and conceptual activities are responsible for how things are; or it might be that our distinction between what's real and what's not is pragmatically constructed—that how we conceive of reality is determined wholly or partly by social factors. Are any of these claims plausible?

There can hardly be a doubt that the distinction we draw between what's real and what's unreal is pragmatically constructed at least in the weak sense—that is, social factors play a role in determining our applications of the distinction. Stepping back from the particular distinction between real/unreal, there are at least two different ways that social factors seem to play an inevitable role in our application of *any* distinction. First, the fact that we have the linguistic and conceptual resources to draw the distinction in question (and that we have any interest in doing so) will always depend upon contingent historical and cultural factors. So the fact that the distinction is available in our conceptual repertoire at all is largely a social matter.

Second, any particular effort (at a particular time) to apply a distinction to something is influenced by social factors. For example, my ability to distinguish effectively As from Bs may depend on my confidence, ignorance, intelligence, bias, the incentives and costs, and so on. So social factors play a role both in determining the content of the distinctions we make and in our efforts to apply them. The real/unreal distinction appears no different from any other in these respects, and I take these points to be completely uncontroversial. So there's at least one sense in which reality is socially constructed: The distinction between real/unreal—in fact, all of the substantive distinctions we employ—are weakly pragmatically constructed. But, as suggested before, it is perfectly compatible with this that our distinctions are accurately capturing genuine—and independent—facts.

So suppose we grant that in this sense, reality is socially constructed: The distinction we draw between what's real and what's not is weakly constructed. Is there any reason this should lead us to be skeptical about there being a world independent of us? It might seem so if we could extend the case for pragmatic construction to show that the real/unreal distinction is *strongly pragmatically constructed*. Remember that a distinction is strongly pragmatically constructed if it is one whose purported applications are wholly determined by social factors and it fails to accurately represent "the facts." If there are arguments to show that the real/unreal distinction is constructed in this strong sense, then it would follow that our use of it is misguided and doesn't "capture" anything; what we take to be reality is simply a fiction. On this view, reality is socially constructed in the sense of being, like intrinsic coolness and Woman's Nature, merely an illusion.

So the question before us now is whether there are further considerations that should lead us from acknowledging the influence of social factors on knowledge to the more controversial suggestion that we should regard the notion of an "independent reality" as a fiction. . . .

### "Objective" Reality

. . . What does the idea [of an independent reality] amount to, and what work does it do for us? . . . The worry is that if the real/unreal distinction . . . is constructed in the sense of being nothing more than a social projection, then we would have to conclude that there are no facts about what's real and what's not, and the idea of an independent reality would be a kind of fiction.

Let us begin again with the acknowledgment that all of our distinctions are weakly pragmatic—what ones we choose to employ and how we do so is at least partly determined by social factors. It follows that our use of the real/unreal distinction is weakly pragmatic. So the question before us now is whether there are further considerations that should lead us from acknowledging the influence of social factors on knowledge to the more controversial suggestion that we should regard the notion of an "independent reality" as a fiction. The following argument is one that can be found explicitly in [the works of] some writers and is implicit in [the works of] many others.[3] . . .

On the picture under attack, knowledge and reality are intimately connected: What is real is what can be objectively known.[4] Objectivity, in this view, is in its primary sense an epistemological[5] notion. Roughly, w+129 P.or

*(ObInq): An inquiry is *objective* in the relevant sense just in case the only factors that determine its outcome are the way the world is, and the rationality of the inquirers.

So an objective view of some subject matter is one that a purely rational inquiry into the subject would eventually yield. This epistemic[6] notion of "objectivity" is then applied derivatively to ontology[7]—as in "objective reality"—by virtue of the following equivalence:

(ObRel): An object or a fact is objectively real just in case it is (or can be) objectively known.

Moreover, on this view there is no notion of reality other than objective reality. (Note that this is only one of many accounts of objectivity; nevertheless, in the remainder of this section I will be using the term "objective" as indicated here.)

*At least in this crude formulation, such a conception of "objective" inquiry is not plausible, and it is now a commonplace to deny that such pure inquiry is possible. For (at least) the reasons sketched above, we must acknowledge that the results of all human inquiry are conditioned by social factors. But if we continue to think that reality must be equated with what is objectively knowable,* then since nothing is objectively knowable (in the relevant sense), it appears that we should conclude that there is no such thing as "reality"—that is, nothing is objectively real. In short, "reality" or "objective reality" are as much an illusion as "pure inquirers" and "objective knowledge."*

IDEA OF OBJ. KNOWLEDGE IS AN ILLUSION.

Having rejected the idea that there is an objective reality, however, it then seems plausible to offer an analysis of our purported references to what's real in line with our previous example of "cool." When we attribute "reality" to something, our attribution does not capture a fact about the object itself (since, by hypothesis, the fact we purport to be attributing is not available); rather, such attributions correspond to a distinction in how things are related to us. In other words, things are graced with the term "real" not by virtue of some intrinsic fact about them, but by virtue of some relevant social fact—for example, our finding them useful or, perhaps, politically expedient. Yet, as in the case of "cool," there is an illusion implicit in our attributions, since the background assumption is that what's real is not a matter of how things are related to us, but rather is an intrinsic feature of things. . . .

## Being Real

That's the sketch of the argument; let's now go through it a bit more carefully. We should note first that the argument is concerned with a particular practice of employing the terms "real," "reality," and their cognates. So far I've spoken vaguely about "our use" of the terms, but this is potentially misleading, since it is unclear who the "we" are whose use is in question.

For the moment, let's just call it the "objectivist use" of the terms, keeping in mind that we are analyzing a particular practice.

The objectivist use of the terms "real" and "unreal" involves both a discrimination between two classes of things (the class of things designated "real" and those designated "unreal") and an interpretation of the basis for that discrimination. In particular, the antiobjectivist argument is directed against those who apply the term "real" rather narrowly, alleging to employ as their criterion whether it is possible to have objective knowledge of the thing. Against this use of the term, the critical argument aims to show, first, that nothing satisfies the alleged criterion and, second, that there is really another criterion being employed in making the relevant discriminations, one that is grounded in certain responses to the things in question.

At this stage, I think we should grant that there's something wrong with an objectivist criterion for applying the term "real" (namely, one requiring "objective knowledge"), so it is implausible that the classes of things the objectivist designates as "real" and "unreal" are being judged accurately by that standard, in spite of his belief that they are. The question is whether there is another criterion, or range of criteria, implicit in the objectivist's discriminations, and what they might be. Here the antiobjectivist will claim that there is always another criterion doing the work, and that more specifically, it is one that draws on social facts or implicates "us" in some way (relating the object in question to our needs, interests, desires, social roles, and so on). Of course, this statement of the point is rather vague, but exactly what social facts are relevant and how "we" are implicated varies depending on which antiobjectivist account you are considering. . . . Moreover, which social factors determine how the terms are used may vary from context to context. But in spite of this vagueness, I think there is reason to be concerned about the whole strategy of argument.

Suppose we do grant there are objectivist uses of the terms "real" and "reality," or that there are ways of determining what is real and what isn't that both purport to be epistemically objective but instead are based on socially loaded criteria. This raises a challenge to the notion of an independent reality only if we accept the thesis that such a reality is *by definition* that which can be objectively known—that is, only if we accept (ObRel) as characterizing what it is to be objectively (or independently) real. This is an easy thesis to reject, especially for one with realist[8] inclinations; for the whole point of speaking of an *independent* reality is to emphasize that there is no necessary connection between what's real and what human beings know or can (in practice) know. Strangely, it appears that the argument as sketched would only be convincing to someone who was already committed to an epistemically constrained conception of reality and should not be convincing to those realists it purportedly sets out to target.

So there are several plausible responses to the argument that "objective reality" is an illusion. We could start by rejecting the most questionable premises: We could reject the proposed link between (objective) knowledge and (objective) reality, as stated in (ObRel). Or we could reject the proposed definition of objective knowledge in (ObInq). I find both of these options appealing. But suppose for the sake of argument that the only way to conceive of an "objective" reality is in terms of what is objectively known—that is, suppose we decide to accept both of these premises. Then we probably should conclude that the correlative idea of reality is equally nonsense. However, even if we grant that there is no *objective* reality, it still doesn't follow that there is no *independent* reality or no genuine facts of the matter that it would be good to know. To give up the idea of "objective reality" as we've been considering it, is simply to give up the idea that there are things that determine, in and of themselves, without any social factors playing a role, how they are known. It seems clear that, because language and knowledge are socially conditioned, there are no things like this.

What's at least partly at stake here is how *we* want to employ the notion of "the real" or "reality." Assuming that the idea of an independent reality can only be defined in terms of objective knowledge grants too much to the objectivist. For, as suggested above, at least one plausible idea of an "independent" reality is one that places no epistemic conditions on what it is to be real. At least initially, we might take the property of being real at face value: To be real is to exist. Or perhaps: For an object to be real is for it to exist; for an event to be real is for it to occur; for a fact to be real is for it to obtain. These explications are unilluminating, to be sure, and may well need further analysis; my point is not to endorse an intentionally naive view, but rather to suggest the first steps of an account that views what's real in nonepistemological and nonsocial terms. We will, of course, need an epistemology (and I think a feminist epistemology) to help us decide what to believe exists, what definitions to accept, and so on. But I see no good reason in the arguments we've considered so far to collapse the epistemology-ontology distinction. When I say that something is real, my assertion is true just in case the thing in question exists; this is so even if the criteria I employ in making the judgment are socially loaded, and even if my utterance also expresses the value it has in my conception of things.

## Conclusion

Are there any general conclusions we can draw from this discussion? How profoundly does the idea of social construction affect our projects in metaphysics[9] and epistemology? There is no doubt that the idea of discursive construction should play a significant role in our ontological theorizing.

Because reality does have a way of conforming itself to our conception of it, the line between artifacts and natural objects must continually be challenged and contested. We must be aware that the classifications we employ in our theorizing may not be capturing differences already there, but may be responsible for creating them. But we have no reason yet to conclude that there are only artifacts, or that our classificatory endeavors are so powerful as to leave nothing untouched.

Moreover, epistemologically we must acknowledge the force of pragmatic construction. Our classificatory schemes, our distinctions, and our judgments are inevitably influenced by many different social factors; and some of our judgments are not tracking any facts but are instead only perpetuating socially meaningful illusions. Moreover, we must be attentive to the possibility that the terms we use are defined by and in the interest of dominant social groups. But from this it does not follow that the only function of judgment is the social one of perpetuating useful stories, or that our judgment can only represent a social world. It may well be that our point of view on the world is always socially conditioned, but there is no reason to conclude that the world we have a point of view on is likewise socially conditioned. We must distance ourselves from the objectivist tendencies to limit our vision of what's real, but we must be careful at the same time not simply to accept perspectivist[10] limitations in their place. I would propose that the task before us is to construct alternative, modestly realist ontologies that enable us to come to more adequate and just visions of what is, what might be, and what should be.

*(handwritten margin note: Don't limit yourself to what you see. Just a woman, black, etc. But you can't just say just a person)*

*(handwritten note above "objectivist": modernist)*

---

▶ NOTES

1. *pragmatic:* practically useful [D. C. ABEL, EDITOR]

2. Sally Haslanger, "On Being Objective and Being Objectified," in *A Mind of One's Own: Feminist Essays on Reason and Objectivity,* ed. Louise M. Anthony and Charlotte Witt (Boulder, Colo.: Westview Press, 1993), pp. 85–125 [S. HASLANGER]

3. My characterization of the argument is much simplified, but I have in mind works such as Richard Rorty, *Philosophy and the Mirror of Nature* (Princeton, N.J.: Princeton University Press, 1979); Catharine A. MacKinnon, *Toward a Feminist Theory of the State* (Cambridge, Mass.: Harvard University Press, 1989); and Sandra Harding, *Whose Science? Whose Knowledge?: Thinking from Women's Lives*, especially Chapter 6 (Ithaca, N.Y.: Cornell University Press, 1991), among others. [S. HASLANGER]

4. For one typical characterization of the objectivist target, see MacKinnon, *Toward a Feminist Theory of the State*, p. 97. [S. HASLANGER]

5. *epistemological:* relating to *epistemology,* the study of the nature and grounds of knowledge [D. C. ABEL]

6. *epistemic:* relating to knowledge [D. C. ABEL]

7. *ontology:* the study of the nature and kinds of reality [D. C. ABEL]

8. *realist:* relating to *realism,* the doctrine that objects of knowledge exist independently of the mind [D. C. ABEL]

9. *metaphysics:* synonym for *ontology* (see note 7) [D. C. ABEL]

10. *perspectivist:* relating to *perspectivism,* the doctrine that all knowledge is conditioned by the perspective of the knower [D. C. ABEL]

# Objective Reality, Male Reality, and Social Construction

Sally Haslanger

### Reading Questions

*According to Haslanger:*

1. Why is a discursive construction "more like a script than a map"?

2. In what sense are adult human beings "a special kind of artifact"?

3. What does it mean for a classification framework (for example, a conceptual distinction) to be "pragmatically constructed"? How does *weak* pragmatic construction differ from *strong* pragmatic construction?

4. In what two ways is the real/unreal distinction a weak pragmatic construction?

5. Why does the fact that real/unreal is a pragmatically weak construction not imply that there is no independent reality?

### Discussion Questions

*In your own view:*

1. Are we who we are, in part, because of what is attributed to us?

2. When we call someone "cool" or "uncool," are we referring to some intrinsic quality of the person, or only to the person's relationship to an in-group?

3. Is all knowledge to some extent socially constructed?

4. If all knowledge is at least partly a social construction, is it possible to know anything as it really is?

5. Can we base a decision to classify something as real or unreal on an understanding of its relation to objective reality?

Bailey–Cuomo: The
Feminist Philosophy
Reader

9. Feminist Epistemologies | Text

© The McGraw–Hill
Companies, 2008

133

CHAPTER 9

# FEMINIST EPISTEMOLOGIES

Epistemology, or theories of knowledge, names the branch of philosophy concerned with the nature, scope, sources, structures, and limits of human knowledge. Western philosophy has been particularly fixated on questions about truth and belief, the nature of the mind, the role reason plays in knowing, and the supremacy of scientific knowledge. These inquiries usually have presupposed that the "perfect knower" is a universal ideal, that all knowing is cognitive, that scientific knowledge is paradigmatic, and that the production of knowledge is politically neutral. Feminist theorists challenge these assumptions by demonstrating how sexism and other harmful biases have shaped presuppositions about the nature of knowing. Feminist epistemology begins with a critique of western scientific and philosophical traditions, and continues with projects that reframe our understandings of what it means to know something, and that reconstruct these understandings on "newer more self-conscious ground" (Alcoff and Potter 1987, 3). Feminists working in epistemology have broadened the field of inquiry by acknowledging the ways knowledge is embodied, emotional, socially situated, and informed by specific experiences and goals. While the principle task of most Anglo-American epistemology has been to refute the skeptic and to determine the conditions for objective knowledge, feminist epistemologies focus on the social and historical circumstances that determine knowledge in particular contexts, and on the relationships between knowledge production and forms of power. So, feminist epistemology does not merely add details to existing accounts of knowledge—it shifts the epistemic framework and raises new questions about agency, cognitive authority, objectivity, and rationality.

In the 1980s, several key critical examinations of traditional theories of science and rationality, and their relationships to canonical views on sex and gender, initiated a terrific wave of feminist work on epistemology. Genevieve Lloyd's *The Man of Reason* (1984), Evelyn Fox Keller's *Reflections on Gender and Science* (1985), and Susan Bordo's *The Flight to Objectivity* (1987) drew clear connections between Enlightenment ideals of rationality, objectivity, and detachment, and the masculine ideals organizing scientific inquiry. In "Purification and Transcendence," Bordo offers a detailed analysis of the work of René Descartes, and especially his canonical *Meditations on First Philosophy* (1641). Bordo argues that the Cartesian epistemic project of seeking god-like certainty and objectivity is grounded in an intellectual "flight" from the (feminine) body, toward a masculine stance that pursues knowledge as pure thought and perception, and that takes knowers to be transcendent and disembodied subjects. The anxieties regarding emotion and the uncontrollable body that ground Descartes' projects create a notion of the body as completely separate and separable from the mind, a fiction that persists in contemporary epistemology and philosophy of mind.

The philosophical ideal of a "disembodied subject" engaging in "pure thought" shows how thoroughly emotions and other feelings have been ignored or dismissed by many influential theories of knowledge. Indeed, in "Love and Knowledge," Alison Jaggar argues that western philosophy, with some exceptions, understands reason in opposition to emotion. Reason, the faculty that supposedly generates knowledge, is associated with male competence and emotion, which allegedly distracts from knowledge, is linked to uncontrollable feminine appetites. The reason/emotion dichotomy is not only misogynist, but also relies on a rather naïve view even of what emotions are. Anticipating some of the key questions in contemporary philosophical writings on mind and emotion, Jaggar develops an alternative account, arguing that emotions are vital for reason, perception, and systematic knowledge.

Another feminist project calls attention to the unseen political dimensions of epistemological endeavors. In "How Is Epistemology Political?," Linda Martín Alcoff clarifies and examines the relation between epistemology and power. As a discipline, epistemology is a social practice engaged in primarily by elite professionals in academic settings where authority is almost always aligned with race, gender, and class privilege. It follows that history, identity, culture, and context often determine methods of hypothesis formation, ideas about what counts as evidence, and beliefs about what is reasonable or justified. In cultures of dominance and subordination, oppressive power

relations may be reinforced by epistemological theories and methods. It is therefore crucial to identify the relations between particular theories and the forms of social power they propagate. As Alcoff argues, attention to those dimensions will inevitably strengthen epistemology as a practice that aims to better understand knowledge.

The problematic ideals and assumptions criticized by Bordo, Jaggar, and Alcoff are not passing fads in the history of philosophy: they ground "S-knows-that-$p$" approaches to questions of knowledge that are standard in contemporary analytic philosophy.[1] In "Taking Subjectivity into Account," Lorraine Code criticizes the propositional focus of epistemology by arguing that it is inattentive to the identities of knowing subjects. The assumptions that ways of knowing are universal and knowers are interchangeable are easy to maintain if we consider only how one comes to know about everyday medium-sized objects like coffee cups and patches of color. But there is no reason that "perception at a distance" should be the template for all knowing practices. For example, knowing other people in personal relationships is at least as important as knowledge of objects. And the "S-knows-that-$p$" template can be harmful to members of groups who are often treated as objects of study and not knowers in their own right. Code proposes that we approach epistemic projects with a "qualified relativism" that will remap the epistemic terrain in ways that are attentive not only to physical geography, but also to subject positions and the sociopolitical structures.

Other approaches consider and construct distinctly feminist theories of knowledge by taking up questions about the relations between bias, truth, and objectivity. They demonstrate the

---

[1] A great deal of standard twentieth-century philosophy took as its leading challenge to discover necessary and sufficient conditions for the truth of sentences of the form "S-knows-that-$p$," where 'S' refers to some subject—a knower—and '$p$' refers to some proposition that is known by the subject. For example, "Sally knows that the glass is on the table." It was then asked, what are the necessary and sufficient conditions for the truth of the assertion "S knows that $p$?"

Bailey–Cuomo: The
Feminist Philosophy
Reader

9. Feminist Epistemologies

Text

© The McGraw–Hill
Companies, 2008

135

ubiquity of political biases in these discussions and go on to argue that "objectivity" can best be served by adding marginalized voices, making the politics behind epistemic and scientific projects visible, or using methodologies that are transparent and self-reflexive. Sandra Harding takes up in "'Strong Objectivity' and Socially Situated Knowledge," arguing that so-called "value-neutral" accounts of objectivity ignore the powerful cultural background beliefs shaping inquiry. In response to this observation she proposes a version of feminist standpoint theory[2] that not only admits to the importance of certain aspects of modern scientific commitment to objectivity, but also acknowledges that deeply stratified societies cannot produce value-free knowledge. Nonetheless, Harding thinks that members of oppressed communities can generate uniquely important knowledge. She argues for "strong objectivity," which includes multiple standpoints, fosters a stronger empiricism, generates a more rigorous objectivity, and produces a more accurate picture of how we know the world.

Certainly it would be a mistake to assume that women everywhere share the same concerns or priorities around questions of knowledge production. So, we might ask, how do different cultural priorities shape the questions that feminist epistemological projects choose to address? In "The Project of Feminist Epistemology: Perspectives from a Nonwestern Feminist," Uma Narayan examines the dangers of theorizing knowledge and

values in ways that ignore nonwestern women's experiences and present western theoretical insights too dogmatically. Her essay outlines several concerns for nonwestern feminists involved in epistemological projects. For example, Narayan notes that westerners' primary critical focus on positivism ignores the fact that religious values, which often shape strongly nonwestern cultural views of gender, are not positivist; and that the political liberalism associated with positivism sometimes offers concepts that are useful for fighting oppression. She also questions the popular idea that members of oppressed groups are epistemically privileged, and that privileged groups can learn to see privilege more clearly by paying attention to the critical insights of the oppressed. In the end, she advocates a more complex theory of epistemic advantage: one that does not romanticize the "double consciousness" of marginalized groups, but instead recognizes the high emotional price many people pay for living the multiple realities that give rise to their unique ways of knowing.

Philosophers have had plenty to say about knowledge, but relatively very little to say about ignorance. Ignorance is not a simple lack of knowing: it is often a social production that is actively fostered and preserved. It is therefore crucial for feminist epistemologies to focus not only on what is known, but also on the practices that systematically erase some forms of knowledge, produce ignorance, and prevent resistance. In "Coming to Understand: Orgasm and the Epistemology of Ignorance," Nancy Tuana examines scientific, feminist, and common-knowledge constructions of female sexual pleasure in order to track the production of knowledge and ignorance about female orgasm. She investigates what we do and do not know about female genitalia and orgasm, and why geographies of the female body have largely excluded or misrepresented the clitoris and other organs of female pleasure. There is the strong correlation between pleasure and knowledge. For this reason questions about whose pleasures are enhanced and whose are suppressed by ignorance must be addressed in any study of the science of sexuality.

[2] Feminist standpoint theory is rooted in the Marxist observation that socially oppressed classes can access knowledge unavailable to the socially privileged—particularly knowledge of power relations. It argues that the epistemic locations of marginalized groups (e.g., women or the proletariat) can yield more comprehensive and accurate questions, observations, and analyses of the world than those of dominant groups. Standpoint theorists make an important distinction between a *woman's perspective* and a *feminist standpoint*. A "standpoint" is a form of understanding that results from political struggle: it is not a form of understanding that one has simply by virtue of having a particular gender identity or body. A feminist standpoint is crafted through gender-sensitive political engagement with the world, and women's perspective is something women are imagined to have by virtue of living their lives as women.

# PURIFICATION AND TRANSCENDENCE IN DESCARTES'S MEDITATIONS

### Susan Bordo

*Me-thinks, I see how all the old Rubbish must be thrown away, and the rotten Buildings be overthrown, and carried away with so powerful an Inundation. These are the days that must lay a new foundation of a more magnificent Philosophy, never to be overthrown . . . a true and permanent Philosophy.*
—Henry Power, *Experimental Philosophy*

## CARTESIANISM AND THE QUEST FOR PURITY

Where there is anxiety, there will almost certainly be found a mechanism of defense against that anxiety. In *Pensées,* VI, 113, Pascal expresses, in one line, what might be seen as the *modus operandi* for the modern struggle for control over the sense of arbitrary allotment of time and place within an indifferent, alien universe. "*Through space,*" he says, "*the universe grasps me and swallows me up like a speck; through thought I grasp it.*" If the impersonal, arbitrary universe of the early modern era is capable of physically "swallowing" him, like a random bit of ontological debris, *he* is nonetheless capable of containing and subduing it—through comprehension, through the "grasp" of the mind. As in much of early modern science and philosophy—in Bacon, most dramatically—the dream of knowledge is here imagined as an explicit revenge fantasy, an attempt to wrest back control from nature.

The fantasy of absolute understanding, of course, motivated Descartes much more than Pascal. But the thought through which Descartes conquered the indifferent, infinite universe was a thought very different from that imagined in Pascal's *Pensées.* To *comprehend*—to contain the

whole within the grasp of the mind—is simply not possible for a finite intelligence, as Descartes makes clear.[1] Rather, what seizes the Cartesian imagination is the possibility of *pure* thought, of *pure* perception. Such perception, far from embracing the whole, demands the disentangling of the various objects of knowledge *from* the whole of things, and beaming a light on the essential separateness of each—its own pure and discrete nature, revealed as *it* is, free of the "distortions" of subjectivity. Arithmetic and geometry are natural models for the science that will result; for, as Descartes says, they "alone deal with an object so pure and uncomplicated, that they need make no assumptions at all which experience renders uncertain" (*Regulae,* HR, I, 5). The "intuitions" of the *Regulae,* the "simples" of the *Discourse,* and the clear and distinct perceptions of the *Meditations* are attempts to describe the possibility of such objects for philosophy, a class of "privileged representations," as Rorty puts it, "so compelling that their accuracy cannot be doubted." Much of Meditation IV, I will argue, turns on the delineation of such a class of ideas.

For these "privileged representations" to reveal themselves, the knower must be purified, too—of all bias, all "perspective," all emotional attachment. And for Descartes, this necessarily involves the transcendence of the body, not only of the "prejudices" acquired through the body-rule of infancy but of all the bodily distractions and passions that obscure our thinking. The *Meditations,* I propose, should be read as providing a guide and exemplar of such bodily transcendence.

The result for Descartes is a new model of knowledge, grounded in *objectivity,* and capable of providing a new epistemological security to replace that which was lost in the dissolution of the medieval world-view. It is a model that, although under attack, is still largely with analytic philosophy today, and that still revolves around the imagery of *purity.* Locke spoke of philosophy as removing the "rubbish lying in the way of knowledge." Three centuries later, Quine wrote

Bailey–Cuomo: The
Feminist Philosophy
Reader

9. Feminist Epistemologies | Text

© The McGraw–Hill
Companies, 2008

137

that the task of the philosopher was "clearing the ontological slums" (p. 275). The image of the philosopher as tidying the mess left by others is more subtly presented by Arthur Danto, who views the philosopher as "executing the tasks of conceptual housekeeping [the sciences and other disciplines] are too robustly busy to tend to themselves" (p. 10).

The creation of a "pure" realm, untouched by uncertainty and risk, always necessitates, as Dewey points out (p. 8), the designation of a contrastingly "impure" realm to absorb or take responsibility for the messy aspects of experience. In the history of philosophy, the role of the unclean and the impure has been played, variously, by material reality, practical activity, change, the emotions, "subjectivity," and most often—as for Descartes—by the *body*. In Locke and Danto's conception of philosophy, the other disciplines play this role: They are the earth to philosophy's spirit, the "matter" to philosophy's "form", providing the "stuff" to be analyzed, organized and corrected by philosophy's purifying scrutiny.[2]

What makes such conceptions peculiarly Cartesian is not just their implicit assumption that the philosopher is in possession of some neutral "matrix" (as Rorty calls it) with which to perform an ultimate critical or conceptual cleansing, but their passion for intellectual separation, demarcation, and *order*. The other disciplines, as Feyerabend says, must be "tamed [and put] in their place" (p. 21); their "robust" effort is fine, so long as there is someone specifically charged to clean up the conceptual debris left in its wake.

Rorty is critical of this conception of the role of the philosopher, according to which the philosopher occupies a space, not within the cultural conversation, but removed, at a distance, linguistically interpreting, logically overseeing, and epistemologically scrutinizing the proceedings. The pretension to do so is not only professionally hubristic, insisting as it does that the philosopher's voice "always has an overriding claim on the attention of other participants in the conversation" (p. 392), but is based on a profound self-deception.

For Rorty, the belief that one may lay claim to an ultimate critical framework of any sort is illusory, an attempt to "escape from history," context, and human finitude (p. 9). Rorty here places himself firmly within the Nietzschean and Deweyan "therapeutic" traditions in philosophy, for whom the intellectual hunger for purity, clarity, and order is revealed to have an "underside"—in the desire for control over the more unruly, "cthonic" dimensions of experience. The sociologist Richard Sennett, too, has described what he calls the "purification urge"—toward ordering the world according to firm, clearly articulated categories permitting of no ambiguity and dissonance—as "the desire to be all-powerful, to control the meanings of experience before encounter so as not to be overwhelmed" (p. 116). Against any possible threat to that organization, strict rules against mixing categories or blurring boundaries must be maintained. The ontological order must be clear and distinct. The anthropologist Mary Douglas has argued that maintaining such pristine ontological integrity—"keeping distinct the categories of creation . . . [through] correct definition, discrimination and order"—animates religious conceptions of purity (1966, p. 53). For the Cartesian, too, ambiguity and contradiction are the worst transgressions. That which cannot be categorized cleanly deserves no place in the universe.

For Descartes, the quest for purity of thought serves more historically specific mechanisms, as well. For, the alien, impersonal nature of the infinite universe—that wasteland of meaninglessness, that terrifying, cold expanse—is precisely what allows it to be known with precision, clarity, and detachment. In a universe in which the spiritual and the physical merge, where body and mind participate in knowledge, objectivity is impossible. (And, in such a world, objectivity is not an ideal.) The quest for objectivity, on the other hand, is capable of transforming the barren landscape of the modern universe into a paradise for analysis, dissection, and "controlled" experimentation. Its barrenness, which filled

Pascal with such existential dread, is, of course, precisely what makes it capable of being "read" mathematically and taken apart with philosophical accuracy—and moral impunity.

## THE PURIFICATION OF THE UNDERSTANDING

At the start of the fourth Meditation, Descartes finds himself on the horns of the dilemma. The proof of the existence of a veracious God has insured him that he is not the victim of a systematic deception and—what amounts to the same thing—that his own capacity for judgment, "doubtless received from God," will not "lead me to err if I use it aright" (HR, I, 172). Yet, of course, we *do* err. How to reconcile this fallibility with his newly established faith in the veracity of God and the fitness of his own faculties?

Descartes, to begin with, considers several solutions of a traditional nature. He first considers that his own nature, not being God-like, but rather somewhere "between the supreme Being and non-being," must "in some degree participate . . . in nought or in non-being." He should not be surprised therefore to find in himself, in addition to the positive faculties given to him by God, *defects* in those faculties. Error need not be attributed to "a special faculty given me by God"; rather, "I fall into error from the fact that the power given me by God for the purpose of distinguishing truth from error is not infinite" (HR, I, 172–3).

But this answer does not satisfy Descartes, "for error is not a pure negation [i.e., is not the simple defect or want of some perfection which ought not to be mine], but it is a lack of some knowledge which it seems I ought to possess" (HR, I, 173). And the seeming failure of God to bestow on me an understanding that would be without such a lack requires explanation.

Perhaps, however, my intellectual defects serve higher ends. It is not, after all, within my capacity to understand all of God's design; for all I know, my own imperfections when considered as "part of the whole universe" are "very perfect." (HR, I, 173). This explanation is not rejected by Descartes, but he does not go any further with it. It appears to function, rather, as a "traditionalist" prelude to what will turn out to be a decidedly innovative approach to the problem of error.

The form of that new approach, like many of Descartes's most radical departures from scholasticism, is itself traditional—an epistemological variant of the Augustinian "solution" to the problem of evil. For Augustine, "God made man but not the sin in him": Human evil is the result of our capacity for free will—given to us by God, and itself good—but meaningless unless the choice of evil is a real possibility. Freedom is not freedom if it is determined to choose the good; in "allowing" us to sin, God is not responsible for evil but for giving us the capacity to behave as moral agents. The will alone is responsible for sin.

Descartes's strategy for dealing with the "problem of error" corresponds to Augustine's approach to the problem of evil. As, for Augustine, God is absolved and the human being charged with sole responsibility for moral fallenness, so, for Descartes, the human being is charged with all responsibility for *epistemological* "fallenness":

> . . . it is not an imperfection in God that He has given me the liberty to give or withhold my assent from certain things as to which He has not placed a clear and distinct knowledge in my understanding: but it is without doubt an imperfection in me not to make good use of my freedom, and to give my judgment readily on matters which I only understand obscurely (HR, I, 177).

It is important to note that judgment here is conceived as an act distinct from the act of understanding. For, "by the understanding alone I [neither assert nor deny anything, but] apprehend the ideas of things as to which I can form a judgement" (HR, I, 174). Judgment is rather an act of the will, as Descartes makes clear in the *Notes*

Bailey–Cuomo: The
Feminist Philosophy
Reader

9. Feminist Epistemologies | Text

© The McGraw–Hill
Companies, 2008

139

Chapter 9 / Feminist Epistemologies

675

*Directed Against a Certain Programme:*

. . . I saw that, over and above perception, which is required as a basis for judgment, there must needs be affirmation, or negation, to constitute the form of the judgment, and that it is frequently open to us to withhold our assent, even if we perceive a thing. I referred the act of judging, which consists in nothing but *assent,* i.e., affirmation or negation, not to the perception of the understanding, but to the determination of the will (HR, I, 446).

Errors, therefore, are acts of the will, or, more precisely, acts of misuse of the will. The way they occur is the following: Although the faculty of will, like the understanding, is "perfect of its kind," being "much wider in its range and compass than the understanding," it sometimes gives its assent to "things which I do not understand" (HR, I, 175). This assent to the obscure or confused represents a misuse of the will, for "the light of nature teaches us that the knowledge of the understanding should always precede the determination of the will" (HR, I, 177; see also *Principle* XLIII, I, 236).

The conception of judgment as an act of will rather than intellect (a radical departure from scholastic tradition), is essential to Descartes's epistemological program in several ways:

1. It is essential to the comprehensibility of Cartesian doubt. For, the methodical "abstent [ion] from giving assent to dubious things" that is Cartesian doubt *is* an act of will rather than intellect. It is an attitude chosen prior to any particular intellectual act, and (even though undertaken to confront a *real* skeptical threat, as I have suggested previously) is deliberately chosen as a route to that goal.

2. As suggested earlier, it exonerates God from the responsibility for error, just as, for Augustine, the attribution of sin to human will exonerates God from the responsibility of having created evil. As such, it is actually the final (though not explicitly presented as such) stage in the full proof of the existence of a veracious God. For, how can I reconcile the veracity of God with the fact of human error? Unless the responsibility for error can be shown to lie elsewhere, the image, if not of an evil genius, then at least of a less than totally veracious God, again could undercut our newly won confidence in our facilities. But since error is the result, instead, of the *wrong use* which we make of the humanly *perfect* faculties given to us by God, the responsibility for it is all ours—and within our control.

3. It serves as an argument for the purity of the understanding. The above correspondence between Descartes's treatment of error and the traditional handling of the "problem of evil" was first described by Etienne Gilson[3] and is ascribed to, in passing, by J. L. Evans (p. 137), Bernard Williams (p. 169), and Hiram Caton (p. 90). The way this correspondence has been formulated, however, has missed something whose significance is crucial to understanding the fourth Meditation. All emphasis, in Gilson's account, has been placed on the exoneration of *God* from the charge of responsibility for error—which indeed is stressed by Descartes, and which is the obvious keynote comparsion to be made *if* the "problem of error" is taken to be *symmetrically* correspondent with the solution to the problem of evil. But it is not symmetrically correspondent. In the context of the problem of evil, the traditional arguments exonerate God alone, not also the will. Whereas, in the context of the problem of intellectual error, on the other hand, in exonerating God, Descartes also exonerated the intellect itself, and not incidentally.[4] In relocating error "outside" the understanding, Descartes is not only placing it in the province of the will, but purging the understanding of what stands in the way of *its* perfection. It therefore counts as an argument for the purity of the understanding as much as an argument for the goodness of God.

The difference is crucial, not only to clarification of the arguments which follow in the

*Meditations,* and to our understanding of the overall project of the *Meditations,* but to our understanding of the philosophical and cultural reconstruction within which Descartes plays such a central role. What we are enabled to see, *in process* as it were, is a historical movement away from a transcendent God as the only legitimate object of worship to the establishing of the *human intellect* as godly, and as appropriately to be revered and submitted to—once "purified" of all that stands in the way of its godliness. Shortly, for modern science, God will indeed become downright superfluous. In the *Meditations,* God most certainly is not. But God's role in that work nonetheless almost approaches the metaphorical: Just as the Evil Genius functions as a personification of the possibility of radical defect in the human faculties of knowing, so a veracious God seems a personification of faith in those faculties. That Descartes's strategy for exonerating God for error is *simultaneously* a strategy for purifying the understanding is suggestive of a merging of foci here. The godly intellect is on the way to becoming the true deity of the modern era.

That Descartes employs an epistemological variant of a traditional solution to the "problem of evil" suggests that *purification* is not too strong a term to describe his project for certifying the perfection of the intellect. The project to conceptually purify one realm, as noted earlier, necessitates a "relocation" of all threatening elements "outside." They become *alien.* This is the strategy employed by Augustine in his answer to the problem of evil, as William James points out in *The Varieties of Religious Experience.* There, James argues that the construal of evil as a "problem" for which God must be absolved of responsibility necessitates transforming "an essential part of our being" into "a waste element, to be sloughed off . . . diseased, inferior, excrementitious stuff" (p. 129).

The strategy, as Mary Douglas points out, is the same, in form and function, as that of social rituals of purification, in which a society establishes some substance or group as impure and "taboo," thus "defining" it as outside the social body. Insuring

that the tabooed thing or group remains separate and does not contaminate the social body sometimes requires violent expulsions, as in witch hunting (1982, pp. 107–124). But usually the taboo functions through the establishment of separate metaphysical "realms"—a good "inside" and a bad "outside"—as, pursuing this analogy, it does for Descartes. Error is not extinguished, but excluded; it is conceptualized as belonging outside an inner circle of purity, in this case, the godly intellect.

Douglas suggests the term "dirt-rejecting" for those philosophers who pursue such purification strategies (1966, p. 164).[5] In terms of such a category, Descartes is an epistemological "dirt-rejecter." Not that he doesn't see confusion and obscurity everywhere ("smudges on the mirror of nature," as a colleague has described it)—for he does. But his entire system is devoted to circumscribing an intellectual arena which is pristinely immune to contamination, a mirror which is impossible to smudge. Here, we should recall the Cartesian imagery of mistaken ideas as spoiled and rotting fruit, capable of corrupting everything that comes into contact with them. Error can no longer be conceptualized as a negation by Descartes (as the medievals had been able to do). For the culture he lived in, unlike the medieval world, uncertainty and confusion seemed so ubiquitous as to suggest that human nature may have been malevolently (or at least mischievously) *designed* to err. But error can be reconceptualized as "belonging" to a faculty other than the intellect (just as evil had been conceived as belonging to *us,* rather than God). In this way the first step is made toward preparing the intellect to enter into a pure, "godly" relation with its objects of knowledge.

## PASSIVITY AND TRUTH

Descartes's initial "purification of the understanding" is, however, *only* a first step. For, the intellect has not quite been purged of all the elements lying in the way of its purity. Denial, assertion, desiring, aversion, and doubting have all become the province of the will. Only the "acts of

Bailey–Cuomo: The
Feminist Philosophy
Reader

9. Feminist Epistemologies | Text

© The McGraw–Hill
Companies, 2008

141

understanding"—perceiving, imagining, conceiving—remain the province of the understanding. In Meditation III, Descartes had described these as the only forms to which the title "idea" should be properly applied, because they alone do not "add something else to the idea which I have of the thing" (HR, I, 159). They are, in other words, *representations*. And, as such, they may of course *mis*represent. Therein lies the problem. If the faculty of judgment is free (as at this point it seems to be) to accept or reject the claims of the ideas that it surveys that they represent the state of things, what is to prevent us from constantly falling into error? The ideas that "pass in review" (to borrow Rorty's phrase) before the "inner eye" of judgment are, after all, a motley array. They include both perceptions that are the result of the acts of volition (imaginatively constructed entities, intelligible objects) and "passive" perceptions, "receive[d] from the things represented by them" (*Passions of the Soul,* HR, I, 340). The latter include the perceptions that occur within dreams and daydreams, bodily perceptions such as pain, heat and cold, the emotions ("the passions of the soul"), and the perceptions of external objects. This is a diverse assemblage, a real democracy of inner representations, united by their common relation to the "inner arena"—the soul—which Descartes likens to the relation between the shapes a piece of wax may take and the wax itself.

> It receives its ideas partly from objects in contact with the senses, partly from impressions in the brain, and partly from precedent dispositions in the soul and motions of the will. Similarly, a piece of wax owes its shapes partly to the pressure of other bodies, partly to its own earlier shape or other qualities such as heaviness and softness, and partly also to its own movement, when, having been pushed it has in itself the power to continue moving (to Mesland, May 2, 1644; PL, 148).

In this analogy, the suggestion is that all our ideas have equal power to impress themselves on the intellect. But for Descartes, the intellect is not quite the democracy of ideas suggested by the analogy with wax. For some ideas are aristocrats and have the power to compel the assent of the will.

> For example, when I lately examined whether anything existed in the world, and found that from the very fact that I considered this question it followed very clearly that I myself existed, I could not prevent myself from believing that a thing I so clearly conceived was true: not that I found myself compelled to do so by some external cause, but simply because from great clearness in my mind there followed a great inclination of my will . . . (Meditation IV, HR, I, 176).
>
> The will of a thinking thing is borne, willingly indeed and freely (for that is the essense of the will), but none the less infallibly, toward the good that it clearly knows (Reply II, HR, II, 56).
>
> For it seems to me certain that *a great light in the intellect is followed by a strong inclination in the will;* so that if we see very clearly that a thing is good for us it is very difficult—and, on my view, impossible, as long as one continues in the same thought—to stop the course of our desire (to Mesland, May 2, 1644; PL, 149).

We are free, to be sure, to cease to *attend* to our clear and distinct perceptions (from this comes the fact that we "earn merit" for the good acts that follow "infallibly" from those perceptions), but to choose to attend is to immediately "ensure that our will follows so promptly the light of our understanding that there is no longer in any way indifference" (to Mesland, PL, 150).[6]

On closer inspection, indeed, it turns out that there is, in fact, only *one* way in which the judgment can *err:* by giving assent to the obscure and confused. This limitation on error runs throughout the Cartesian corpus, from the *Regulae,* which instructs us "never to assume what is false is true" (HR, I, 9), but does not mention the converse, to the *Principles:* "We deceive ourselves *only* when we form judgments about anything insufficiently known to us" (HR, I, 232). And, of course, in the *Meditations:*

> Whence then come my errors? They come from the sole fact that . . . I do not restrain [the will] within [the bounds of the understanding], but extend it

also to things which I do not understand: and as the will is of itself indifferent to these, it easily falls into error and sin, and chooses the evil for the good, or the false for the true (HR, I, Meditation IV, 175–176).

In the above quotation, what Descartes calls the "understanding" is *identified* with the capacity to *correctly* (i.e., clearly and distinctly) understand, rather than with the general faculty of receiving, recalling, or combining ideas. His inconsistency is not my focus here, however. What is important is that a new mental arena has been designated, one which is normatively delineated—by the qualities of clearness and distinctness. And the capacity to fall into error has been circumscribed as well. It is connected, not with the freedom of the will but with the *indifference* of the will. These, for Descartes, are two very different things. To explain this will require some sorting out of the Cartesian doctrine of the will: the faculty of will itself is simply

> the power of choosing to do a thing or not to do it (that is, to affirm or deny, to pursue or to shun it), or rather it consists alone in the fact that in order to affirm or deny, pursue or shun those things placed before us by the understanding, we act so that we are unconscious that any outside force constrains us in doing so (Meditation IV, HR, I, 175).

It is important to note that for Descartes the power of the will to choose a course of action is not simply "negative" freedom—is not simply the absence of force or constraint on our actions—a "freedom" shared by animals, who do not *will* their activities, and who cannot therefore be said to be truly "free" (to Mesland, PL, 150). Rather, the power of the will is the "positive faculty of determining oneself to one or other of two contraries" (to Mesland, February 9, 1645; PL, 161), the power, in other words, of acting *voluntarily* (and not merely automatically or instinctually).

Within this general freedom, Descartes notes, there are different grades of freedom. The highest—the "greater liberty," as Descartes calls it—consists in one of two things: *either* "a great

faculty in determining oneself" through "follow[ing] the course which appears to have the most reasons in its favor" *or* "a greater use of the positive power which we have of following the worse, although we see the better" (to Mesland, PL, 160). The latter refers to those special cases when we "hold back from pursuing a clearly known good, or from admitting a clearly perceived truth [because] we consider it a good thing to demonstrate the freedom of our will by doing so" (to Mesland, PL, 160). The former reconciles the *freedom* of the will with the will's assent to the clear and distinct perception. Indeed, Descartes affirms that the "greater the inclination of the will" that follows from the "clearness of the mind," the "greater [the] freedom or spontaneity" of the act (Meditation IV, HR, I, 176).

This reconciliation is similar to the reconciliation of determinism and freedom offered by so-called "soft determinists," who replace the traditional opposition between these two with an opposition between freedom and external compulsion. For the soft determinist, I am free, not insofar as my actions are *undetermined,* but insofar as they are determined by my *own* inclinations rather than an external force. And for Descartes, indeed, the "lowest degree of liberty" is *indifference:* the state in which nothing in the self determines us to any direction, when the will "is not impelled one way rather than another by any perception of truth or goodness" (to Mesland, PL, 159).

The capacity to err derives, as we have seen, from this state of indifference. Correspondingly, when we *cannot* maintain indifference—when we are irresistibly drawn to one side rather than another—we can be assured that we are in the presence of truth.

The Cartesian clear and distinct perception is very like an emotion (as emotions are conceived by Descartes) in its capacity to *overtake* us, to absorb us, to render us passive in the face of its strength. But while the emotions may overtake us in ways that obscure our intellectual vision (that is, in the traditional picture that comes down to us from Descartes), the clear and distinct idea

Bailey–Cuomo: The
Feminist Philosophy
Reader

9. Feminist Epistemologies    Text

© The McGraw–Hill
Companies, 2008

143

overtakes the propensity to error itself. *Our* very passivity in the face of a clear and distinct idea is the mark of *its* truth.

Passivity in the face of an idea—the inability to say "no" to an idea—is a hallmark of epistemological reassurance to one degree or another throughout the *Meditations.* We encounter it first in the fleeting moments of the first and second Meditations when the pull of the clear and distinct perception temporarily subdues doubt. Even *before* it is demonstrated that "all that I know clearly is true," "my mind is such that I could not prevent myself from holding [my perception] to be true so long as I conceive them clearly" (HR, I, 180). This passivity, however, is not to be trusted, for my mind may be such, too, that it is fundamentally flawed, and responds to the false as though it were true (HR, I, 184). I need to be assured that I may trust my own responses (that God has not created me such that I am systematically deceived) before I can take them as guides to the truth of things.

The *cogito,* too, is a case—though a special one—of an idea that compels assent. It is special, as I have argued previously, because it is one of a very small class of ideas whose denial, paradoxically, involves assent. It is more resilient to doubt, therefore, than other clear and distinct perceptions, since even if I am sure that my mind is fundamentally flawed, I am still "sure," that is, *thinking* something. But the compelling nature of the *cogito,* in any case, does not assure me that the compelling nature of all other clear and distinct ideas will "as a general rule" insure me of their truth.

For that assurance Descartes needs God. And he needs, in addition (and what amounts to the same thing, but in an "epistemological" form that is a working model of *knowing*), to be assured that we will not be drawn to error in submitting to the force of the intellect. This is what the fourth Meditation accomplishes: *first,* by identifying (if somewhat inconsistently) the intellect with the arena of the clear and distinct, and *second,* by attributing error, not just to the will, but to the *indifferent* will. The will that is compelled by the intellect can never err.

*Now* the passivity of the soul can be more fully trusted, and we may let our ideas "speak to us," attending to those we can answer and those we cannot. In Meditation IV, for example, the following argument occurs, in which the fact that our perceptions of external objects are not subject to voluntary control turns out to be a strong reason for believing that they proceed from the things they seem to represent.

> There is certainly further in me a certain passive faculty of perception, that is, of receiving and recognizing the ideas of sensible things, but this would be useless to me . . . if there were not either in me or in some other thing another active faculty capable of forming and producing these ideas. But this active faculty cannot exist in me . . . seeing that it does not presuppose thought, and also that those ideas are often produced in me without my contributing in any way to the same, and often even against my will; it is thus necessarily the case that the faculty resides in some substance different from me in which all the reality which is objectively in the ideas that are produced by this faculty is formally or eminently contained, as I remarked before (HR, I, 191).

This argument does not differ significantly from the argument that Descartes recalls from his naïve, pre-doubting days:

> . . . It was not without reason that I believed myself to perceive objects quite different from my thought, to wit, bodies from which those ideas proceeded; for I found by experience that these ideas presented themselves to me without my consent being requisite, so that I could not perceive any object, however desirous I might be, unless it were present to the organs of sense; and it was not in my power not to perceive it, when it was present. (HR, I, 187–188).

The difference is not a difference in argument, but a difference in self-trust. Prior to the proofs of God and the account of error, even the strongest natural inclination may be looked on as suspect, once the immediacy of the moment has passed.

> For since nature *seemed* to cause me to lean towards many things from which reason repelled me, I did

not believe that I should trust much to the teachings of nature. And although the ideas which I receive by the senses do not depend on my will, I did not think that one should for that reason conclude that they proceeded from things different from myself, since possibly some faculty might be discovered in me—though hitherto unknown to me—which produced them (HR, I, 189; emphasis added).

The qualification "seemed to" is important, for the fourth Meditation has established that this "seeming" was an illusion—that error is always the result of indifference (allowed for only by the obscure and confused perception) and not of real inclination. It is significant, too, that Descartes says that his new-found self-trust is the result, not just of knowing "more clearly the author of my being," but of "know[ing] myself better" (HR, I, 189). The latter was the point of the fourth Meditation—to translate my knowledge that this is God's world into a new model of the human intellect. This new model is one in which indifference rather than inclination is the hallmark of error, and in which, therefore, a class of "godly" ideas—"king," as Dewey puts it, "to any beholding mind that may gaze upon it" (p. 23)—could reign supreme. Having attributed judgment to the will, for Descartes it is doubly imperative to circumscribe a set of realities within the intellect that are capable of bending judgment to their authority. The very last thing that Descartes would want is a Jamesian "will to believe," in which the belief in truth itself is "but a passionate affirmation of desire," and behind every particular intellectual position lies "fear and hope, prejudice and passion" (1897, p. 9). Objective evidence and certainty may be "fine ideals to play with," says James, "but where on this moonlit and dream-visited planet are they found?" (p. 14); "Pretend as we may, the whole man within us is at work when we form our philosophical opinions" (p. 92). The clear and distinct idea, on the contrary, assures us that it is precisely when we form our philosophical opinions that the "whole man" may be *passified*—quite literally—by the purity and authority of the object.

This is, of course, no new theme in the history of philosophy, which is studded with metaphors suggesting spectatorship rather than participation, the "known" specifically conceived as that realm in which the distorting effects of human interest and activity are eliminated, and in which fixity and purity thus rule. But before the sixteenth and seventeenth centuries, such conceptions had been reserved for the sort of knowing that has formal, immutable, or immaterial "reality" as its object. It is only with Descartes that fixity and purity—"the immutable state of mind"—began to be demanded of the knowledge necessary to certify concrete perceptions of the self (that I have hands, eyes, senses, etc.), of particular "corporeal things" (other animals, inanimate things) and, indeed, of *anything* external to consciousness. And it is only in the sixteenth and seventeenth centuries that earthly science, insofar as it is trustworthy, is equated with "spectatorship" and the passive reception of ideas.[7] It is in the work of Descartes that we find the official philosophical birth of the notion of mind as "mirror of nature."

## THE TRANSCENDENCE OF THE BODY

The Cartesian purification of the understanding, at this point, is still abstract and conceptual—not methodological. How does one do it? Some *method* of purification must be supplied, some rules to direct the understanding. On this score, of course, Descartes is emphatic: We must learn *how* to achieve the proper sort of receptivity to ideas. And although all persons are capable of learning this, "there are very few who rightly distinguish between what is really perceived and what they fancy they perceive, because but few are accustomed to clear and distinct perceptions" (Reply VII, HR, II, 307).

Descartes recognizes that people may be wrong about what they take to be the clearness and distinctness of ideas. He has even proven himself guilty of it at various points in the progress of the *Meditations.* He agrees with Gassendi that without a method "which will direct and show us when we are in error and when not, so often as we think we clearly and distinctly perceive anything" (HR, II, 152), we are thrown back on each individual's sense of conviction, a psychological datum that cannot be trustworthy in all cases. But, then, in which cases, and for what reasons is testimony to personal conviction trustworthy? The problem is further compounded by the similarities between the workings of the clear and distinct perceptions, which irresistibly dispose the will through the power of intellectual insight, and the emotions, which irresistibly dispose the will through the force of the bodily—the attendant "commotion" in the heart, blood and "animal spirits" which "prevents the soul from being able at one to change or arrest its passions" (HR, I, 352).[8] To be sure, the clear and distinct perception is "seen" with the mind, whereas the emotions are felt by the body. But the issue at stake here is not how to distinguish between the two; rather, what is at issue is the epistemological trustworthiness of the "irresistible" *qua* irresistible: If the will can be overtaken and bent in directions that oppose reason (as it is often by the body [I, 353]), then how can the will's passivity itself serve as a mark that reason has conducted itself to the truth (as it is supposed to via the clear and distinct perception)?

We need to recall now that what principally stands in the way of the "habit" of clear and distinct perception (taken as an activity now, rather than a content or object) is what Descartes generally calls "prejudice," but which, on closer inspection, turns out to be a specific sort of prejudice—that of "seeing" with one's *body* rather than one's *mind.* This, as we have seen, is the original, and most formidable legacy of infancy, a time in which the mind, "newly united" to the body, was "wholly occupied in perceiving or feeling the ideas of pain, pleasure, heat, cold and other similar ideas which arise from its union and intermingling with the body" (to Hyperaspistes, August 1641, PL, 111). "The body is

always a hindrance to the mind in its thinking," he tells Burman, "and this was especially true in youth" (B, 8).

That Descartes views the "prison of the body" as the chief, if not sole, source of our inability to perceive clearly and distinctly is evidenced by a remarkable passage in the letter to Hyperaspistes, in which Descartes maintains that the infant "has in itself the ideas of God, itself, and all such truths as are called self-evident . . . if it were taken out of the prison of the body it would find [those ideas] within itself" (PL, 111). That this "prison" can, in fact, be transcended in adulthood is no less in doubt for Descartes.

> Nothing in metaphysics causes more trouble than the making the perception of its primary notions clear and distinct. For, though in their own nature they are as intelligible as, or even more intelligible than those the geometricians study, yet being contradicted by the many preconceptions of our senses to which we have since our earliest years been accustomed, they cannot be perfectly apprehended *except by those who give strenuous attention and study to them, and withdraw their minds as far as possible from matters corporeal* (Reply II, HR, II, 49–50; emphasis added).

In *The Passions of the Soul,* Descartes explicitly opposes his own view—that the body is the source of all in us that is "opposed to reason"—to the traditional view that it is the inferior, appetitive, or sensuous part of the soul itself that wars with the rational (HR, I, 353). He is thus able, given the "real distinction between soul and body" (see *Principle* LX, HR, I, 243; Meditation VI, HR, I, 190; *Discourse,* HR, I, 101; to Reneri, April 1638, PL, 52) to conceptualize the possibility of complete intellectual transcendence of the appetitive and sensuous. Although the soul "can have its operations disturbed by the bad disposition of the bodily organs" (PL, 52) or the passions, "even those who have the feeblest souls can acquire a very absolute dominion over all their passions if sufficient industry is applied in training and guiding them" (*Passions,* HR, I, 356).

Such "training" is largely a matter of accumulating, in the moments when the soul's operations are undisturbed, a strong arsenal of rational truth to rely on when agitation threatens. The resolution to carry out what reason recommends, at such time, is the essence of human happiness, as Descartes tells Elizabeth (August 4, 1645, PL, 165). When Elizabeth (quite understandably) expressed skepticism over this, pointing out that there are diseases that overpower the faculty of reason "and with it the satisfaction proper to a rational mind," Descartes confidently replied that repetition is the key: ". . . if one often has a certain thought while one's body was at liberty, it returns again no matter how indisposed the body may be." He himself, he assured her, had in this way completely eliminated bad dreams from his sleep (PL, 168). He presumably did not notice that they return in the first Meditation.

Not only, however, may the properly trained mind overcome the passions. In certain mental acts, as Margaret Wilson points out (in Hooker, 99), it actually does "think without the body," as Descartes claims it can in the letter to Reneri (PL, 52) and in Meditation VI (HR, I, 193). These are the acts of "pure intellection" or "pure understanding," which not only have no "imagic" content (e.g., the chiliagon, the idea of God, the idea of a thinking thing), but no corporeal correlates at all. Unlike sensation, imagery and memory, acts of "pure understanding" (and the memory of them) are not only "phenomenologically" independent of the body, but independent of all physical processes whatever. In a letter to Mesland, for example (PL, 148), Descartes argues that the memory of intellectual things, unlike those of material things, depends on "traces" left in thought itself, not in the brain. And in the Gassendi Replies he states quite emphatically that "I have often also shown distinctly that mind can act independently of the brain; for certainly the brain can be of no use in pure thought: its only use is for imagining and perceiving" (HR, I, 212).[9]

To achieve this autonomy, the mind must be gradually liberated from the body: it must *become*

a "pure mind." First, constant vigilance must be maintained against the distractions of the body. Throughout the *Meditations,* emphasis is placed on training oneself in nonreliance on the body and practice in the art of "pure understanding." It is virtually a kind of mechanistic yoga.

> I shall now close my eyes, I shall stop my ears, I shall call away all my senses, I shall efface even from my thoughts all the images of corporeal things, or at least (for that is hardly possible) I shall esteem them as vain and false; and thus holding converse only with myself and considering my own nature, I shall try little by little to reach a better knowledge of and a more familiar acquaintanceship with myself (Meditation III, HR, I, 157).

Indeed, much of the *Meditations* may be read as prescribing rules for the liberation of mind from the various seductions of the body, in order to cleanse and prepare it for the reception of clear and distinct ideas. The initial requirement is to "deliver [the] mind from every care . . . and agitat[ion from the] passions" (HR, I, 145). Since, as we have seen, our passionate inclinations can bend the will in directions which oppose reason, it is essential that we not be susceptible to their coercive power while we are pursuing truth. The field must be cleared of such influence, so we will be receptive to the coerciveness exercised by ideas alone.

The next step is to topple the "prejudices" acquired through the body-rule of infancy and childhood. These prejudices have their origin in a hyperabsorption in the senses. But their precise form, as we have seen, is the inability to properly distinguish what is happening solely "inside" the subject from what has an external existence—e.g., the attribution of heat, cold, etc., to the object, of greater "reality" to rocks than water because of their greater heaviness, and so on. As an infant "swamped" inside the body, one simply did not have a perspective from which to discriminate, to judge. In Meditation I, Descartes re-creates that state of utter entrapment, by luring the reader, first, through the continuities between madness and dreaming—that state

Bailey–Cuomo: The
Feminist Philosophy
Reader

9. Feminist Epistemologies | Text

© The McGraw–Hill
Companies, 2008

147

each night when all of us lose our adult clarity and detachment—and then to the possibility that the whole of our existence may be like a dream, a grand illusion so encompassing that there is no conceivable perspective from which to judge its correspondence with reality. The difference, of course, is that in childhood, we *assumed* that what we felt was a measure of external reality; now, as mature Cartesian doubters, we reverse that prejudice. We assume nothing. We refuse to let our bodies mystify us. And we begin afresh, as pure minds.

This reading of the *Meditations* suggests that a long-standing issue for Cartesian scholars may be founded on a mistake about the nature of Descartes's epistemological program. From Gassendi and Leibniz to Prichard, Ashworth, and Gewirth, commentators have criticized and wrestled with the seeming lack of "objective" criteria for the clearness and distinctness of ideas; with the seeming need for a method, as Gassendi put it, "which will direct and show us when we are in error and when not, so often as we think that we clearly and distinctly perceive anything" (HR, II, 152). Gassendi was struck, as Montaigne had been before him, by the vicissitudes of human certainty and the tenacity with which people may cling to their ever-shifting convictions. He was impressed with, and reminded Descartes of, the number of people willing to die for false beliefs, beliefs that those people presumably perceived as true. Descartes's answer—that he has *supplied* the needed method of discrimination in the procedure of the *Meditations,* "where I first laid aside all prejudices, and afterward enumerated all the chief ideas, distinguishing the clear from the obscure and confused" (HR, II, 214)—did not satisfy Gassendi. It seemed to him to beg the question, like many of Descartes's replies to his critics. Descartes, for his part, was unimpressed with Gassendi's example of those who face death for the sake of (possibly false) opinions, because "it can never be proved that they clearly and distinctly perceive what they pertinaciously affirm" (HR, II, 214). Is Descartes's reasoning

hopelessly circular, as Ashworth, following Gassendi, claims (p. 102)?

I would suggest that when Descartes tells Gassendi that he has "attended" to the problem of "finding a method for deciding whether we err or not when we think that we perceive something clearly" (HR, II, 214), he does *not* mean that he believes himself to have supplied criteria for the clearness and distinctness of ideas. He has "attended" to the problem, rather, by supplying "rules for the direction of the mind" (read: rules for the transcendence of the body) that will prepare the mind to be swayed by nothing but the peculiar coerciveness of ideas, that will methodically eliminate all seductions except for the purely intellectual. Once that state of mental readiness has been achieved (something one can only know for oneself. Descartes would insist), the mind's *subjective* responses—its convictions—can be trusted. While Gassendi and other critics have complained of the lack of an "objective" test of ideas, Descartes, I propose, was up to something entirely different: He was offering a program of purification and training—for the liberation of *res cogitans* from the confusion and obscurity of its bodily swamp.

## THE CARTESIAN WAY WITH DUALISM

Disdain for the body, the conception of it as an alien force and an impediment to the soul, is, of course, very old in our Greco-Christian traditions. Descartes was not the first philosopher to charge the body with responsibility for obscurity and confusion in our thinking. Rather, as Plato says in the *Phaedo,* ". . . it is characteristic of the philosopher to despise the body" (65). And, according to Plato, this disdain is well-founded: "A source of countless distractions by reason of the mere requirement of food, liable also to diseases which overtake and impede us in the pursuit of truth: [the body] fills us full of loves, and lusts, and fears, and fancies of all kinds, and endless foolery, and in very truth, as men say, takes away from us the power of thinking at all" (66c).

Chapter 9 / Feminist Epistemologies

Descartes, then, was not the first philosopher to view the body with disdain. Platonic and neo-Platonic thought, and the Christian traditions that grew out of them, all exhibit such a strain. Nor was Descartes the first to view human existence as bifurcated into the realms of the physical and the spiritual, with the physical cast in the role of the alien and impure. For Plato, the body is often described via the imagery of separateness from the self: It is "fastened and glued" to me, "nailed" and "riveted" to me (83d). Images of the body-as-confinement from which the soul struggles to escape—"prison," "cage"—abound in Plato, as they do in Descartes. For Plato, as for Augustine later, the body is the locus of all that which threatens our attempts at control. It overtakes, it overwhelms, it erupts and disrupts. This situation becomes an incitement to battle the unruly forces of the body. Although less methodically than Descartes, Plato provides instruction on how to gain control over the body, how to achieve intellectual independence from the lure of its illusions and become impervious to its distractions. A central theme of the *Phaedo,* in fact, is the philosopher's training in developing such independence from the body.

But while dualism runs deep in our traditions, it is only with Descartes that body and mind are *defined* in terms of mutual exclusivity. For Plato (and Aristotle), the living body is permeated with soul, which can only depart the body at death. For Descartes, on the other hand, soul and body become two distinct substances. The body is pure *res extensa*—unconscious, extended stuff, brute materiality. "Every kind of thought which exists in us," he says in the *Passions of the Soul,* "belongs to the soul" (HR, I, 332). The soul, on the other hand, is pure *res cogitans*—mental, incorporeal, without location, *bodyless:* ". . . in its nature entirely independent of body, and not in any way derived from the power of matter" *(Discourse,* HR, I, 118).

The mutual exclusivity of mind and body has important consequences. Plato's and Aristotle's view that "soul" is a principle of life is one which

Descartes takes great pains to refute in the *Passions of the Soul.* For Descartes, rather, the "life" of the body is a matter of purely mechanical functioning.

> [W]e may judge that the body of a living man differs from that of a dead man just as does a watch or other automaton (i.e., a machine that moves of itself), when it is wound up and contains in itself the corporeal principle of those movements for which it is designated along with all that is requisite for its action, from the same watch or other machine when it is broken and when the principle of its movement ceases to act (HR, I, 333).

While the body is thus likened to a machine, the mind (having been conceptually purified of all material "contamination") is defined by precisely and only those qualities which the human being shares with God: freedom, will, consciousness. For Descartes there is no ambiguity or complexity here. The body is excluded from all participation, all connection with God; the soul alone represents the godliness and the goodness of the human being.

In Plato and Aristotle, the lines simply cannot be drawn in so stark a fashion. In the *Symposium,* we should remember, the love of the body is the first, and necessary, step on the spiritual ladder which leads to the glimpsing of the eternal form of beauty. For the Greek philosophers, the body is not simply an impediment to knowledge; it may also function as a spur to spiritual growth. Its passions may motivate the quest for knowledge and beauty. Moreover, since soul is inseparable from body except at death, any human aspirations to intellectual "purity" during one's lifetime are merely wishful fantasy. "While in company with the body the soul cannot have pure knowledge," Plato unequivocally declares in the *Phaedo.*

For the Greeks, then, there are definite limits to the human intellect. For Descartes, on the other hand, epistemological hubris knows few bounds.[10] The dream of purity is realizable during one's lifetime. For, given the right method, one can transcend the body. This is, of course, what Descartes believed himself to have accomplished

Bailey–Cuomo: The
Feminist Philosophy
Reader

9. Feminist Epistemologies | Text

© The McGraw–Hill
Companies, 2008

149

in the *Meditations*. Addressing Gassendi as "O flesh!" he describes himself as "a mind so far withdrawn from corporeal things that it does not even know that anyone has existed before it" (HR, II, 214).

That such a radical program of mental purification is so central to the Cartesian epistemological program is not surprising. For, the body is not only the organ of the deceptive senses, and the site of disruption and "commotion" in the heart, blood, and animal spirits. It is also the most brute, pressing and ubiquitous reminder of how *located* and perspectival our experience and thought is, how bounded in time and space. "Birth, the past, contingency, the necessity of a point of view . . . such is the body," says Sartre. The Cartesian knower, on the other hand, being without a body, not only has "no need of any place" (*Discourse,* HR, I, p. 101) but actually is "no place." He[11] therefore cannot "grasp" the universe—which would demand a place "outside" the whole. But, assured of his own transparency, he can relate with absolute neutrality to the objects he surveys, unfettered by the perspectival nature of embodied vision. He has become, quite literally, *"objective."*

Not only, in this way, is the spectre of "subjectivity" laid to rest, but the very impersonality of the post-Copernican universe is turned to human advantage. For impersonality has become the mark of the truth of the known. Resistant to human will, immune to every effort of the knower to make it what *he* would have it be rather than what it "is," purified of all "inessential" spiritual associations and connections with the rest of the universe, the clear and distinct idea is both compensation for and conqueror of the cold, new world.

## NOTES

1. Even to assert the fact of infinity, for Descartes, is to transcend the bounds of human knowledge. For, although it "is impossible to prove or even to conceive that there are bounds to the matter of which the world is made," there may nonetheless

be limits "which are known to God though inconceivable to me" (PL, 221). The most we can say about the extent of the universe is that it is "from [our] own point of view . . . indefinite"; only God can be "positively conceive[d] as infinite" (PL, 242), since this infinity is necessarily contained in his essence. And even the "positive" knowledge that God is infinite does not entail the ability to "grasp" the infinite. For, although we are certain that God, unlike the universe, can have no limits (*Principle* XXVII, HR, I, 230):

> . . . our soul, being finite, cannot comprehend or conceive Him. In the same way we can touch a mountain with our hands but we cannot put our arms around it as we could put them around a tree or something else not too large for them. To comprehend something is to embrace it in one's thought; to know something it is sufficient to touch it with one's thought (To Mersenne, May 27, 1630, PL, 15. See also Reply, I, II, 18).

By *v*irtue of our finitude, then—although we can "touch" the infinite with our thought—we can neither completely comprehend the scope of the universe nor can we comprehend the infinite *qua* infinite. Neither of these limitations disturbs Descartes; indeed, they are essential to his system: If the human being's comprehension were *not* limited, neither of the third Meditation's proofs of the existence of God could gain a foothold. For, the proof from the idea of God depends upon my recognition that I lack the formal reality (infinite goodness, wisdom, and power) required for *me* to be the cause of the idea of a being with such qualities. And the "causal" argument depends upon the same recognition, but as entailing the necessity of postulating something other than *me* as the cause of myself (for if it had been me, why would I have created myself so imperfect?) (HR, I, 168).

2. Mary Douglas (1966, 1982) has written of the frequency with which social orders are demarcated into a pure "us" and a taboo "them" group. The strategy not only allows the projection of responsibility for disorder onto the outsider group, it also, as Richard Sennet has emphasized, confers the illusion of stable identity and

solidarity on the insider group—"the pleasure in recognizing 'us' and 'who we are' " (p. 31). Bruce Wilshire, in a profound and insightful study of the development of professionalism in academia, has explored how these dynamics function, albeit in disguised and mystified form, in the extreme insularity of professional academic disciplines (*Professionalism and the Eclipse of University Teaching: Dynamics of Purification and Exclusion,* manuscript in progress).

3. *The Cartesian Doctrine of Freedom.* See Kenny, 1972, p.8.

4. To exonerate God from responsibility for error, as Kenny points out, it would have been sufficient for Descartes to have made judgment a *voluntary* act of the intellect (as walking is a voluntary act of the body). He needn't have gone so far as to make it an act of the *will.* Imagining and conceiving, for example, appear to be such voluntary acts of the intellect for Descartes. They require the participation of the will (see *Passions of the Soul,* HR, I, 340; PL, 177–78), but are not themselves *acts* of the will. Judgment is, and Kenny puzzles over this, suggesting that it may have something to do with Descartes's desire to preserve a continuity between error and moral fault (1972, p. 8). Without disagreeing with this, I want to note that if the exoneration of the *intellect* is an aim of the fourth Meditation, this could *not* be accomplished by making judgment a voluntary act of the intellect. It requires a "relocation" of the sources of error to an arena distinct from the intellect.

5. "Dirt-affirming" philosophies, by contrast, are those within whose system everything actual has a function. For James, Hegel is the paradigm example of this (Douglas, 1982, p. 164).

6. There has been a scholarly debate about whether this capacity of clear and distinct ideas to "determine" the will is in tension with the Cartesian doctrine of the will as infinite. Kenny (1972, p. 8) and Williams (p. 180) see this as a genuine tension. Hiram Caton, on the other hand, resolves the apparent contradiction by noting that for Descartes, truth and falsity are not "symmetrical values in a binary matrix" (p. 92). Rather, he maintains, Descartes holds to a *rationalist* theory of truth, in which "judgement plays no role" and "clear ideas are known to be true *per se,*" and a *voluntarist* theory of error, in which judgment is required for the commission of error (p. 93). Although I do not wish to comment on this debate as such, my own reading of the fourth Meditation, as presented in this essay, can be seen to have a greater affinity with Caton's views on the matter.

7. These function in the context of epistemological "purification rituals" for authors other than Descartes, too. Evelyn Fox Keller, in her inspired and fascinating reading of Bacon's *Masculine Birth of Time,* attempts to correct the popular misconception that seventeenth-century science is *only* about aggression and control of nature, by focusing on Bacon's model of mind, which, like Descartes's, emphasizes the ideals of *submissiveness* and *receptivity* to the "true native rays" of things. To achieve this receptivity, however, requires that the mind first purify and cleanse *itself* of "idols" and "false preconceptions." As Keller describes Bacon's project:

> To receive God's truth, the mind must be pure and clean, submissive and open. Only then can it give birth to a masculine and virile science. That is, if the mind is pure, receptive, and submissive in its relation with God, it can be transformed by God into a forceful, potent, and virile agent in its relation to nature. Cleansed of contamination, the mind can be impregnated by God and, in that act, virilized: made potent and capable of generating virile offspring in its union with Nature (p. 38).

8. Although Descartes maintains that the emotions can "indirectly" be governed by the will (e.g., through the decision to try to "reason through" or talk oneself out of a particular fear [I, 352]), we can never simply will ourselves *not* to be afraid, or depressed, or jealous. Once an emotion is experienced, "the most that the will can do . . . is not to yield to its effects and to restrain many of the movements to which it disposes the body" (I, 252).

9. Phenomenologically, the distinguishing feature of acts of the pure intellect is, besides their lack of imagic content (PL, 107), that they formed through *reflection of the mind on itself* (see to Mersenne, October 16, 1639, PL, 66). This is not to say that they are formed through reflection on *thinking.* Rather, the exercise of pure intellect

Bailey–Cuomo: The
Feminist Philosophy
Reader

9. Feminist Epistemologies | Text

© The McGraw–Hill
Companies, 2008

151

is an inquiry into the *ideas* of the mind (e.g., of the idea of the wax, of the self, of God, of mind, of body). It is an investigation which sets as its goal what the mind *cannot conceive* the object in question as being without, lest the object cease to be what it is (Gewirth, 1955, pp. 271–273). This, determined through a rigorous series of "reductions," as Gewirth calls them, in which the mind has "reduced [ideas] to their elements and tried to separate and combine them in various ways" will be the essence of the object, its "true and immutable nature" (in Doney, 276). (Thus, God cannot be conceived without existence, nor wax without extension, nor myself without thought, etc.)

This operation, if performed successfully, will result in the conviction that the mind has reached the limits of its freedom of imagination and will: It will find itself coerced and compelled "by the internal meaning of ideas" (Gewirth, 1955, p. 274). But it is important to note that the culminating compulsion is reached as a result of an arduous and deliberately undertaken process; the mind must *subject* itself to the coerciveness exercised by the internal meanings of ideas. To do this it has to learn to "see" with *its* eye and not that of the body.

10. See endnote #1 for a discussion of the Cartesian limits to human understanding.

11. The male pronoun is the appropriate one here.

# LOVE AND KNOWLEDGE: EMOTION IN FEMINIST EPISTEMOLOGY

**Alison M. Jaggar**

## INTRODUCTION: EMOTION IN WESTERN EPISTEMOLOGY

Within the western philosophical tradition, emotions usually have been considered as potentially or actually subversive of knowledge.[1] From Plato until the present, with a few notable exceptions, reason rather than emotion has been regarded as the indispensable faculty for acquiring knowledge.[2]

Typically, although again not invariably, the rational has been contrasted with the emotional, and this contrasted pair then often has been linked with other dichotomies. Not only has reason been contrasted with emotion, but it has also been associated with the mental, the cultural, the universal, the public and the male, whereas emotion has been associated with the irrational, the physical, the natural, the particular, the private, and of course, the female.

Although western epistemology has tended to give pride of place to reason rather than emotion, it has not always excluded emotion completely from the realm of reason. In the *Phaedrus*, Plato portrayed emotions, such as anger or curiosity, as irrational urges (horses) that must always be controlled by reason (the charioteer). On this model, the emotions did not need to be totally suppressed, but rather needed to be directed by reason: for example, in a genuinely threatening situation, it was thought not irrational but foolhardy not to be afraid.[3] The split between reason and emotion was not absolute, therefore, for the Greeks. Instead, the emotions were thought to provide indispensable motive power that needed to be channeled appropriately. Without horses, after all, the skill of the charioteer would be worthless.

The contrast between reason and emotion was sharpened in the seventeenth century by redefining reason as a purely instrumental faculty. For both the Greeks and the medieval philosophers, reason had been linked with value insofar as reason provided access to the objective structure or order of reality, seen as simultaneously natural and morally justified. With the rise of modern science, however, the realms of nature and value were separated: nature was stripped of value and reconceptualized as an inanimate mechanism of no intrinsic worth. Values were relocated in human beings, rooted in human preferences and emotional responses. The separation of supposedly natural fact from human value meant that reason, if it were to provide trustworthy insight into reality, had to be uncontaminated by or abstracted from value. Increasingly, therefore, though never universally,[4] reason was reconceptualized as the ability to make valid inferences from premises established elsewhere, the ability to calculate means but not to determine ends. The validity of logical inferences was thought independent of human attitudes and preferences; this was now the sense in which reason was taken to be objective and universal.[5]

The modern redefinition of rationality required a corresponding reconceptualization of emotion. This was achieved by portraying emotions as nonrational and often irrational urges that regularly swept the body, rather as a storm sweeps over the land. The common way of referring to the emotions as the "passions" emphasized that emotions happened to or were imposed upon an individual, something she suffered rather than something she did.

The epistemology associated with this new ontology rehabilitated sensory perception that, like emotion, typically had been suspected or even discounted by the western tradition as a reliable source of knowledge. British empiricism, succeeded in the nineteenth century by positivism, took its epistemological task to be the formulation of rules of inference that would guarantee the derivation of certain knowledge from the "raw data" supposedly given directly to the senses. Empirical testability became accepted as the hallmark of natural science; this, in turn, was viewed as the paradigm of genuine knowledge. Epistemology often was equated

with the philosophy of science, and the dominant methodology of positivism prescribed that truly scientific knowledge must be capable of intersubjective verification. Because values and emotions had been defined as variable and idiosyncratic, positivism stipulated that trustworthy knowledge could be established only by methods that neutralized the values and emotions of individual scientists.

Recent approaches to epistemology have challenged some fundamental assumptions of the positivist epistemological model. Contemporary theorists of knowledge have undermined once-rigid distinctions between analytic and synthetic statements, between theories and observations and even between facts and values. Thus far, however, few challenged the purported gap between emotion and knowledge. In this essay, I wish to begin bridging this gap through the suggestion that emotions may be helpful and even necessary rather than inimical to the construction of knowledge. My account is exploratory in nature and leaves many questions unanswered. It is not supported by irrefutable arguments or conclusive proofs; instead, it should be viewed as a preliminary sketch for an epistemological model that will require much further development before its workability can be established.

## EMOTION

### What Are Emotions?

The philosophical question, "What are emotions?" requires both explicating the ways in which people ordinarily speak about emotion and evaluating the adequacy of those ways for expressing and illuminating experience and activity. Several problems confront someone trying to answer this deceptively simple question. One set of difficulties results from the variety, complexity, and even inconsistency of the ways in which emotions are viewed, both in daily life and in scientific contexts. It is in part this variety that makes emotions into a "question" and at the

Bailey–Cuomo: The
Feminist Philosophy
Reader

9. Feminist Epistemologies | Text

© The McGraw–Hill
Companies, 2008

153

same time precludes answering that question by simple appeal to ordinary usage. A second difficulty is the wide range of phenomena covered by the term "emotion": these extend from apparently instantaneous "knee-jerk" responses of fright to lifelong dedication to an individual or a cause; from highly civilized aesthetic responses to undifferentiated feelings of hunger and thirst,[6] from background moods such as contentment or depression to intense and focused involvement in an immediate situation. It may well be impossible to construct a manageable account of emotion to cover such apparently diverse phenomena.

A further problem concerns the criteria for preferring one account of emotion to another. The more one learns about the ways in which other cultures conceptualize human faculties, the less plausible it becomes that emotions constitute what philosophers call a "natural kind." Not only do some cultures identify emotions unrecognized in the west, but there is reason to believe that the concept of emotion itself is a historical invention, like the concept of intelligence (Lewontin 1982) or even the concept of mind (Rorty 1979). For instance, anthropologist Catherine Lutz argues that the "dichotomous categories of 'cognition' and 'affect' are themselves Euroamerican cultural constructions, master symbols that participate in the fundamental organization of our ways of looking at ourselves and others, both in and outside of social science" (Lutz 1987: 308, citing Lutz 1985, 1986). If this is true, then we have even more reason to wonder about the adequacy of ordinary western ways of talking about emotion. Yet we have no access either to our own emotions or to those of others independent of or unmediated by the discourse of our culture.

In the face of these difficulties, I shall sketch an account of emotion with the following limitations. First, it will operate within the context of western discussions of emotion: I shall not question, for instance, whether it would be possible or desirable to dispense entirely with anything

resembling our concept of emotion. Second, although this account attempts to be consistent with as much as possible of western understandings of emotion, it is intended to cover only a limited domain, not every phenomenon that may be called an emotion. On the contrary, it excludes as genuine emotions both automatic physical responses and nonintentional sensations, such as hunger pangs. Third, I do not pretend to offer a complete theory of emotion; instead, I focus on a few specific aspects of emotion that I take to have been neglected or misrepresented, especially in positivist and neopositivist accounts. Finally, I would defend my approach not only on the ground that it illuminates aspects of our experience and activity that are obscured by positivist and neopositivist construals but also on the ground that it is less open than these to ideological abuse. In particular, I believe that recognizing certain neglected aspects of emotion makes possible a better and less ideologically biased account of how knowledge is, and so ought to be, constructed.

## Emotions as Intentional

Early positivist approaches to understanding emotion assumed that an adequate account required analytically separating emotion from other human faculties. Just as positivist accounts of sense perception attempted to distinguish the supposedly raw data of sensation from their cognitive interpretations, so positivist accounts of emotion tried to separate emotion conceptually from both reason and sense perception. As one way of sharpening these distinctions, positivist construals of emotion tended to identify emotions with the physical feelings or involuntary bodily movements that typically accompany them, such as pangs or qualms, flushes or tremors; emotions were also assimilated to the subduing of physiological function or movement, as in the case of sadness, depression, or boredom. The continuing influence of such supposedly scientific conceptions of emotion can be seen in the fact that "feeling" is often used colloquially as a synonym for emotion, even though the more central meaning of "feeling" is physiological sensation. On such accounts, emotions were not seen as being *about* anything; instead, they were contrasted with and seen as potential disruptions of other phenomena that *are* about some thing, phenomena such as rational judgments, thoughts, and observations. The positivist approach to understanding emotion has been called the Native View (Spelman 1982).

The Native View of emotion is quite untenable. For one thing, the same feeling or physiological response is likely to be interpreted as various emotions, depending on the context of experience. This point often is illustrated by reference to the famous Schachter and Singer experiment; excited feelings were induced in research subjects by the injection of adrenalin, and the subjects then attributed to themselves appropriate emotions depending on their context (Schachter and Singer 1969). Another problem with the Native View is that identifying emotions with feelings would make it impossible to postulate that a person might not be aware of her emotional state, because feelings by definition are a matter of conscious awareness. Finally, emotions differ from feelings, sensations, or physiological responses in that they are dispositional rather than episodic. For instance, we may assert truthfully that we are outraged by, proud of, or saddened by certain events, even if at that moment we are neither agitated nor tearful.

In recent years, contemporary philosophers have tended to reject the Native View of emotion and have substituted more intentional or cognitivist understandings. These newer conceptions emphasize that intentional judgments as well as physiological disturbances are integral elements in emotion.[7] They define or identify emotions not by the quality or character of the physiological sensation that may be associated with them but rather by their intentional aspect, the associated judgment. Thus, it is the content of my associated thought or judgment that determines whether my physical agitation and restlessness are defined as "anxiety about my daughter's lateness" rather than as "anticipation of tonight's performance."

Cognitivist accounts of emotion have been criticized as overly rationalist and inapplicable to allegedly spontaneous, automatic, or global emotions, such as general feelings of nervousness, contentedness, angst, ecstasy, or terror. Certainly, these accounts entail that infants and animals experience emotions, if at all, in only a primitive, rudimentary form. Far from being unacceptable, however, this entailment is desirable because it suggests that humans develop and mature in emotions as well as in other dimensions, increasing the range, variety and subtlety of their emotional responses in accordance with their life experiences and their reflections on these.

Cognitivist accounts of emotion are not without their own problems. A serious difficulty with many is that they end up replicating within the structure of emotion the very problem they are trying to solve—namely, that of an artificial split between emotion and thought—because most cognitivist accounts explain emotion as having two "components": an affective or feeling component and a cognition that supposedly interprets or identifies the feelings. Such accounts, therefore, unwittingly perpetuate the positivist distinction between the shared, public, objective world of verifiable calculations, observations, and facts, and the individual, private, subjective world of idiosyncratic feelings and sensations. This sharp distinction breaks any conceptual links between our feelings and the "external" world: if feelings still are conceived as blind or raw or undifferentiated, then we can give no sense to the notion of feelings fitting or failing to fit our perceptual judgments, that is, being appropriate or inappropriate. When intentionality is viewed as intellectual cognition and moved to the center of our picture of emotion, the affective elements are pushed to the periphery and become shadowy conceptual danglers whose relevance to emotion is obscure or even negligible. An adequate cognitive account of emotion must overcome this problem.

Bailey–Cuomo: The
Feminist Philosophy
Reader

9. Feminist Epistemologies | Text

© The McGraw–Hill
Companies, 2008

155

Most cognitivist accounts of emotion thus remain problematic insofar as they fail to explain the relation between the cognitive and the affective aspects of emotion. Moreover, insofar as they prioritize the intellectual aspect over feelings, they reinforce the traditional western preference for mind over body.[8] Nevertheless, they do identify a vital feature of emotion overlooked by the Native View—namely, its intentionality.

## Emotions as Social Constructs

We tend to experience our emotions as involuntary individual responses to situations, responses that are often (though, significantly, not always) private in the sense that they are not perceived as directly and immediately by other people as they are by the subject of the experience. The apparently individual and involuntary character of our emotional experience often is taken as evidence that emotions are presocial, instinctive responses, determined by our biological constitution. This inference, however, is quite mistaken. Although it is probably true that the physiological disturbances characterizing emotions (facial grimaces, changes in the metabolic rate, sweating, trembling, tears and so on) are continuous with the instinctive responses of our prehuman ancestors, and also that the ontogeny of emotions to some extent recapitulates their phylogeny, mature human emotions are neither instinctive nor biologically determined. Instead, they are socially constructed on several levels.

The most obvious way in which emotions are socially constructed is that children are taught deliberately what their culture defines as appropriate responses to certain situations: to fear strangers, to enjoy spicy food, or to like swimming in cold water. On a less conscious level, children also learn what their culture defines as the appropriate ways to express the emotions that it recognizes. Although there may be cross-cultural similarities in the expression of some apparently universal emotions, there are also wide divergences in what are recognized as expressions of grief, respect,

contempt, or anger. On an even deeper level, cultures construct divergent understandings of what emotions are. For instance, English metaphors and metonymies are said to reveal a "folk" theory of anger as a hot fluid contained in a private space within an individual and liable to dangerous public explosion (Lakoff and Kovecses 1987). By contrast, the Ilongot, a people of the Philippines, apparently do not understand the self in terms of a public/private distinction and consequently do not experience anger as an explosive internal force: for them, rather, it is an interpersonal phenomenon for which an individual may, for instance, be paid (Rosaldo 1984).

Further aspects of the social construction of emotion are revealed through reflection on emotion's intentional structure. If emotions necessarily involve judgments, then obviously they require concepts, which may be seen as socially constructed ways of organizing and making sense of the world. For this reason, emotions simultaneously are made possible and limited by the conceptual and linguistic resources of a society. This philosophical claim is borne out by empirical observation of the cultural variability of emotion. Although there is considerable overlap in the emotions identified by many cultures (Wierzbicka 1986), at least some emotions are historically or culturally specific, including perhaps *ennui, angst,* the Japanese *amai* (in which one clings to another, affiliative love) and the response of "being a wild pig," which occurs among the Gururumba, a horticultural people living in the New Guinea Highlands (Averell 1980: 158). Even apparently universal emotions, such as anger or love, may vary crossculturally. We have just seen that the Ilongot experience of anger apparently is quite different from the contemporary western experience. Romantic love was invented in the Middle Ages in Europe and since that time has been modified considerably; for instance, it is no longer confined to the nobility, and it no longer needs to be extramarital or unconsummated. In some cultures, romantic love does not exist at all.[9]

Thus there are complex linguistic and other social preconditions for the experience, that is, for the existence of human emotions. The emotions that we experience reflect prevailing forms of social life. For instance, one could not feel or even be betrayed in the absence of social norms about fidelity: it is inconceivable that betrayal or indeed any distinctively human emotion could be experienced by a solitary individual in some hypothetical presocial state of nature. There is a sense in which any individual's guilt or anger, joy or triumph, presupposes the existence of a social group capable of feeling guilt, anger, joy, or triumph. This is not to say that group emotions historically precede or are logically prior to the emotions of individuals; it is to say that individual experience is simultaneously social experience.[10] In later sections, I shall explore the epistemological and political implications of this social rather than individual understanding of emotion.

### Emotions as Active Engagements

We often interpret our emotions as experiences that overwhelm us rather than as responses we consciously choose: that emotions are to some extent involuntary is part of the ordinary meaning of the term "emotion." Even in daily life, however, we recognize that emotions are not entirely involuntary and we try to gain control over them in various ways, ranging from mechanistic behavior modification techniques designed to sensitize or desensitize our feeling responses to various situations to cognitive techniques designed to help us think differently about situations. For instance, we might try to change our response to an upsetting situation by thinking about it in a way that will either divert our attention from its more painful aspects or present it as necessary for some larger good.

Some psychological theories interpret emotions as chosen on an even deeper level, interpreting them as actions for which the agent disclaims responsibility. For instance, the psychologist

Averell likens the experience of emotion to playing a culturally recognized role: we ordinarily perform so smoothly and automatically that we do not realize we are giving a performance. He provides many examples demonstrating that even extreme and apparently totally involving displays of emotion in fact are functional for the individual and/or the society.[11] For example, when students were asked to record their experiences of anger or annoyance over a two-week period, they came to realize that their anger was not as uncontrollable and irrational as they had assumed previously, and they noted the usefulness and effectiveness of anger in achieving various social goods. Averell, notes, however, that emotions often are useful in attaining their goals only if they are interpreted as passions rather than as actions. He cites the case of one subject led to reflect on her anger, who later wrote that it was less useful as a defense mechanism when she became conscious of its function.

The action/passion dichotomy is too simple for understanding emotion, as it is for other aspects of our lives. Perhaps it is more helpful to think of emotions as habitual responses that we may have more or less difficulty in breaking. We claim or disclaim responsibility for these responses depending on our purposes in a particular context. We could never experience our emotions entirely as deliberate actions, for then they would appear nongenuine and inauthentic, but neither should emotions be seen as nonintentional, primal, or physical forces with which our rational selves are forever at war. As they have been socially constructed, so may they be reconstructed, although describing how this might happen would require a long and complicated story.

Emotions, then, are wrongly seen as necessarily passive or involuntary responses to the world. Rather, they are ways in which we engage actively and even construct the world. They have both "mental" and "physical" aspects, each of which conditions the other; in some respects, they are chosen, but in others they are involuntary; they presuppose language and a social

Bailey–Cuomo: The
Feminist Philosophy
Reader

9. Feminist Epistemologies

Text

© The McGraw–Hill
Companies, 2008

157

order. Thus, they can be attributed only to what are sometimes called "whole persons," engaged in the ongoing activity of social life.

## Emotion, Evaluation and Observation

Emotions and values are closely related. The relation is so close, indeed, that some philosophical accounts of what it is to hold or express certain values reduce these phenomena to nothing more than holding or expressing certain emotional attitudes. When the relevant conception of emotion is the Native View, then simple emotivism certainly is too crude an account of what it is to hold a value; on this account, the intentionality of value judgments vanishes and value judgments become nothing more than sophisticated grunts and groans. Nevertheless, the grain of important truth in emotivism is its recognition that values presuppose emotions to the extent that emotions provide the experiential basis for values. If we had no emotional responses to the world, it is inconceivable that we should ever come to value one state of affairs more highly than another.

Just as values presuppose emotions, so emotions presuppose values. The object of an emotion—that is, the object of fear, grief, pride, and so on—is a complex state of affairs that is appraised or evaluated by the individual. For instance, my pride in a friend's achievement necessarily incorporates the value judgment that my friend has done something worthy of admiration.

Emotions and evaluations, then, are logically or conceptually connected. Indeed, many evaluative terms derive directly from words for emotions: "desirable," "admirable," "contemptible," "despicable," "respectable," and so on. Certainly it is true (pace J. S. Mill) that the evaluation of a situation as desirable or dangerous does not entail it is universally desired or feared but it does entail that desire (or fear) is viewed generally as an appropriate response to the situation. If someone is unafraid in a situation generally perceived as dangerous, her lack of fear requires further explanation; conversely, if someone is afraid without evident danger, then her fear is denounced as irrational or pathological. Thus, every emotion presupposes an evaluation of some aspect of the environment while, conversely, every evaluation or appraisal of the situation implies that those who share that evaluation will share, *ceteris paribus,* a predictable emotional response to the situation.

The rejection of the Native View and the recognition of intentional elements in emotion already incorporate a realization that observation influences and indeed partially constitutes emotion. We have seen already that distinctively human emotions are not simple instinctive responses to situations or events; instead, they depend essentially on the ways that we perceive those situations and events, as well on the ways that we have learned or decided to respond to them. Without characteristically human perceptions of and engagements in the world, there would be no characteristically human emotions.

Just as observation directs, shapes, and partially defines emotion, so too emotion directs, shapes, and even partially defines observation. Observation is not simply a passive process of absorbing impressions or recording stimuli; instead, it is an activity of selection and interpretation. What is selected and how it is interpreted are influenced by emotional attitudes. On the level of individual observation, this influence always has been apparent to common sense, which notes that we remark very different features of the world when we are happy, depressed, fearful, or confident. Social scientists are now exploring this influence of emotion on perception. One example is the so-called Honi phenomenon, named after the subject Honi who, under identical experimental conditions, perceived strangers' heads as changing in size but saw her husband's head as remaining the same.[12]

The most obvious significance of this sort of example is to illustrate how the individual experience of emotion focuses our attention selectively, directing, shaping and even partially defining our observations, just as our observations direct, shape and partially define our emotions. In addition, the example argues for the social construction of what are taken in any situation to be undisputed facts. It shows how these facts rest on intersubjective agreements that consist partly in shared assumptions about "normal" or appropriate emotional responses to situations (McLaughlin 1985). Thus these examples suggest that certain emotional attitudes are involved on a deep level in all observation, in the intersubjectively verified and so supposedly dispassionate observations of science as well as in the common perceptions of daily life. In the next section, I shall elaborate this claim.

## EPISTEMOLOGY

### The Myth of Dispassionate Investigation

As we have seen already, western epistemology has tended to view emotion with suspicion and even hostility.[13] This derogatory western attitude towards emotion, like the earlier western contempt for sensory observation, fails to recognize that emotion, like sensory perception, is necessary to human survival. Emotions prompt us to act appropriately, to approach some people and situations and to avoid others, to caress or cuddle, fight or flee. Without emotion, human life would be unthinkable. Moreover, emotions have an intrinsic as well as an instrumental value. Although not all emotions are enjoyable or even justifiable, as we shall see, life without any emotion would be life without any meaning.

Within the context of western culture, however, people often have been encouraged to control or even suppress their emotions. Consequently, it is not unusual for people to be unaware of their emotional state or to deny it to themselves and others. This lack of awareness, especially combined with a neopositivist understanding of emotion that construes it just as a feeling of which one is aware, lends plausibility to the myth of dispassionate investigation. But lack of awareness of emotions certainly does not mean

that emotions are not present subconsciously or unconsciously, or that subterranean emotions do not exert a continuing influence on people's articulated values and observations, thoughts and actions.[14]

Within the positivist tradition, the influence of emotion usually is seen only as distorting or impeding observation or knowledge. Certainly it is true that contempt, disgust, shame, revulsion, or fear may inhibit investigation of certain situations or phenomena. Furiously angry or extremely sad people often seem quite unaware of their surroundings or even their own conditions; they may fail to hear or may systematically misinterpret what other people say. People in love are notoriously oblivious to many aspects of the situation around them.

In spite of these examples, however, positivist epistemology recognizes that the role of emotion in the construction of knowledge is not invariably deleterious and that emotions may make a valuable contribution to knowledge. But the positivist tradition will allow emotion to play only the role of suggesting hypotheses for emotion. Emotions are allowed this because the so-called logic of discovery sets no limits on the idiosyncratic methods that investigators may use for generating hypotheses.

When hypotheses are to be tested, however, positivist epistemology imposes the much stricter logic of justification. The core of this logic is replicability, a criterion believed capable of eliminating or cancelling out what are conceptualized as emotional as well as evaluative biases on the part of individual investigators. The conclusions of western science thus are presumed "objective," precisely in the sense that they are uncontaminated by the supposedly "subjective" values and emotions that might bias individual investigators (Nagel 1968: 33–4).

But if, as has been argued, the positivist distinction between discovery and justification is not viable, then such a distinction is incapable of filtering out values in science. For example, although such a split, when built into the western

Bailey–Cuomo: The
Feminist Philosophy
Reader

9. Feminist Epistemologies | Text

© The McGraw–Hill
Companies, 2008

159

scientific method, generally is successful in neutralizing the idiosyncratic or unconventional values of individual investigators, it has been argued that it does not, indeed cannot, eliminate generally accepted social values. These values are implicit in the identification of the problems that are considered worthy of investigation, in the selection of the hypotheses that are considered worthy of testing, and in the solutions to the problems that are considered worthy of acceptance. The science of past centuries provides ample evidence of the influence of prevailing social values, whether seventeenth century atomistic physics (Merchant 1980) or nineteenth century competitive interpretations of natural selection (Young 1985).

Of course, only hindsight allows us to identify clearly the values that shaped the science of the past and thus to reveal the formative influence on science of pervasive emotional attitudes, attitudes that typically went unremarked at the time because they were shared so generally. For instance, it is now glaringly evident that contempt for (and perhaps fear of) people of color is implicit in nineteenth century anthropology's interpretations and even constructions of anthropological facts. Because we are closer to them, however, it is harder for us to see how certain emotions, such as sexual possessiveness or the need to dominate others, currently are accepted as guiding principles in twentieth century sociobiology or even defined as part of reason within political theory and economics (Quinby 1986).

Values and emotions enter into the science of the past and the present not only on the level of scientific practice but also on the metascientific level, as answers to various questions: What is science? How should it be practiced? And what is the status of scientific investigation versus nonscientific modes of enquiry? For instance, it is claimed with increasing frequency that the modern western conception of science, which identifies knowledge with power and views it as a weapon for dominating nature, reflects the imperialism, racism and misogyny of the societies that created it. Several feminist theorists have argued that modern epistemology itself may be viewed as an expression of certain emotions alleged to be especially characteristic of males in certain periods, such as separation anxiety and paranoia (Flax 1983; Bordo 1987) or an obsession with control and fear of contamination (Scheman 1985; Schott 1988).

Positivism views values and emotions as alien invaders that must be repelled by a stricter application of the scientific method. If the forgoing claims are correct, however, the scientific method and even its positivist construals themselves incorporate values and emotions. Moreover, such an incorporation seems a necessary feature of all knowledge and conceptions of knowledge. Therefore, rather than repressing emotion in epistemology it is necessary to rethink the relation between knowledge and emotion and construct a conceptual model that demonstrates the mutually constitutive rather than oppositional relation between reason and emotion. Far from precluding the possibility of reliable knowledge, emotion as well as value must be shown as necessary to such knowledge. Despite its classical antecedents and like the ideal of disinterested enquiry, the ideal of dispassionate enquiry is an impossible dream, but a dream nonetheless, or perhaps a myth that has exerted enormous influence on western epistemology. Like all myths, it is a form of ideology that fulfills certain social and political functions.

### The Ideological Function of the Myth

So far, I have spoken very generally of people and their emotions, as though everyone experienced similar emotions and dealt with them in similar ways. It is an axiom of feminist theory, however, that all generalizations about "people" are suspect. The divisions in our society are so deep, particularly the divisions of race, class, and gender, that many feminist theorists would claim that talk about people in general is ideologically dangerous because such talk obscures the fact that no one is simply a person but instead is constituted fundamentally by race, class and gender.

Race, class, and gender shape every aspect of our lives, and our emotional constitution is not excluded. Recognizing this helps us to see more clearly the political functions of the myth of the dispassionate investigator.

Feminist theorists have pointed out that the western tradition has not seen everyone as equally emotional. Instead, reason has been associated with members of dominant political, social, and cultural groups and emotion with members of subordinate groups. Prominent among those subordinate groups in our society are people of color, except for supposedly "inscrutable orientals," and women.[15]

Although the emotionality of women is a familiar cultural stereotype, its grounding is quite shaky. Women appear to be more emotional than men because they, along with some groups of people of color, are permitted and even required to express emotion more openly. In contemporary western culture, emotionally inexpressive women are suspect as not being real women,[16] whereas men who express their emotions freely are suspected of being homosexual or in some other way deviant from the masculine ideal. Modern western men, in contrast with Shakespeare's heroes, for instance, are required to present a facade of coolness, lack of excitement, even boredom, to express emotion only rarely and then for relatively trivial events, such as sporting occasions, where the emotions expressed are acknowledged to be dramatized and so are not taken entirely seriously. Thus, women in our society form the main group allowed or even expected to feel emotion. A woman may cry in the face of disaster, and a man of color may gesticulate, but a white man merely sets his jaw.[17]

White men's control of their emotional expression may go to the extremes of repressing their emotions, failing to develop emotionally, or even losing the capacity to experience many emotions. Not uncommonly, these men are unable to identify what they are feeling, and even they may be surprised, on occasion, by their own apparent lack of emotional response to a situation, such as a death, where emotional reaction is perceived as appropriate. In some married couples, the wife implicitly is assigned the job of feeling emotion for both of them. White, college-educated men increasingly enter therapy in order to learn how to "get in touch with" their emotions, a project other men may ridicule as weakness. In therapeutic situations, men may learn that they are just as emotional as women but less adept at identifying their own or others' emotions. In consequence, their emotional development may be relatively rudimentary; this may lead to moral rigidity or insensitivity. Paradoxically, men's lacking awareness of their own emotional responses frequently results in their being more influenced by emotion rather than less.

Although there is no reason to suppose that the thoughts and actions of women are any more influenced by emotion than the thoughts and actions of men, the stereotypes of cool men and emotional women continue to flourish because they are confirmed by an uncritical daily experience. In these circumstances, where there is a differential assignment of reason and emotion, it is easy to see the ideological function of the myth of the dispassionate investigator. It functions, obviously, to bolster the epistemic authority of the currently dominant groups, composed largely of white men, and to discredit the observations and claims of the currently subordinate groups including, of course, the observations and claims of many people of color and women. The more forcefully and vehemently the latter groups express their observations and claims, the more emotional they appear and so the more easily they are discredited. The alleged epistemic authority of the dominant groups then justifies their political authority.

The previous section of this essay argued that dispassionate inquiry was a myth. This section has shown that the myth promotes a conception of epistemological justification vindicating the silencing of those, especially women, who are defined culturally as the bearers of emotion and so are perceived as more "subjective," biased, and

Bailey–Cuomo: The
Feminist Philosophy
Reader

9. Feminist Epistemologies

Text

© The McGraw–Hill
Companies, 2008

161

irrational. In our present social context, therefore, the ideal of the dispassionate investigator is a classist, racist, and especially masculinist myth.[18]

## Emotional Hegemony and Emotional Subversion

As we have seen already, mature human emotions are neither instinctive nor biologically determined, although they may have developed out of presocial, instinctive responses. Like everything else that is human, emotions in part are socially constructed; like all social constructs, they are historical products, bearing the marks of the society that constructed them. Within the very language of emotion, in our basic definitions and explanations of what it is to feel pride or embarrassment, resentment or contempt, cultural norms and expectations are embedded. Simply describing ourselves as angry, for instance, presupposes that we view ourselves as having been wronged, victimized by the violation of some social norm. Thus, we absorb the standards and values of our society in the very process of learning the language of emotion, and those standards and values are built into the foundation of our emotional constitution.

Within a hierarchical society, the norms and values that predominate tend to serve the interest of the dominant groups. Within a capitalist, white supremacist, and male-dominant society, the predominant values will tend to be those that serve the interests of rich white men. Consequently, we are all likely to develop an emotional constitution that is quite inappropriate for feminism. Whatever our color, we are likely to feel what Irving Thalberg has called "visceral racism"; whatever our sexual orientation, we are likely to be homophobic; whatever our class, we are likely to be at least somewhat ambitious and competitive; whatever our sex, we are likely to feel contempt for women. The emotional responses may be rooted in us so deeply that they are relatively impervious to intellectual argument and may recur even when we pay lip service to changed intellectual convictions.[19]

By forming our emotional constitution in particular ways, our society helps to ensure its own perpetuation. The dominant values are implicit in responses taken to be precultural or acultural, our so-called gut responses. Not only do these conservative responses hamper and disrupt our attempts to live in or prefigure alternative social forms but also, and insofar as we take them to be natural responses, they limit our vision theoretically. For instance, they limit our capacity for outrage; they either prevent us from despising or encourage us to despise; they lend plausibility to the belief that greed and domination are inevitable human motivations; in sum, they blind us to the possibility of alternative ways of living.

This picture may seem at first to support the positivist claim that the intrusion of emotion only disrupts the process of seeking knowledge and distorts the results of that process. The picture, however, is not complete; it ignores the fact that people do not always experience the conventionally acceptable emotions. They may feel satisfaction rather than embarrassment when their leaders make fools of themselves. They may feel resentment rather than gratitude for welfare payments and hand-me-downs. They may be attracted to forbidden modes of sexual expression. They may feel revulsion for socially sanctioned ways of treating children or animals. In other words, the hegemony that our society exercises over people's emotional constitution is not total. People who experience conventionally unacceptable, or what I call "outlaw," emotions often are subordinated individuals who pay a disproportionately high price for maintaining the status quo. The social situation of such people makes them unable to experience the conventionally prescribed emotions: for instance, people of color are more likely to experience anger than amusement when a racist joke is recounted, and women subjected to male sexual banter are less likely to be flattered than uncomfortable or even afraid.

When unconventional emotional responses are experienced by isolated individuals, those concerned may be confused, unable to name their experience; they may even doubt their own sanity. Women may come to believe that they are "emotionally disturbed" and that the embarrassment or fear aroused in them by male sexual innuendo is prudery or paranoia. When certain emotions are shared or validated by others, however, the basis exists for forming a subculture defined by perceptions, norms, and values that systematically oppose the prevailing perceptions, norms, and values. By constituting the basis for such a subculture, outlaw emotions may be politically (because epistemologically) subversive.

Outlaw emotions are distinguished by their incompatibility with the dominant perceptions and values, and some, though certainly not all, of these outlaw emotions are potentially or actually feminist emotions. Emotions become feminist when they incorporate feminist perceptions and values, just as emotions are sexist or racist when they incorporate sexist or racist perceptions and values. For example, anger becomes feminist anger when it involves the perception that the persistent importuning endured by one woman is a single instance of a widespread pattern of sexual harassment, and pride becomes feminist pride when it is evoked by realizing that a certain person's achievement was possible only because that individual overcame specifically gendered obstacles to success.[20]

Outlaw emotions stand in a dialectical relation to critical social theory: at least some are necessary to developing a critical perspective on the world, but they also presuppose at least the beginnings of such a perspective. Feminists need to be aware of how we can draw on some of our outlaw emotions in constructing feminist theory and also of how the increasing sophistication of feminist theory can contribute to the reeducation, refinement, and eventual reconstruction of our emotional constitution.

## Outlaw Emotions and Feminist Theory

The most obvious way in which feminist and other outlaw emotions can help in developing alternatives to prevailing conceptions of reality is by motivating new investigations. This is possible because, as we saw earlier, emotions may be long-term as well as momentary; it makes sense to say that someone continues to be shocked or saddened by a situation, even if she is at the moment laughing heartily. As we have seen already, theoretical investigation is always purposeful, and observation is always selective. Feminist emotions provide a political motivation for investigation and so help to determine the selection of problems as well as the method by which they are investigated. Susan Griffin makes the same point when she characterizes feminist theory as following "a direction determined by pain, and trauma, and compassion and outrage" (Griffin 1979:31).

As well as motivating critical research, outlaw emotions may also enable us to perceive the world differently than we would from its portrayal in conventional descriptions. They may provide the first indications that something is wrong with the way alleged facts have been constructed, with accepted understandings of how things are. Conventionally unexpected or inappropriate emotions may precede our conscious recognition that accepted descriptions and justifications often conceal as much as reveal the prevailing state of affairs. Only when we reflect on our initially puzzling irritability, revulsion, anger, or fear, may we bring to consciousness our "gut-level" awareness that we are in a situation of coercion, cruelty, injustice, or danger. Thus, conventionally inexplicable emotions, particularly, though not exclusively, those experienced by women, may lead us to make subversive observations that challenge dominant conceptions of the status quo. They may help us to realize that what are taken generally to be facts have been constructed in a way that obscures the reality of subordinated people, especially women's reality.

But why should we trust the emotional responses of women and other subordinated groups? How can we determine which outlaw emotions we should endorse or encourage and which reject? In what sense can we say that some emotional responses are more appropriate than others? What reason is there for supposing that certain alternative perceptions of the world, perceptions informed by outlaw emotions, are to be preferred to perceptions informed by conventional emotions? Here I can indicate only the general direction of an answer, whose full elaboration must await another occasion.[21]

I suggest that emotions are appropriate if they are characteristic of a society in which all humans (and perhaps some nonhuman life too) thrive, or if they are conducive to establishing such a society. For instance, it is appropriate to feel joy when we are developing or exercising our creative powers, and it is appropriate to feel anger and perhaps disgust in those situations where humans are denied their full creativity or freedom. Similarly, it is appropriate to feel fear if those capacities are threatened in us.

This suggestion obviously is extremely vague and may even verge on the tautological. How can we apply it in situations where there is disagreement over what is or is not disgusting or exhilarating or unjust? Here I appeal to a claim for which I have argued elsewhere: the perspective on reality that is available from the standpoint of the oppressed, which in part at least is the standpoint of women, is a perspective that offers a less partial and distorted and therefore more reliable view (Jaggar 1983: chap. 11). Oppressed people have a kind of epistemological privilege insofar as they have easier access to this standpoint and therefore a better chance of ascertaining the possible beginnings of a society in which all could thrive. For this reason, I would claim that the emotional responses of oppressed people in general, and often of women in particular, are more likely to be appropriate than the emotional responses of the dominant class. That is, they are more likely to incorporate reliable appraisals of situations.

Even in contemporary science, where the ideology of dispassionate inquiry is almost overwhelming, it is possible to discover a few examples that seem to support the claim that certain emotions are more appropriate than others in both a moral and epistemological sense. For instance, Hilary Rose claims that women's practice of caring, even though warped by its containment in the alienated context of a coercive sexual division of labor, nevertheless has generated more accurate and less oppressive understandings of women's bodily functions, such as menstruation (Rose 1983). Certain emotions may be both morally appropriate and epistemologically advantageous in approaching the nonhuman and even the inanimate world. Jane Goodall's scientific contribution to our understanding of chimpanzee behavior seems to have been made possible only by her amazing empathy with or even love for these animals (Goodall 1987). In her study of Barbara McClintock, Evelyn Fox Keller describes McClintock's relation to the objects of her research—grains of maize and their genetic properties—as a relation of affection, empathy and "the highest form of love: love that allows for intimacy without the annihilation of difference." She notes that McClintock's "vocabulary is consistently a vocabulary of affection, of kinship, of empathy" (Keller 1984:164). Examples like these prompt Hilary Rose to assert that a feminist science of nature needs to draw on heart as well as hand and brain.

## Some Implications of Recognizing the Epistemic Potential of Emotion

Accepting that appropriate emotions are indispensable to reliable knowledge does not mean, of course, that uncritical feeling may be substituted for supposedly dispassionate investigation. Nor does it mean that the emotional responses of women and other members of the underclass are to be trusted without question. Although our emotions are epistemologically indispensable, they are not epistemologically indisputable. Like all our faculties, they may be misleading, and their data, like all data, are always subject to reinterpretation and revision. Because emotions are not presocial, physiological responses to unequivocal situations, they are open to challenge on various grounds. They may be dishonest or self-deceptive, they may incorporate inaccurate or partial perceptions, or they may be constituted by oppressive values. Accepting the indispensability of appropriate emotions to knowledge means no more (and no less) than that discordant emotions should be attended to seriously and respectfully rather than condemned, ignored, discounted, or suppressed.

Just as appropriate emotions may contribute to the development of knowledge so the growth of knowledge may contribute to the development of appropriate emotions. For instance, the powerful insights of feminist theory often stimulate new emotional responses to past and present situations. Inevitably, our emotions are affected by the knowledge that the women on our faculty are paid systematically less than the men, that one girl in four is subjected to sexual abuse from heterosexual men in her own family, and that few women reach orgasm in heterosexual intercourse. We are likely to feel different emotions towards older women or people of color as we reevaluate our standards of sexual attractiveness or acknowledge that Black is beautiful. The new emotions evoked by feminist insights are likely in turn to stimulate further feminist observations and insights, and these may generate new directions in both theory and political practice. There is a continuous feedback loop between our emotional constitution and our theorizing such that each continually modifies the other and is in principle inseparable from it.

The ease and speed with which we can reeducate our emotions unfortunately is not great. Emotions are only partially within our control as individuals. Although affected by new information, they are habitual responses not quickly unlearned. Even when we come to believe consciously that our fear or shame or revulsion is unwarranted, we may still continue to experience emotions inconsistent with our conscious politics. We may still continue to be anxious for male approval, competitive with our comrades

and sisters and possessive with our lovers. These unwelcome, because apparently inappropriate, emotions should not be suppressed or denied; instead, they should be acknowledged and subjected to critical scrutiny. The persistence of such recalcitrant emotions probably demonstrates how fundamentally we have been constituted by the dominant world view, but it may also indicate superficiality or other inadequacy in our emerging theory and politics.[22] We can only start from where we are—beings who have been created in a cruelly racist, capitalist, and male-dominated society that has shaped our bodies and our minds, our perceptions, our values and our emotions, our language and our systems of knowledge.

The alternative epistemological model that I suggest displays the continuous interaction between how we understand the world and who we are as people. It shows how our emotional responses to the world change as we conceptualize it differently and how our changing emotional responses then stimulate us to new insights. The model demonstrates the need for theory to be self-reflexive, to focus not only on the outer world but also on ourselves and our relation to that world, to examine critically our social location, our actions, our values, our perceptions and our emotions. The model also shows how feminist and other critical social theories are indispensable psychotherapeutic tools because they provide some insights necessary to a full understanding of our emotional constitution. Thus, the model explains how the reconstruction of knowledge is inseparable from the reconstruction of ourselves.

A corollary of the reflexivity of feminist and other critical theory is that it requires a much broader construal than positivism accepts of the process of theoretical investigation. In particular, it requires acknowledging that a necessary part of theoretical process is critical self-examination. Time spent in analyzing emotions and uncovering their sources should be viewed, therefore, neither as irrelevant to theoretical investigation nor even as a prerequisite for it; it is not a kind of

Bailey–Cuomo: The
Feminist Philosophy
Reader

9. Feminist Epistemologies | Text

© The McGraw–Hill
Companies, 2008

165

clearing of the emotional decks, "dealing with" our emotions so that they will not influence our thinking. Instead, we must recognize that our efforts to reinterpret and refine our emotions are necessary to our theoretical investigation, just as our efforts to reeducate our emotions are necessary to our political activity. Critical reflection on emotion it not a self-indulgent substitute for political analysis and political action. It is itself a kind of political theory and political practice, indispensable for an adequate social theory and social transformation.

Finally, the recognition that emotions play a vital part in developing knowledge enlarges our understanding of women's claimed epistemic advantage. We can now see that women's subversive insights owe much to women's outlaw emotions, themselves appropriate responses to the situations of women's subordination. In addition to their propensity to experience outlaw emotions, at least on some level, women are relatively adept at identifying such emotions, in themselves and others, in part because of their social responsibility for caretaking, including emotional nurturance. It is true that women (like all subordinated peoples, especially those who must live in close proximity with their masters) often engage in emotional deception and even self-deception as the price of their survival. Even so, women may be less likely than other subordinated groups to engage in denial or suppression of outlaw emotions. Women's work of emotional nurturance has required them to develop a special acuity in recognizing hidden emotions and in understanding the genesis of those emotions. This emotional acumen can now be recognized as a skill in political analysts and validated as giving women a special advantage both in understanding the mechanisms of domination and in envisioning freer ways to live.

## CONCLUSION

The claim that emotion is vital to systematic knowledge is only the most obvious contrast between the conception of theoretical investigation that I have sketched here and the conception provided by positivism. For instance, the alternative approach emphasizes that what we identify as emotion is a conceptual abstraction from a complex process of human activity that also involves acting, sensing, and evaluating. This proposed account of theoretical construction demonstrates the simultaneous necessity for and interdependence of faculties that our culture has abstracted and separated from each other: emotion and reason, evaluation and perception, observation and action. The model of knowing suggested here is nonhierarchical and antifoundationalist; instead, it is appropriately symbolized by the radical feminist metaphor of the upward spiral. Emotions are neither more basic than observation, reason, or action in building theory, nor secondary to them. Each of these human faculties reflects an aspect of human knowing inseparable from the other aspects. Thus, to borrow a famous phrase from a Marxian context, the development of each of these faculties is a necessary condition for the development of all.

In conclusion, it is interesting to note that acknowledging the importance of emotion for knowledge is not an entirely novel suggestion within the western epistemological tradition. The archrationalist, Plato himself, came to accept in the end that knowledge required (a very purified form of) love. It may be no accident that in the *Symposium* Socrates learns this lesson from Diotima, the wise woman!

## NOTES

I wish to thank the following individuals who commented helpfully on earlier drafts of this paper or made me aware of further resources: Lynne Arnault, Susan Bordo, Martha Bolton, Cheshire Calhoun, Randy Cornelius, Shelagh Crooks, Ronald De Sousa, Tim Diamond, Dick Foley, Ann Garry, Judy Gerson, Mary Gibson, Sherry Gorelick, Marcia Lind, Helen Longino, Catherine Lutz, Andy McLaughlin, Uma Narayan, Linda Nicholson, Bob Richardson, Sally Ruddick, Laurie Shrage, Alan Soble, Vicky Spelman, Karsten

*Chapter 9 / Feminist Epistemologies*

Struhl, Joan Tronto, Daisy Quarm, Naomi Quinn and Alison Wylie. I am also grateful to my colleagues in the fall of 1985 Women's Studies Chair Seminar at Douglass College, Rutgers University, and to audiences at Duke University, Georgia University Centre, Hobart and William Smith Colleges, Northeastern University, the University of North Carolina at Chapel Hill and Princeton University, for their responses to earlier versions of this paper. In addition, I received many helpful comments from members of the Canadian Society for Women in Philosophy and from students in Lisa Heldke's classes in feminist epistemology at Carleton College and Northwestern University. Thanks, too, to Delia Cushway, who provided a comfortable environment in which I wrote the first draft.

1. Philosophers who do not conform to this generalization and constitute part of what Susan Bordo calls a "recessive" tradition in western philosophy include Hume and Nietzsche, Dewey and James (Bordo 1987:114–118).

2. The western tradition as a whole has been profoundly rationalist, and much of its history may be viewed as a continuous redrawing of the boundaries of the rational. For a survey of this history from a feminist perspective, see Lloyd 1984.

3. Thus, fear and other emotions were seen as rational in some circumstances. To illustrate this point, E. V. Spelman quotes Aristotle as saying (in the *Nicomachean Ethics*, Bk. IV, ch. 5): "[Anyone] who does not get angry when there is reason to be angry, or who does not get angry in the right way at the right time and with the right people, is a dolt" (Spelman 1982:1).

4. Descartes, Leibnitz, and Kant are among the prominent philosophers who did not endorse a wholly stripped-down, instrumentalist conception of reason.

5. The relocation of values in human attitudes and preferences in itself was not grounds for denying their universality, because they could have been conceived as grounded in a common or universal human nature. In fact, however, the variability, rather than the commonality, of human preferences and responses was emphasized; values gradually came to be viewed as individual, particular, and even idiosyncratic rather than as universal and objective. The only exception to the variability of human desires was the supposedly universal urge to egoism and the motive to maximize one's own utility, whatever that consisted of. The value of autonomy and liberty, consequently, was seen as perhaps the only value capable of being justified objectively because it was a precondition for satisfying other desires.

6. For instance, Julius Moravcsik has characterized as emotions what I would call "plain" hunger and thirst, appetites that are not desires for any particular food or drink (Moravcsik 1982: 207–224). I myself think that such states, which Moravcsik also calls instincts or appetites, are understood better as sensations than emotions. In other words, I would view so-called instinctive, nonintentional feelings as the biological raw material from which full-fledged human emotions develop.

7. Even adherents of the Native View recognize, of course, that emotions are not entirely random or unrelated to an individual's judgments and beliefs; in other words, they note that people are angry or excited *about* something, afraid or proud *of* something. On the Native View, however, the judgments or beliefs associated with an emotion are seen as its causes and thus as related to it only externally.

8. Cheshire Calhoun pointed this out to me in private correspondence.

9. Recognition of the many levels on which emotions are socially constructed raises the question whether it makes sense even to speak of the possibility of universal emotions. Although a full answer to this question is methodologically problematic, one might speculate that many of what we westerners identify as emotions have functional analogues in other cultures. In other words, it may be that people in every culture behave in ways that fulfill at least some social functions of our angry or fearful behavior.

10. The relationship between the emotional experience of an individual and the emotional experience of the group to which the individual belongs may perhaps be clarified by analogy to the relation between a word and the language of which it is a part. That a word has meaning presupposes that it is part of a linguistic system without which it has no meaning; yet the language itself has no meaning over and above

Bailey–Cuomo: The
Feminist Philosophy
Reader

9. Feminist Epistemologies | Text

© The McGraw–Hill
Companies, 2008

167

Chapter 9 / Feminist Epistemologies

*703*

the meaning of the words of which it is composed, together with their grammatical ordering. Words and language presuppose and mutually constitute each other. Similarly, both individual and group emotion presuppose and mutually constitute each other.

11. Averell cites dissociative reactions by military personnel at Wright Paterson Air Force Base and shows how these were effective in mustering help to deal with difficult situations while simultaneously relieving the individual of responsibility or blame (Averell 1980:157).

12. These and similar experiments are described in Kilpatrick 1961: ch.10, cited by McLaughlin 1985:296.

13. The positivist attitude toward emotion, which requires that ideal investigators be both disinterested and dispassionate, may be a modern variant of older traditions in western philosophy that recommended that people seek to minimize their emotional responses to the world and develop instead their powers of rationality and pure contemplation.

14. It is now widely accepted that the suppression and repression of emotion has damaging if not explosive consequences. There is general acknowledgement that no one can avoid at some time experiencing emotions she or he finds unpleasant, and there is also increasing recognition that the denial of such emotions is likely to result in hysterical disorders of thought and behavior, in projecting one's own emotions on to others, in displacing them to inappropriate situations, or in psychosomatic ailments. Psychotherapy, which purports to help individuals recognize and "deal with" their emotions, has become an enormous industry, especially in the U.S. In much conventional psychotherapy, however, emotions still are conceived as feelings or passions, "subjective" disturbances that afflict individuals or interfere with their capacity for rational thought and action. Different therapies, therefore, have developed a wide variety of techniques for encouraging people to "discharge" or "vent" their emotions, just as they would drain an abscess. Once emotions have been discharged or vented they are supposed to be experienced less intensely, or even to vanish entirely, and consequently to exert less

influence on individuals' thoughts and actions. This approach to psychotherapy clearly demonstrates its kinship with the "folk" theory of anger mentioned earlier, and it equally clearly retains the traditional western assumption that emotion is inimical to rational thought and action. Thus, such approaches fail to challenge and indeed provide covert support for the view that "objective" knowers are not only disinterested but also dispassionate.

15. E.V. Spelman (1982) illustrates this point with a quotation from the well known contemporary philosopher, R. S. Peters, who wrote "we speak of emotional outbursts, reactions, upheavals and women" (*Proceedings of the Aristotelian Society,* New Series, vol. 62).

16. It seems likely that the conspicuous absence of emotion shown by Mrs Thatcher is a deliberate strategy she finds necessary to counter the public perception of women as too emotional for political leadership. The strategy results in her being perceived as a formidable leader, but as an Iron Lady rather than a real woman. Ironically, Neil Kinnock, leader of the British Labor Party and Thatcher's main opponent in the 1987 General Election, was able to muster considerable public support through television commercials portraying him in the stereotypically feminine role of caring about the unfortunate victims of Thatcher economics. Ultimately, however, this support was not sufficient to destroy public confidence in Mrs Thatcher's "masculine" competence and gain Kinnock the election.

17. On the rare occasions when a white man cries, he is embarrassed and feels constrained to apologize. The one exception to the rule that men should be emotionless is that they are allowed and often even expected to experience anger. Spelman (1982) points out that men's cultural permission to be angry bolsters their claim to authority.

18. Someone might argue that the viciousness of this myth was not a logical necessity. In the egalitarian society, where the concepts of reason and emotion were not gender-bound in the way they still are today, it might be argued that the ideal of the dispassionate investigator could be epistemologically beneficial. Is it possible that, in such socially and conceptually egalitarian

circumstances, the myth of the dispassionate investigator could serve as a heuristic device, an ideal never to be realized in practice but nevertheless helping to minimize "subjectivity" and bias? My own view is that counterfactual myths rarely bring the benefits advertised and that this one is no exception. This myth fosters an equally mythical conception of pure truth and objectivity, quite independent of human interests or desires, and in this way it functions to disguise the inseparability of theory and practice, science and politics. Thus, it is part of an antidemocratic world view that mystifies the political dimension of knowledge and unwarrantedly circumscribes the arena of political debate.

19. Of course, the similarities in our emotional constitutions should not blind us to systematic differences. For instance, girls rather than boys are taught fear and disgust for spiders and snakes, affection for fluffy animals, and shame for their naked bodies. It is primarily, though not exclusively, men rather than women whose sexual responses are shaped by exposure to visual and sometimes violent pornography. Girls and women are taught to cultivate sympathy for others; boys and men are taught to separate themselves emotionally from others. As I have noted already, more emotional expression is permitted for lower-class and some nonwhite men than for ruling-class men, perhaps because the expression of emotion is thought to expose vulnerability. Men of the upper classes learn to cultivate an attitude of condescension, boredom, or detached amusement. As we shall see shortly, differences in the emotional constitution of various groups may be epistemologically significant in so far as they both presuppose and facilitate different ways of perceiving the world.

20. A necessary condition for experiencing feminist emotions is that one already be a feminist in some sense, even if one does not consciously wear that label. But many women and some men, even those who would deny that they are feminist, still experience emotions compatible with feminist values. For instance, they may be angered by the perception that someone is being mistreated just because she is a woman, or they may take special pride in the achievement of a woman. If those who experience such emotions

are unwilling to recognize them as feminist, their emotions are probably better described as potentially feminist or prefeminist emotions.

21. I owe this suggestion to Marcia Lind.

22. Within a feminist context, Berenice Fisher suggests that we focus particular attention on our emotions of guilt and shame as part of a critical reevaluation of our political ideals and our political practice (Fisher 1964).

## REFERENCES

Averell, James R. 1980. "The Emotions." In *Personality: Basic Aspects and Current Research,* ed. Ervin Staub. Englewood Cliffs, N.J.: Prentice Hall.

Bordo, Susan R. 1987. *The Flight to Objectivity: Essays on Cartesianism and Culture.* Albany, N.Y.: SUNY Press.

Fisher, Berenice. 1984. "Guilt and Shame in the Women's Movement: The Radical Ideal of Action and its Meaning for Feminist Intellectuals." *Feminist Studies* 10:185–212.

Flax, Jane. 1983. "Political Philosophy and the Patriarchal Unconscious: A Psychoanalytic Perspective on Epistemology and Metaphysics." In *Discovering Reality: Feminist Perspectives on Epistemology, Metaphysics, Methodology and Philosophy of Science,* ed. Sandra Harding and Merrill Hintikka. Dordrecht, Holland: D. Reidel Publishing.

Goodall, Jane. 1986. *The Chimpanzees of Bombe: Patterns of Behavior.* Cambridge, Mass.: Harvard University Press.

Griffin, Susan. 1979. *Rape: The Power of Consciousness.* San Francisco: Harper & Row.

Hinman, Lawrence. 1986. "Emotion, Morality and Understanding." Paper presented at Annual Meeting of the Central Division of the American Philosophical Association, St. Louis, Missouri, May 1986.

Jaggar, Alison M. 1983. *Feminist Politics and Human Nature.* Totowa, N.J.: Rowman and Allanheld; Brighton, UK: Harvester Press.

Keller, Evelyn Fox. 1984. *Gender and Science.* New Haven, Conn.: Yale University Press.

Kilpatrick, Franklin P., ed. 1961. *Explorations in Transactional Psychology.* New York: New York University Press.

Lakoff, George and Zoltan Kovecses. 1987. "The Cognitive Model of Anger Inherent in American English." In *Cultural Models in Language and*

Bailey–Cuomo: The
Feminist Philosophy
Reader

9. Feminist Epistemologies    Text

© The McGraw–Hill
Companies, 2008

169

*Thought,* ed. N. Quinn and D. Holland. New York: Cambridge University Press.

Lewontin, R. C. 1982. "Letter to the Editor." *New York Review of Books,* 4 (February): 40–1. This letter was drawn to my attention by Alan Soble.

Lloyd, Genevieve. 1984. *The Man of Reason: 'Male' and 'Female' in Western Philosophy.* Minneapolis: University of Minnesota Press.

Lutz, Catherine. 1985. "Depression and the Translation of Emotional Worlds." In *Culture and Depression: Studies in the Anthropology and Cross-cultural Psychiatry of Affect and Disorder,* ed. A. Kleinman and B. Good. Berkeley, Calif: University of California Press, 63–100.

Lutz, Catherine. 1986. "Emotion, Thought, and Estrangement: Emotion as a Cultural Category." *Cultural Anthropology* 1:287–309.

Lutz, Catherine. 1987. "Goals, Events and Understanding in Ifaluck and Emotion Theory." In *Cultural Models in Language and Thought,* ed. N. Quinn and D. Holland. New York: Cambridge University Press.

McLaughlin, Andrew. 1985. "Images and Ethics of Nature." *Environmental Ethics* 7:293–319.

Merchant, Carolyn M. 1980. *The Death of Nature: Women, Ecology and the Scientific Revolution.* New York: Harper & Row.

Moravcsik, J. M. E. 1982. "Understanding and the Emotions." *Dialectics* 36, 2–3:207–224.

Nagel, Ernest. 1968. "The Subjective Nature of Social Subject Matter." In *Readings in the Philosophy of the Social Sciences,* ed. May Brodbeck. New York: Macmillan.

Quinby, Lee. 1986. Discussion following talk at Hobart and William Smith Colleges, April 1986.

Rorty, Richard. 1979. *Philosophy and the Mirror of Nature.* Princeton: Princeton University Press.

Rosaldo, Michelle Z. 1984. "Toward an Anthropology of Self and Feeling." In *Culture Theory,* ed. Richard A. Shweder and Robert A. LeVine. New York: Cambridge University Press.

Rose, Hilary. 1983. "Hand, Brain, and Heart: A Feminist Epistemology for the Natural Sciences." *Signs: Journal of Women in Culture and Society* 9, 1:73–90.

Schachter, Stanley and Jerome B. Singer. 1969. "Cognitive, Social and Psychological Determinants of Emotional State." *Psychological Review* 69:379–399.

Scheman, Naomi. "Women in the Philosophy Curriculum." Paper presented at the Annual Meeting of the Central Division of the American Philosophical Association, Chicago, April 1985.

Schott, Robin M. 1988. *Cognition and Eros: A Critique of the Kantian Paradigm.* Boston, Mass: Beacon Press.

Spelman, Elizabeth V. 1982. "Anger and Insubordination." Manuscript; early version read to Midwest chapter of the Society for Women in Philosophy, Spring 1982.

Wierzbicka, Anna. 1986. "Human Emotions: Universal or Culture-Specific?" *American Anthropologist* 88:584–594.

Young, Robert M. 1985. *Darwin's Metaphor: Nature's Place in Victorian Culture.* Cambridge: Cambridge University Press.

# HOW IS EPISTEMOLOGY POLITICAL?

### Linda Martín Alcoff

Epistemology is typically understood as that branch of philosophy which seeks to have knowledge about knowledge itself. Though this was once considered to be above the fray of politics, increasingly epistemology is charged with having a politics, usually an oppressive one. From some Continental philosophers comes the charge that epistemology seeks a totalizing standard of justification that would narrow the scope of debate and authorize only certain privileged speakers, thus supporting current structures of social domination and even totalitarianism.[1] From radical philosophers of various types we hear that epistemology frames its inquiry in such a way as

*Chapter 9 / Feminist Epistemologies*

to exclude the possibility of interrogating the social and political identities of knowing subjects or the impact of these identities on the knowledge produced, thus rendering epistemology's political biases immune from criticism.[2] And from an increasing number of philosophers of science we hear that epistemology rarely takes into account the fact that scientific knowledge emerges from a social praxis that occurs in the interface between scientific and political/economic institutions, and that the latter have determinate effects not only on the priorities of research but on which hypotheses are considered plausible.[3]

If these charges are mostly right, as I think they are, the problems that they identify must result from a more general but unacknowledged relationship between epistemology and politics, a relationship that is necessary rather than contingent. In this essay my principal aim is to elucidate this more general relationship and to clarify the ways in which it might be said that epistemology is political or has a necessary relationship to politics or political phenomena. But this thesis immediately raises further questions that need to be explored, such as: If epistemology is indeed political, can a self-consciousness of that fact peacefully coexist with the tradition itself? Or, as some have argued, should epistemology be replaced with the sociology of knowledge or with hermeneutics? If the answer to that question is no, then what are the implications of the political character of epistemology for it as a philosophical practice and a program of inquiry? And finally, are the politics of epistemology necessarily conservative or oppressive, as some critics have maintained?

Before we can consider answers to these questions, however, we need to clarify the sense in which it can plausibly be maintained that epistemology is political. It strikes me that there are three principal ways in which it might be argued that a significant relationship between epistemology and politics obtains. First, it could be argued that the conditions for the production of epistemologies are political in the sense that these

conditions reflect social hierarchies of power and privilege to determine who can participate in epistemological discussions and whose views on epistemology have the potential to gain wide influence. Thus, on this view, epistemology is political in its conditions of production. Second, it could be argued that specific theories of knowledge produced by epistemologists reflect the social locatedness of the particular theorist(s). Thus, the social and political identity of theorists will have a substantive effect on the epistemology they devise. This argument implies a rejection of the view that theories and minds can be separated from theorists and bodies, where bodies are understood to have social location and meaning. Third, it could be argued that epistemologies have political effects insofar as they are discursive interventions in specific discursive and political spaces. Thus, certain theories of justification will have the effect of authorizing or disauthorizing certain kinds of voices and may legitimate or delegitimate given discursive hierarchies and arrangements of speaking.

These three possibilities can mutually coexist, in any given combination. Let us look at each in turn.

## THE CONDITIONS OF PRODUCTION

The first option highlights the fact that epistemology is not simply a collection of texts but a social practice engaged in by specific kinds of participants in prescribed situations. For the most part, thinking about thinking itself goes on among professional philosophers, at least in its formalized and published manifestations.[4] And it goes on in academic institutions that are themselves constrained and determined by their embeddedness within larger socioeconomic institutions. The result of this process is that epistemology is primarily a conversation between relatively privileged males; indeed, if one looks at the *Philosophers' Index* for recent articles in epistemology or attends the epistemology sessions at the American Philosophical Association, epistemology is

Bailey–Cuomo: The
Feminist Philosophy
Reader

9. Feminist Epistemologies | Text

© The McGraw–Hill
Companies, 2008

171

striking among all the various branches of philosophy for its gender and race exclusivity.

It could be argued that this exclusivity results from a meritocracy in academic institutions, such that only those most gifted at epistemology are able to participate in it. Such a position would then have to maintain that those most gifted are generally middle- and upper-class white males.[5] This argument is obviously politically offensive, but it can be countered on other grounds as well. The high cost of tuition, the hierarchical differences between the higher education available to the rich and poor, and the class divisions exacerbated by racism and sexism in U.S. society could all be pointed out to show that who gets to do philosophy is not determined solely or primarily by merit, if we assume for the moment that the characterization of merit itself can be made without political considerations.[6] We might also point to the fact that first-generation college students—the group most likely to include larger numbers of people of color and working-class students—generally tend away from the humanities and more toward programs that can guarantee well-paying jobs. They also sometimes gravitate toward careers that can contribute more directly to their communities.

It could be countered that merit is not so much at play here as interest and that the segment of the population that engages in epistemology is that segment most interested in pursuing it. But the factors listed above that contraindicate merit as the determining factor also contraindicate interest as a primary cause. Interest and merit may play a determining role within that group of students that has reasonable access to philosophy, to determine who among this group become epistemologists; but this group is just the group of (primarily) upper- and middle-class white males. The conclusion to which we are thus compelled is that the political relationships of power and privilege in any given society have determinate effects on the conditions in which epistemology is practiced. This fact does not obtain merely when the society is not egalitarian, but would

also obtain in an egalitarian society, since there too relations of power and privilege (in this case, fair ones) would determine the possibility of merit and interest becoming primary causal factors in delimiting the class of epistemologists.

The sense in which it is true that the conditions of the production of epistemology are political can be broadened beyond consideration of who ends up in humanities programs to a consideration of the informal but no less powerful systems of discursive hierarchy and authority. In our society processes of socialization produce a situation in which there exists a presumption in favor of the views and arguments advanced by certain kinds of people over others. Thus men's views tend to be given more weight than women's, white's over non-white's, and persons of a professional-managerial class over persons of the working class. It is true that the subject matter under discussion can have a legitimate effect on who is accorded discursive authority, such that those with direct experience are more credible than those without it, but there are so many systematic divergences from this general rule that it seems ineffectual. For example, in terms of general and universal claims, which philosophy understands itself most often to be making, although one might guess that the logic of the situation would dictate that anyone at all could have the right to make such claims, in fact discursive authority is accorded by class, race, sexuality, and gender. African Americans may be considered experts on African Americans but rarely will an African American political candidate be seen by whites as capable of understanding the situation of the whole community, whereas whites more often assume that white candidates can achieve this universal point of view. In the analogous arena of literary theory, bell hooks has argued that Black writers are too often read by whites as writing about "blackness," whereas white writers are assumed to write about "life."[7]

There are many more such instances where the hierarchy of discursive authority goes against apparent logic or the basic rules of empiricism in order to maintain systems of privilege. Thus, for example, children who have been victimized by sexual abuse are less likely to be believed by adult jurors than the accused adults.[8] Midwives with extensive experience attending to women in labor as well as their own personal experience of childbirth are less likely to be believed than male obstetricians fresh out of medical school. Assembly-line workers with decades of experience are routinely ignored in decisions about how to increase efficiency on the line, and deference is instead given to college-trained efficiency "experts." Because these instances contradict basic empiricist rules or what passes for "common sense" so sharply, they reveal that there are political forces at work in determining who gets discursive credibility. And this suggests that many if not most discursive situations are political in the sense that who is allowed to speak, who is listened to with attention, who has the presumption of credibility in their favor, and who is likely to be ignored or disbelieved is partly a function of the hierarchy of political status existent in the society. Given that epistemology is similarly produced in discursive situations, whether written or spoken, the conditions of its production will be affected by these social conventions of discursive hierarchy, consciously or unconsciously, thus influencing whose arguments are considered plausible enough to be given consideration.

Of course, some might concede that for the reasons described above, epistemology has a necessary relationship to politics, but then argue that this relationship remains at the extrinsic level and has no substantive bearing on the content or character of epistemological work itself. If we turn here, however, to the second form of the relationship between epistemology and politics, we find arguments that show why it is of substantive epistemic concern who the people doing epistemology are.

## THE IDENTITY OF THEORISTS

The majority of the work showing that the identity of epistemic theorists is epistemologically relevant has been done by feminist philosophers.

Naomi Scheman, for example, has argued that the predominance of skepticism as the determining problem for epistemology is correlated with common features of socialized masculine identity formation.[10] Susan Bordo has shown correlations between such features as a fear of the feminine and the dominant Cartesian paradigm of disembodied objective knowing.[11] Elizabeth Potter has demonstrated a connection between Robert Boyle's articulation of experimental methods and his preoccupation with gender dimorphism.[12] Andrea Nye has argued that Western formulations of logic from Parmenides through Frege exemplify the desire of aristocratic males to maintain their own authority and control over the behavior of all social subjects, and thus to maintain a system of strictly controlled hierarchical relations that benefit them.[13] Genevieve Lloyd has shown that the ideals of reason developed throughout the history of Western philosophy are integrally connected to ideals of masculinity.[14] For a more contemporary case, Lorraine Code has argued that Richard Foley's epistemology commits the error of assuming that he can generalize from his own experience to the experience of all other human beings, an assumption usually found (and sometimes accorded to) dominant groups but less commonly found in subordinate groups. Her argument suggests not only that Foley's assumption is mistaken, but that there is a noncoincidental connection between Foley's epistemic conclusions and the fact that he is a male.[15] None of the works I have cited argues for a gender reductionism, or what might be called "vulgar feminism," in the sense that the evaluation of epistemology and philosophy could be *reduced* to an issue of gender identity. Such a reductionism, which is a caricature of existing feminist philosophy, is a straw position put forward only (so far as I know) by the detractors of this work.

It is also important to note that the work outlined above is not suggesting a causal relationship between epistemology and morphology or certain metaphysical entities such as sex. Within feminist philosophy, in general, the term "maleness"

Bailey–Cuomo: The
Feminist Philosophy
Reader

9. Feminist Epistemologies | Text

© The McGraw–Hill
Companies, 2008

173

does not merely or primarily connote a physiological condition as it connotes a social and political one. That is, maleness, like femaleness and whiteness and so forth, is a socially constructed identity with specified attributes of privilege and authority, a range of possible freedoms, and a designated hierarchical relationship to other possible identities. If we think of it as a social location in this way, it is easier to understand that maleness brings a particular perspective, shared assumptions and values, and social meanings.

But if the connection posited by this growing body of work is not arguing for a gender reductionism or a morphological determinism, what is it arguing for? It argues that there exists a relationship of partial determination between theories and the social identity of theorists, in general, which applies to epistemology as well. Helen Longino has provided a conception of theory-choice that can help us to make sense of this phenomenon without positing all epistemologists as intentionally promoting their own privilege or as uniformly unwilling to use available unbiased methods of argument. Longino argues that no such "pure" methods are available, since background assumptions which contain metaphysical commitments as well as contextual values enter necessarily into the process of knowing.[16] The influence of these assumptions and values cannot be restricted to the so-called "context of discovery" because they have an important impact on the formulation of hypotheses, which hypotheses are taken to be plausible, the kinds of analogies and models that get seriously entertained, and the determination of the kind of evidence considered sufficient to justify theories. After all these factors are set in place, the process of theory-choice may indeed conform to a paradigm of objectivity since, as Longino and others have pointed out, once you determine the scale that will be used to assess temperature, the determination of the temperature is really an objective matter. But the realm of objectivity in this traditional sense does not extend very far. The models of justification that are considered plausible and

thus are up for debate and consideration, the goals of epistemology itself, its unexamined assumptions about the locus and contours of knowing that set up the problematic of epistemological research—all these elements are significantly influenced by contextual values that are themselves a function in part of who the epistemologist is.

To give just one example, traditional epistemology has most often assumed that knowing occurs between an individual and an object or world.[17] This typically Western assumption of individualism (which operates as both an ontological assumption and a value) dictates the kinds of problems and hurdles epistemologists set themselves to overcome: how can I (by myself) justify my beliefs; how can the massive number of beliefs I hold be justified on the basis of my own narrow observational input; and, for naturalized epistemology, how can we describe the complex brain states involved in various epistemic functions. But little knowledge is actually achieved individually—most knowledge is produced through collective endeavor and is largely dependent on the knowledge produced by others. If epistemology were to dispense with its individualist assumption and begin with a conception of knowing as collective, a different agenda of issues would suggest itself. For example, we would need a more complicated understanding of the epistemic interrelationships of a knowing community; we would want to understand the relation between modes of social organization and the types of beliefs that appear reasonable; and we would need to explore the influence of the political relationship between individuals on their epistemic relationships.

This analysis indicates that the formative assumptions and values of any group of epistemologists, whether privileged European American males or a national minority, can have a significant impact on the epistemological theories thus produced. This need not devolve into a dysfunctional, absolute relativism, especially if we begin to acknowledge such influences so that they can be identified as far as possible and raised for debate and discussion. To assume that the interdiction of political issues entails a radical relativism is to assume that political debate is doomed to irrationality. But political issues are no less susceptible to rational consideration and discussion than epistemological ones.

## DISCURSIVE EFFECTS

This brings us to the third possible formulation of the relationship between politics and epistemology. It should be clear by this point that I am defining politics as anything having to do with relationships of power and privilege between persons, and the way in which these relationships are maintained and reproduced or contested and transformed. It should also be clear that given this definition, politics is ubiquitous in the social landscape. To the extent that discourse is produced and circulated through social practices, all discourse has political involvements. The analysis thus far given could be applied to any social knowledge or project of inquiry. Epistemology cannot be singled out as having a connection to political relations and structures, and therefore it may seem as if the targeting of epistemology as a special case is unnecessary and even unfair.

Although it is true that the general features of epistemology's relationship to and involvement with politics are not unique, it is also true that there are specificities to this relationship that bear exploration. For one thing, it is an important task to identify the connections between particular and influential epistemological theories and traditions and the political identities or social locatedness of epistemological theorists, a task that the feminist work cited above has initiated. And moreover, there are reasons why such a critique of epistemology has a unique importance. As many have pointed out, philosophy is not just one discourse among many discourses of knowledge; it is, rather, the discourse that sets out the structures of legitimation for all other discourses. This is particularly true of epistemology, which takes as its objective the delineation

of a conceptual apparatus by which all knowledge claims can be judged. Like Marx, I reject the view that philosophy, as a body of texts and ideas, actually is the causal mechanism making possible the emergence of other discourses; like Hegel, I hold, rather, that philosophy comes usually afterward and in the midst of emerging dominant discourses and provides the arguments and theories that then "justify" these discourses' dominance. Even without absolute causal power, however, philosophy and epistemology are critical discursive sites because they are influential in the crafting of what Lyotard calls narratives of legitimation or delegitimation for essentially all other discourses that claim knowledge.

Epistemology thus has a particularly strong relationship to other discourses, a relationship that is thematized in epistemology's own self-definition. Epistemology presents itself as the theory of knowledge, and thus presents itself as the arbiter of all claims to know. It is in this light that the third possible way to formulate the relationship between epistemology and politics as listed above has a particular importance. This possibility, it will be recalled, held that epistemology is political in the sense that epistemologies have political effects as discursive interventions in specific spaces, for example, to authorize or disauthorize certain kinds of voices, certain kinds of discourses, and certain hierarchical structures between discourses.

There is again a wealth of work that has explored such political effects. One of Marx's most important philosophical contributions was to begin this materialist critique of philosophy itself. On his view, the tendency under conditions of commodity production to develop positivist conceptions of knowledge, to conceal or deny the influence of social and political factors on the development of conceptual frameworks, and to remove theories from their historical embeddedness produces a reification of knowledge as absolute, uncontestable, and unchanging—just as capitalist ideology promotes the idea that capitalism as an economic system is absolute,

Bailey–Cuomo: The
Feminist Philosophy
Reader

9. Feminist Epistemologies | Text

© The McGraw–Hill
Companies, 2008

175

uncontestable, and unchangeable. Thus, the de-historicized view of knowledge dominant in "bourgeois" philosophy has the political effect of producing a fatalism about the status quo. When such an epistemology is taken up within the social sciences, theoretical descriptions of a reified, unchangeable human nature are produced.

Adorno and Horkheimer further argued that the ontology of nature as an inert object and the privileging of "prediction and control" as the goal of scientific inquiry are noncoincidentally functional for the capitalist project of maximizing the exploitation of resources and the domination of nature without constraint. This mechanistic conceptualization of nature as inert is correlated with the ontology of truth that involves a detached thing-in-itself, without subjectivity, and thus unresistant to human manipulation. The need to demythologize and desubjectify nature led to a conception of inquiry as involving an active knower and an inert, passive thing-in-itself. And this conception had the political effect of making it easier to exploit natural resources by making the nonreciprocal relationship of unchecked exploitation between "Man" and nature appear to be a natural one. Moreover, when the object of inquiry is not nature but other human beings, the result of this ontology becomes not only the exploitation of nature but the domination and oppression of large sectors of humanity.

More recently, feminist philosophers have argued that dominant epistemological frameworks and theories have had the political effect of (unjustifiably) excluding women's voices and disauthorizing women's claims to know. For example, Elizabeth Potter has argued that Locke's development of an empiricist epistemology in the seventeenth century had the political effect of silencing the emerging voices of lower-class sectarian women and thus altering the progress of women's liberation.[18] With Vrinda Dalmiya, I have argued that the requirement for justification that a knowledge claim be capable of being rendered into propositional form has had the political effect of helping to disauthorize much of women's traditional knowledge, including the wealth of knowledge of midwifery.[19] Much of the feminist work cited in the previous section also shows that the mind–body dualism and disembodied conceptions of objectivity found in the Cartesian tradition of epistemology work to undermine women's ability to claim knowledge given their socially constructed association with the body, emotion, and nature—elements that are considered more of a hindrance than a help in the achievement of epistemic justification. The tyranny of this subject-less, value-less conception of objectivity has had the effect of authorizing those scientific voices that have universalist pretensions and disauthorizing personalized voices that argue with emotion, passion, and open political commitment. Most recently, this struggle has been framed as a conflict between the (correctly) apolitical and the "politically correct." Only the latter group, which includes disproportionate numbers of scholars who are working-class, white women, and/or persons of color, is said to have a politics, which is then said to disqualify them from the academy. This notion of objective inquiry, then, continues to have significant political effects in censoring certain kinds of voices and obscuring the real political content of others.

These examples establish that epistemologies have political effects on the development and contestation of discourses, though these effects will be determined as much by the specific political struggles and the array of forces that exist in particular social contexts where the epistemologies emerge as by the content of the epistemologies themselves.[20]

## BUT WHAT ABOUT TRUTH?

But, one might ask here, what about truth? The preceding discussion may appear to have conveniently left out the fact that epistemology is most fundamentally a project in the pursuit of truth. And if truth has a relationship to politics, then it may appear that there is no possibility of achieving "real" truth, epistemology must

dissolve in the face of skepticism, and the whole
project of this essay dissolves into incoherence as well to the extent that it is making truth
claims.

In response to this point, it can first be noted
that it is not necessary to hold that truth has a
relationship to politics in order to hold that epistemology does. Epistemology is concerned not
only with truth but also with belief and standards
of justification, and we can show that there is a
connection between politics and the latter two
without any danger of incoherence.

Second, truth, it needs to be remembered, is
also a human idea with a genealogy, historical
location, and variability in the way it is conceptualized and defined. The metaphors and models
by which we characterize the nature of truth are
likely to contain both metaphysical and political
background assumptions. The belief that truth is
outside history, above politics, and that therefore
science and philosophy are likewise immune
from political evaluation and historical analysis
is a belief that both can and has served a variety of political ends, arguably both positive and
negative ones.

Finally, we need to remember that truth can
be given a variety of definitions. Truth has been
defined as correspondence to an independent reality, as coherence between beliefs or between
theories and models of reality, as instrumental
success, and as a state of subjective certainty.
Which alternative is chosen may have political
ramifications, and certain definitions may have
clear political connections, such as the definition
of truth as instrumental success arising in a capitalist era in which all value is put on the "bottom
line" and practical, usable results.

To acknowledge these points does not require
that we collapse truth into an issue of political
debate or replace epistemic considerations with
political ones. Both epistemic and political considerations need to be taken into account in the
work that goes on within epistemology, given that
it cannot "transcend" its political involvements
or social and historical embeddedness. But how

should epistemic and political considerations be
combined? Or should the political considerations
be included in sociologies of knowledge rather
than epistemology?

Given the depth and degree of the relationship
between epistemology and politics, it seems obvious that such a segregation will only weaken
epistemology by keeping it blind to its own political assumptions and involvements. If there is
danger in a total replacement of epistemic with
political considerations in theory-choice within
epistemology, there is also danger in continuing
to ignore the political elements at work within
the discipline. Thus, acknowledging and exploring the political content of epistemology is a necessity for epistemic reasons, so that this content
can no longer operate as a silent, unanalyzed influence. And it is also our political responsibility
to acknowledge and explore the political effects
of our program of work and the ways in which it
may be enhancing or undermining current struggles for political progress. In the concluding section, then, I explore what kinds of concrete and
specific changes should be made in the practice
of epistemology itself once we acknowledge its
connections to politics.

## AN EPISTEMOLOGY WITHOUT
## BAD FAITH

It is not possible to disinvest epistemology of its
relationship to politics. To the extent that epistemology is done by people, debated between people, and engaged in through the use of discourse
in a Foucauldian sense, epistemology will be of
necessity political, since all persons, their interrelationships, and their discourses have political
identities and associations, power differentials,
and political assumptions, goals, and effects. But
this need not lead to a quietism or despair that our
enterprise is unalterably mired in irrational power
struggles. It is more likely that the acknowledgment and exploration of the relationship of epistemology to politics will improve epistemology
rather than sound its death knell, since such an

exploration will increase the accuracy of epistemology's self-understanding and enhance its ability for self-critique. For this to occur, the internal methods of theory-development and debate will need to be transformed. There needs to be a change in the conditions of the production of epistemology, in its procedures of criticism and debate, and in the bases on which critiques can be made. Such transformations will not eradicate the influence of politics on epistemology but will alter the form and nature of that influence.

In regard to the first type of relationship between epistemology and politics—the fact that the conditions of epistemology's production involve political relationships of subordination and domination—it seems obvious that our goal should be to make it possible for the group of epistemologists to be chosen or selected not by unfair privilege and prejudice or by economic and discursive advantage, but by merit, or aptitude, and interest. This can be accomplished only through a social transformation sufficiently radical to eliminate the major structures of domination in our society, certainly a utopian goal but one worthy of pursuit. It should be noted, however, that the achievement of such a goal would not eliminate political influence over the conditions of epistemology's production, but would rather transform the political relationships that determine those conditions.

This project, difficult as it is, is further complicated by the fact that the determination of what counts as having a merit for or aptitude in epistemology is itself political as well. Merit is presumably judged on the basis of the ability to produce "good" epistemological work, but what counts as "good" work is subject to variable judgment, itself affected by background assumptions and contextual values. Given this, we need to find alternatives to a scenario in which the current group of epistemologists, a group that was not created primarily by merit and interest, is judging the merit of all the new candidates to the profession. We need, in other words, a form of affirmative action for the judgment and development

of new work in epistemology, not because the new works may not yet have sufficient quality, but because the determination of quality itself is subject to group-related assumptions and values. Like affirmative action programs in general, such an affirmative action would be based not on the argument that work of an inferior quality should be accepted in order to increase inclusiveness, but on the idea that quality itself is in part a political determination.

The practical implications of the second claim—that is, that there are determinate relations between the epistemologies produced and the theorists of those epistemologies—are simply that we need to do genealogies of these relationships. This is simply to continue the project begun by some feminist epistemologists. Such genealogies will be informative and enlightening for their own sake, but they will also shed light on how to incorporate the fact of the social embeddedness of epistemological theories within the process of critique and the methods of analysis that theories are subjected to within epistemology. This will most likely entail that the informal fallacy known as the "genetic fallacy" will be transformed or abolished, since it stipulates that issues involving the genesis of theories are not germane to philosophical criticism. Thus, in general, such genealogies will be able to specify further ways in which the discipline needs to be transformed.

The third way in which epistemology is connected to politics—in that epistemologies have political effects as discursive interventions in specific contexts—suggests similarly that an analysis of those effects, or the projected effects, of given theories should become a standard feature of the analysis and evaluation of epistemological alternatives. Such an analysis of effects has an impetus in both epistemic and political considerations. On political grounds, if, for example, one has a commitment to maximize discursive democracy as far as possible, or the ability and right of as many people to speak and be given credibility as possible, then one will want to know how a given theory of epistemic justification will contribute to that project. On epistemic grounds, it seems likely that if a given theory of epistemic justification has the effect of authorizing only privileged voices, helping to legitimate an oppressive status quo or buttressing colonialist and racist conceptions about which cultures are "advanced" and which are "backward," this is a good indication that extraepistemic and spurious assumptions or commitments are involved in the development and influence of such a theory of justification. What epistemically reputable reasons might be given for maintaining a system of discursive privilege so suspiciously parallel to current social hierarchies? Given that a positive answer to this question is implausible, then, if such effects obtain or are likely to obtain, the epistemic reasons given for the theory and its framing within epistemic debates should be carefully interrogated. In other words, undemocratic political effects provide a presumption against a theory's epistemic credibility.

Moreover, Hilary Putnam has recently argued, à la Dewey, that the full development of science and the most adequate interpretations of its maxims will be maximized in some proportion to the degree of democratic inclusiveness of the enterprise.[21] This conclusion follows once we acknowledge that science rarely involves deductive deliberation and more often involves processes of interpretation of data and application of maxims that admit of variability. Such processes of *decision making* will be epistemically more adequate when all the viable alternatives are available for consideration. A lone scientist or a small, homogeneous research team is less likely to be able to produce or imagine all the viable alternatives than a more heterogeneous group. On this view, science has an intrinsic reason to pursue social democracy.

This argument can be used to support the claim that epistemologies need to have a liberatory agenda for epistemic reasons. Given that the primary political effects of epistemologies are effects on the ability of certain groups of people to speak and be accorded credibility, I define a liberatory agenda in epistemology as one that seeks to maximize both the number and the diversity of persons who have such discursive possibilities. Conversely, an oppressive agenda is one that would minimize discursive access and in particular restrict it to those groups in power. We do not need to uphold the relativist notion that everyone's view has an equal claim to truth in order to hold that truth is more likely to be obtained through a process that includes the articulation and examination of all possible views. The artificial exclusion of views, or their exclusion from the realm of debate on the basis of non-epistemic reasons such as racism or sexism, is a matter of epistemic concern since it will have a deleterious effect on the strength and comprehensiveness of the view(s) that win dominance. And this means that it is not the influence of politics per se we need to eliminate from epistemology; it is the influence of oppressive politics.[22]

Despite the radical nature of the transformations thus far suggested (a radicalness that is simply a testimony to the stubborn persistence of epistemology's political blind spot), these suggestions indicate that epistemology itself as a project of inquiry about knowledge need not be eradicated. It is not epistemology itself but particular epistemological theories that have oppressive political effects, contra Heidegger and Derrida. Richard Rorty too makes the conflation between epistemology as a project of inquiry about the nature and conditions of knowledge and as a specific and substantive epistemological tradition that has been dominant in Western philosophy since Descartes or, on some readings, since Plato. This tradition—which has encompassed Cartesianism, mind–body dualism, a mirror theory of representation, scientism, and certain incarnations of positivism—has had significant oppressive effects. Moreover, this tradition, given its reliance on a de-contextualized conception of knowledge, will not be able to coexist peacefully with a developed awareness of epistemology's political connections. Though

I cannot develop the argument here, I hold that other epistemological traditions, such as pragmatism, coherentism, and naturalized epistemology, are more flexible or accommodating.

My conclusion, then, is that epistemology, as a project of inquiry into knowledge, can survive the development of its own self-consciousness, so to speak, or an awareness of its own political character. Moreover, such a redescription and transformation of epistemology will provide a new counter-argument to those who would dismiss it on the grounds that it is a sterile, irrelevant discussion without connection to social life.

## FINAL OBSTACLES

There remain two further obstacles that a revisionist epistemology must overcome.

First, an argument fashioned from Foucault's writings could be developed along the lines of the following: "Epistemology is necessarily reactionary because it presumes to sit in judgment on all other discourses. Thus it seeks discursive hegemony, creates hierarchies between discourses, and then helps to oppress and subjugate subordinate discourses." The fact that epistemology presumes to sit in judgment on all other discourses, however, does not guarantee its active or actual hegemony, as Foucault would be the first to admit. No discourse has absolute power over the discursive field. And epistemology is itself a discursive field that is internally contested and heterogeneous. Moreover, the existence of hierarchical relations between discourses is inevitable—an absolute proliferation of discourses without distinction is neither possible nor desirable. Structured frameworks are required to create discourses, and, in whatever way knowledge is defined, the identification of knowledge necessitates the ability to identify that which is not knowledge. Thomas Kuhn argues this in connection to the work of "normal" science, and Donald Davidson makes this argument in connection to meaning and errors in understanding.

Even Foucault makes a similar claim in connection to the manner in which power operates: according to him, it is implausible to understand power as operating merely on the basis of repression and constraint. Its influence, persistence, and ubiquitousness require that we understand power as also creating and producing pleasures, discourses, and possibilities for action and experience. On Foucault's view, discourses are created through the structured relations among meaning, power/knowledge, and desire, and power should be generally understood not as a system for constraint and oppression but simply as a field of structured possibilities. Foucault found all such structures to be "dangerous," and he therefore advocated a kind of cognitive skepticism (or the epistemic equivalent of a permanent revolution) characterized by a constant vigilance and critique. But Foucault was not so unrealistic as to argue that all such structured relations can be dispensed with, and he even asserted that power exists everywhere. Therefore, notwithstanding his own rejection of (analytic) epistemology, these views suggest that a wholesale repudiation of epistemology on the grounds that it attempts to create structured relationships between discourses is naive. The point of critique should concern the form and nature of the structure, or its range and degree of effective hegemony, not its very existence.

A second objection to my thesis might go like this: "Epistemology is indelibly tainted by its absolutist, ahistorical orientation. Therefore, it would be wiser to replace it than to try and reform it. And besides, we need an altogether new project that refuses the separation between sociology and epistemology, as well as other disciplines. Our new understanding of knowledge shows precisely that it cannot be adequately theorized within the field of philosophy as traditionally understood."

Of course, it is relatively trivial which particular name is given to the project of inquiry that I have been discussing. The more important issue is the nature of the project. Nonetheless, I argue that because epistemology has always included heterogeneous orientations and been a contested field, it is not monolithically incapable of transforming in the ways I have suggested. Retaining the name does imply a continuation of that which has gone before, but there are some elements in the history of epistemological work with which it will be useful to maintain a continuity. Moreover, retaining the name might reflect more accurately epistemology's heterogeneous past and counteract the distorted histories that homogenize the field and erase the existence of discontinuities and radical oppositions.

This raises the philosophical issue of how philosophy is itself understood. Some see it as the exploration of a closed set of "fundamental" questions, and when a thinker is not grappling with a question within that set, then she or he is said to be doing something other than philosophy. Such a view is ahistorical and dogmatic. It understands philosophy in terms of a dogma that in this case is a set of questions, and it rejects the view that this set exists within history and is subject to historical change. But historical changes in philosophy can mean and often have meant that the questions themselves are altered, in their framing and their assumptions, and also that new questions replace old ones. And these changes have also affected the way in which the various branches of philosophy are defined and demarcated.

A nondogmatic, historically conscious view of philosophy would therefore understand philosophy's set of questions, the tasks that it sets for itself, as open-ended rather than closed. What is attractive to many students about philosophy, I wager, is the feeling that here, ultimately, everything is open for discussion. No question can be regarded as nonsensical and out of bounds for all time, though philosophy like every other discipline needs its period of "normal" science. Because of its emphasis on reflection and the criticism of thinking itself, the project of philosophy seems uniquely situated to engage in transformative critiques. But if this commitment to reflection is to avoid dogmatism, it must include the possibility of the transformation of philosophy itself up to and including its own eradication.

At this historical juncture, philosophy in general and epistemology in particular need a major overhaul. We must become more self-conscious of the machinations of power and desire in our own field, in both our theories and our research agenda. At the same time, like the theorists of the Frankfurt School, I believe that the present era needs reflective thinking more than ever, and needs a space where thinking can occur outside the dynamics of commodity production and the demand for instrumental usefulness toward the maintenance of this system (or as much outside as possible), and outside a closed set of prescribed questions deemed fruitful for social maintenance. And one of the most critical areas of work in which reflection is needed is in the area of knowledge. It has been said that a defining feature of postmodern society is its crisis and confusion in regard to what can count as knowledge, even while there are more and conflicting knowledge claims bombarding the consumer every day. This crisis of knowledge is positive only to the extent that it can lead to a critique of authoritarian epistemologies and the development of better, more self-aware, and liberatory ones. We need the project of epistemology to continue in such a way that it can contribute to this important work.

Given the connections between epistemology and politics, and a clearer understanding of the nature of belief-formation and justification, however, it is also the case that an exploration of knowledge necessitates the combining of traditional philosophical methods and concerns with sociological, psychological, and historical ones. This move, which was called for over a century ago in the writings of Marx, is finally occurring under the banner of naturalized epistemology, though psychology and cognitive science are more often brought into play than history and sociology.[23] But what this move already implies is that the traditional way in which the academic disciplines have been divided and categorized

Bailey–Cuomo: The
Feminist Philosophy
Reader

9. Feminist Epistemologies | Text

© The McGraw–Hill
Companies, 2008

181

needs radical transformation. An orientation toward border control between disciplines serves no legitimate intellectual purpose and is usually promoted out of institutional conservatism and narrow career pragmatism.

Thus I agree that the project of inquiry into knowledge, as I have understood epistemology to be, requires a new configuration of disciplinary identities. The contours of such a configuration are beyond my ability to determine, but I am certain that ongoing work in the interface between politics and epistemology can begin to reveal the future path our project should take.

## NOTES

1. See, e.g., Jean-François Lyotard, *The Postmodern Condition: A Report on Knowledge,* trans. G. Bennington and B. Massumi (Minneapolis: University of Minnesota Press, 1984); and Michel Foucault, *Power/Knowledge: Selected Interviews and Other Writings,* ed. Colin Gordon, trans. Colin Gordon et al. (New York: Pantheon Books, 1980).

2. See, e.g., Sandra Harding, *The Science Question in Feminism* (Ithaca, N.Y.: Cornell University Press, 1986); Lorraine Code, *What Can She Know? Feminist Theory and the Construction of Knowledge* (Ithaca, N.Y.: Cornell University Press, 1991); Andrea Nye, *Words of Power: A Feminist Reading of the History of Logic* (New York: Routledge, 1990); Stephen A. Resnick and Richard D. Woolf, *Knowledge and Class: A Marxian Critique of Political Economy* (Chicago: University of Chicago Press, 1987).

3. See, e.g., Helen Longino, *Science as Social Knowledge: Values and Objectivity in Scientific Inquiry* (Princeton: Princeton University Press, 1990); Joseph Rouse, *Knowledge and Power: Toward a Political Philosophy of Science* (Ithaca, N.Y.: Cornell University Press, 1987); Lynn Hankinson Nelson, *Who Knows: From Quine to a Feminist Empiricism* (Philadelphia: Temple University Press, 1990); *Ideology of/in the Natural Sciences,* ed. Hilary Rose and Steven Rose (Cambridge, Mass.: Schenkman, 1976).

4. Here and throughout this chapter my frame of reference is Western Europe, the United States, and Australia.

5. Such an argument is not unheard-of among philosophers. See Michael Levin's apologia for the white domination in philosophy in his letter to the *Proceedings and Addresses of the APA,* 63, 5 (Jan. 1990): 62–63.

6. For an excellent history of racism in the history of U.S. education, see Meyer Weinberg, *A Chance to Learn: A History of Race and Education in the United States* (Cambridge: Cambridge University Press, 1977).

7. bell hooks, *Yearning: Race, Gender, and Cultural Politics* (Boston: South End Press, 1990).

8. In this scenario, where it is a child's word against an adult's, one might think that neither should get presumptive credibility. Or one might argue that the child should, on the grounds that it is extremely difficult and costly to any child to report such a crime, whereas adult denials are in line with their own interest. And the notion that children tend to lie about such things has been adequately disproved. See Florence Rush, *The Best Kept Secret: Sexual Abuse of Children* (New York: McGraw-Hill, 1980), pp. 155–57.

9. Such discursive hierarchies are also a function of the dominant conception of objectivity, of mind–body dualism, and of the fact that natural science is most often taken to be the paradigm of knowledge, but whether these conceptual commitments are causes or effects of systems of discursive hierarchy should not be assumed without argument. This is discussed further on.

10. Scheman, "Othello's Doubt/Desdemona's Death: The Engendering of Skepticism," in *Power, Gender, Values,* ed. Judith Genova (Edmonton, Canada: Academic Printing and Publishing, 1987), pp. 113–34.

11. Bordo, *The Flight to Objectivity: Essays on Cartesianism and Culture* (Albany: SUNY Press, 1987).

12. Potter, "Making Gender/Making Science: Gender Ideology and Boyle's Experimental Philosophy," forthcoming in her book *Gender Politics in Seventeenth-Century Science.*

13. Nye, *Words of Power.*

14. Lloyd, *The Man of Reason: "Male" and "Female" in Western Philosophy* (Minneapolis: University of Minnesota Press, 1984).

15. Code, *What Can She Know?* pp. 8, 302, 310. See also her "Taking Subjectivity into Account," in *Feminist Epistemologies,* ed. Linda Alcoff and Elizabeth Potter (New York: Routledge, 1993). Code points out that Foley's assumption is not at all uncharacteristic of work in analytic epistemology, and she uses him as an example only because of the specific clarity his work affords her case.

16. This analysis is taken from her *Science as Social Knowledge,* which, although primarily directed at knowing within science, can be applied to epistemology as well.

17. This example is discussed in Nelson, *Who Knows* (sec esp. chap. 6).

18. Potter, "Locke's Epistemology and Women's Struggles," forthcoming in *Critical Feminist Essays in the History of Western Philosophy,* ed. Bat-Ami Bar On.

19. Alcoff and Dalmiya, "Are Old Wives' Tales Justified?" in *Feminist Epistemologies,* ed. Alcoff and Potter (New York: Routledge, 1993).

20. These effects do not imply the existence of intentions of any type on the part of epistemologists: the effects are not dependent on the existence of intentions and may very well counter the political intentions of the theorist. This is also true of the two other types of relationships between epistemology and politics which we have discussed; neither of them entails or requires an ascription of political intentions on the part of the epistemologist.

21. Putnam, "Moral Objectivism and Pragmatism," presented at the World Institute for Development Economics Research conference "Human Capabilities: Women, Men, and Equality," Helsinki, August 1991.

22. It could be argued here that assessing epistemologies in terms of their effects runs into incoherence given the fact that the determination of effects will, of course, require that we be able to make truth claims and thus have an epistemology already in place. This sort of difficulty faces every epistemology and is sometimes referred to as the problem of the criterion. One solution to this problem is to provide a coherentist account that would require coherence between levels, such that the criteria of adequacy we impose on an epistemology should be consistent with that epistemology itself. In this way, an epistemology can give an account of itself, or account for its legitimation on its own terms.

23. Incorrectly, in my view. This focus is due to the fact that those epistemologists continue to see knowing as fundamentally an individual enterprise, such that the facts about individual psychological development and brain behavior are regarded as more important than group dynamics or social phenomena. See Nelson's alternative orientation to naturalized epistemology in her *Who Knows.*

# TAKING SUBJECTIVITY INTO ACCOUNT

**Lorraine Code**

## 1. THE PROBLEM

Suppose epistemologists should succeed in determining a set of necessary and sufficient conditions for justifying claims that "*S* knows that *p*" across a range of "typical" instances. Furthermore, suppose that these conditions could silence the skeptic who denies that human beings can have certain knowledge of the world. Would the epistemological project then be completed? I maintain that it would not.

There is no doubt that a discovery of necessary and sufficient conditions that offered a response to the skeptic would count as a major epistemological breakthrough. But once one seriously entertains the hypothesis that knowledge is a *construct* produced by cognitive agents within social practices and acknowledges the variability

Bailey–Cuomo: The
Feminist Philosophy
Reader

9. Feminist Epistemologies | Text

© The McGraw–Hill
Companies, 2008

183

of agents and practices across social groups, the possible scope even of "definitive" justificatory strategies for S-knows-that-p claims reveals itself to be very narrow indeed. My argument here is directed, in part, against the breadth of scope that many epistemologists accord to such claims. I am suggesting that necessary and sufficient conditions in the "received" sense—by which I mean conditions that hold for any knower, regardless of her or his identity, interests, and circumstances (i.e., her or his subjectivity)—could conceivably be discovered only for a narrow range of artificially isolated and purified empirical knowledge claims, which might be paradigmatic by fiat but are unlikely to be so 'in fact.'

In this essay I focus on S-knows-that-p claims and refer to S-knows-that-p epistemologies because of the emblematic nature of such claims in the Anglo-American epistemology. My suggestion is not that discerning necessary and sufficient conditions for the justification of such claims is the sole, or even the central, epistemological preoccupation. Rather, I use this label, S-knows-that-p, for three principal reasons as a trope that permits easy reference to the epistemologies of the mainstream. First, I want to mark the positivist-empiricist orientation of these epistemologies, which is both generated and enforced by appeals to such paradigms. Second, I want to show that these paradigms prompt and sustain a belief that universally necessary and sufficient conditions can indeed be found. Finally—and perhaps most importantly—I want to distance my discussion from analyses that privilege scientific knowledge, as do S-knows-that-p epistemologies implicitly and often explicitly, and hence to locate it within an "epistemology of everyday lives."

Coincidentally—but only, I think, coincidentally—the dominant epistemologies of modernity with their Enlightenment legacy and later infusion with positivist-empiricist principles, have defined themselves around ideals of pure objectivity and value-neutrality. These ideals are best suited to govern evaluations of the knowledge of knowers who can be considered capable of achieving a

"view from nowhere"[1] that allows them, through the autonomous exercise of their reason, to transcend particularity and contingency. The ideals presuppose a universal, homogeneous, and essential "human nature" that allows knowers to be substitutable for one another. Indeed, for S-knows-that-p epistemologies, knowers worthy of that title can act as "surrogate knowers," who are able to put themselves in anyone else's place and know his or her circumstances and interests in just the same way as she or he would know them.[2] Hence those circumstances and interests are deemed epistemologically irrelevant. Moreover, by virtue of their detachment, these ideals erase the possibility of analyzing the interplay between emotion and reason and obscure connections between knowledge and power. They lend support to the conviction that cognitive products are as neutral—as politically innocent—as the processes that allegedly produce them. Such epistemologies implicitly assert that if one cannot see "from nowhere" (or equivalently, from an ideal observation position that could be anywhere and everywhere)—if one cannot take up an epistemological position that mirrors the "original position" of "the moral point of view"—then one cannot know anything at all. If one cannot transcend subjectivity and the particularities of its "location," then there is no knowledge worth analyzing.

The strong prescriptions and proscriptions that I have highlighted reveal that S-knows-that-p epistemologies work with a closely specified kind of knowing. That knowledge is by no means representative of "human knowledge" or "knowledge in general" (if such terms retain a legitimate reference in these postmodern times), either diachronically (across recorded history) or synchronically (across the late twentieth-century epistemic terrain). Nor have theories of knowledge throughout the history of philosophy developed uniformly around these same exclusions and inclusions. Neither Plato, Spinoza, nor Hume, for example, would have denied that there are interconnections between reason and "the passions"; neither Stoics, Marxists, phenomenologists, pragmatists, nor followers of the later Wittgenstein would represent knowledge seeking as a disinterested pursuit, disconnected from everyday concerns. And these are but a few exceptions to the "rule" that has come to govern the epistemology of the Anglo-American mainstream.

The *positivism* of positivist-empiricist epistemologies has been instrumental in ensuring the paradigmatic status of *S-knows-that-p* claims and all that is believed to follow from them.[3] For positivist epistemologists, sensory observation in ideal observation conditions is the privileged source of knowledge, offering the best promise of certainty. Knowers are detached, neutral spectators, and the objects of knowledge are separate from them; they are inert items in the observational knowledge-gathering process. Findings are presented in *propositions* (e.g., *S-knows-that-p*), which are verifiable by appeals to the observational data. Each individual knowledge-seeker is singly and separately accountable to the evidence; however, the belief is that *his* cognitive efforts are replicable by any other individual knower in the same circumstances. The aim of knowledge seeking is to achieve the capacity to predict, manipulate, and control the behavior of the objects known.

The fact/value distinction that informs present-day epistemology owes its strictest formulation to the positivist legacy. For positivists, value statements are not verifiable and hence are meaningless; they must not be permitted to distort the facts. And it is in the writings of the logical positivists and their heirs that one finds the most definitive modern articulations of the supremacy of scientific knowledge (for which read "the knowledge attainable in physics"). Hence, for example, Karl Popper writes: "Epistemology I take to be the theory of *scientific knowledge*."[4]

From a positivistically derived conception of scientific knowledge comes the ideal objectivity that is alleged to be achievable by any knower who deserves the label. Physical science is represented as the site of ideal, controlled, and objective knowing at its best; its practitioners are held to be knowers *par excellence*. The

positivistic separation of the contexts of discovery and justification produces the conclusion that even though information gathering (discovery) may sometimes be contaminated by the circumstantial peculiarities of everyday life, justificatory procedures can effectively purify the final cognitive product—knowledge—from any such taint. Under the aegis of positivism, attempts to give epistemological weight to the provenance of knowledge claims—to grant justificatory or explanatory significance to social- or personal-historical situations, for example—risk committing the "genetic fallacy." More specifically, claims that epistemological insight can be gained from understanding the psychology of knowers or analyzing their socio-cultural locations invite dismissal either as "psychologism" or as projects belonging to the sociology of knowledge. For epistemological purists, many of these pursuits can provide anecdotal information, but none contributes to the real business of epistemology.

In this sketch I have represented the positivist credo at its starkest because it is these stringent aspects of its program that have trickled down not just to produce the tacit ideals of the epistemological orthodoxy but to inform even well-educated laypersons' conceptions of what it means to be objective and of the authoritative status of modern science.[5] Given the spectacular successes of science and technology, it is no wonder that the scientific method should appear to offer the best available route to reliable, objective knowledge not just of matters scientific but of everything one could want to know, from what makes a car run to what makes a person happy. It is no wonder that reports to the effect that "Science has proved . . ." carry an immediate presumption of truth. Furthermore, the positivist program offered a methodology that would extend not just across the natural sciences, but to the human/social sciences as well. All scientific inquiry—including inquiry in the human sciences—was to be conducted on the model of natural scientific inquiry, especially as practiced in physics.[6] Knowledge of people could be scientific to the extent that it

Bailey–Cuomo: The
Feminist Philosophy
Reader

9. Feminist Epistemologies

Text

© The McGraw–Hill
Companies, 2008

185

could be based on empirical observations of predictable, manipulable patterns of behavior.

I have focused on features of mainstream epistemology that tend to sustain the belief that a discovery of necessary and sufficient conditions for justifying $S$-knows-that-$p$ claims could count as the last milestone on the epistemological journey. Such claims are distilled, simplified observational knowledge claims that are objectively derived, propositionally formulable, and empirically testable. The detail of the role they play varies according to whether the position they figure in is foundational or coherentist, externalist or internalist. My intent is not to suggest that $S$-knows-that-$p$ formulations capture the essence of these disparate epistemic orientations or to reduce them to one common principle. Rather, I am contending that certain reasonably constant features of their diverse functions across a range of inquiries—features that derive at least indirectly from the residual prestige of positivism and its veneration of an idealized scientific methodology—produce epistemologies for which the places $S$ and $p$ can be indiscriminately filled across an inexhaustible range of subject matters. The legislated (not "found") context-independence of the model generates the conclusion that knowledge worthy of the name must transcend the particularities of experience to achieve objective purity and value neutrality. This is a model within which the issue of taking subjectivity into account simply does not arise.

Yet despite the disclaimers, hidden subjectivities produce these epistemologies and sustain their hegemony in a curiously circular process. It is true that, in selecting examples, the context in which $S$ knows or $p$ occurs is rarely considered relevant, for the assumption is that only in abstraction from contextual confusion can clear, unequivocal knowledge claims be submitted for analysis. Yet those examples tend to be selected—whether by chance or by design—from the experiences of a privileged group of people and to be presented as paradigmatic for all knowledge. Hence a certain range of contexts is,

in effect, presupposed. Historically, the philosopher arrogated that privilege to himself, maintaining that an investigation of his mental processes could reveal the workings of human thought. In Baconian and later positivist-empiricist thought, as I have suggested, paradigmatic privilege belongs more specifically to standardized, faceless observers or to scientists. (The latter, at least, have usually been white and male.) Their ordinary observational experiences provide the "simples" of which knowledge is comprised: observational simples caused, almost invariably, by medium-sized physical objects such as apples, envelopes, coins, sticks, and colored patches. The tacit assumptions are that such objects are part of the basic experiences of every putative knower and that more complex knowledge—or scientific knowledge—consists in elaborated or scientifically controlled versions of such experiences. Rarely in the literature, either historical or modern, is there more than a passing reference to knowing other people, except occasionally to a recognition (i.e., observational information) that this is a man—whereas that is a door or a robot. Neither with respect to material objects nor to other people is there any sense of how these "knowns" figure in a person's life.

Not only do these epistemic restrictions suppress the context in which objects are known, they also account for the fact that, apart from simple objects—and even there it is questionable—one cannot, on this model, know anything well enough to do very much with it. One can only *perceive* it, usually at a distance. In consequence, most of the more complex, contentious, and locationally variable aspects of cognitive practice are excluded from epistemological analysis. Hence the knowledge that epistemologists analyze is not of concrete or unique aspects of the physical/social world. It is of *instances* rather than particulars; the norms of formal sameness obscure practical and experiential differences to produce a picture of a homogeneous epistemic community, comprised of discrete individuals with uniform access to the stuff of which knowledge is made.

*Chapter 9 / Feminist Epistemologies*

The project of remapping the epistemic terrain that I envisage is subversive, even anarchistic, in challenging and seeking to displace some of the most sacred principles of standard Anglo-American epistemologies. It abandons the search for and denies the possibility of the disinterested and dislocated view from nowhere. More subversively, it asserts the political investedness of most knowledge-producing activity and insists upon the accountability—the epistemic responsibilities—of knowing subjects to the community, not just to the evidence.[7]

Because my engagement in the project is specifically prompted by a conviction that *gender* must be put in place as a primary analytic category, I start by assuming that it is impossible to sustain the presumption of gender-neutrality that is central to standard epistemologies: the presumption that gender has nothing to do with knowledge, that the mind has no sex, that reason is alike in all men, and man "embraces" woman.[8] But gender is not an enclosed category, for it is always interwoven with such other sociopolitical-historical locations as class, race, and ethnicity, to mention only a few. It is experienced differently, and it plays differently into structures of power and dominance at its diverse intersections with other specificities. From these multiply describable locations, the world looks quite different from the way it might look from nowhere. Homogenizing those differences under a range of standard or typical instances always invites the question, "standard or typical for whom?"[9] Answers to that question must necessarily take subjectivity into account.

My thesis, then, is that a "variable construction" hypothesis[10] requires epistemologists to pay as much attention to the nature and situation—the location—of S as they commonly pay to the content of p; I maintain that a constructivist reorientation requires epistemologists to take subjective factors—factors that pertain to the circumstances of the subject, S—centrally into account in evaluative and justificatory procedures. Yet the socially located, critically dialogical nature of

the reoriented epistemological project preserves a realist orientation, ensuring that it will not slide into subjectivism. This caveat is vitally important. Although I shall conclude this essay with a plea for a hybrid breed of relativism, my contention will be that realism and relativism are by no means incompatible. Although I argue the need to excise the positivist side of the positivist-empiricist couple, I retain a modified commitment to the empiricist side for several reasons.

I have suggested that the stark conception of objectivity that characterizes much contemporary epistemology derives from the infusion of empiricism with positivistic values. Jettison those values, and an empiricist core remains that urges both the survival significance and emancipatory significance of achieving reliable knowledge of the physical and social world.[11] People need to be able to explain the world and to explain their circumstances as part of it; hence they need to be able to assume its 'reality' in some minimal sense. The fact of the world's intractability to intervention and wishful thinking is the strongest evidence of its independence from human knowers. Earthquakes, trees, disease, attitudes, and social arrangements are *there* requiring different kinds of reaction and (sometimes) intervention. People cannot hope to transform their circumstances and hence to realize emancipatory goals if their explanations cannot at once account for the intractable dimensions of the world and engage appropriately with its patently malleable features. Therefore it is necessary to achieve some match between knowledge and "reality," even when the reality at issue consists, primarily in social productions such as racism or tolerance, oppression or equality of opportunity. A reconstructed epistemological project has to retain an empirical-realist core that can negotiate the fixities and less stable constructs of the physical-social world, while refusing to endorse the objectivism of the positivist legacy or the subjectivism of radical relativism.

Bailey–Cuomo: The
Feminist Philosophy
Reader

9. Feminist Epistemologies

Text

© The McGraw–Hill
Companies, 2008

187

## 2. AUTONOMOUS SOLIDARITY

Feminist critiques of epistemology and philosophy of science/social science have demonstrated that the ideals of the autonomous reasoner—the dislocated, disinterested observer—and the epistemologies they inform are the artifacts of a small, privileged group of educated, usually prosperous, white men.[12] Their circumstances enable them to believe that they are materially and even affectively autonomous and to imagine that they are nowhere or everywhere, even as they occupy an unmarked position of privilege. Moreover, the ideals of rationality and objectivity that have guided and inspired theorists of knowledge throughout the history of western philosophy have been constructed through processes of excluding the attributes and experiences commonly associated with femaleness and underclass social status: emotion, connection, practicality, sensitivity, and idiosyncracy.[13] These systematic excisions of "otherness" attest to a presumed—and willed—belief in the stability of a social order that the presumers have good reasons to believe that they can ensure, because they occupy the positions that determine the norms of conduct and enquiry. Yet all that these convictions demonstrate is that ideal objectivity is a generalization from the *subjectivity* of quite a small social group, albeit a group that has the power, security, and prestige to believe that it can generalise its experiences and normative ideals across the social order, thus producing a group of like-minded practitioners ("we") and dismissing "others" as deviant, aberrant ("they").

Richard Foley's book *The Theory of Epistemic Rationality* illustrates my point. Foley bases his theory on a criterion of first-person persuasiveness, which he calls a "subjective foundationalism." He presents exemplary knowledge claims in the standard *S*-knows-that-*p* rubric. Whether or not a propositional knowledge claim turns out to be warranted for any putative knower/believer will depend upon its being "uncontroversial," "argument-proof" *for that individual,* "in the sense

that all possible arguments against it are implausible."[14] Foley is not concerned that his "subjective" appeal could force him into subjectivism or solipsism. His unconcern, I suggest, is precisely a product of the confidence with which he expands his references to *S* into "we." Foley's appeals to *S*'s normality—to his being "one of us" "just like the rest of us"—to his not having "crazy, bizarre [or] outlandish beliefs,"[15] "weird goals," or "weird perceptions,"[16] underpin his assumption that in speaking for *S* he is speaking for everyone—or at least for "all of *us*." Hence he refers to what "any normal individual on reflection would be likely to think,"[17] without pausing to consider the presumptuousness of the terminology. There are no problems, no politics of "we-saying" visible here; this is an epistemology oblivious to its experiential and political specificity. Yet its appeals to a taken-for-granted normality, achieved through commonality, align it with all of the positions of power and privilege that unthinkingly consign to epistemic limbo people who profess "crazy, bizarre, or outlandish" beliefs and negate their claims to the authority that knowledge confers. In its assumed political innocence, it prepares the ground for the practices that make 'knowledge' an honorific and ultimately exclusionary label, restricting it to the products of a narrow subset of the cognitive activities of a closely specified group. The histories of women and other "others" attempting to count as members of that group are justifiably bitter. In short, the assumptions that accord *S*-knows-that-*p* propositions a paradigmatic place generate epistemologies that derive from a privileged subjective specificity to inform sociopolitical structures of dominance and submission. Such epistemologies—and Foley's is just one example—mask the specificity of their origins beneath the putative neutrality of the rubric.

Therefore, although subjectivity does not figure in any explicit sense in the formulaic, purely place-holder status of *S* in Foley's theory, there is no doubt that the assumptions that allow him to presume *S*'s normality—and apolitical status—in effect work to install a very specific conception of subjectivity in the *S*-place: a conception that demands analysis if the full significance of the inclusions and exclusions it produces are to be understood. These "subjects" are interchangeable only across a narrow range of implicit group membership. And the group in question is the dominant social group in western capitalist societies: propertied, educated, white men. Its presumed political innocence needs to be challenged. Critics must ask for whom this epistemology exists; whose interests it serves; and whose it neglects or suppresses in the process.[18]

I am not suggesting that *S*-knows-that-*p* epistemologies are the only ones that rely on silent assumptions of solidarity. Issues about the implicit politics of "we-saying" infect even the work of such an antifoundationalist, anti-objectivist, anti-individualist as Richard Rorty, whom many feminists are tempted to see as an ally in their successor epistemology projects. Again, the manner in which these issues arise is instructive.

In that part of his work with which feminist and other revisionary epistemologists rightly find an affinity,[19] Rorty develops a sustained argument to the effect that the "foundational" (for which read "empiricist-positivist and rationalist") projects of western philosophy have been unable to fulfill their promise. That is to say, they have not been successful in establishing their claims that knowledge must—and can—be grounded in absolute truth and that necessary and sufficient conditions can be ascertained. Rorty turns his back on the (in his view) ill-conceived project of seeking absolute epistemic foundations to advocate a process of "continuing conversation rather than discovering truth."[20] The conversation will be informed and inspired by the work of such "edifying philosophers" as Dewey, Wittgenstein, Heidegger, and (latterly) Gadamer. It will move away from the search for foundations to look within communally created and communably available history, tradition, and culture for the only possible bases for truth claims. Relocating questions about knowledge and truth to positions within the conversations of humankind does

seem to break the thrall of objectivist detachment and to create a forum for dialogic, cooperative debate of the epistemological issues of everyday, practical life. Yet the question is how open that forum would—or could—be; who would have a voice in Rorty's conversations? They are not likely, I suspect, to be those who fall under Foley's exclusions.

In his paper "Solidarity or Objectivity?", Rorty reaffirms his repudiation of objectivist epistemologies to argue that "for the pragmatist [i.e., for him, as pragmatist] . . . knowledge is, like 'truth,' simply a compliment paid to the beliefs which *we* think so well justified that, for the moment, further justification is not needed."[21] He eschews epistemological analysis of truth, rationality, and knowledge to concentrate on questions about "what self-image our society should have of itself."[22] Contending that philosophy is a frankly ethnocentric project and affirming that "'there is only the dialogue,' only *us*," he advocates throwing out "the last residue of transcultural rationality."[23] It is evidently his belief that communal solidarity, guided by principles of liberal tolerance—and of Nietzschean irony—will both provide solace in this foundationless world *and* check the tendencies of ethnocentricity to oppress, marginalize, or colonize.

Yet as Nancy Fraser aptly observes: "Rorty homogenizes social space, assuming tendentiously that there are no deep social cleavages capable of generating conflicting solidarities and opposing 'we's."[24] Hence he can presume that there will be no disagreement about the best self-image of "our" society; he can fail to note—or at least to take seriously—the androcentricity, class-centricity, and all of the other centricities that his solidarity claims produce. The very goal of achieving "as much intersubjective agreement as possible," of extending "the reference of 'us' as far as we can,"[25] with the belief that tolerance will do the job when conflicts arise, is unlikely to convince members of groups who have never felt solidarity with the represeners of the self-image of the society. The very promise of inclusion in the extension of that "we" is as likely to occasion anxiety as it is to offer hope. Naming ourselves as "we" empowers us, but it always risks disempowering others. The we-saying, then, of assumed or negotiated solidarity must always be submitted to critical analysis.

Now it is neither surprising nor outrageous that epistemologies should derive out of specific human interests. Indeed, it is much less plausible to contend that they do not; human cognitive agents, after all, have made them. Why would they not bear the marks of their makers? Nor does the implication of human interests in theories of knowledge, prima facie, invite censure. It does alert epistemologists to the need for case-by-case analysis and critique of the sources out of which claims to objectivity and neutrality are made.[26] More pointedly, it forces the conclusion that if the ideal of objectivity cannot pretend to have been established in accordance with its own demands, then it has no right to the theoretical hegemony to which it lays claim.

Central to the program of taking subjectivity into account that feminist epistemological inquiry demands, then, is a critical analysis of that very politics of "we-saying" that objectivist epistemologies conceal from view. Whenever an *S*-knows-that-*p* claim is declared paradigmatic, the first task is to analyze the constitution of the group(s) by whom and for whom it is accorded that status.

## 3. SUBJECTS AND OBJECTS

I have noted that the positivist-empiricist influence on the principal epistemologies of the mainstream manifests itself in assumptions that verifiable knowledge—knowledge worthy of the name—can be analyzed into observational simples; that the methodology of the natural sciences, and especially physics, is a model for productive enquiry; and that the goal of developing a "unified science" translates into a "unity of knowledge" project in which all knowledge—including everyday and social-scientific knowledge about people—would

be modeled on the knowledge ideally obtainable in physics. Reliance upon *S*-knows-that-*p* paradigms sustain these convictions. In the preceding section I have shown that these paradigms, in practice, are problematic with respect to the subjects (knowers) who occupy the *S* position, whose subjectivity and accountability are effaced in the formal structure. In this section I shall show that they are ultimately oppressive for subjects who come to occupy the *p* position—who become objects of knowledge—because their subjectivity and specificity are reduced to interchangeable, observable variables. When more elaborated knowledge claims are at issue—theories and interpretations of human behaviors and institutions are the salient examples here—these paradigms generate a presumption in favor of apolitical epistemic postures that is at best deceptive and at worst dangerous, both politically and epistemologically.

This last claim requires some explanation. The purpose of singling out *paradigmatic* knowledge claims is to establish exemplary instances that will map, feature by feature, onto knowledge that differs from the paradigm in content across a wide range of possibilities. Strictly speaking, paradigms are meant to capture just the formal, structural character of legitimate (appropriately verifiable) knowledge. But their paradigmatic status generates presumptions in favor of much wider resemblances across the epistemic terrain than the strictest reading of the model would permit. Hence it looks as if it is not just the paradigm's purely formal features that are generalizable to knowledge that differs not just in complexity but in kind from the simplified, paradigmatic example. Of particular interest in the present context is the fact that paradigms are commonly selected from mundane experiences of virtually indubitable facticity ("Susan knows that the door is open"); they are distilled from simple objects in the world that seem to be just neutrally *there*. There appear to be no political stakes in knowing such a fact. Moreover, it looks (at least from the vantage point of the epistemologist) as though the poorest, most "weird," and most marginalized of knowers would have access to and know about these things in exactly the same way. Hence the substitutionalist assumption that the paradigm relies on points to the conclusion that *all* knowing—knowing theories, institutions, practices, life forms, *and* forms of life—is just as objective, transparent, and apolitical an exercise.

My contention that subjectivity has to be taken into account takes issue with the belief that epistemologists need only to understand the conditions for propositional, observationally derived knowledge, and all the rest will follow. It challenges the concommitant belief that epistemologists need only to understand how such knowledge claims are made and justified by individual, autonomous, self-reliant reasoners to understand all the rest. Such beliefs derive from conceptions of detached and faceless cognitive agency that mask the variability of the experiences and practices from which knowledge is constructed.

Even if necessary and sufficient conditions cannot yet be established, say in the form of unassailable foundations or seamless coherence, there are urgent questions for epistemologists to address. They bear not primarily upon criteria of evidence, justification, and warrantability but upon the "nature" of inquirers: upon their interests in the inquiry, their emotional involvement and background assumptions, and their character; upon their material, historical, and cultural circumstances. Answers to such questions will rarely offer definitive assessments of knowledge claims and hence are not ordinarily open to the charge that they commit the genetic fallacy; but they can be instructive in debates about the worth of such claims. I am thinking of questions about how credibility is established, about connections between knowledge and power, about political agendas and epistemic responsibilities, and about the place of knowledge in ethical and aesthetic judgments. These questions are less concerned with individual, monologic cognitive projects than with the workings of epistemic communities as they are manifested in structures of authority

and expertise and in the processes through which knowledge comes to inform public opinion. Such issues will occupy a central place in reconstructed epistemological projects that eschew formalism in order to engage with cognitive practices and to promote emancipatory goals.

The epistemic and moral/political ideals that govern inquiry in technologically advanced, capitalist, free-enterprise western societies are an amalgam of liberal-utilitarian moral values and the empiricist-positivist intellectual values that I have been discussing in this essay. These ideals and values shape both the intellectual enterprises that the society legitimates and the language of liberal individualism that maps out the rhetorical spaces where those enterprises are carried out. The ideal of tolerance and openness is believed to be the right attitude from which, initially, to approach truth claims. It combines with the assumptions that objectivity and value-neutrality govern the rational conduct of scientific and social-scientific research to produce the philosophical commonplaces of late twentieth-century anglo-American societies, not just in "the academy" but in the public perception—the "common sense," in Gramsci's terms—that prevails about the academy and the scientific community.[27] (Recall that for Rorty, tolerance is to ensure that postepistemological societies will sustain productive conversations.) I have noted that a conversational item introduced with the phrase "Science has proved . . ." carries a presumption in favor of its reliability *because of* its objectivity and value-neutrality—a presumption that these facts can stand up to scrutiny *because* they are products of an objective, disinterested process of inquiry. (It is ironic that this patently "genetic" appeal—that is, to the genesis of cognitive products in a certain kind of process—is normally cited to discredit other genetic accounts!) Open and fair-minded consumers of science will recognize its claims to disinterested, tolerant consideration.

I want to suggest that these ideals are inadequate to guide epistemological debates about contentious issues and hence that it is deceptive and

Bailey–Cuomo: The
Feminist Philosophy
Reader

9. Feminist Epistemologies | Text

© The McGraw–Hill
Companies, 2008

191

dangerous to ignore questions about subjectivity in the name of objectivity and value-neutrality. (Again, this is why simple observational paradigms are so misleading.) To do so, I turn to an example that is now notorious, at least in Canada.

Psychologist Philippe Rushton claims to have demonstrated that "Orientals as a group are more intelligent, more family-oriented, more law-abiding and less sexually promiscuous than whites, and that whites are superior to blacks in all the same respects."[28] Presented as "facts" that "science [i.e., an allegedly scientific psychology] has proved . . ." by using an objective statistical methodology, Rushton's findings carry a presumption in favor of their reliability *because* they are products of objective research.[29] The "Science has proved . . ." rhetoric creates a public presumption in favor of taking them at face value, believing them true until they are proven false. It erects a screen, a blind, behind which the researcher, like any other occupant of the *S* place, can abdicate accountability to anything but "the facts" and can present himself as a neutral, infinitely replicable vehicle through which data passes en route to becoming knowledge. He can claim to have fulfilled his epistemic obligations if, "withdraw[ing] to his professional self,"[30] he can argue that he has been "objective," detached and disinterested in his research. The rhetoric of objectivity and value-neutrality places the burden of proof on the challenger rather than the fact-finder and judges her guilty of intolerance, dogmatism, or ideological excess if she cannot make her challenge good. That same rhetoric generates a conception of knowledge for its own sake that at once effaces accountability requirements and threatens the dissolution of viable intellectual and moral community.

I have noted that the "Science has proved . . ." rhetoric derives from the sociopolitical influence of the philosophies of science that incorporate and are underwritten by *S*-knows-that-*p* epistemologies. Presented as the findings of a purely neutral observer who "discovered" facts about racial inferiority and superiority in controlled observation conditions so that he could not rationally withhold assent, Rushton's results ask the community to be equally objective and neutral in assessing them. These requirements are at once reasonable and troubling. They are reasonable because the empiricist-realist component that I maintain is vital to any emancipatory epistemology makes it a mark of competent, reasonable inquiry to approach even the most unsavory truth claims seriously, albeit critically. But the requirements are troubling in their implicit appeal to a doxastic involuntarism that becomes an escape hatch from the demands of subjective accountability. The implicit claim is that empirical inquiry is not only a neutral and impersonal process but also an inexorable one; it is compelling, even coercive, in what it turns up to the extent that a rational inquirer *cannot* withhold assent. He has no choice but to believe that *p,* however unpalatable the findings may be. The individualism and presumed disinterestedness of the paradigm reinforces this claim.

It is difficult, however, to believe in the coincidence of Rushton's discoveries; they could only be compelling in that strong sense if they could be shown to be purely coincidental—brute fact—something he came upon as he might bump into a wall. Talk about his impartial reading of the data assumes such hard facticity: the facticity of a blizzard or a hot sunny day. "Data" is the problematic term here, suggesting that facts presented themselves neutrally to Rushton's observing eye as though they were literally given, not sought or made. Yet it is not easy to conceive of Rushton's "data" in perfect independence from ongoing debates about race, sex, and class.

These difficulties are compounded when Rushton's research is juxtaposed against analogous projects in other places and times. In her book, *Sexual Science*.[31] Cynthia Russett documents the intellectual climate of the nineteenth century, when claims for racial and sexual equality were threatening upheavals in the social order. She notes that there was a concerted effort just at that time among scientists to produce studies that would demonstrate the "natural" sources of racial and sexual *in*equality. Given its aptness to the climate of the times, it is hard to believe that this research was "dislocated," prompted by a disinterested spirit of objective, neutral fact-finding. It is equally implausible, at a time when racial and sexual unrest is again threatening the complacency of the liberal dream—and meeting with strong conservative efforts to contain it—that it could be purely by coincidence that Rushton reaches the conclusion he does. Consider Rushton's contention that the brain has increased in size and the genitals have shrunk correspondingly over the course of human evolution; blacks have larger genitals, ergo. . . . Leaving elementary logical fallacies aside, it is impossible not to hear echoes of nineteenth-century medical science's "proofs" that excessive mental activity in women interferes with the proper functioning of the uterus; hence, permitting women to engage in higher intellectual activity impedes performance of their proper reproductive roles.

The connections Rushton draws between genital and brain size, and conformity to idealized patterns of good liberal democratic citizenship, trade upon analogous normative assumptions. The rhetoric of stable, conformist family structure as the site of controlled, utilitarian sexual expression is commonly enlisted to sort the "normal" from the "deviant" and to promote conservative conceptions of the self-image a society should have of itself.[32] The idea that the dissolution of "the family" (the nuclear, two-parent, patriarchal family) threatens the destruction of civilized society has been deployed to perpetuate white male privilege and compulsory heterosexuality, especially for women. It has been invoked to preserve homogeneous WASP values from disruption by "unruly" (not law-abiding, sexually promiscuous) elements. Rushton's contention that "naturally occurring" correlations can explain the demographic distribution of tendencies to unruliness leaves scant room for doubt about what he believes a society concerned about

its self-image should do: suppress unruliness. As Julian Henriques puts a similar point, by a neat reversal, the "black person becomes the cause of racism whereas the white person's prejudice is seen as a natural effect of the information-processing mechanisms."[33] The "facts" that Rushton produces are simply presented to the scholarly and lay communities so that they allegedly "speak for themselves" on two levels: both roughly as data and in more formal garb as research findings. What urgently demands analysis is the process by which these "facts" are inserted into a public arena that is prepared to receive them, with the result that inquiry stops right where it should begin.[34]

My point is that it is not enough just to be more rigorously empirical in adjudicating such controversial knowledge claims with the expectation that biases that may have infected the "context of discovery" will be eradicated in the purifying process of justification. Rather, the scope of epistemological investigation has to expand to merge with moral-political inquiry, acknowledging that "facts" are always infused with values and that both facts and values are open to ongoing critical debate. It would be necessary to demonstrate the innocence of descriptions (their derivation from pure data) and to show the perfect congruence of descriptions with "the described" in order to argue that descriptive theories have no normative force. Their assumed innocence licenses an evasion of the accountability that socially concerned communities have to demand of their producers of knowledge. Only the most starkly positivistic epistemology merged with the instrumental rationality it presupposes could presume that inquirers are accountable only to the evidence. Evidence is *selected,* not found, and selection procedures are open to scrutiny. Nor can critical analysis stop there, for the funding and institutions that enable inquirers to pursue certain projects and not others explicitly legitimize the work.[35] So the lines of accountability are long and interwoven; only a genealogy of their multiple strands can begin to unravel the issues.

Bailey–Cuomo: The
Feminist Philosophy
Reader

9. Feminist Epistemologies | Text

© The McGraw–Hill
Companies, 2008

193

What, then, should occur within epistemic communities to ensure that scientists and other knowers cannot conceal bias and prejudice or claim *a right not to know* about their background assumptions and the significance of their locations?

The crux of my argument is that the phenomenon of the disinterested inquirer is the exception rather than the rule; there are no dislocated truths, and some facts about the locations and interests at the source of inquiry are always pertinent to questions about freedom and accountability. Hence I am arguing, with Naomi Scheman, that

> Feminist epistemologists and philosophers of science [who] *along with others who have been the objects of knowledge-as-control* [have to] understand and . . . pose alternatives to the epistemology of modernity. As it has been central to this epistemology to guard its products from contamination by connection to the particularities of its producers, it must be central to the work of its critics and to those who would create genuine alternatives to remember those connections . . .[36]

There can be no doubt that research is—often imperceptibly—shaped by presuppositions and interests external to the inquiry itself, which cannot be filtered out by standard, objective, disinterested epistemological techniques.[37]

In seeking to explain what makes Rushton possible,[38] the point cannot be to exonerate him as a mere product of his circumstances and times. Rushton accepts grants and academic honors in his own name, speaks "for himself" in interviews with the press, and claims credit where credit is to be had. He upholds the validity of his findings. Moreover, he participates fully in the rhetoric of the autonomous, objective inquirer. Yet although Rushton is plainly accountable for the sources and motivations of his projects, he is not singly responsible. Such research is legitimized by the community and speaks in a discursive space that is available and prepared for it. So scrutinizing Rushton's "scientific" knowledge claims demands an examination of the moral and intellectual health of

a community that is infected by racial and sexual injustices at every level. Rushton may have had reasons to believe that his results would be welcome.

Equally central, then, to a feminist epistemological program of taking subjectivity into account are case-by-case analyses of the political and other structural circumstances that generate projects and lines of inquiry. Feminist critique—with critiques that center on other marginalizing structures—needs to act as an "experimental control" in epistemic practice so that every inquiry, assumption, and discovery is analyzed for its place in and implications for the prevailing sex/gender system, in its intersections with the systems that sustain racism, homophobia, and ethnocentrism.[39] The burden of proof falls upon inquirers who claim neutrality. In all "objective" inquiry, the positions and power relations of *gendered* and otherwise located subjectivity have to be submitted to piece-by-piece scrutiny that will vary according to the field of research. The task is intricate, because the subjectivity of the inquirer is always also implicated and has to be taken into account. Hence, the inquiry is at once critical and self-critical. But this is no monologic, self-sufficient enterprise. Conclusions are reached and immoderate subjective omissions and commissions become visible in dialogic processes among inquirers and—in social science—between inquirers and the subjects of their research.

It emerges from this analysis that although the ideal objectivity of the universal knower is neither possible nor desirable, a realistic commitment to achieving empirical adequacy that engages in situated analyses of the subjectivities of both the knower and (where appropriate) the known is both desirable and possible. This exercise in supposing that the places in the *S*-knows-that-*p* formula could be filled by asserting "Rushton knows that blacks are inferior" shows that simple, propositional knowledge claims that represent inquirers as purely neutral observers of unignorable data cannot be permitted to count as paradigms of knowledge. Objectivity *requires* taking subjectivity into account.

## 4. KNOWING SUBJECTS

Women—and other "others"—are *produced* as "objects of knowledge-as-control" by *S*-knows-that-*p* epistemologies and the philosophies of science/social science that they inform. When subjects become objects of knowledge, reliance upon simple observational paradigms has the consequence of assimilating those subjects to physical objects, reducing their subjectivity and specificity to interchangeable, observable features.

*S*-knows-that-*p* epistemologies take for granted that observational knowledge of everyday objects forms the basis from which all knowledge is constructed. Prima facie, this is a persuasive belief. Observations of childhood development (at least in materially advantaged, "normal" western families) suggest that simple observational truths are the first bits of knowledge an infant acquires in learning to recognize and manipulate everyday objects. Infants seem to be objective in this early knowing: they *come across* objects and learn to deal with them; apparently without preconceptions and without altering the properties of the objects. Objects ordinarily remain independent of a child's knowing; these same objects—cups, spoons, chairs, trees, and flowers—seem to be the simplest and surest things that every adult knows. They are *there* to be known and are reasonably constant through change. In the search for examples of what standard knowers know "for sure," such knowledge claims are obvious candidates. So it is not surprising that they have counted as paradigmatic.

I want to suggest, however, that when one considers how basic and crucial *knowing other people* is in the production of human subjectivity, paradigms and objectivity take on a different aspect.[40] If epistemologists require paradigms or other less formal exemplary knowledge claims, knowing other people in personal relationships is at least as worthy a contender as knowledge of everyday objects. Developmentally, learning what she or he can expect of other people is one of the first and most essential kinds of knowledge a child acquires. She or he learns to respond *cognitively* to the people who are a vital part of and provide access to her or his environment *long before* she or he can recognize the simplest physical objects. Other people are the point of origin of a child's entry into the material/physical environment both in providing or inhibiting access to that environment—in *making* it—and in fostering entry into the language with which children learn to name. Their initial induction into language generates a framework of presuppositions that prompts children, from the earliest stages, to construct their environments variously, according to the quality of their affective, intersubjective locations. Evidence about the effects of sensory and emotional deprivation on the development of cognitive agency shows that a child's capacity to make sense of the world (and the manner of engaging in that process) is intricately linked with her or his caregivers' construction of the environment.

Traditionally, theories of knowledge tend to be derived from the experiences of uniformly educated, articulate, epistemically "positioned" adults who introspect retrospectively to review what they must once have known most simply and clearly. Locke's *tabula rasa* is one model; Descartes's radical doubt is another. Yet this introspective process consistently bypasses the epistemic significance of early experiences with other people, with whom the relations of these philosophers must surely have been different from their relations to objects in their environment. As Seyla Benhabib wryly notes, it is a strange world from which this picture of knowledge is derived: a world in which "individuals are grown up before they have been born; in which boys are men before they have been children; a world where neither mother, nor sister, nor wife exist."[41] Whatever the historical variations in childraising practices, evidence implicit

Bailey–Cuomo: The
Feminist Philosophy
Reader

9. Feminist Epistemologies

Text

© The McGraw–Hill
Companies, 2008

195

in (similarly evolving) theories of knowledge points to a noteworthy constancy. In separated adulthood, the knowledge that enables a knower to give or withhold trust as a child—and hence to survive—is passed over as unworthy of philosophical notice. It is tempting to conclude that theorists of knowledge must either be childless or so disengaged from the rearing of children as to have minimal developmental awareness. Participators in childraising could not easily ignore the primacy of knowing and being known by other people in cognitive development, nor could they denigrate the role such knowledge plays throughout an epistemic history. In view of the fact that disengagement throughout a changing history and across a range of class and racial boundaries has been possible primarily for *men* in western societies, this aspect of the androcentricity of objectivist epistemologies is not surprising.

Knowing other people in relationships requires constant learning: how to be with them, respond to them, and act toward them. In this respect it contrasts markedly with the immediacy of common, sense-perceptual paradigms. In fact, if exemplary "bits" of knowledge were drawn from situations where people have to *learn* to know, rather than from taken-for-granted adult expectations, the complexity of knowing even the simplest things would not so readily be masked, and the fact that knowledge is *qualitatively* variable would be more readily apparent. Consider the strangeness of traveling in a country and culture where one has to suspend judgment about how to identify and deal with things like simple artifacts, flora and fauna, customs and cultural phenomena. These experiences remind epistemologists of how tentative the process of making everyday observations and judgments really is.

Knowledge of other people develops, operates, and is open to interpretation at various levels; it admits of degree in ways that knowing that a book is red does not. Such knowledge is not primarily propositional; I can know that Alice is clever and not *know* her very well at all in a "thicker" sense. Knowing "facts" (the standard

$S$-knows-that-$p$ substitutions) is part of such knowing, but the knowledge involved is more than and different from its propositional parts. Nor is this knowledge reducible to the simple observational knowledge of the traditional paradigms. The fact that it is acquired differently, interactively, and relationally differentiates it both as process and as product from standard propositional knowledge. Yet its status as knowledge disturbs the smooth surface of the paradigm's structure. The contrast between its multidimensional, multiperspectival character and the stark simplicity of standard paradigms requires philosophers to reexamine the practice of granting exemplary status to those paradigms. "Knowing how" and "knowing that" are implicated, but they do not begin to tell the whole story.

The contention that people are *knowable* may sit uneasily with psychoanalytic decenterings of conscious subjectivity and postmodern critiques of the unified subject of Enlightenment humanism. But I think this is a tension that has to be acknowledged and maintained. In practice, people often know one another well enough to make good decisions about who can be counted on and who cannot, who makes a good ally and who does not. Yet precisely because of the fluctuations and contradictions of subjectivity, this process is ongoing, communicative, and interpretive. It is never fixed or complete; any fixity claimed for "the self" will be a fixity in flux. Nonetheless, I argue that something must be fixed to "contain" the flux even enough to permit references to and ongoing relationships with "this person." Knowing people always occurs within the terms of this tension.

Problems about determining criteria for justifying claims to know another person—the utter availability of necessary and sufficient conditions, the complete inadequacy of $S$-knows-that-$p$ paradigms—must account for philosophical reluctance to count this as knowledge that bears epistemological investigation. Yet my suggestion that such knowledge is a model for a wide range of knowledge and is not merely inchoate and unmanageable recommends itself the more strongly in view of the extent to which cognitive practice is grounded upon such knowledge. I am thinking not just of everyday interactions with other people, but of the specialized knowledge—such as Rushton's—that claims institutional authority. Educational theory and practice, psychology, sociology, anthropology, law, some aspects of medicine and philosophy, politics, history, and economics all depend for their credibility upon knowing people. Hence it is all the more curious that observation-based knowledge of material objects and the methodology of the physical sciences hold such relatively unchallenged sway as the paradigm—and paragon—of intellectual achievement. The results of according continued veneration to observational paradigms are evident in the reductive approaches of behaviorist psychology. They are apparent in parochial impositions of meaning upon the practices of other cultures which is still characteristic of some areas of anthropology, and in the simple translation of present-day descriptions into past cultural contexts that characterizes some historical and archaeological practice. But feminist, hermeneutic, and postmodern critiques are slowly succeeding in requiring objectivist social scientists to reexamine their presuppositions and practices. In fact, it is methodological disputes within the social sciences—and the consequent unsettling of positivistic hegemony—that, according to Susan Hekman, have set the stage for the development of a productive, postmodern approach to epistemology for contemporary feminists.[42]

I am not proposing that knowing other people should become *the* new epistemological paradigm but rather that it has a strong claim to exemplary status in the epistemologies that feminist and other case-by-case analyses will produce. I am proposing further that if epistemologists require a model drawn from "scientific" inquiry, then a reconstructed, interpretive social science, liberated from positivistic constraints, will be a better resource than natural science—or physics—for knowledge as such.

Social science of whatever stripe is constrained by the factual-informational details that constrain all attempts to know people; physical, historical, biographical, environmental, social-structural, and other *facts* constitute its "objects" of study. These facts are available for objective analysis, yet they also lend themselves to varying degrees of interpretation and ideological construction. Social science often focuses upon meanings, upon purposeful and learned behavior, preferences, and intentions, with the aim of explaining what Sandra Harding calls "the origins, forms and prevalence of apparently irrational but culturewide patterns of human belief and action."[43] Such phenomena cannot be measured and quantified to provide results comparable to the results of a controlled physics experiment. Yet this constraint neither precludes social-scientific objectivity nor reclaims the methodology of physics as paradigmatic. Harding is right to maintain that "the totally reasonable exclusion of intentional and learned behavior from the subject matter of physics is a good reason to regard enquiry in physics as atypical of scientific knowledge-seeking."[44] I am arguing that it is equally atypical of everyday knowledge-seeking. Interpretations of intentional and learned behavior are indeed subjectively variable; taking subjectivity into account does not *entail* abandoning objectivity. Rabinow and Sullivan put the point well: "Discourse being about something, one must understand the world in order to interpret it . . . Human action and interpretation are subject to many *but not infinitely many* constructions."[45] When theorists acknowledge the oddity and peculiar insularity of physics-derived paradigms with their suppression of subjectivity, it is clear that their application to areas of inquiry in which subjectivities are the "objects" of study has to be contested.

The problem about claiming an exemplary role for personal-knowledge paradigms is to show how the kinds of knowledge integral to human relationships could work in situations where the object of knowledge is inanimate. The case has to be made by analogy and not by requiring knowers to convert from being objective observers to being friends with tables and chairs, chemicals, particles, cells, planets, rocks, trees, and insects. There are obvious points of disanalogy, not the least of which derives from the fact that chairs and plants and rocks cannot reciprocate in the ways that people can. There will be none of the mutual recognition and affirmation between observer and observed that there is between people. But Heisenberg's "uncertainty principle" suggests that not even physical objects are inert in and untouched by observational processes. If there is any validity to this suggestion, then it is not so easy to draw rigid lines separating responsive from unresponsive objects. Taking knowledge of other people as a model does not, *per impossibile,* require scientists to begin talking to their rocks and cells or to admit that the process is not working when the rocks fail to respond. It calls, rather, for a recognition that rocks, cells, and scientists are located in multiple relations to one another, all of which are open to analysis and critique. Singling out and privileging the asymmetrical observer–observed relation is but one possibility.

A more stubborn point of disanalogy may appear to attach to the belief that it is *possible* to know physical objects, whereas it is never possible really to know other people. But this apparent disanalogy appears to prevent the analogy from going through because of another feature of the core presupposition of empiricist-objectivist theories.

According to the standard paradigms, empirical observation can produce knowledge that is universally and uncontrovertibly established for all time. Whether or not such perfect knowledge has ever been achieved is an open question; a belief in its possibility guides and regulates mainstream epistemologies and theories of science. The presumption that knowing other people is difficult to the point of near impossibility is declared by contrast with those paradigms, whose realization may only be possible in contrived, attenuated instances. By *that* standard, knowing other people, however well, does look like as pale an approximation as it was for Descartes,

by contrast with the "clear and distinct ideas" he was otherwise able to achieve. The question, again, is why *that* standard, which governs so minuscule a part of the epistemic lives even of members of the privileged professional class and gender, should regulate legitimate uses of the label "knowledge."

If the empiricist-positivist standard were displaced by more complex analyses in which knowledge claims are provisional and approximate, knowing other people might not seem to be so different. Current upheavals in epistemology point to the productivity of hermeneutic, interpretive, literary methods of analysis and explanation in the social sciences. The skills these approaches require are not so different from the interpretive skills that human relationships require. The extent of their usefulness for the natural sciences is not yet clear. But one point of the challenge is to argue that natural-scientific enquiry has to be located differently, where it can be recognized as a sociopolitical-historical activity in which knowing who the scientist is can reveal important epistemological dimensions of her or his inquiry.

A recognition of the space that needs to be kept open for reinterpretation of the contextualizing that adequate knowledge requires becomes clearer in the light of the "personal" analogy. Though the analogy is not perfect, it is certainly no more preposterous to argue that people should try to know physical objects in the nuanced way that they know their friends than it is to argue that they should try to know people in the unsubtle way that they often claim to know physical objects.

Drawing upon such an interpretive approach across the epistemic terrain would guard against reductivism and rigidity. Knowing other people occurs in a persistent interplay between opacity and transparency, between attitudes and postures that elude a knower's grasp and patterns that are clear and relatively constant. Hence knowers are kept on their cognitive toes. In its need to accommodate change and growth, this knowledge contrasts further with traditional paradigms that deal, on the whole, with objects that can be treated as permanent. In knowing other people, a knower's subjectivity is implicated from its earliest developmental stages; in such knowing, her or his subjectivity is produced and reproduced. Analogous reconstructions often occur in the subjectivity of the person(s) she or he knows. Hence such knowledge works from a conception of subject–object relations different from that implicit in simple empirical paradigms. Claims to know a person are open to negotiation between knower and "known," where the "subject" and "object" positions are always, in principle, interchangeable. In the process, it is important to watch for discrepancies between a person's sense of her or his own subjectivity and a would-be knower's conception of how things are for her or him; neither the self-conception nor the knower-conception can claim absolute authority, because the limits of self-consciousness constrain the process as closely as the interiority of mental processes and experiential constructs and their unavailability to observation.

That an agent's subjectivity is so clearly implicated may create the impression that this knowledge is, indeed, purely subjective. But such a conclusion would be unwarranted. There *are* facts that have to be respected: facts that constitute "the person one is" at any historical moment.[46] Only certain stories can accurately be told; others simply cannot. "External" facts are obvious constraints: facts about age, sex, place and date of birth, height, weight, and hair color—the information that appears on a passport. They would count as objective even on a fairly traditional understanding of the term. Other information is reasonably objective as well: facts about marriage or divorce, childbirth, siblings, skills, education, employment, abode, and travel. But the intriguing point about knowing people—and another reason why it is epistemologically instructive—is that even knowing all the *facts* about someone does not count as knowing her as the person she is. No more can knowing all the facts about oneself, past and present, guarantee self-knowledge.

Yet none of these problems raise doubts that there is such a creature as the person I am or the person anyone else is now. Nor do they indicate the impossibility of knowing other people. If the limitations of these accumulated factual claims were taken seriously with respect to empirical knowledge more generally, the limitations of an epistemology built from *S*-knows-that-*p* claims would be more clearly apparent.

That perfect, objective knowledge of other people is not possible gives no support to a contention *either* that "other minds" are radically unknowable *or* that people's claims to know one another never merit the label "knowledge." Residual assumptions to the effect that people are opaque to one another may explain why this knowledge has had minimal epistemological attention. Knowledge, as the tradition defines it, is *of* objects; only by assimilating people to objects can one hope to know them. This long-standing assumption is challenged by my claims that knowing other people is an exemplary kind of knowing and that subjectivity has always to be taken into account in making and assessing knowledge claims of any complexity.

## 5. RELATIVISM AFTER ALL?

The project I am proposing, then, requires a new *geography* of the epistemic terrain: one that is no longer primarily a physical geography, but a population geography that develops qualitative analyses of subjective positions and identities and the sociopolitical structures that produce them. Because differing social positions generate variable constructions of reality and afford different perspectives on the world, the revisionary stages of this project will consist of case-by-case analyses of the knowledge produced in specific social positions. These analyses derive from a recognition that knowers are always *somewhere*— and at once limited and enabled by the specificities of their locations.[47] It is an interpretive project, alert to the possibility of finding generalities and commonalities within particulars and

Bailey–Cuomo: The
Feminist Philosophy
Reader

9. Feminist Epistemologies | Text

© The McGraw–Hill
Companies, 2008

199

hence of the explanatory potential that opens up when such commonalities can be delineated. But it is wary of the reductivism that results when commonalities are presupposed or forced. It has no ultimate foundation, but neither does it float free, because it is grounded in experiences and practices, in the efficacy of dialogic negotiation and of action.

All of this having been said, my argument in this essay points to the conclusion that necessary and sufficient conditions for establishing empirical knowledge claims cannot be found, at least where experientially significant knowledge is at issue. Hence it poses the question whether feminist epistemologists must, after all, "come out" as relativists. In view of what I have been arguing, the answer to that question will have to be a qualified "yes." Yet the relativism that my argument generates is sufficiently nuanced and sophisticated to escape the scorn—and the anxiety—that "relativism, after all" usually occasions. To begin with, it refuses to occupy the negative side of the traditional absolutism/relativism dichotomy. It is at once realist, rational, and significantly objective; hence it is not forced to define itself within or against the oppositions between realism and relativism, rationality and relativism, or objectivism and relativism.[48] Moreover, it takes as its starting point a recognition that the "positive" sides of these dichotomies have been caricatured to affirm a certainty that was never rightfully theirs.

The opponents of relativism have been so hostile, so thoroughly scornful in their dismissals, that it is no wonder that feminists, well aware of the folk-historical identification of women with the forces of unreason, should resist the very thought that the logic of feminist emancipatory analyses points in that direction.[49] Feminists know, if they know anything at all, that they have to develop the best possible explanations—the "truest" explanations—of how things are if they are to intervene effectively in social structures and institutions. The intransigence of material circumstances constantly reminds them

that their world-making possibilities are neither unconstrained nor infinite; they have to be able to produce accurate, transformative analyses of things as they *are*. In fact, many feminists are vehement in their resistance to relativism precisely because they suspect—not without reason—that only the supremely powerful and privileged, the self-proclaimed sons of God, could believe that they can make the world up as they will and practice that supreme tolerance in whose terms all possible constructions of reality are equally worthy. Their fears are persuasive. Yet even at the risk of speaking within the oppositional mode, it is worth thinking seriously about the alternative. For there is no doubt that only the supremely powerful and privileged could believe, in the face of all the evidence to the contrary, that there is only one true view, and it is theirs; that they alone have the resources to establish universal, incontrovertible, and absolute Truth. Donna Haraway aptly notes that: "Relativism is a way of being nowhere and claiming to be everywhere"[50] but absolutism is a way of being everywhere while pretending to be nowhere—and neither one, in its starkest articulation, will do. For this reason alone, it is clear that the absolutism/relativism dichotomy needs to be displaced because it does not, as a true dichotomy must, use up all of the alternatives.[51]

The position I am advocating is one for which knowledge is always *relative to* (i.e., a perspective *on,* a standpoint *in*) specifiable circumstances. Hence it is constrained by a realist, empiricist commitment according to which getting those circumstances right is vital to effective action. It may appear to be a question-begging position, for it does assume that the circumstances can be known, and it relies heavily upon pragmatic criteria to make good that assumption. It can usually avoid regress, for although the circumstances in question may have to be specified *relative to* other circumstances, prejudgments, and theories, it is never (as with Neurath's raft) necessary to take away all of the pieces—all of the props—at once. Inquiry grows out of and turns back to practice, to action; inquirers are always *in media res,* and the *res* are both identifiable and constitutive of perspectives and possibilities for action. Practice will show, not once and for all but case by case, whether conclusions are reasonable and workable. Hence the position at once allows for the development of practical projects and for their corrigibility.

This "mitigated relativism" has a skeptical component: a consequence many feminists will resist even more vigorously than they will resist my claim for relativism. Western philosophy is still in thrall to an Enlightenment legacy that equates skepticism with nihilism: the belief that if no absolute foundations—no necessary and sufficient conditions—can be established, then there can be no knowledge.[52] Nothing is any more reasonable or rational than anything else; there is nothing to believe in. This is the skepticism that necessary and sufficient conditions are meant to forestall.

But there are other skepticisms which are resourceful, not defeatist. The ancient skepticisms of Pyrrho and Sextus Empiricus were declarations not of nihilism but of the impossibility of certainty, of the need to withhold definitive judgment. They advocated continual searching in order to prevent error by suspending judgment. They valued a readiness to reconsider and warned against hasty conclusions. These were skepticisms about the possibility of definitive knowledge but not about the existence of a (knowable?) reality. For Pyrrhonists, skepticism was a moral stance that was meant to ensure the inner quietude (*ataraxia*) that was essential to happiness.[53]

My suggestion that feminist epistemologists can find a resource in such skepticisms cannot be pushed to the point of urging that they take on the whole package. There is no question that the quietude of *ataraxia* could be the achievement that feminists are after. Nor could they take on a skepticism that would immobilize them by negating all possibilities for action: a quietism born of a theorized incapacity to choose or take a

stand. So the skepticism that flavors the position I am advocating is better characterized as a common-sense, practical skepticism of everyday life than as a technical, philosophers' skepticism. It resembles the "healthy skepticism" that parents teach their children about media advertising and the skepticism that marks cautiously informed attitudes to politicians' promises.

Above all, feminists cannot opt for a skepticism that would make it impossible to know that certain practices and institutions are *wrong* and likely to remain so. The political ineffectiveness of universal tolerance no longer needs demonstrating: sexism is only the most obvious example of an undoubted intolerable. (Seyla Benhabib notes that Rorty's "admirable demand to 'let a hundred flowers bloom' is motivated by a desire to depoliticize philosophy."[54]) So even the skepticism that I am advocating is problematic in the sense that it has to be carefully measured and articulated if it is not to amount merely to "an apology for the existing order."[55] Its heuristic, productive dimensions are best captured by Denise Riley's observation that "an active skepticism about the integrity of the sacred category 'women' would be no merely philosophical doubt to be stifled in the name of effective political action in the world. On the contrary, it would be a condition *for* the latter."[56] It is in "making strange," loosening the hold of taken-for-granted values, ideals, categories, and theories, that skepticism demonstrates its promise.

Michel Foucault is one of the most articulate late twentieth-century successors of the ancient skeptics. A skeptic in his refusal of dogmatic unities, essences, and labels, Foucault examines changing practices of knowledge rather than taking the standard epistemological route of assuming a unified rationality or science. He eschews totalizing, universalist assumptions in his search for what John Rajchman calls the "invention of specific forms of experience which are taken up and transformed again and again."[57] His is a skepticism about the certainty and stability of systems of representation. Like the

Bailey–Cuomo: The
Feminist Philosophy
Reader

9. Feminist Epistemologies | Text

© The McGraw–Hill
Companies, 2008

201

ancient skeptics, Foucault can be cast as a realist. He never doubts that there *are* things, institutions, and practices whose genealogies and archaeologies can be written. His position recommends itself for the freedom that its skeptical component offers. Hence he claims

> All my analyses are against the idea of universal necessities in human existence. They show the arbitrariness of institutions and show which space of freedom we can still enjoy and how many changes can still be made.[58]

Yet this is by no means an absolute freedom, for Foucault also observes

> My point is not that everything is bad, but that everything is dangerous, which is not exactly the same as bad. If everything is dangerous, then we always have something to do. So my position leads not to apathy but to a hyper- and pessimistic activism. . . . [T]he ethico-political choice we have to make . . . is to determine which is the main danger.[59]

One of the most urgent tasks that Foucault has left undone is that of showing how we can *know* what is dangerous.

There are many tensions within the strands that my skeptical-relativist recommendations try to weave together. For these I do not apologize. At this critical juncture in the articulation of emancipatory epistemological projects it is impossible to have all of the answers, to resolve all of the tensions and paradoxes. I have exposed some ways in which *S*-knows-that-*p* epistemologies are dangerous and have proposed one route toward facing and disarming those dangers: taking subjectivity into account. The solutions that route affords and the further dangers it reveals will indicate the directions that the next stages of this enquiry must take.[60]

## NOTES

1. I allude here to the title of Thomas Nagel's book, *A View From Nowhere* (Oxford: Oxford University Press, 1986).
2. I owe the phrase *surrogate knower* to Naomi Scheman, which she coined in her paper "Descartes and Gender," presented to the conference "Reason, Gender, and the Moderns," University of Toronto, February 1990. I draw on this idea to make a set of points rather different from these in my "Who Cares? The Poverty of Objectivism for Moral Epistemology," in Alan Megill, ed., *Rethinking Objectivity Annals of Scholarship* 9 (1992).
3. For an account of the central tenets of logical positivism, a representative selection of articles, and an extensive bibliography, see A. J. Ayer, ed., *Logical Positivism* (New York: The Free Press, 1959).
4. Karl Popper, *Objective Knowledge* (Oxford: Clarendon Press, 1972), 108; emphasis in original.
5. Mary Hesse advisedly notes that philosophers of science would now more readily assert than they would have done in the heyday of positivism that facts in both the natural and social sciences are "value-laden." [See Mary Hesse, *Revolutions and Reconstructions in the Philosophy of Science* (Bloomington: Indiana University Press, 1980), 172–73.] I am claiming, however, that everyday conceptions of scientific authority are still significantly informed by a residual positivistic faith.
6. For classic statements of this aspect of the positivistic program see, for example, Rudolf Carnap, "Psychology in Physical Language"; and Otto Neurath, "Sociology and Physicalism," in Ayer, ed., *Logical Positivism*.
7. I discuss such responsibilities in my *Epistemic Responsibility* (Hanover, N.H.: University Press of New England, 1987).
8. See, for example, Joan Wallach Scott, "Is Gender a Useful Category of Historical Analysis?" in her book *Gender and the Politics of History* (New York: Columbia University Press, 1989).
9. Paul Moser, for example, in reviewing my *Epistemic Responsibility*, takes me to task for not announcing "the necessary and sufficient conditions for one's being epistemically responsible." He argues that even if, as I claim throughout the book, epistemic responsibility does not lend itself to analysis in those terms, "we could still provide necessary and sufficient conditions for the wide range of typical instances, and then

*Chapter 9 / Feminist Epistemologies*

handle the wayward cases independently" [Paul Moser, review of *Epistemic Responsibility,* in *Philosophical Books* 29 (1988): 154–56]. Yet it is precisely their "typicality" that I contest. Moser's review is a salient example of the tendency of dominant epistemologies to claim as their own even those positions that reject their central premises.

10. See p. 1 of this essay for a formulation of this thesis.

11. These aims are continuous with some of the aims of recent projects to naturalize epistemology by drawing on the resources of cognitive psychology. See especially W. V. Quine, "Epistemology Naturalized," in *Ontological Relativity and Other Essays* (New York: Columbia University Press, 1969), Hilary Kornblith, ed. *Naturalizing Epistemology* (Cambridge, Mass.: MIT Press, 1985); and his paper "The Naturalistic Project in Epistemology: A Progress Report," presented to the American Philosophical Association, Los Angeles, April 1990; and Alvin I. Goldman, *Epistemology and Cognition* (Cambridge, Mass.: Harvard University Press, 1986). Feminist epistemologists who are developing this line of inquiry are Jane Duran, *Toward a Feminist Epistemology* (Savage, MD: Rowman and Littlefield, 1991); and Lynn Hankinson Nelson, *Who Knows: From Quine to a Feminist Empiricism* (Philadelphia: Temple University Press, 1990). Feminists who find a resource in this work have to contend with the fact that the cognitive psychology that informs it presupposes a constancy in "human nature," exemplified in "representative selves" who have commonly been white, male, and middle class. They have also to remember the extent to which appeals to "nature" have oppressed women and other marginal groups.

12. For an extensive bibliography of such critiques up to 1989, see Alison Wylie, Kathleen Okruhlik, Sandra Morton, and Leslie Thielen-Wilson, "Philosophical Feminism: A Bibliographic Guide to Critiques of Science," *Resources for Feminist Research/Documentation sur la Recherche Feministe* 19, 2 (June 1990): 2–36.

13. For an analysis of the androcentricity—the 'masculinity' of these ideals—and their 'feminine' exclusions in theories of knowledge

see Genevieve Lloyd, *The Man of Reason* (Minneapolis: University of Minnesota Press, 1984); and Susan Bordo, *The Flight to Objectivity* (Albany: State University of New York Press, 1987). For discussions of the scientific context, see Evelyn Fox Keller, *Reflections on Gender and Science* (New Haven: Yale University Press, 1985); Sandra Harding, *The Science Question in Feminism* (Ithaca: Cornell University Press, 1986); and Nancy Tuana, ed., *Feminism and Science* (Bloomington: Indiana University Press, 1989).

14. Richard Foley, *The Theory of Epistemic Rationality* (Cambridge, Mass.: Harvard University Press, 1987), 48.

15. Ibid., 114.

16. Ibid., 140.

17. Ibid., 54.

18. I have singled out Foley's book because it is such a good example of the issues I am addressing. But he is by no means atypical. Space does not permit a catalogue of similar positions, but Lynn Hankinson Nelson notes that "Quine apparently assumes that at a given time "we" will agree about the question worth asking and the standards by which potential answers are to be judged, so he does not consider social arrangements as epistemological factors" (*Who Knows,* 170). Quine assumes, further, that "in the relevant community . . . we will all . . . see the same thing" (p. 184).

19. Here I am thinking of Richard Rorty, *Philosophy and the Mirror of Nature,* (Princeton: Princeton University Press, 1979); and *Consequences of Pragmatism* (Minneapolis: University of Minnesota Press, 1982).

20. *Philosophy and the Mirror of Nature,* 373.

21. Richard Rorty, "Solidarity or Objectivity?" in John Rajchman and Cornel West, eds., *Post-Analytic Philosophy* (New York: Columbia University Press, 1985), 7; emphasis added.

22. Ibid., 11.

23. Ibid., 15.

24. Nancy Fraser, "Solidarity or Singularity? Richard Rorty between Romanticism and Technocracy," in Nancy Fraser, *Unruly Practices: Power, Discourse and Gender in Contemporary Social Theory* (Minneapolis: University of Minnesota Press, 1989), 104.

Bailey–Cuomo: The
Feminist Philosophy
Reader

9. Feminist Epistemologies

Text

© The McGraw–Hill
Companies, 2008

203

25. Rorty, "Solidarity or Objectivity?," 5.

26. I borrow the idea, if not the detail, of the potential of case-by-case analysis from Roger A. Shiner, "From Epistemology to Romance Via Wisdom," in Ilham Dilman, ed., *Philosophy and Life: Essays on John Wisdom* (The Hague: Martinus Nijhoff, 1984), 291–314.

27. See Antonio Gramsci, *Selections from the Prison Notebooks,* trans. and ed. Quintin Hoare and Geoffrey Nowell Smith (New York: International Publishers, 1971).

28. Rudy Platiel and Stephen Strauss, *The Globe and Mail,* 4 February 1989. I cite the newspaper report because the media produce the public impact that concerns me here. I discuss neither the quality of Rushton's research practice nor the questions his theories and pedagogical practice pose about academic freedom. My concern is with how structures of knowledge, power, and prejudice grant him an epistemic place.

29. Commenting on the psychology of occupational assessment, Wendy Hollway observes: "That psychology is a science and that psychological assessment is therefore objective is a belief which continues to be fostered in organizations." She further notes: "The legacy of psychology as science is the belief that the individual can be understood through measurement" [Wendy Hollway, "Fitting work: psychological assessment in organizations," in Julian Henriques, Wendy Hollway, Cathy Urwin, Couze Venn, and Valerie Walkerdine, *Changing the Subject: Psychology, social regulation and subjectivity* (London: Methuen, 1984), 35, 55].

30. The phrase is Richard Schmitt's, from "Murderous Objectivity: Reflections on Marxism and the Holocaust," in Roger S. Gottlieb, ed., *Thinking the Unthinkable: Meanings of the Holocaust* (New York: Paulist Press, 1990), 71. I am grateful to Richard Schmitt for helping me to think about the issues I discuss in this section.

31. Cynthia Eagle Russett, *Sexual Science: The Victorian Construction of Womanhood* (Cambridge, Mass.: Harvard University Press, 1989). In this connection, see also Lynda Birke, *Women, Feminism, and Biology* (Brighton: Harvester Press, 1986); and Janet Sayers, *Biological Politics* (London: Tavistock Publications, 1982).

32. The best-known contemporary discussion of utilitarian, controlled sexuality is Michel Foucault, *The History of Sexuality Volume I: An Introduction,* trans. Robert Hurley (New York: Vintage Books, 1980). In Foucault's analysis, sexuality is utilitarian both in reproducing the population and in cementing the family bond.

33. Julian Henriques, "Social psychology and the politics of racism," in Henriques et al., *Changing the Subject,* 74.

34. Clifford Geertz comments: "It is not . . . the validity of the sciences, real or would-be, that is at issue. What concerns me, and should concern us all, are the axes that, with an increasing determination bordering on the evangelical, are being busily ground with their assistance" ["Anti Anti-Relativism," in Michael Krausz, ed., *Relativism: Interpretation and Confrontation* (Notre Dame: University of Notre Dame Press, 1989), 20].

35. Philippe Rushton has received funding from the Social Sciences and Humanities Research Council of Canada and the Guggenheim Foundation in the USA, agencies whose status in the North American intellectual community confers authority and credibility. He has also received funding from the Pioneer Fund, an organization with explicit white supremacist commitments.

36. Naomi Scheman, "Commentary," in the Symposium on Sandra Harding's 'The Method Question' *APA Feminism and Philosophy Newsletter* 88.3 (1989): 42.

37. Helen Longino observes: ". . . How one determines evidential relevance, why one takes some state of affairs as evidence for one hypothesis rather than for another, depends on one's other beliefs, which we can call background beliefs or assumptions" (p. 43). And "When, for instance, background assumptions are shared by all members of a community, they acquire an invisibility that renders them unavailable for criticism" (p. 80). In *Science as Social Knowledge: Values and Objectivity in Scientific Inquiry* (Princeton: Princeton University Press, 1990).

38. Here I am borrowing a turn of phrase from Michel Foucault, when he writes in quite a different context: "And it was this network that made possible the individuals we term Hobbes, Berkeley,

Hume, or Condillac" [Michel Foucault, *The Order of Things: An Archaeology of the Human Sciences* (New York: Random House, 1971), 63].

39. I owe this point to the Biology and Gender Study Group, in "The Importance of Feminist Critique for Contemporary Cell Biology," in Nancy Tuana, ed., *Feminism and Science* (Bloomington: Indiana University Press, 1989), 173.

40. The argument about the primacy of knowing other people is central to the position I develop in my *What Can She Know? Feminist Theory and the Construction of Knowledge* (Ithaca: Cornell University Press, 1991). Portions of this section of this essay are drawn, with modifications, from the book.

41. Seyla Benhabib, "The Generalized and the Concrete Other," in Seyla Benhabib and Drucilla Cornell, eds., *Feminism As Critique* (Minneapolis: University of Minnesota Press, 1987), 85.

42. See Susan Hekman, *Gender and Knowledge: Elements of a Postmodern Feminism* (Boston: Northeastern University Press, 1990), especially p. 3. For an introduction to these disputes, see Paul Rabinow and William M. Sullivan, eds., *Interpretive Social Science: A Second Look* (Berkeley: University of California Press, 1987).

43. Sandra Harding, *The Science Question in Feminism.* (Ithaca: Cornell University Press, 1986), 47. Harding contends that "a critical and self-reflective social science should be the model for all science, and . . . if there are any special requirements for adequate explanations in physics, they are just that—special" (Ibid., 44).

44. Ibid., 46.

45. Introduction, "The Interpretive Turn," in Rabinow and Sullivan, *Interpretive Social Science,* 13; emphasis added.

46. The phrase is Elizabeth V. Spelman's, in "On Treating Persons as Persons," *Ethics* 88 (1978): 151.

47. Here I borrow a phrase from Susan Bordo, "Feminism, Postmodernism, and Gender-Scepticism," in Linda Nicholson, ed., *Feminism/Postmodernism* (New York: Routledge, 1990), 145.

48. I allude here to three now-classic treatments of the relativism question: Anne Seller, "Realism versus Relativism: Toward a Politically Adequate Epistemology," in Morwenna Griffiths and Margaret Whitford, eds., *Feminist Perspectives in Philosophy* (Bloomington: Indiana University Press, 1988); Martin Hollis and Steven Lukes, eds., *Rationality and Relativism* (Cambridge, Mass.: MIT Press, 1982), and Richard Bernstein, *Beyond Objectivism and Relativism* (Philadelphia: University of Pennsylvania Press, 1983).

49. Sandra Harding resists endorsing relativism even in her discussions of standpoint and postmodern epistemologies. In a recent piece she introduces the neologism "interpretationism" as a solution, noting that "relativism is a consequence, but not always the intent, of interpretationism." (See her "Feminism, Science, and the Anti-Enlightenment Critiques," in Linda Nicholson, ed., *Feminism/Postmodernism,* 102, n. 5.) By contrast, I am uring the value of endorsing a reconstructed relativism, shorn of its enfeebling implications.

50. Donna Haraway, "Situated Knowledges: The Science Question in Feminism and the Privilege of Partial Perspective," *Feminist Studies* 14, 3 (Fall 1988).

51. See Nancy Jay, "Gender and Dichotomy," *Feminist Studies* 7 (1981) for a discussion of the exclusiveness of dichotomies.

52. Peter Unger, in *Ignorance: A Case for Skepticism* (Oxford: Clarendon Press, 1975), argues that because no knowledge claim can meet the exacting standards of formulation in absolute terms, there is only conjecture, opinion, and fantasy. People are doomed to ignorance and should simply avow their skepticism.

53. In thinking about Pyrrhonian skepticism I am indebted to David R. Hiley, "The Deep Challenge of Pyrrhonian Skepticism," *Journal of the History of Philosophy* 25, 2 (April 1987): 185–213.

54. Seyla Benhabib, "Epistemologies of Postmodernism: A Rejoinder to Jean-Francois Lyotard," in Linda Nicholson, ed., *Feminism/Postmodernism,* 124.

55. The phrase is Hiley's, p. 213.

56. Denise Riley, *"Am I That Name?" Feminism and the Category of Women in History* (Minneapolis: University of Minnesota Press, 1988), 113.

57. John Rajchman, *Michel Foucault: The Freedom of Philosophy* (New York: Columbia University Press, 1985), 3.

58. Rux Martin, "Truth, Power, Self: An Interview with Michel Foucault, October 25, 1982," in Luther H. Martin, Huck Gutman and Patrick H.

Bailey–Cuomo: The
Feminist Philosophy
Reader

9. Feminist Epistemologies | Text

© The McGraw–Hill
Companies, 2008

205

Hutton, eds., *Technologies of the Self: A Seminar
with Michel Foucault* (Amherst: University of
Massachusetts Press, 1988), 11.

59. Michel Foucault, "On the Genealogy of Ethics:
An Overview of Work in Progress." After-
word, in Hubert L. Dreyfus and Paul Rabinow,
*Michel Foucault: Beyond Structuralism and
Hermeneutics,* 2nd ed. (Chicago: University of
Chicago Press, 1983), 231.

60. Earlier versions of this paper were presented at
the American Philosophical Association conference at Los Angeles and to the Departments of
Philosophy at McMaster University and McGill
University. I am grateful to participants in those
discussions—especially to Susan Dwyer, Hilary
Kornblith, and Doug Odegard—for their comments and to Linda Alcoff and Libby Potter for
their valuable editorial suggestions.

# "STRONG OBJECTIVITY" AND SOCIALLY SITUATED KNOWLEDGE

### Sandra Harding

I argued that a feminist standpoint theory can direct the production of less partial and less distorted
beliefs. This kind of scientific process will not
merely acknowledge the social-situatedness—the
historicity—of the very best beliefs any culture
has arrived at or could in principle "discover" but
will use this fact as a resource for generating those
beliefs.[1] Nevertheless, it still might be thought
that this association of objectivity with socially
situated knowledge is an impossible combination.
Has feminist standpoint theory really abandoned
objectivity and embraced relativism? Or, alternatively, has it remained too firmly entrenched in a
destructive objectivism that increasingly is criticized from many quarters?

## THE DECLINING STATUS OF "OBJECTIVISM"

Scientists and science theorists working in many
different disciplinary and policy projects have

objected to the conventional notion of a value-
free, impartial, dispassionate objectivity that is
supposed to guide scientific research and without which, according to conventional thought
one cannot separate justified belief from mere
opinion, or real knowledge from mere claims to
knowledge. From the perspective of this conventional notion of objectivity—sometimes referred
to as "objectivism"—it has appeared that if one
gives up this concept, the only alternative is not
just a cultural relativism (the sociological assertion that what is thought to be a reasonable claim
in one society or subculture is not thought to be
so in another) but, worse, a judgmental or epistemological relativism that denies the possibility
of any reasonable standards for adjudicating between competing claims. Some fear that to give
up the possibility of one universally and eternally
valid standard of judgment is perhaps even to be
left with no way to argue rationally against the
possibility that *each person's* judgment about the
regularities of nature and their underlying causal
tendencies must be regarded as equally valid. The
reduction of the critic's position to such an absurdity provides a powerful incentive to question no
further the conventional idea that objectivity requires value-neutrality. From the perspective of
objectivism, judgmental relativism appears to be
the only alternative.

Insistence on this division of epistemological
stances between those that firmly support value-
free objectivity and those that support judgmental

---

[1] See Donna Haraway, "Situated Knowledges: *The Science
Question in Feminism* and the Privilege of Partial Perspective," *Feminist Studies* 14:3 (1988).

*Chapter 9 / Feminist Epistemologies*

relativism—a dichotomy that unfortunately has gained the consent of many critics of objectivism as well as its defenders—has succeeded in making value-free objectivity look much more attractive to natural and social scientists than it should. It also makes judgmental relativism appear far more progressive than it is. Some critics of the conventional notion of objectivity have openly welcomed judgmental relativism.[2] Others have been willing to tolerate it as the cost they think they must pay for admitting the practical ineffectualness, the proliferation of confusing conceptual contradictions, and the political regressiveness that follow from trying to achieve an objectivity that has been defined in terms of value-neutrality. But even if embracing judgmental relativism could make sense in anthropology and other social sciences, it appears absurd as an epistemological stance in physics or biology. What would it mean to assert that no reasonable standards can or could in principle be found for adjudicating between one culture's claim that the earth is flat and another culture's claim that the earth is round?

The literature on these topics from the 1970s and 1980s alone is huge and located in many disciplines. Prior to the 1960s the issue was primarily one of ethical and cultural absolutism versus relativism. It was the concern primarily of philosophers and anthropologists and was considered relevant only to the social sciences, not the natural sciences. But since then, the recognition has emerged that cognitive, scientific, and epistemic absolutism are both implicated in ethical and cultural issues and are also independently problematic. One incentive to the expansion was Thomas Kuhn's account of how the natural sciences have developed in response to what scientists have found "interesting," together with the subsequent post-Kuhnian philosophy and social studies of the natural sciences.[3] Another has been the widely recognized failure of the social

sciences to ground themselves in methods and theoretical commitments that can share in the scientificity of the natural sciences. Paradoxically, the more "scientific" social research becomes, the less objective it becomes.[4]

Further incentives have been such political tendencies as the U.S. civil rights movement, the rise of the women's movement, the decentering of the West and criticisms of Eurocentrism in international circles, and the increasing prominence within U.S. political and intellectual life of the voices of women and of African Americans and other people of Third World descent. From these perspectives, it appears increasingly arrogant for defenders of the West's intellectual traditions to continue to dismiss the scientific and epistemological stances of Others as caused mainly by biological inferiority, ignorance, underdevelopment, primitiveness, and the like. On the other hand, although diversity, pluralism, relativism, and difference have their valuable political and intellectual uses, embracing them resolves the political-scientific-epistemological conflict to almost no one's satisfaction.

I make no attempt here to summarize the arguments of these numerous and diverse writings.[5]

---

[2] See, e.g., David Bloor, *Knowledge and Social Imagery* (London: Routledge & Kegan Paul, 1977); and many of the papers in *Knowledge and Reflexivity,* ed. Steve Woolgar (Beverly Hills, Calif.: Sage, 1988).

[3] Thomas Kuhn, *The Structure of Scientific Revolutions* (Chicago: University of Chicago Press, 1962).

[4] This is an important theme in Richard Bernstein, *Beyond Objectivism and Relativism* (Philadelphia: University of Pennsylvania Press, 1983). Similar doubts about the ability of legal notions of objectivity to advance justice appear in many of the essays in "Women in Legal Education: Pedagogy, Law, Theory, and Practice," *Journal of Legal Education* 38 (1988), special issue, ed. Carrie Menkel-Meadow, Martha Minow, and David Vernon.

[5] Discussions on one or more of these focuses can be found in Martin Hollis and Steven Lukes, eds., *Rationality and Relativism* (Cambridge, Mass: Harvard University Press, 1982); Michael Krausz and Jack Meiland, eds., *Relativism: Cognitive and Moral* (Notre Dame, Ind.: University of Notre Dame Press, 1982); Richard Bernstein, *Beyond Objectivism;* and S. P. Mohanty, "Us and Them: On the Philosophical Bases of Political Criticism," *Yale Journal of Criticism* 2:2 (1989). A good brief bibliographic essay on the recent philosophy of science within and against which the particular discussion of this essay is located is Steve Fuller, "The Philosophy of Science since Kuhn: Readings on the Revolution That Has Yet to Come," *Choice,* December 1989. For more extended studies that are not incompatible with my arguments here, see Steve Fuller, *Social Epistemology* (Bloomington: Indiana University Press, 1988); and Joseph Rouse, *Knowledge and Power: Toward a Political Philosophy of Science* (Ithaca: Cornell University Press, 1987).

Bailey–Cuomo: The
Feminist Philosophy
Reader

9. Feminist Epistemologies | Text

© The McGraw–Hill
Companies, 2008

207

My concern is more narrowly focused: to state as clearly as possible how issues of objectivity and relativism appear from the perspective of a feminist standpoint theory.

Feminist critics of science and the standpoint theorists especially have been interpreted as supporting either an excessive commitment to value-free objectivity or, alternatively, the abandonment of objectivity in favor of relativism. Because there are clear commitments within feminism to tell less partial and distorted stories about women, men, nature, and social relations, some critics have assumed that feminism must be committed to value-neutral objectivity. Like other feminists, however, the standpoint theorists have also criticized conventional sciences for their arrogance in assuming that they could tell one true story about a world that is out there, ready-made for their reporting, without listening to women's accounts or being aware that accounts of nature and social relations have been constructed within men's control of gender relations. Moreover, feminist thought and politics as a whole are continually revising the ways they bring women's voices and the perspectives from women's lives to knowledge-seeking, and they are full of conflicts between the claims made by different groups of feminists. How could feminists in good conscience do anything but abandon any agenda to legitimate one over another of these perspectives? Many feminists in literature, the arts, and the humanities are even more resistant than those in the natural and social sciences to claims that feminist images or representations of the world hold any special epistemological or scientific status. Such policing of thought is exactly what they have objected to in criticizing the authority of their disciplinary canons on the grounds that such authority has had the effect of stifling the voices of marginalized groups. In ignoring these views, feminist epistemologists who are concerned with natural or social science agendas appear to support an epistemological divide between the sciences and humanities, a divide that feminism has elsewhere criticized.

The arguments of this essay move away from the fruitless and depressing choice between value-neutral objectivity and judgmental relativism. This essay draws on some assumptions underlying the analyses of earlier chapters in order to argue that the conventional notion of objectivity against which feminist criticisms have been raised should be regarded as excessively weak. A feminist standpoint epistemology requires strengthened standards of objectivity. The standpoint epistemologies call for recognition of a historical or sociological or cultural relativism—but not for a judgmental or epistemological relativism. They call for the acknowledgment that all human beliefs—including our best scientific beliefs—are socially situated, but they also require a critical evaluation to determine which social situations tend to generate the most objective knowledge claims. They require, as judgmental relativism does not, a scientific account of the relationships between historically located belief and maximally objective belief. So they demand what I shall call *strong objectivity* in contrast to the weak objectivity of objectivism and its mirror-linked twin, judgmental relativism. This may appear to be circular reasoning—to call for scientifically examining the social location of scientific claims—but if so, it is at least not viciously circular.[6]

---

[6] Additional writings informing this essay include esp. Haraway, "Situated Knowledges"; Donna Haraway, *Primate Visions: Gender, Race, and Nature in the World of Modern Science* (New York: Routledge, 1989); Jane Flax, *Thinking Fragments: Psychoanalysis, Feminism, and Postmodernism in the Contemporary West* (Berkeley: University of California Press, 1990); and the writings of standpoint theorists themselves, esp. Nancy Hartsock, "The Feminist Standpoint: Developing the Ground for a Specifically Feminist Historical 'Materialism,'" in *Discovering Reality: Feminist Perspectives on Epistemology, Metaphysics, Methodology, and Philosophy of Science,* ed. Sandra Harding and Merrill Hintikka (Dordrecht: Reidel, 1983); Dorothy Smith, *The Everyday World as Problematic: A Feminist Sociology* (Boston: Northeastern University Press, 1987); Hilary Rose, "Hand, Brain, and Heart: A Feminist Epistemology for the Natural Sciences," *Signs* 9:1 (1983); Patricia Hill Collins, "Learning from the Outsider Within: The Sociological Significance of Black Feminist Thought," *Social Problems* 33(1986)—though each of these theorists would no doubt disagree with various aspects of my argument.

This essay also considers two possible objections to the argument presented, one that may arise from scientists and philosophers of science, and another that may arise among feminist themselves.

## OBJECTIVISM'S WEAK CONCEPTION OF OBJECTIVITY

The term "objectivism" is useful for the purposes of my argument because its echoes of "scientism" draw attention to ways in which the research prescriptions called for by a value-free objectivity only mimic the purported style of the most successful scientific practices without managing to produce their effects. Objectivism results only in semi-science when it turns away from the task of critically identifying all those broad, historical social desires, interests, and values that have shaped the agendas, contents, and results of the sciences much as they shape the rest of human affairs. Objectivism encourages only a partial and distorted explanation of why the great moments in the history of the natural and social sciences have occurred.

Let me be more precise in identifying the weaknesses of this notion. It has been conceptualized both too narrowly and too broadly to be able to accomplish the goals that its defenders claim it is intended to satisfy. Taken at face value it is ineffectively conceptualized, but this is what makes the sciences that adopt weak standards of objectivity so effective socially: objectivist justifications of science are useful to dominant groups that, consciously or not, do not really intend to "play fair" anyway. Its internally contradictory character gives it a kind of flexibility and adaptability that would be unavailable to a coherently characterized notion.

Consider, first, how objectivism operationalizes too narrowly the notion of maximizing objectivity. The conception of value-free, impartial, dispassionate research is supposed to direct the identification of all social values and their elimination from the results of research, yet it has been operationalized to identify and eliminate *only* those social values and interests that differ among the researchers and critics who are regarded by the scientific community as competent to make such judgments. If the community of "qualified" researchers and critics systematically excludes, for example, all African Americans and women of all races, and if the larger culture is stratified by race and gender and lacks powerful critiques of this stratification, it is not plausible to imagine that racist and sexist interests and values would be identified within a community of scientists composed entirely of people who benefit—intentionally or not—from institutional racism and sexism.

This kind of blindness is advanced by the conventional belief that the truly scientific part of knowledge-seeking—the part controlled by methods of research—is only in the context of justification. The context of discovery, where problems are identified as appropriate for scientific investigation, hypotheses are formulated, key concepts are defined—this part of the scientific process is thought to be unexaminable within science by rational methods. Thus "real science" is restricted to those processes controllable by methodological rules. The methods of science—or, rather, of the special sciences—are restricted to procedures for the testing of already formulated hypotheses. Untouched by these careful methods are those values and interests entrenched in the very statement of what problem is to be researched and in the concepts favored in the hypotheses that are to be tested. Recent histories of science are full of cases in which broad social assumptions stood little chance of identification or elimination through the very best research procedures of the day.[7]

---

[7] This is the theme of many feminist, left, and antiracist analyses of biology and social sciences. See, e.g., Anne Fausto-Sterling, *Myths of Gender: Biological Theories about Women and Men* (New York: Basic Books, 1985); Stephen Jay Gould, *The Mismeasure of Man* (New York: Norton, 1981); Robert V. Guthrie, *Even the Rat Was White: A Historical View of Psychology* (New York: Harper & Row, 1976); Haraway, *Primate Visions;* Sandra Harding, ed., *Feminism and Methodology: Social Science Issues* (Bloomington: Indiana University Press, 1987); Joyce Ladner, ed., *The Death of White Sociology* (New York: Random House, 1973); Hilary Rose and Steven Rose, eds., *Ideology of/in the Natural Sciences* (Cambridge, Mass.: Schenkman, 1979); Londa Schiebinger, *The Mind Has No Sex: Women in the Origins of Modern Science* (Cambridge, Mass.: Harvard University Press, 1989).

Bailey–Cuomo: The
Feminist Philosophy
Reader

9. Feminist Epistemologies | Text

© The McGraw–Hill
Companies, 2008

209

Thus objectivism operationalizes the notion of objectivity in much too narrow a way to permit the achievement of the value-free research that is supposed to be its outcome.

But objectivism also conceptualizes the desired value-neutrality of objectivity too broadly. Objectivists claim that objectivity requires the elimination of *all* social values and interests from the research process and the results of research. It is clear, however, that not all social values and interests have the same bad effects upon the results of research. Some have systematically generated less partial and distorted beliefs than others— or than purportedly value-free research—as has earlier been argued.

Nor is this so outlandish an understanding of the history of science as objectivists frequently intimate. Setting the scene for his study of nineteenth-century biological determinism, Stephen Jay Gould says:

> I do not intend to contrast evil determinists who stray from the path of scientific objectivity with enlightened antideterminists who approach data with an open mind and therefore see truth. Rather, I criticize the myth that science itself is an objective enterprise, done properly only when scientists can shuck the constraints of their culture and view the world as it really is. . . . Science, since people must do it, is a socially embedded activity. It progresses by hunch, vision, and intuition. Much of its change through time does not record a closer approach to absolute truth, but the alteration of cultural contexts that influence it so strongly.[8]

Other historians agree with Gould.[9] Modern science has again and again been reconstructed by a set of interests and values—distinctively Western, bourgeois, and patriarchal—which

were originally formulated by a new social group that intentionally used the new sciences in their struggles against the Catholic Church and feudal state. These interests and values had both positive and negative consequences for the development of the sciences. Political and social interests are not "add-ons" to an otherwise transcendental science that is inherently indifferent to human society; scientific beliefs, practices, institutions, histories, and problematics are constituted in and through contemporary political and social projects, and always have been. It would be far more startling to discover a kind of human knowledge-seeking whose products could—alone among all human products—defy historical "gravity" and fly off the earth, escaping entirely their historical location. Such a cultural phenomenon would be cause for scientific alarm; it would appear to defy principles of "material" causality upon which the possibility of scientific activity itself is based.[10]

Of course, people in different societies arrive at many of the same empirical claims. Farmers, toolmakers, and child tenders in every culture must arrive at similar "facts" about nature and social relations if their work is to succeed. Many of the observations collected by medieval European astronomers are preserved in the data used by astronomers today. But what "facts" these data refer to, what further research they point to, what theoretical statements they support and how such theories are to be applied, what such data signify in terms of human social relations and relations to nature—all these parts of the sciences can differ wildly, as the contrast between medieval and contemporary astronomy illustrates.

There are yet deeper ways in which political values permeate modern science. For even relatively conservative tendencies in the

[8] Gould, *Mismeasure of Man,* 21–22.
[9] E.g., William Leiss, *The Domination of Nature* (Boston: Beacon Press, 1972); Carolyn Merchant, *The Death of Nature: Women, Ecology, and the Scientific Revolution* (New York: Harper & Row, 1980); Wolfgang Van den Daele, "The Social Construction of Science," in *The Social Production of Scientific Knowledge,* ed. Everett Mendelsohn, Peter Weingart, and Richard Whitley (Dordrecht: Reidel, 1977).

[10] Rouse, *Knowledge and Power,* provides a good analysis of the implications for science of Foucauldian notions of politics and power.

post-Kuhnian philosophies of science, the sciences' power to manipulate the world is considered the mark of their success. The "new empiricism" contrasts in this respect with conventional empiricism. As Joseph Rouse puts the point:

> If we take the new empiricism seriously, it forces us to reappraise the relation between power and knowledge in a more radical way. The central issue is no longer how scientific claims can be distorted or suppressed by polemic, propaganda, or ideology. Rather, we must look at what was earlier described as the achievement of power through the application of knowledge. But the new empiricism also challenges the adequacy of this description in terms of "application." The received view distinguishes the achievement of knowledge from its subsequent application, from which this kind of power is supposed to derive. New empiricist accounts of science make this distinction less tenable by shifting the locus of knowledge from accurate representation to successful manipulation and control of events. Power is no longer external to knowledge or opposed to it: power itself becomes the mark of knowledge.[11]

The best as well as the worst of the history of the natural sciences has been shaped by—or, more accurately, constructed through and within—political desires, interests, and values. Consequently, there appear to be no grounds left from which to defend the claim that the objectivity of research is advanced by the elimination of all political values and interests from the research process. Instead, the sciences need to legitimate *within scientific research,* as part of practicing science, critical examination of historical values and interests that may be so shared within the scientific community, so invested in by the very constitution of this or that field of study, that they will not show up as a cultural bias between experimenters or between research communities. What objectivism cannot conceptualize is the need for critical examination of the "intentionality of nature"—meaning not that nature is no different from humans (in having intentions, desires, interests, and values or in constructing its own meaningful "way of life," and so on) but that nature as-the-object-of-human-knowledge never comes to us "naked"; it comes only as already constituted in social thought.[12] Nature-as-object-of-study simulates in this respect an intentional being. This idea helps counter the intuitively seductive idea that scientific claims are and should be an epiphenomenon of nature. It is the development of strategies to generate just such critical examination that the notion of strong objectivity calls for.

Not everyone will welcome such a project; even those who share these criticisms of objectivism may think the call for strong objectivity too idealistic, too utopian, not realistic enough. But is it more unrealistic than trying to explain the regularities of nature and their underlying causal tendencies scientifically but refusing to examine *all* their causes? And even if the ideal of identifying all the causes of human beliefs is rarely if ever achievable, why not hold it as a desirable standard? Anti-litter laws improve social life even if they are not always obeyed.[13]

Weak objectivity, then, is a contradictory notion, and its contradictory character is largely responsible for its usefulness and its widespread appeal to dominant groups. It offers hope that scientists and science institutions, themselves admittedly historically located, can produce claims that will be regarded as objectively valid without their having to examine critically their

---

[11] Rouse, *Knowledge and Power,* 19. Among the "new empiricist" works that Rouse has in mind are Larry Laudan, *Progress and Its Problems: Toward a Theory of Scientific Growth* (Berkeley: University of California Press, 1977); Mary Hesse, *Revolutions and Reconstructions in the Philosophy of Science* (Bloomington: University of Indiana Press, 1980); Nancy Cartwright, *How the Laws of Physics Lie* (Oxford: Oxford University Press, 1983).

[12] See Haraway, *Primate Visions,* esp. chap. 10, for analysis of differences between the Anglo-American, Japanese, and Indian constructions of "nature" which shape the objects of study in primatology.

[13] Fuller uses the anti-litter law example in another context in *Social Epistemology.*

Bailey–Cuomo: The
Feminist Philosophy
Reader

9. Feminist Epistemologies | Text

© The McGraw–Hill
Companies, 2008

211

own historical commitments, from which—intentionally or not—they actively construct their scientific research. It permits scientists and science institutions to be unconcerned with the origins or consequences of their problematics and practices, or with the social values and interests that these problematics and practices support. It offers the possibility of enacting what Francis Bacon promised: "The course I propose for the discovery of sciences is such as leaves but little to the acuteness and strength of wits, but places all wits and understandings nearly on a level." His "way of discovering sciences goes far to level men's wits, and leaves but little to individual excellence; because it performs everything by surest rules and demonstrations."[14]

For those powerful forces in society that want to appropriate science and knowledge for their own purposes, it is extremely valuable to be able to support the idea that ignoring the constitution of science within political desires, values, and interests will somehow increase the reliability of accounts of nature and social life. The ideal of the disinterested rational scientist advances the self-interest of both social elites and, ironically, scientists who seek status and power. Reporting on various field studies of scientific work, Steve Fuller points out that Machiavellian judgments

> simulate those of the fabled "rational" scientist, since in order for the Machiavellian to maximize his advantage he must be ready to switch research programs when he detects a change in the balance of credibility—which is, after all, what philosophers of science would typically have the rational scientist do. To put the point more strikingly, it would seem that as the scientist's motivation approximates total *self-interestedness* (such that he is always able to distance his own interests from those of any social group which supports what may turn out to be a research program with diminishing credibility), his behavior approximates total

*disinterestedness.* And so we can imagine the ultimate Machiavellian scientist pursuing a line of research frowned upon by most groups in the society—perhaps determining the racial component in intelligence is an example—simply because he knows of its potential for influencing the course of future research and hence for enhancing his credibility as a scientist.[15]

The history of science shows that research directed by maximally liberatory social interests and values tends to be better equipped to identify partial claims and distorting assumptions, even though the credibility of the scientists who do it may not be enhanced during the short run. After all, antiliberatory interests and values are invested in the natural inferiority of just the groups of humans who, if given real equal access (not just the formally equal access that is liberalism's goal) to public voice, would most strongly contest claims about their purported natural inferiority. Antiliberatory interests and values silence and destroy the most likely sources of evidence against their own claims. That is what makes them rational for elites.

## STRONG OBJECTIVITY: A COMPETENCY CONCEPT

At this point, what I mean by a concept of strong objectivity should be clear. In an important sense, our cultures have agendas and make assumptions that we as individuals cannot easily detect. Theoretically unmediated experience, that aspect of a group's or an individual's experience in which cultural influences cannot be detected, functions as part of the evidence for scientific claims. Cultural agendas and assumptions are part of the background assumptions and auxiliary hypotheses that philosophers have identified. If the goal is to make available for critical scrutiny *all* the evidence marshaled for or against a scientific hypothesis, then this evidence too requires critical examination *within* scientific research processes.

---

[14] Quoted in Van den Daele, "Social Construction of Science," 34.

[15] Fuller, *Social Epistemology,* 267.

In other words, we can think of strong objectivity as extending the notion of scientific research to include systematic examination of such powerful background beliefs. It must do so in order to be competent at maximizing objectivity.

The strong objectivity that standpoint theory requires is like the "strong programme" in the sociology of knowledge in that it directs us to provide symmetrical accounts of both "good" and "bad" belief formation and legitimation.[16] We must be able to identify the social causes of good beliefs, not just of the bad ones to which the conventional "sociology of error" and objectivism restrict causal accounts. However, in contrast to the "strong programme," standpoint theory requires causal analyses not just of the micro processes in the laboratory but also of the macro tendencies in the social order, which shape scientific practices. Moreover, a concern with macro tendencies permits a more robust notion of reflexivity than is currently available in the sociology of knowledge or the philosophy of science. In trying to identify the social causes of good beliefs, we will be led also to examine critically the kinds of bad beliefs that shape our own thought and behaviors, not just the thought and behavior of others.

To summarize the argument of the last chapter, in a society structured by gender hierarchy, "starting thought from women's lives" increases the objectivity of the results of research by bringing scientific observation and the perception of the need for explanation to bear on assumptions and practices that appear natural or unremarkable from the perspective of the lives of men in the dominant groups. Thinking from the perspective of women's lives makes strange what had appeared familiar, which is the beginning of any scientific inquiry.[17]

Why is this gender difference a scientific resource? It leads us to ask questions about nature and social relations from the perspective of devalued and neglected lives. Doing so begins research in the perspective from the lives of "strangers" who have been excluded from the culture's ways of socializing the "natives," who are at home in its institutions and who are full-fledged citizens. It starts research in the perspective from the lives of the systematically oppressed, exploited, and dominated, those who have fewer interests in ignorance about how the social order actually works. It begins research in the perspective from the lives of people on the "other side" of gender battles, offering a view different from the "winner's stories" about nature and social life which men's interpretations of men's lives tend to produce. It starts thought in everyday life, for which women are assigned primary responsibility and in which appear consequences of dominant group activities—consequences that are invisible from the perspective of those activities. It starts thought in the lives of those people to whom is assigned the work of mediating many of the culture's ideological dualisms—especially the gap between nature and culture. It starts research in the lives not just of strangers or outsiders but of "outsiders within," from which the relationship between outside and inside, margin and center, can more easily be detected. It starts thought in the perspective from the life of the Other, allowing the Other to gaze back "shamelessly" at the self who had reserved for himself the right to gaze "anonymously" at whomsoever he chooses. It starts thought in the lives of people who are unlikely to permit the denial of the interpretive core of all knowledge claims. It starts thought in the perspective from lives that at this moment in history are especially revealing of broad social contradictions. And no doubt there are additional ways in which thinking from the perspective of women's lives is especially revealing of regularities in nature and social relations and their underlying causal tendencies.

It is important to remember that in a certain sense there are no "women" or "men" in the

---

[16] I use "good" and "bad" here to stand for "true" and "false," "better confirmed" and "less well confirmed," "plausible" and "implausible," and so on.

[17] Starting thought from women's lives is something that both men and women must *learn* to do. Women's telling their experiences is not the same thing as thinking from the perspective of women's lives.

Bailey–Cuomo: The
Feminist Philosophy
Reader

9. Feminist Epistemologies | Text

© The McGraw–Hill
Companies, 2008

213

world—there is no "gender"—but only women, men, and gender constructed through particular historical struggles over just which races, classes, sexualities, cultures, religious groups, and so forth, will have access to resources and power. Moreover, standpoint theories of knowledge, whether or not they are articulated as such, have been advanced by thinkers concerned not only with gender and class hierarchy (recollect that standpoint theory originated in class analyses) but also with other "Others."[18] To make sense of any actual woman's life or the gender relations in any culture, analyses must begin in real, historic women's lives, and these will be women of particular races, classes, cultures, and sexualities. The historical particularity of women's lives is a problem for narcissistic or arrogant accounts that attempt, consciously or not, to conduct a cultural monologue. But it is a resource for those who think that our understandings and explanations are improved by what we could call an intellectual participatory democracy.

The notion of strong objectivity welds together the strengths of weak objectivity and those of the "weak subjectivity" that is its correlate, but excludes the features that make them only weak. To enact or operationalize the directive of strong objectivity is to value the Other's perspective and to pass over in thought into the social condition that creates it—not in order to stay there, to "go native" or merge the self with the Other, but in order to look back at the self in all its cultural particularity from a more distant, critical, objectifying location. One can think of

the subjectivism that objectivism conceptualizes as its sole alternative as only a "premodern" alternative to objectivism; it provides only a premodern solution to the problem we have here and now at the moment of postmodern criticisms of modernity's objectivism. Strong objectivity rejects attempts to resuscitate those organic, occult, "participating consciousness" relationships between self and Other which are characteristic of the premodern world.[19] Strong objectivity requires that we investigate the relation between subject and object rather than deny the existence of, or seek unilateral control over, this relation.

## HISTORICAL RELATIVISM VERSUS JUDGMENTAL RELATIVISM

It is not that historical relativism is in itself a bad thing. A respect for historical (or sociological or cultural) relativism is always useful in starting one's thinking. Different social groups tend to have different patterns of practice and belief and different standards for judging them; these practices, beliefs, and standards can be explained by different historical interests, values, and agendas. Appreciation of these empirical regularities are especially important at this moment of unusually deep and extensive social change, when even preconceived schemes used in liberatory projects are likely to exclude less-well-positioned voices and to distort emerging ways of thinking that do not fit easily into older schemes. Listening carefully to different voices and attending thoughtfully to others' values and interests can enlarge our vision and begin to correct for inevitable enthnocentrisms. (The dominant values, interests, and voices are not among these "different" ones; they are the

---

[18] See, e.g., Samir Amin, *Eurocentrism* (New York: Monthly Review Press, 1989); Bettina Aptheker, *Tapestries of Life: Women's Work, Women's Consciousness, and the Meaning of Daily Life* (Amherst: University of Massachusetts Press, 1989); Collins, "Learning from the Outsider Within"; Walter Rodney, *How Europe Underdeveloped Africa* (Washington, D.C.: Howard University Press, 1982); Edward Said, *Orientalism* (New York: Pantheon Books, 1978); Edward Said, Foreword to *Selected Subaltern Studies,* ed. Ranajit Guha and Gayatri Chakravorty Spivak (New York: Oxford University Press, 1988), viii.

[19] See Morris Berman, *The Reenchantment of the World* (Ithaca: Cornell University Press, 1981), for an analysis of the world that modernity lost, and lost for good. Some feminists have tried to dismantle modernist projects with premodernist tools.

powerful tide against which "difference" must swim.)

To acknowledge this historical or sociological fact, as I have already argued, does not commit one to the further epistemological claim that there are therefore no rational or scientific grounds for making judgments between various patterns of belief and their originating social practices, values, and consequences. Many thinkers have pointed out that judgmental relativism is internally related to objectivism. For example, science historian Donna Haraway argues that judgmental relativism is the other side of the very same coin from "the God trick" required by what I have called weak objectivity. To insist that no judgments at all of cognitive adequacy can legitimately be made amounts to the same thing as to insist that knowledge can be produced only from "no place at all": that is, by someone who can be every place at once.[20] Critical preoccupation with judgmental relativism is the logical complement to the judgmental absolutism characteristic of Eurocentrism. Economist Samir Amin criticizes the preoccupation with relativism in some Western intellectual circles as a kind of "inverted Eurocentrism":

> The view that any person has the right—and even the power—to judge others is replaced by attention to the relativity of those judgments. Without a doubt, such judgments can be erroneous, superficial, hasty, or relative. No case is ever definitely closed; debate always continues. But that is precisely the point. It is necessary to pursue debate and not to avoid it on the grounds that the views that anyone forms about others are and always will be false: that the French will never understand the Chinese (and vice versa), that men will never understand women, etc; or, in other words, that there is no human species, but only "people." Instead, the claim is made that only Europeans can truly understand Europe, Chinese China, Christians

Christianity, and Moslems Islam; the Eurocentrism of one group is completed by the inverted Eurocentrism of others.[21]

Historically, relativism appears as a problematic intellectual possibility only for dominating groups at the point where the hegemony of their views is being challenged. Though the recognition that other cultures do, in fact, hold different beliefs, values, and standards of judgment is as old as human history, judgmental relativism emerged as an urgent intellectual issue only in nineteenth-century Europe, with the belated recognition that the apparently bizarre beliefs and behaviors of Others had a rationality and logic of their own. Judgmental relativism is not a problem originating in or justifiable in terms of the lives of marginalized groups. It did not arise in misogynous thought about women; it does not arise from the contrast feminism makes between women's lives and men's. Women do not have the problem of how to accommodate intellectually both the sexist claim that women are inferior in some way or another and the feminist claim that they are not. Here relativism arises as a problem only from the perspective of men's lives. Some men want to appear to acknowledge and accept feminist arguments without actually giving up any of their conventional androcentric beliefs and the practices that seem to follow so reasonably from such beliefs. "It's all relative, my dear," is a convenient way to try to accomplish these two goals.

We feminists in higher education may have appeared to invite charges of relativism in our language about disseminating the results of feminist research and scholarship beyond women's studies programs into the entire curriculum and canon. We speak of "mainstreaming"

---

[20] Haraway, "Situated Knowledges" makes these points and uses the phrase "the God trick."

[21] Amin, *Eurocentrism,* 146–47. Amin further makes clear that it takes more than *mere* debate—i.e., only intellectual work—to come to understand the lives or point of view of "people" who are on trajectories that oppose one's own in political struggles. The following paragraph draws on "Introduction: Is There a Feminist Method?" in *Feminism and Methodology,* p. 10.

Bailey–Cuomo: The
Feminist Philosophy
Reader

9. Feminist Epistemologies | Text

© The McGraw–Hill
Companies, 2008

215

and "integrating" the research, scholarship, and curriculum of Other programs and of encouraging "inclusiveness" in scholarship and the curriculum. We enroll our women's studies courses in campuswide projects to promote "cultural diversity" and "multiculturalism," and we accept students into such courses on these terms. Do these projects conflict with the standpoint logic? Yes and no. They conflict because the notions involved are perfectly coherent with the maintenance of elitist knowledge production and systems. Let me make the point in terms of my racial identity as white. "They (those people of color at the margins of the social order) are to be integrated with us (whites at the center), leaving us unchanged and the rightful heirs of the center of the culture. They are to give up their agendas and interests that conflict with ours in order to insert their contributions into the research, scholarship, or curriculum that has been structured to accommodate our agendas and interests." This is just as arrogant a posture as the older cultural absolutism. From the perspective of racial minorities, integration has never worked as a solution to ethnic or race relations in the United States. Why is there reason to think it will work any better for the marginalized projects in intellectual circles?

Should we therefore give up attempts at an "inclusive curriculum" and "cultural diversity" because of their possible complicity with sexism, racism, Eurocentrism, heterosexism, and class oppression? Of course the answer must be no. It is true that this kind of language appears to betray the compelling insights of the standpoint epistemology and to leave feminist programs in the compromised position of supporting the continued centering of white, Western, patriarchal visions. But many feminist projects—including women's studies programs themselves—are forced to occupy whatever niches they can find within institutional structures that are fundamentally opposed to them or, at least, "prefeminist." An implicit acceptance of pluralism, if not judgmental relativism—at least at the institutional level—appears to be the

only condition under which women's voices and feminist voices, male and female, can be heard at all.

After all, isn't feminism just one "equal voice" among many competing for everyone's attention? The nineteenth-century "natives" whose beliefs and behaviors Europeans found bizarre were not in any real sense competing for an equal voice within European thought and politics. They were safely off in Africa, the Orient, and other faraway places. The chances were low that aborigines would arrive in Paris, London, and Berlin to study and report back to their own cultures the bizarre beliefs and behaviors that constituted the "tribal life" of European anthropologists and *their* culture. More important, there was no risk at all that they could have used such knowledge to assist in imposing their rule on Europeans in Europe. Women's voices, while certainly far from silent, were far more effectively contained and muted than is possible today. As a value, a moral prescription, relativism was a safe stance for Europeans to choose; the reciprocity of respect it appeared to support had little chance of having to be enacted. Today, women and feminists are not safely off and out of sight at all. They are present, speaking, within the very social order that still treats women's beliefs and behaviors as bizarre. Moreover, their speech competes for attention and status as most plausible not only with that of misogynists but also with the speech of other Others: African Americans, other peoples of color, gay rights activists, pacifists, ecologists, members of new formations of the left, and so on. Isn't feminism forced to embrace relativism by its condition of being just one among many countercultural voices?

This description of the terrain in which feminists struggle to advance their claims, however, assumes that people must either choose only one among these countercultures as providing an absolute standard for sorting knowledge claims, or else regard all of them as competing and assign them equal cognitive status. Actually, it is a different scenario that the countercultures

*Chapter 9 / Feminist Epistemologies*

can envision and even occasionally already enact: the fundamental tendencies of each must permeate each of the others in order for each movement to succeed. Feminism should center the concerns of each of these movements, and each of them must move feminist concerns to its center.

To summarize, then, a strong notion of objectivity requires a commitment to acknowledge the historical character of every belief or set of beliefs—a commitment to cultural, sociological, historical relativism. But it also requires that judgmental or epistemological relativism be rejected. Weak objectivity is located in a conceptual interdependency that includes (weak) subjectivity and judgmental relativism. One cannot simply give up weak objectivity without making adjustments throughout the rest of this epistemological system.

## RESPONDING TO OBJECTIONS

Two possible objections to the recommendation of a stronger standard for objectivity must be considered here. First, some scientists and philosophers of science may protest that I am attempting to specify standards of objectivity for all the sciences. What could it mean to attempt to specify *general* standards for increasing the objectivity of research? Shouldn't the task of determining what counts as adequate research be settled within each science by its own practitioners? Why should practicing scientists revise their research practices because of what is thought by a philosopher or anyone else who is not an expert in a particular science?

But the issue of this essay is an epistemological issue—a metascientific one—rather than an issue within any single science. It is more like a directive to operationalize theoretical concepts than like a directive to operationalize in a certain way some particular theoretical notion within physics or biology. The recommended combination of strong objectivity with the acknowledgment of historical relativism would, if adopted, create a

culturewide shift in the kind of epistemology regarded as desirable. Certainly, strategies for enacting commitments to strong objectivity and the acknowledgment of historical relativism would have to be developed within each particular research program; plenty of examples already exist in biology and the social sciences. My position is that the natural sciences are backward in this respect; they are not immune from the reasonableness of these directives, as conventionalists have assumed.

The notion of strong objectivity developed here represents insights that have been emerging from thinkers in a number of disciplines for some decades—not just "wishful thinking" based on no empirical sciences at all. Criticisms of the dominant thought of the West from both inside and outside the West argue that its partiality and distortions are the consequence in large part of starting that thought only from the lives of the dominant groups in the West. Less partiality and less distortion result when thought starts from peasant life, not just aristocratic life; from slaves' lives, not just slaveowners' lives; from the lives of factory workers, not just those of their bosses and managers; from the lives of people who work for wages and have also been assigned responsibility for husband and child care, not just those of persons who are expected to have little such responsibility. This directive leaves open to be determined within each discipline or research area what a researcher must do to start thought from women's lives or the lives of people in other marginalized groups, and it will be easier—though still difficult—to provide reasonable responses to such a request in history or sociology than in physics or chemistry. But the difficulty of providing an analysis in physics or chemistry does not signify that the question is an absurd one for knowledge-seeking in general, or that there are no reasonable answers for those sciences too.

The second objection may come from feminists themselves. Many would say that the notion of objectivity is so hopelessly tainted by its

Bailey–Cuomo: The
Feminist Philosophy
Reader

9. Feminist Epistemologies | Text

© The McGraw–Hill
Companies, 2008

217

historical complicity in justifying the service of science to the dominant groups that trying to make it function effectively and progressively in alternative agendas only confuses the matter. If feminists want to breathe new life into such a bedraggled notion as objectivity, why not at least invent an alternative term that does not call up the offenses associated with the idea of value-neutrality, that is not intimately tied to a faulty theory of representation, to a faulty psychic construction of the ideal agent of knowledge, and to regressive political tendencies.

Let us reorganize some points made earlier in order to get the full force of this objection. The goal of producing results of research that are value-free is part of the notion of the ideal mind as a mirror that can reflect a world that is "out there," ready-made. In this view, value-free objectivity can locate an Archimedean perspective from which the events and processes of the natural world appear in their proper places. Only false beliefs have social causes—human values and interests that blind us to the real regularities and underlying causal tendencies in the world, generating biased results of research. True beliefs have only natural causes: those regularities and underlying causal tendencies that are *there,* plus the power of the eyes to see them and of the mind to reason about them. This theory of representation is a historically situated one: it is characteristic only of certain groups in the modern West. Can the notion of objectivity really be separated from this implausible theory of representation?

Value-free objectivity requires also a faulty theory of the ideal agent—the subject—of science, knowledge, and history. It requires a notion of the self as a fortress that must be defended against polluting influences from its social surroundings. The self whose mind would perfectly reflect the world must create and constantly police the borders of a gulf, a no-man's-land, between himself as the subject and the object of his research, knowledge, or action. Feminists have been among the most pointed critics of this

self-versus-Other construct,[22] referring to it as "abstract masculinity."[23] Moreover, its implication in Western constructions of the racial Other against which the "white" West would define its admirable projects is also obvious.[24] Can the notion of objectivity be useful in efforts to oppose such sexism and racism?

Equally important, the notion of value-free objectivity is morally and politically regressive for reasons additional to those already mentioned. It justifies the construction of science institutions and individual scientists as "fast guns for hire." It has been used to legitimate and hold up as the highest ideal institutions and individuals that are, insofar as they are scientific, to be studiously unconcerned with the origins or consequences of their activities or with the values and interests that these activities advance. This nonaccidental, determined, energetic lack of concern is supported by science education that excludes training in critical thought and that treats all expressions of social and political concern—the concerns of the torturer and the concerns of the tortured—as being on the same low level of scientific "rationality." Scandalous examples of the institutional impotence of the sciences as sciences to speak to the moral and political issues that shape their problematics, consequences, values, and interests have been identified for decades. The construction of a border between scientific method and violations of human and, increasingly, animal

---

[22] See, e.g., Nancy Chodorow, *The Reproduction of Mothering* (Berkeley: University of California Press, 1978); Dorothy Dinnerstein, *The Mermaid and the Minotaur: Sexual Arrangements and Human Malaise* (New York: Harper & Row, 1976); Carol Gilligan, *In a Different Voice: Psychological Theory and Women's Development* (Cambridge, Mass.: Harvard University Press, 1982); Evelyn Fox Keller, *Reflections on Gender and Science* (New Haven, Conn.: Yale University Press, 1984).

[23] Hartsock, "The Feminist Standpoint."

[24] See, e.g., Sander Gilman, *Difference and Pathology: Stereotypes of Sexuality, Race, and Madness* (Ithaca: Cornell University Press, 1985); V. Y. Mudimbe, *The Invention of Africa: Gnosis, Philosophy, and the Order of Knowledge* (Bloomington: Indiana University Press, 1988); Said, *Orientalism,* and Foreword to Guha and Spivak. *Subaltern Studies.*

Chapter 9 / Feminist Epistemologies

rights must be conducted "outside" that method, by government statements about what constitutes acceptable methods of research on human and animal subjects, what constitutes consent to experimentation, the subsequent formation of "ethics committees," and so on. Can the notion of objectivity be extracted from the morals and politics of "objective science" as a "fast gun for hire"?

These are formidable objections. Nevertheless, the argument of this book is that the notion of objectivity not only can but should be separated from its shameful and damaging history. Research is socially situated, and it can be more objectively conducted without aiming for or claiming to be value-free. The requirements for achieving strong objectivity permit one to abandon notions of perfect, mirrorlike representations of the world, the self as a defended fortress, and the "truly scientific" as disinterested with regard to morals and politics, yet still apply rational standards to sorting less from more partial and distorted belief. Indeed, my argument is that these standards are more rational and more effective at producing maximally objective results than the ones associated with what I have called weak objectivity.

As I have been arguing, objectivity is one of a complex of inextricably linked notions. Science and rationality are two other terms in this network. But it is not necessary to accept the idea that there is only one correct or reasonable way to think about these terms, let alone that the correct way is the one used by dominant groups in the modern West. Not all reason is white, masculinist, modern, heterosexual, Western reason. Not all modes of rigorous empirical knowledge-seeking are what the dominant groups think of as science—to understate the point. The procedures institutionalized in conventional science for distinguishing between how we want the world to be and how it is are not the only or best ways to go about maximizing objectivity. It is important to work and think outside the dominant modes, as the minority movements

have done. But it is important, also, to bring the insights developed there into the heart of conventional institutions, to disrupt the dominant practices from within by appropriating notions such as objectivity, reason, and science in ways that stand a chance of compelling reasoned assent while simultaneously shifting and displacing the meanings and referents of the discussion in ways that improve it. It is by thinking and acting as "outsiders within" that feminists and others can transform science and its social relations for those who remain only insiders or outsiders.

One cannot afford to "just say no" to objectivity. I think there are three additional good reasons to retain the notion of objectivity for future knowledge-seeking projects but to work at separating it from its damaging historical associations with value-neutrality.

First, it has a valuable political history. There have to be standards for distinguishing between how I want the world to be and how, in empirical fact, it is. Otherwise, might makes right in knowledge-seeking just as it tends to do in morals and politics. The notion of objectivity is useful because its meaning and history support such standards. Today, as in the past, there are powerful interests ranged against attempts to find out the regularities and underlying causal tendencies in the natural and social worlds. Some groups do not want exposed to public scrutiny the effect on the environment of agribusiness or of pesticide use in domestic gardening. Some do not want discussed the consequences for Third World peasants, for the black underclass in the United States, and especially for women in both groups of the insistence on economic production that generates profit for elites in the West. The notion of achieving greater objectivity has been useful in the past and can be today in struggles over holding people and institutions responsible for the fit between their behavior and the claims they make.

Second, objectivity also can claim a glorious intellectual history. The argument of this essay

Bailey–Cuomo: The
Feminist Philosophy
Reader

9. Feminist Epistemologies | Text

© The McGraw–Hill
Companies, 2008

219

has emphasized its service to elites, but it also has been invoked to justify unpopular criticisms of partisan but entrenched beliefs. Standpoint theory can rightfully claim that history as its legacy.

Finally, the appeal to objectivity is an issue not only between feminist and prefeminist sciences but within each feminist and other emancipatory movement. There are many feminisms, some of which result in claims that distort the racial, class, sexuality, and gender relationships in society. Which ones generate less and which more partial and distorted accounts of nature and social life? The notion of objectivity is useful in providing a way to think about the gap we want between how any individual or group wants the world to be and how in fact it is.

The notion of objectivity—like such ideas as science and rationality, democracy and feminism— contains progressive as well as regressive tendencies. In each case, it is important to develop the progressive and to block the regressive ones.

## REFLEXIVITY REVISITED

The notion of "strong objectivity" conceptualizes the value of putting the subject or agent of knowledge in the same critical, causal plane as the object of her or his inquiry. It permits us to see the scientific as well as the moral and political advantages of this way of trying to achieve a reciprocal relationship between the agent and object of knowledge. The contrast developed here between weak and strong notions of objectivity permits the parallel construction of weak versus strong notions of reflexivity.

Reflexivity has tended to be seen as a problem in the social sciences—and only there. Observation cannot be as separated from its social consequences as the directives of "weak objectivity," originating in the natural sciences, have assumed. In social inquiry, observation changes the field observed. Having recognized his complicity in the lives of his objects of study, the researcher is then supposed to devise various strategies to try

to democratize the situation, to inform the "natives" of their options, to make them participants in the account of their activities, and so forth.[25]

Less commonly, reflexivity has been seen as a problem because if the researcher is under the obligation to identify the social causes of the "best" as well as the "worst" beliefs and behaviors of those he studies, then he must also analyze his own beliefs and behaviors in conducting his research project—which have been shaped by the same kinds of social relations that he is interested to identify as causes of the beliefs and behaviors of others. (Here, reflexivity can begin to be conceptualized as a "problem" for the natural sciences, too.) Sociologists of knowledge in the recent "strong programme" school and related tendencies, who emphasize the importance of identifying the social causes of "best belief," have been aware of this problem from the very beginning but have devised no plausible way of resolving it—primarily because their conception of the social causes of belief in the natural sciences (the subject matter of their analyses) is artificially restricted to the micro processes of the laboratory and research community, explicitly excluding race, gender, and class relations. This restricted notion of what constitutes appropriate subject matter for analyses of the social relations of the sciences is carried into their understanding of their own work. It generates ethnographies of their own and the natural science communities

---

[25] A fine account of the travails of such a project reports Robert Blauner and David Wellman's dawning recognition that nothing they did could eliminate the colonial relationship between themselves and their black informants in the community surrounding Berkeley: see their "Toward the Decolonization of Social Research," in Ladner, *The Death of White Sociology.* Economist Vernon Dixon argues that from the perspective of an African or African American world view, the idea that observation would not change the thing observed appears ridiculous; see his "World Views and Research Methodology," in *African Philosophy: Assumptions and Paradigms for Research on Black Persons,* ed. L. M. King, Vernon Dixon, and W. W. Nobles (Los Angeles: Fanon Center, Charles R. Drew Postgraduate Medical School, 1976), and my discussion of the congruence between African and feminine world views in *The Science Question in Feminism* (Ithaca: Cornell University Press, 1986), chap. 7.

*Chapter 9 / Feminist Epistemologies*

which are complicitous with positivist tendencies in insisting on the isolation of research communities from the larger social, economic, and political currents in their societies. (These accounts are also flawed by their positivist conceptions of the object of natural science study).[26]

These "weak" notions of reflexivity are disabled by their lack of any mechanism for identifying the cultural values and interests of the researchers, which form part of the evidence for the results of research in both the natural and social sciences. Anthropologists, sociologists, and the like, who work within social communities, frequently appear to desire such a mechanism or standard; but the methodological assumptions of their disciplines, which direct them to embrace either weak objectivity or judgmental relativism, have not permitted them to develop one. That is, individuals express "heartfelt desire" not to harm the subjects they observe, to become aware of their own cultural biases, and so on, but such reflexive goals remain at the level of desire rather than competent enactment. In short, such weak reflexivity has no possible operationalization, or no competency standard, for success.

A notion of strong reflexivity would require that the objects of inquiry be conceptualized as gazing back in all their cultural particularity and that the researcher, through theory and methods, stand behind them, gazing back at his own socially situated research project in all its cultural particularity and its relationships to other projects of his culture—many of which (policy development in international relations, for example, or industrial expansion) can be seen only from locations far away from the scientist's actual daily work. "Strong reflexivity" requires the development of oppositional theory from the perspective of the lives of those Others ("nature" as already socially constructed, as well as other peoples), since intuitive experience, for reasons discussed earlier, is frequently not a reliable guide to the regularities of nature and social life and their underlying causal tendencies.

Standpoint theory opens the way to stronger standards of both objectivity and reflexivity. These standards require that research projects use their historical location as a resource for obtaining greater objectivity.

---

[26] See, e.g., Bloor, *Knowledge and Social Imagery;* and Steve Woolgar's nevertheless interesting paper, "Reflexivity Is the Ethnographer of the Text," as well as other (somewhat bizarre) discussions of reflexivity in Woolgar, *Knowledge and Reflexivity.*

---

# THE PROJECT OF FEMINIST EPISTEMOLOGY: PERSPECTIVES FROM A NONWESTERN FEMINIST

### Uma Narayan

A fundamental thesis of feminist epistemology is that our location in the world as women makes it possible for us to perceive and understand different aspects of both the world and human activities in ways that challenge the male bias of existing perspectives. Feminist epistemology is a particular manifestation of the general insight that the nature of women's experiences as individuals and as social beings, our contributions to work, culture, knowledge, and our history and political interests have been systematically ignored or misrepresented by mainstream discourses in different areas.

Women have been often excluded from prestigious areas of human activity (for example, politics or science) and this has often made these activities seem clearly "male." In areas where women were not excluded (for example, subsistence work), their contribution has been misrepresented as secondary and inferior to that of men. Feminist epistemology sees mainstream theories about various human enterprises, including mainstream theories about human knowledge, as one-dimensional and deeply flawed because of the exclusion and misrepresentation of women's contributions.

Feminist epistemology suggests that integrating women's contribution into the domain of science and knowledge will not constitute a mere adding of details; it will not merely widen the canvas but result in a shift of perspective enabling us to see a very different picture. The inclusion of women's perspective will not merely amount to women participating in greater numbers in the existing practice of science and knowledge, but it will change the very nature of these activities and their self-understanding.

It would be misleading to suggest that feminist epistemology is a homogenous and cohesive enterprise. Its practitioners differ both philosophically and politically in a number of significant ways (Harding 1986). But an important theme on its agenda has been to undermine the abstract, rationalistic, and universal image of the scientific enterprise by using several different strategies. It has studied, for instance, how contingent historical factors have colored both scientific theories and practices and provided the (often sexist) metaphors in which scientists have conceptualized their activity (Bordo 1986; Keller 1985; Harding and O'Barr 1987). It has tried to reintegrate values and emotions into our account of our cognitive activities, arguing for both the inevitability of their presence and the importance of the contributions they are capable of making to our knowledge (Gilligan 1982). It has also attacked various sets of dualisms characteristic of western philosophical thinking—reason versus emotion, culture versus nature, universal versus particular—in which the first of each set is identified with science, rationality, and the masculine and the second is relegated to the nonscientific, the nonrational, and the feminine (Harding and Hintikka 1983; Lloyd 1984; Wilshire essay in this volume).

At the most general level, feminist epistemology resembles the efforts of many oppressed groups to reclaim for themselves the value of their own experience. The writing of novels that focused on working-class life in England or the lives of black people in the United States shares a motivation similar to that of feminist epistemology—to depict an experience different from the norm and to assert the value of this difference.

In a similar manner, feminist epistemology also resembles attempts by third-world writers and historians to document the wealth and complexity of local economic and social structures that existed prior to colonialism. These attempts are useful for their ability to restore to colonized peoples a sense of the richness of their own history and culture. These projects also mitigate the tendency of intellectuals in former colonies who are westernized through their education to think that anything western is necessarily better and more "progressive." In some cases, such studies help to preserve the knowledge of many local arts, crafts, lore, and techniques that were part of the former way of life before they are lost not only to practice but even to memory.

These enterprises are analogous to feminist epistemology's project of restoring to women a sense of the richness of their history, to mitigate our tendency to see the stereotypically "masculine" as better or more progressive, and to preserve for posterity the contents of "feminine" areas of knowledge and expertise—medical lore, knowledge associated with the practices of childbirth and child rearing, traditionally feminine crafts, and so on. Feminist epistemology, like these other enterprises, must attempt to balance the assertion of the value of a different culture or experience against the dangers of romanticizing it to the extent that the limitations and oppressions it confers on its subjects are ignored.

My essay will attempt to examine some dangers of approaching feminist theorizing and epistemological values in a noncontextual and nonpragmatic way, which could convert important feminist insights and theses into feminist epistemological dogmas. I will use my perspective as a nonwestern, Indian feminist to examine critically the predominantly Anglo-American project of feminist epistemology and to reflect on what such a project might signify for women in nonwestern cultures in general and for nonwestern feminists in particular. I will suggest that different cultural contexts and political agendas may cast a very different light on both the "idols" and the "enemies" of knowledge as they have characteristically been typed in western feminist epistemology.

In keeping with my respect for contexts, I would like to stress that I do not see nonwestern feminists as a homogenous group and that none of the concerns I express as a nonwestern feminist may be pertinent to or shared by *all* nonwestern feminists, although I do think they will make sense to many.

In the first section, I will show that the enterprise of feminist epistemology poses some political problems for nonwestern feminists that it does not pose, in the same way, for western feminists. In the second section, I will explore some problems that nonwestern feminists may have with feminist epistemology's critical focus on positivism. In the third section, I will examine some political implications of feminist epistemology's thesis of the "epistemic privilege" of oppressed groups for nonwestern feminists. And in the last section, I will discuss the claim that oppressed groups gain epistemic advantages by inhabiting a larger number of contexts, arguing that such situations may not always confer advantages and may sometimes create painful problems.

## NONWESTERN FEMINIST POLITICS AND FEMINIST EPISTEMOLOGY

Some themes of feminist epistemology may be problematic for nonwestern feminists in ways that they are not problematic for western feminists. Feminism has a much narrower base in most nonwestern countries. It is primarily of significance to some urban, educated, middle-class, and hence relatively westernized women, like myself. Although feminist groups in these countries do try to extend the scope of feminist concerns to other groups (for example, by fighting for childcare, women's health issues, and equal wages issues through trade union structures), some major preoccupations of western feminism—its critique of marriage, the family, compulsory heterosexuality—presently engage the attention of mainly small groups of middle-class feminists.

These feminists must think and function within the context of a powerful tradition that, although it systematically oppresses women, also contains within itself a discourse that confers a high value on women's place in the general scheme of things. Not only are the roles of wife and mother highly praised, but women also are seen as the cornerstones of the spiritual well-being of their husbands and children, admired for their supposedly higher moral, religious, and spiritual qualities, and so on. In cultures that have a pervasive religious component, like the Hindu culture with which I am familiar, everything seems assigned a place and value as long as it keeps to its place. Confronted with a powerful traditional discourse that values woman's place as long as she keeps to the place prescribed, it may be politically counterproductive for nonwestern feminists to echo uncritically the themes of western feminist epistemology that seek to restore the value, cognitive and otherwise, of "women's experience."

The danger is that, even if the nonwestern feminist talks about the value of women's experience in terms totally different from those of the traditional discourse, the difference is likely to be drowned out by the louder and more powerful voice of the traditional discourse, which will then claim that "what those feminists say" vindicates its view that the roles and experiences it assigns to women have value and that women should stick to those roles.

I do not intend to suggest that this is not a danger for western feminism or to imply that there is no tension for western feminists between being

Bailey–Cuomo: The
Feminist Philosophy
Reader

9. Feminist Epistemologies  |  Text

© The McGraw–Hill
Companies, 2008

223

critical of the experiences that their societies have provided for women and finding things to value in them nevertheless. But I am suggesting that perhaps there is less at risk for western feminists in trying to strike this balance. I am inclined to think that in nonwestern countries feminists must still stress the negative sides of the female experience within that culture and that the time for a more sympathetic evaluation is not quite ripe.

But the issue is not simple and seems even less so when another point is considered. The imperative we experience as feminists to be critical of how our culture and traditions oppress women conflicts with our desire as members of once colonized cultures to affirm the value of the same culture and traditions.

There are seldom any easy resolutions to these sorts of tensions. As an Indian feminist currently living in the United States, I often find myself torn between the desire to communicate with honesty the miseries and oppressions that I think my own culture confers on its women and the fear that this communication is going to reinforce, however unconsciously, western prejudices about the "superiority" of western culture. I have often felt compelled to interrupt my communication, say on the problems of the Indian system of arranged marriages, to remind my western friends that the experiences of women under their system of "romantic love" seem no more enviable. Perhaps we should all attempt to cultivate the methodological habit of trying to understand the complexities of the oppression involved in different historical and cultural settings while eschewing, at least for now, the temptation to make comparisions across such settings, given the dangers of attempting to compare what may well be incommensurable in any neat terms.

## THE NONPRIMACY OF POSITIVISM AS A PROBLEMATIC PERSPECTIVE

As a nonwestern feminist, I also have some reservations about the way in which feminist epistemology seems to have picked positivism as its main target of attack. The choice of positivism as

the main target is reasonable because it has been a dominant and influential western position and it most clearly embodies some flaws that feminist epistemology seeks to remedy.

But this focus on positivism should not blind us to the facts that it is not our only enemy and that nonpositivist frameworks are not, by virtue of that bare qualification, any more worthy of our tolerance. Most traditional frameworks that nonwestern feminists regard as oppressive to women are not positivist, and it would be wrong to see feminist epistemology's critique of positivism given the same political importance for nonwestern feminists that it has for western feminists. Traditions like my own, where the influence of religion is pervasive, are suffused through and through with values. We must fight not frameworks that assert the separation of fact and value but frameworks that are pervaded by values to which we, as feminists, find ourselves opposed. Positivism in epistemology flourished at the same time as liberalism in western political theory. Positivism's view of values as individual and subjective related to liberalism's political emphasis on individual rights that were supposed to protect an individual's freedom to live according to the values she espoused.

Nonwestern feminists may find themselves in a curious bind when confronting the interrelations between positivism and political liberalism. As colonized people, we are well aware of the facts that many political concepts of liberalism are both suspicious and confused and that the practice of liberalism in the colonies was marked by brutalities unaccounted for by its theory. However, as feminists, we often find some of its concepts, such as individual rights, very useful in our attempts to fight problems rooted in our traditional cultures.

Nonwestern feminists will no doubt be sensitive to the fact that positivism is not our only enemy. Western feminists too must learn not to uncritically claim any nonpositivist framework as an ally; despite commonalities, there are apt to be many differences. A temperate look at positions we espouse as allies is necessary since "the enemy of my enemy is my friend" is a principle likely to be as misleading in epistemology as it is in the domain of Realpolitik.

The critical theorists of the Frankfurt School will serve well to illustrate this point. Begun as a group of young intellectuals in the post-World War I Weimar Republic, the members were significantly influenced by Marxism, and their interests ranged from aesthetics to political theory to epistemology. Jürgen Habermas, the most eminent critical theorist today, has in his works attacked positivism and the claim of scientific theories to be value neutral or "disinterested." He has attempted to show the constitutive role played by human interests in different domains of human knowledge. He is interested, as are feminists, in the role that knowledge plays in the reproduction of social relations of domination. But, as feminist epistemology is critical of all perspectives that place a lopsided stress on reason, it must also necessarily be critical of the rationalist underpinnings of critical theory.

Such rationalist foundations are visible, for example, in Habermas's "rational reconstruction" of what he calls "an ideal speech situation," supposedly characterized by "pure intersubjectivity," that is, by the absence of any barriers to communication. That Habermas's "ideal speech situation" is a creature of reason is clear from its admitted character as a "rationally reconstructed ideal" and its symmetrical distribution of chances for all of its participants to choose and apply speech acts.

This seems to involve a stress on formal and procedural equality among speakers that ignores substantive differences imposed by class, race, or gender that may affect a speaker's knowledge of the facts or the capacity to assert herself or command the attention of others. Women in academia often can testify to the fact that, despite not being forcibly restrained from speaking in public forums, they have to overcome much conditioning in order to learn to assert themselves. They can also testify as to how, especially in male-dominated disciplines,

their speech is often ignored or treated with condescension by male colleagues.

Habermas either ignores the existence of such substantive differences among speakers or else assumes they do not exist. In the latter case, if one assumes that the speakers in the ideal speech situation are not significantly different from each other, then there may not be much of significance for them to speak about. Often it is precisely our differences that make dialogue imperative. If the ideal speakers of the ideal speech situation are unmarked by differences, there may be nothing for them to surmount on their way to a "rational consensus." If there are such differences between the speakers, then Habermas provides nothing that will rule out the sorts of problems I have mentioned.

Another rationalist facet of critical theory is revealed in Habermas's assumption that justifiable agreement and genuine knowledge arise only out of "rational consensus." This seems to overlook the possibility of agreement and knowledge based on sympathy or solidarity. Sympathy or solidarity may very well promote the uncovering of truth, especially in situations when people who divulge information are rendering themselves vulnerable in the process. For instance, women are more likely to talk about experiences of sexual harassment to other women because they would expect similar experiences to have made them more sympathetic and understanding. Therefore, feminists should be cautious about assuming that they necessarily have much in common with a framework simply because it is nonpositivist. Nonwestern feminists may be more alert to this error because many problems they confront arise in nonpositivist contexts.

## THE POLITICAL USES OF "EPISTEMIC PRIVILEGE"

Important strands in feminist epistemology hold the view that our concrete embodiments as members of a specific class, race, and gender as well

Bailey–Cuomo: The
Feminist Philosophy
Reader

9. Feminist Epistemologies | Text

© The McGraw–Hill
Companies, 2008

225

as our concrete historical situations necessarily play significant roles in our perspective on the world; moreover, no point of view is "neutral" because no one exists unembedded in the world. Knowledge is seen as gained not by solitary individuals but by socially constituted members of groups that emerge and change through history.

Feminists have also argued that groups living under various forms of oppression are more likely to have a critical perspective on their situation and that this critical view is both generated and partly constituted by critical emotional responses that subjects experience vis-à-vis their life situations. This perspective in feminist epistemology rejects the "Native View" of emotions and favors an intentional conception that emphasizes the cognitive aspect of emotions. It is critical of the traditional view of the emotions as wholly and always impediments to knowledge and argues that many emotions often help rather than hinder our understanding of a person or situation.

Bringing together these views on the role of the emotions in knowledge, the possibility of critical insights being generated by oppression, and the contextual nature of knowledge may suggest some answers to serious and interesting political questions. I will consider what these epistemic positions entail regarding the possibility of understanding and political cooperation between oppressed groups and sympathetic members of a dominant group—say, between white people and people of color over issues of race or between men and women over issues of gender.

These considerations are also relevant to questions of understanding and cooperation between western and nonwestern feminists. Western feminists, despite their critical understanding of their own culture, often tend to be more a part of it than they realize. If they fail to see the contexts of their theories and assume that their perspective has universal validity for all feminists, they tend to participate in the dominance that western culture has exercised over nonwestern cultures.

Our position must explain and justify our dual need to criticize members of a dominant group (say men or white people or western feminists) for their lack of attention to or concern with problems that affect an oppressed group (say, women or people of color or nonwestern feminists, respectively), as well as for our frequent hostility toward those who express interest, even sympathetic interest, in issues that concern groups of which they are not a part.

Both attitudes are often warranted. On the one hand, one cannot but be angry at those who minimize, ignore, or dismiss the pain and conflict that racism and sexism inflict on their victims. On the other hand, living in a state of siege also necessarily makes us suspicious of expressions of concern and support from those who do not live these oppressions. We are suspicious of the motives of our sympathizers or the extent of their sincerity, and we worry, often with good reason, that they may claim that their interest provides a warrant for them to speak for us, as dominant groups throughout history have spoken for the dominated.

This is all the more threatening to groups aware of how recently they have acquired the power to articulate their own points of view. Nonwestern feminists are especially aware of this because they have a double struggle in trying to find their own voice: they have to learn to articulate their differences, not only from their own traditional contexts but also from western feminism.

Politically, we face interesting questions whose answers hinge on the nature and extent of the communication that we think possible between different groups. Should we try to share our perspectives and insights with those who have not lived our oppressions and accept that they may fully come to share them? Or should we seek only the affirmation of those like ourselves, who share common features of oppression, and rule out the possibility of those who have not lived these oppressions ever acquiring a genuine understanding of them?

*Chapter 9 / Feminist Epistemologies*

I argue that it would be a mistake to move from the thesis that knowledge is constructed by human subjects who are socially constituted to the conclusion that those who are differently located socially can never attain *some* understanding of our experience or *some* sympathy with our cause. In that case, we would be committed to not just a perspectival view of knowledge but a relativistic one. Relativism, as I am using it, implies that a person could have knowledge of only the sorts of things she had experienced personally and that she would be totally unable to communicate any of the contents of her knowledge to someone who did not have the same sorts of experiences. Not only does this seem clearly false and perhaps even absurd, but it is probably a good idea not to have any a priori views that would imply either that all our knowledge is always capable of being communicated to every other person or that would imply that some of our knowledge is necessarily incapable of being communicated to some class of persons.

"Nonanalytic" and "nonrational" forms of discourse, like fiction or poetry, may be better able than other forms to convey the complex life experiences of one group to members of another. One can also hope that being part of one oppressed group may enable an individual to have a more sympathetic understanding of issues relating to another kind of oppression—that, for instance, being a woman may sensitize one to issues of race and class even if one is a woman privileged in those respects.

Again, this should not be reduced to some kind of metaphysical presumption. Historical circumstances have sometimes conspired, say, to making working-class men more chauvinistic in some of their attitudes than other men. Sometimes one sort of suffering may simply harden individuals to other sorts or leave them without energy to take any interest in the problems of other groups. But we can at least try to foster such sensitivity by focusing on parallels, not identities, between different sorts of oppressions.

Our commitment to the contextual nature of knowledge does not require us to claim that those who do not inhabit these contexts can never have any knowledge of them. But this commitment does permit us to argue that it is *easier* and *more likely* for the oppressed to have critical insights into the conditions of their own oppression than it is for those who live outside these structures. Those who actually *live* the oppressions of class, race, or gender have faced the issues that such oppressions generate in a variety of different situations. The insights and emotional responses engendered by these situations are a legacy with which they confront any new issue or situation.

Those who display sympathy as outsiders often fail both to understand fully the emotional complexities of living as a member of an oppressed group and to carry what they have learned and understood about one situation to the way they perceive another. It is a commonplace that even sympathetic men will often fail to perceive subtle instances of sexist behavior or discourse.

Sympathetic individuals who are not members of an oppressed group should keep in mind the possibility of this sort of failure regarding their understanding of issues relating to an oppression they do not share. They should realize that nothing they may do, from participating in demonstrations to changing their lifestyles, can make them one of the oppressed. For instance, men who share household and child-rearing responsibilities with women are mistaken if they think that this act of choice, often buttressed by the gratitude and admiration of others, is anything like the woman's experience of being forcibly socialized into these tasks and of having others perceive this as her natural function in the scheme of things.

The view that we can understand much about the perspectives of those whose oppression we do not share allows us the space to criticize dominant groups for their blindness to the facts of oppression. The view that such an understanding,

Bailey–Cuomo: The
Feminist Philosophy
Reader

9. Feminist Epistemologies | Text

© The McGraw–Hill
Companies, 2008

227

despite great effort and interest, is likely to be incomplete or limited, provides us with the ground for denying total parity to members of a dominant group in their ability to understand our situation.

Sympathetic members of a dominant group need not necessarily defer to our views on any particular issue because that may reduce itself to another subtle form of condescension, but at least they must keep in mind the very real difficulties and possibility of failure to fully understand our concerns. This and the very important need for dominated groups to control the means of discourse about their own situations are important reasons for taking seriously the claim that oppressed groups have an "epistemic advantage."

## THE DARK SIDE OF "DOUBLE VISION"

I think that one of the most interesting insights of feminist epistemology is the view that oppressed groups, whether women, the poor, or racial minorities, may derive an "epistemic advantage" from having knowledge of the practices of both their own contexts and those of their oppressors. The practices of the dominant groups (for instance, men) govern a society; the dominated group (for instance, women) must acquire some fluency with these practices in order to survive in that society.

There is no similar pressure on members of the dominant group to acquire knowledge of the practices of the dominated groups. For instance, colonized people had to learn the language and culture of their colonizers. The colonizers seldom found it necessary to have more than a sketchy acquaintance with the language and culture of the "natives." Thus, the oppressed are seen as having an "epistemic advantage" because they can operate with two sets of practices and in two different contexts. This advantage is thought to lead to critical insights because each framework provides a critical perspective on the other.

I would like to balance this account with a few comments about the "dark side," the disadvantages, of being able to or of having to inhabit two mutually incompatible frameworks that provide differing perspectives on social reality. I suspect that nonwestern feminists, given the often complex and troublesome interrelationships between the contexts they must inhabit, are less likely to express unqualified enthusiasm about the benefits of straddling a multiplicity of contexts. Mere access to two different and incompatible contexts is not a guarantee that a critical stance on the part of an individual will result. There are many ways in which she may deal with the situation.

First, the person may be tempted to dichotomize her life and reserve the framework of a different context for each part. The middle class of nonwestern countries supplies numerous examples of people who are very westernized in public life but who return to a very traditional lifestyle in the realm of the family. Women may choose to live their public lives in a "male" mode, displaying characteristics of aggressiveness, competition, and so on, while continuing to play dependent and compliant roles in their private lives. The pressures of jumping between two different lifestyles may be mitigated by justifications of how each pattern of behavior is appropriate to its particular context and of how it enables them to "get the best of both worlds."

Second, the individual may try to reject the practices of her own context and try to be as much as possible like members of the dominant group. Westernized intellectuals in the nonwestern world often may almost lose knowledge of their own cultures and practices and be ashamed of the little that they do still know. Women may try both to acquire stereotypically male characteristics, like aggressiveness, and to expunge stereotypically female characteristics, like emotionality. Or the individual could try to reject entirely the framework of the dominant group and assert the virtues of her own despite the risks of being marginalized from the power structures of the society; consider, for example, women who seek a certain sort of security in traditionally defined roles.

The choice to inhabit two contexts critically is an alternative to these choices and, I would argue, a more useful one. But the presence of alternative contexts does not by itself guarantee that one of the other choices will not be made. Moreover, the decision to inhabit two contexts critically, although it may lead to an "epistemic advantage," is likely to exact a certain price. It may lead to a sense of totally lacking roots or any space where one is at home in a relaxed manner.

This sense of alienation may be minimized if the critical straddling of two contexts is part of an ongoing critical politics, due to the support of others and a deeper understanding of what is going on. When it is not so rooted, it may generate ambivalence, uncertainty, despair, and even madness, rather than more positive critical emotions and attitudes. However such a person determines her locus, there may be a sense of being an outsider in both contexts and a sense of clumsiness or lack of fluency in both sets of practices. Consider this simple linguistic example: most people who learn two different languages that are associated with two very different cultures seldom acquire both with equal fluency; they may find themselves devoid of vocabulary in one language for certain contexts of life or be unable to match real objects with terms they have acquired in their vocabulary. For instance, people from my sort of background would know words in Indian languages for some spices, fruits, and vegetables that they do not know in English. Similarly, they might be unable to discuss "technical" subjects like economics or biology in their own languages because they learned about these subjects and acquired their technical vocabularies only in English.

The relation between the two contexts the individual inhabits may not be simple or straightforward. The individual subject is seldom in a position to carry out a perfect "dialectical synthesis" that preserves all the advantages of both contexts and transcends all their problems. There may be a number of different "syntheses," each of which avoids a different subset of the problems and preserves a different subset of the benefits.

No solution may be perfect or even palatable to the agent confronted with a choice. For example, some Indian feminists may find some western modes of dress (say trousers) either more comfortable or more their "style" than some local modes of dress. However, they may find that wearing the local mode of dress is less socially troublesome, alienates them less from more traditional people they want to work with, and so on. Either choice is bound to leave them partly frustrated in their desires.

Feminist theory must be temperate in the use it makes of this doctrine of "double vision"—the claim that oppressed groups have an epistemic advantage and access to greater critical conceptual space. Certain types and contexts of oppression certainly may bear out the truth of this claim. Others certainly do not seem to do so; and even if they do provide space for critical insights, they may also rule out the possibility of actions subversive of the oppressive state of affairs.

Certain kinds of oppressive contexts, such as the contexts in which women of my grandmother's background lived, rendered their subjects entirely devoid of skills required to function as independent entities in the culture. Girls were married off barely past puberty, trained for nothing beyond household tasks and the rearing of children, and passed from economic dependency on their fathers to economic dependency on their husbands to economic dependency on their sons in old age. Their criticisms of their lot were articulated, if at all, in terms that precluded a desire for any radical change. They saw themselves sometimes as personally unfortunate, but they did not locate the causes of their misery in larger social arrangements.

I conclude by stressing that the important insight incorporated in the doctrine of "double vision" should not be reified into a metaphysics that

Bailey–Cuomo: The
Feminist Philosophy
Reader

9. Feminist Epistemologies | Text

© The McGraw–Hill
Companies, 2008

229

serves as a substitute for concrete social analysis. Furthermore, the alternative to "buying" into an oppressive social system need not be a celebration of exclusion and the mechanisms of marginalization. The thesis that oppression may bestow an epistemic advantage should not tempt us in the direction of idealizing or romanticizing oppression and blind us to its real material and psychic deprivations.

## REFERENCES

Bordo, S. 1986. "The Cartesian Masculinization of Thought." *Signs* 11:439–456.

Gilligan, C. 1982. *In A Different Voice: Psychological Theory and Women's Development.* Cambridge, Mass.: Harvard University Press.

Harding, S. 1986. *The Science Question in Feminism.* Ithaca, N.Y.: Cornell University Press.

Harding, S., and M. Hintikka. 1983. *Discovering Reality: Feminist Perspectives on Epistemology, Metaphysics, Methodology, and Philosophy of Science.* Dordrecht: Reidel.

Harding, S., and J. O'Barr, eds. 1987. *Sex and Scientific Inquiry.* Chicago: University of Chicago Press.

Keller, E. F. 1985. *Reflections on Gender and Science.* New Haven, Conn.: Yale University Press.

Lloyd, G. 1984. *The Man of Reason.* Minneapolis: University of Minnesota Press.

# COMING TO UNDERSTAND: ORGASM AND THE EPISTEMOLOGY OF IGNORANCE

**Nancy Tuana**

*Lay understanding and scientific accounts of female sexuality and orgasm provide a fertile site for demonstrating the importance of including epistemologies of ignorance within feminist epistemologies. Ignorance is not a simple lack. It is often constructed, maintained, and disseminated and is linked to issues of cognitive authority, doubt, trust, silencing, and uncertainty. Studying both feminist and nonfeminist understandings of female orgasm reveals practices that suppress or erase bodies of knowledge concerning women's sexual pleasures.*

It is a common tenet of theorists working in the sociology of scientific knowledge (SSK) that an account of the conditions that result in scientists accepting apparently true beliefs and theories is as crucial as an analysis of those that result in

their holding to apparently false theories and beliefs. In outlining the Strong Programme in SSK studies, David Bloor (1976) argues against the asymmetry position common to philosophies of science. On such a position, only false beliefs that have had a history of influence upon science, such as views about ether, humors, or phlogiston, are in need of a sociological account. True beliefs or theories, however, are viewed as in need of no such explanation in that their acceptance can be accounted for simply by their truth. Bloor and other SSK theorists argue that such appeals to truth are inadequate, insisting that the acceptance of a belief as true, even in science, involves social factors. The appeal to reality thus does not suffice in explaining why a belief has come to be accepted by scientists.

In a similar fashion it is important that our epistemologies not limit attention simply to what is known or believed to be known. If we are to fully understand the complex practices of knowledge production and the variety of features that account for why something is known, we must also understand the practices that account for *not* knowing, that is, for our *lack* of knowledge about a phenomenon or, in some cases, an account of the practices that resulted in a group *unlearning* what was once a realm of knowledge. In other words, those who would strive to understand how we know must also develop epistemologies of ignorance.[1]

Ignorance, far from being a simple lack of knowledge that good science aims to banish, is better understood as a practice with supporting social causes as complex as those involved in knowledge practices. As Robert Proctor argued in his study of the politics of cancer research and dissemination, *Cancer Wars,* we must "study the social construction of ignorance. The persistence of controversy is often not a natural consequence of imperfect knowledge but a political consequence of conflicting interests and structural apathies. Controversy can be engineered: ignorance and uncertainty can be manufactured, maintained, and disseminated" (1995, 8).

An important aspect of an epistemology of ignorance is the realization that ignorance should not be theorized as a simple omission or gap but is, in many cases, an active production. Ignorance is frequently constructed and actively preserved, and is linked to issues of cognitive authority, doubt, trust, silencing, and uncertainty. Charles Mills, for example, argues that matters related to race in Europe and the United States involve an active production and preservation of ignorance: "On matters related to race, the Racial Contract prescribes for its signatories an inverted epistemology, an epistemology of ignorance, a particular pattern of localized and global cognitive dysfunctions (which are psychologically and socially functional), producing the ironic outcome that whites will in general be unable to understand the world they themselves have made" (1997, 18).

Although such productions are not always linked to systems of oppression, it is important to be aware of how often oppression works through and is shadowed by ignorance. As Eve Kosofsky Sedgwick argues in her *Epistemology of the Closet,* "ignorance effects can be harnessed, licensed, and regulated on a mass scale for striking

enforcements" (1990, 5). Indeed, tracing what is not known and the politics of such ignorance should be a key element of epistemological *and* social/political analyses, for it has the potential to reveal the role of power in the construction of what is known and to provide a lens for the political values at work in our knowledge practices.

Epistemologies that view ignorance as an arena of not-yet-knowing will also overlook those instances where knowledge once had has been lost. What was once common knowledge or even common scientific knowledge can be transferred to the realm of ignorance not because it is refuted and seen as false, but because such knowledge is no longer seen as valuable, important, or functional. Obstetricians in the United States, for example, no longer know how to turn a breech, not because such knowledge, in this case a knowing-how, is seen as false, but because medical practices, which are in large part fueled by business and malpractice concerns, have shifted knowledge practices in cases of breech births to Caesareans. Midwives in most settings and physicians in many other countries still possess this knowledge and employ it regularly. Epistemologies of ignorance must focus not only on cases where bodies of knowledge have been completely erased, or where a realm has never been subject to knowledge production, but also on these in-between cases where what was once common knowledge has been actively "disappeared" amongst certain groups. We must also ask the question now common to feminist and postcolonialist science studies of who benefits and who is disadvantaged by such ignorance (see, for example, Harding 1998; Tuana 1996b).

While we must abandon the assumption that ignorance is a passive gap in what we know, awaiting scientific progress and discovery, it would be premature to seek out a theory of ignorance with the expectation of finding some universal calculus of the "justified true belief" model. Why we do not know something, whether it has remained or been made unknown, who knows and who is ignorant, and how each of these shift

Bailey–Cuomo: The
Feminist Philosophy
Reader

9. Feminist Epistemologies

Text

© The McGraw–Hill
Companies, 2008

231

historically or from realm to realm, are all open to question. Furthermore, while the movements and productions of ignorance often parallel and track particular knowledge practices, we cannot assume that their logic is similar to the knowledge that they shadow. The question of how ignorance is sustained, cultivated, or allowed is one that must be asked explicitly and without assuming that the epistemic tools cultivated for understanding knowledge will be sufficient to understanding ignorance. The general point, however, still holds that we cannot fully account for what we know without also offering an account of what we do not know and who is privileged and disadvantaged by such knowledge/ignorance.

Female sexuality is a particularly fertile area for tracking the intersections of power/knowledge-ignorance.[2] Scientific and common-sense knowledge of female orgasm has a history that provides a rich lens for understanding the importance of explicitly including epistemologies of ignorance alongside our theories of knowledge. And so it is women's bodies and pleasures that I embrace.

## EPISTEMOLOGIES OF ORGASM

Following in the footsteps of foremothers as interestingly diverse as Mary Daly (1978) and Donna Haraway (2000), I adopt the habit of invoking a material-semiotic presence. I write under the sign of Inanna, the Sumerian Queen of Heaven and Earth.[3] Let her be a reminder that sign and flesh are profoundly interconnected.[4]

*What I tell you*
*Let the singer weave into song.*
*What I tell you,*

*Let it flow from ear to mouth,*
*Let it pass from old to young:*

*My vulva, the horn,*
*The Boat of Heaven,*
*Is full of eagerness like the young moon.*
*My untilled land lies fallow.*

*As for me, Inanna,*
*Who will plow my vulva?*
*Who will plow my high field?*
*Who will plow my wet ground?*
                    *(—Inanna 1983, 36–37)*

No doubt it sounds strange to ears schooled by a Foucaultian sensitivity to things sexual for me to frame an epistemology of ignorance around women's sexuality in general, and their orgasms in particular. Indeed, it was Michel Foucault who warned that the disciplining practices of the nineteenth century had constructed sex as "a problem of truth": "[T]he truth of sex became something fundamental, useful, or dangerous, precious or formidable; in short, that sex was constituted as a problem of truth" (1990, 56). Can my investigations of the power dimensions of ignorance concerning women's orgasms not fall prey to a constructed desire for the "truth of sex?"

One might suggest that I follow Foucault's admonition to attend to bodies and pleasures rather than sexual desire to avoid this epistemic trap. And indeed, I do desire to trace bodies and pleasures as a source of subversion. The bodies of my attention are those of women, the pleasures those of orgasm. But bodies and pleasures are not outside the history and deployment of sex-desire. Bodies and pleasures will not remove me, the epistemic subject, from the practice of desiring truth. Bodies and pleasures, as Foucault well knew, have histories. Indeed the bodies that I trace are material-semiotic interactions of organisms/environments/cultures.[5] Bodies and their pleasures are not natural givens, not even deep down. Nor do I believe in a true female sexuality hidden deep beneath the layers of oppressive socialization. But women's bodies and pleasures provide a fertile lens for understanding the workings of power/knowledge-ignorance in which we can trace who desires what knowledge; that is, we can glimpse the construction of desire (or lack thereof) for knowledge of women's sexuality. I also believe that women's bodies and pleasures can, at this historical moment, be a wellspring for resisting sexual normalization.[6] Although my focus in this essay will be on the former concern, I hope to provide sufficient development of the latter to tantalize.

I have no desire in this essay to trace the normalizing and pathologizing of sexual subjectivities. My goal is to understand what "we" do and do not know about women's orgasms, and why. My "we"s include scientific communities, both feminist and nonfeminist, and the common knowledges of everyday folk, both feminist and nonfeminist. Of course I cannot divorce normalizing sexualities from such a study of women's orgasms, for, as we will see, what we do and do not know of women's bodies and pleasures interact with these practices. Although part of my goal is to trace an epistemology of orgasm, I do so because of a firm belief that as we come to understand our orgasms, we will find a site of pleasure that serves as a resource for resisting sexual normalization through the practices of becoming sexual.

In coming to understand, I suggest that we begin at the site of the clitoris.

## UNVEILING THE CLITORIS

*Inanna placed the* shugurra, *the crown of the steppe, on her head.*
*She went to the sheepfold, to the shepherd.*
*She leaned back against the apple tree.*
*When she leaned against the apple tree,*
    *her vulva was wondrous to behold.*
*Rejoicing at her wondrous vulva,*
    *the young woman Inanna applauded herself.*
            —Inanna: Queen of Heaven and Earth:
                Her Stories and Hymms from Sumer

What we do and do not know about women's genitalia is a case study of the politics of ignorance. The "we"s I speak of here are both the "we"s of the general population in the United States[7] and the "we"s of scientists. Let me begin with the former. I teach a popular, large lecture course on sexuality. I have discovered that the students in the class know far more about male genitals than they

do about female genitals. Take, for example, the clitoris. The vast majority of my female students have no idea how big their clitoris is, or how big the average clitoris is, or what types of variations exist among women. Compare to this the fact that most of my male students can tell you the length *and* diameter of their penis both flaccid and erect, though their information about the average size of erect penises is sometimes shockingly inflated—a consequence, I suspect, of the size of male erections in porn movies. An analogous pattern of knowledge-ignorance also holds across the sexes. That is, both women and men alike typically know far more about the structures of the penis than they do about those of the clitoris.

This is not to say that women do not know anything about their genitalia. But what they, and the typical male student, know consists primarily in a more or less detailed knowledge of the menstrual cycle and the reproductive organs. Women and men can typically draw a relatively accurate rendition of the vagina, uterus, fallopian tubes, and ovaries, but when asked to provide me with a drawing (from memory) of an external and an internal view of female sexual organs, they often do not include a sketch of the clitoris; and when they do, it is seldom detailed.

This pattern of knowledge-ignorance mirrors a similar pattern in scientific representations of female and male genitalia. Although the role of the clitoris in female sexual satisfaction is scientifically acknowledged, and well known by most of us, the anatomy and physiology of the clitoris, particularly its beginnings and ends, is still a contested terrain. A brief history of representations of the clitoris provides an interesting initial entry into this epistemology of ignorance. Let me begin with the "facts."

As I and many other theorists have argued, until the nineteenth century, men's bodies were believed to be the true form of human biology and the standard against which female structures—bones, brains, and genitalia alike—were to be compared (see Laqueur 1990; Gallagher and Laqueur 1987; Schiebinger 1989; and Tuana 1993). The clitoris fared no differently. Medical science held the male

Bailey–Cuomo: The
Feminist Philosophy
Reader

9. Feminist Epistemologies | Text

© The McGraw–Hill
Companies, 2008

233

*The twelfth Figure, of the Wombe.*

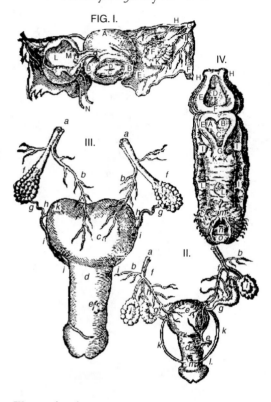

**Illustration 1**
*The workes of that famous chirurgion Ambrose
Pare,* translated out of Latine and compared with the
French by Thomas Johnson. London, Printed by
T. Cotes and R. Young, Anno 1634. Page 127.

genitals to be the true form, of which women's
genitals were a colder, interior version (see Illustration 1). As Luce Irigaray (1985) would say, through
this speculum women's genitals were simply those
of a man turned inside out and upside down. It
thus comes as no surprise that the clitoris would
be depicted as, at best, a diminutive homologue to
the penis. A history of medical views of the clitoris is not a simple tale. It includes those of Ambroise Paré, the sixteenth-century biologist, who,
while quite content to chronicle and describe the
various parts and functions of women's reproductive organs, refused to discuss what he called this
"obscene part," and admonished "those which desire to know more of it" to read the work of anatomists such as Renaldus Columbus and Gabriello
Fallopius (Paré 1968, 130). A history of the clitoris

must also include the subject, well dissected by
Thomas Laqueur (1989, 1986), whether, despite the
proliferation of terms such as *kleitoris, columnella,
virga* (rod), and *nympha* in texts from Hippocrates
to the sixteenth century, these meant anything
quite like what "clitoris" meant after the sixteenth
century when the link between it and pleasure was
bridged.

What was so "discovered" was, of course,
complex. Renaldus Columbus, self-heralded as he
who discovered the clitoris, refers us to "protuberances, emerging from the uterus near that opening
which is called the mouth of the womb" (1559,
11.16.447; Laqueur 1989, 103). He described
the function of these protuberances as "the seat
of women's delight" which "while women are eager for sex and very excited as if in a frenzy and
aroused to lust . . . you will find it a little harder
and oblong to such a degree that it shows itself a
sort of male member," and when rubbed or touched
"semen swifter than air flows this way and that on
account of the pleasure even with them unwilling"
(1559, 11.16.447–8; Laqueur 1989, 103).Though
a different clitoris than we are used to, I will later
argue that Columbus provides an interesting rendition of this emerging flesh relevant to an epistemology of knowledge-ignorance.

While much pleasure can result from a thorough history of the clitoris, let me forebear and
leap ahead to more contemporary renditions of
this seat of pleasure. Even after the "two-sex"
model became dominant in the nineteenth century,
with its view of the female not as an underdeveloped male but as a second gender with distinctive gender differences, the clitoris got short
shrift. It was often rendered a simple nub, which
though carefully labeled, was seldom fleshed out
or made a focus of attention (see Illustration 2).
Even more striking is the emerging practice from
the 1940s to the 1970s of simply omitting even
the nub of this seat of pleasure when offering a
cross-sectional image of female genitalia (see
Illustrations 3 and 4). It is important to remember
that this display, or lack thereof, is happening at
a time when displays of the penis are becoming
ever more complex (see Illustration 5).

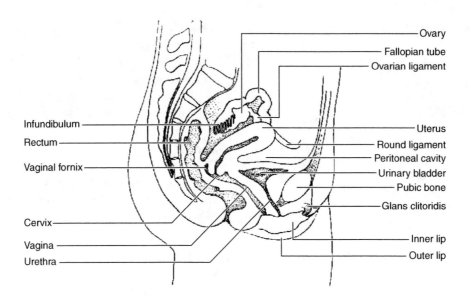

**Illustration 2**

Figure 4.3, Sagittal section of female internal anatomy (Rosen and Rosen 1981, 138).

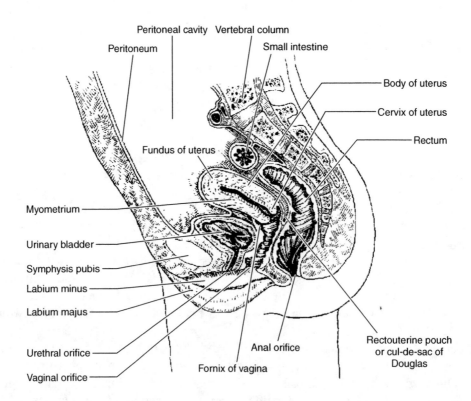

**Illustration 3**

Figure 24–6, Median sagittal section of female pelvis (Kimber, Gray, Stackpole, Leavell, and Miller 1966, 712).

Bailey–Cuomo: The
Feminist Philosophy
Reader

9. Feminist Epistemologies

Text

© The McGraw–Hill
Companies, 2008

235

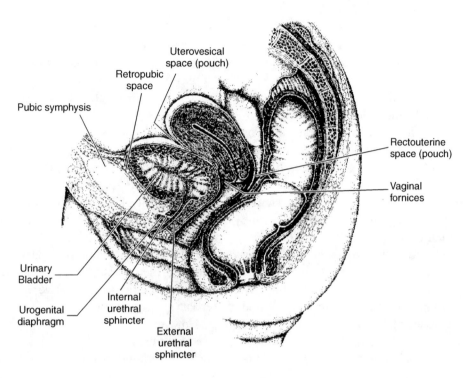

**Illustration 4**

Figure 5–13, Female pelvic organs (Christensen and Telford 1978, 182).

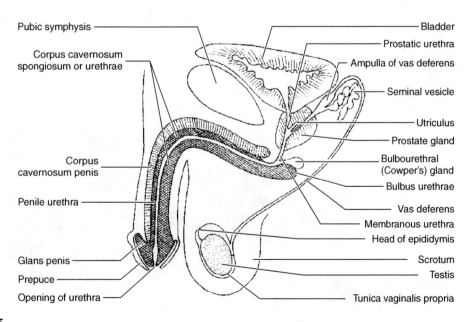

**Illustration 5**

Figure 24–3, Diagram of midsagittal section of male reproductive organs (Kimber, Gray, Stackpole, Leavell, and Miller 1966, 708).

Enter the women's health movement, and illustrations of women's genitals shift yet again, at least in some locations. Participants in the self-help women's movement, ever believers in taking matters into our own hands, not only took up the speculum as an instrument of knowledge and liberation but questioned standard representations of our anatomy. The nub that tended to disappear in standard anatomical texts took on complexity and structure in the hands of these feminists. In the 1984 edition of the Boston Women Health Collective's book, *Our Bodies, Ourselves,* the clitoris expanded in size and configuration to include three structures: the shaft, the glans, and the crura. This new model received its most loving rendition thanks to the leadership of the Federation of Feminist Women's Health Centers and the illustrative hands of Suzann Gage (1981) in *A New View of Woman's Body* (see Illustration 6).

On such accounts, the lower two-thirds of the clitoris is hidden beneath the skin of the vulva. The clitoral glans surmounts the shaft, or body of the clitoris, which is partly visible, and then extends under the muscle tissue of the vulva (see Illustration 7). To this is attached the crura, two stems of tissue, the corpora cavernosa, which arc out toward the thighs and obliquely toward the vagina. The glans of the clitoris, they explain, is a bundle of nerves containing 8,000 nerve fibers, twice the number in the penis, and which, as you know, respond to pressure, temperature, and touch. The "new view" presented to us provides not only far more detail about the clitoral structures, but also depicts the clitoris as large and largely internal. Unlike typical nonfeminist depictions of the clitoris as largely an external genitalia (see Illustration 8), the new view rendered visible the divide between external and internal (see Illustration 9).

Now to be fair, some very recent nonfeminist anatomical texts have included this trinity of shaft, glans, and crura.[8] But none of these texts focus attention on coming to understand the sexual response patterns of these and other bits.[9]

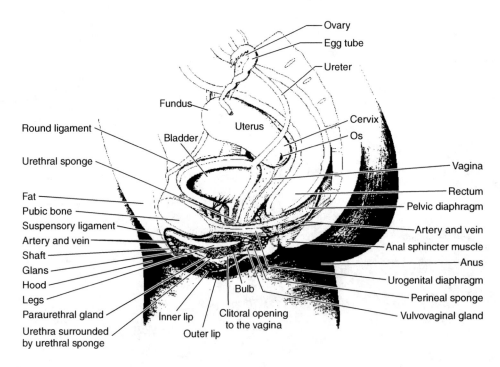

**Illustration 6**
Figure 3.9, A cross section of the clitoris (Federation of Feminist Women's Health Centers 1981, 41).

Bailey–Cuomo: The
Feminist Philosophy
Reader

9. Feminist Epistemologies    Text

© The McGraw–Hill
Companies, 2008

237

*Chapter 9 / Feminist Epistemologies*                    *773*

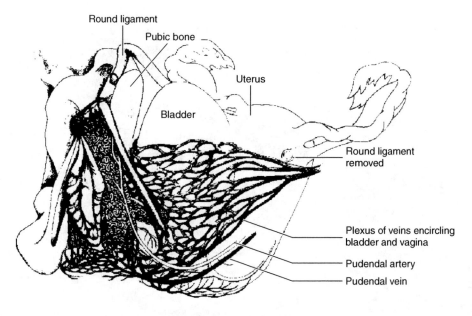

**Illustration 7**

Figure 3.10, How the clitoris is situated in the pelvis (Federation of Feminist Women's Health Centers 1981, 42).

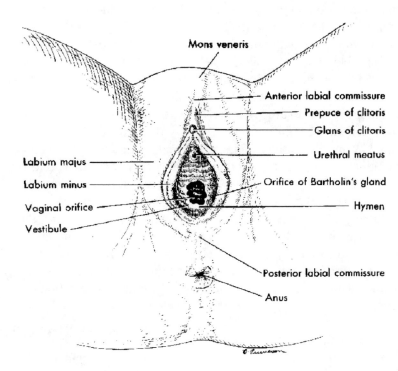

**Illustration 8**

Figure 24–8, External female genitalia (Kimber, Gray, Stackpole, Leavell, and Miller 1966, 717).

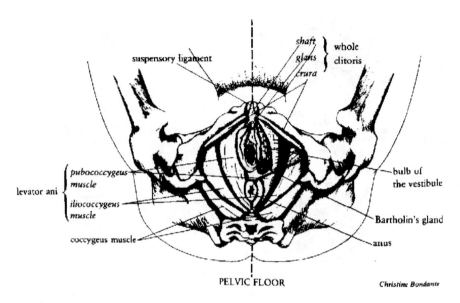

**Illustration 9**
Figure of the pelvic floor, clitoris, etc. (Boston Women's Health Book Collective 1984, 206).

Feminist imagery diverges significantly from non-feminist in providing us far more detailed views of the impact of sexual stimulation on the glans and crura of the clitoris, as well as the labia majora and the bulbs of the vestibule, the latter of which possess a very extensive blood vessel system that becomes very engorged during arousal, doubling, even tripling in size, we are told, during sexual arousal (see Illustration 10). The always-found illustrations of male erections (see Illustration 11), are now accompanied by an illustration of female erections (see Illustration 12), something absent in nonfeminist texts. Feminist texts also lovingly detail the other bits that are part of our seat of delight. Reminding us that the clitoris, impressive though it be, is not our only sensitive bit, feminists also provide us with images of the urethral sponge that lies between the front wall of the vagina and the urethra, which expands with blood during sexual arousal (see Illustration 13). It was this structure that was allegedly "discovered" with Columbus-like gusto (Christopher, this time, not Renaldus) by Ernst Grafenburg (1950) and popularized as the "G-spot." Although a few nonfeminist anatomical illustrators, post-Grafenburg, provide us

glimpses of this pleasurable sponge (see Illustration 14), apparently neither they nor Grafenburg have gotten the hang of the feminist speculum, for they continue to overlook feminist presentations of the other sponge, the perineal sponge located between the vagina and the rectum, which also engorges when a woman is sexually aroused (see Illustration 15). Pressure on any of these engorged structures can result in pleasure and orgasm.

We have a classic case of separate and unequal when it comes to contemporary nonfeminist depictions of female and male genitals. All the abovementioned contemporary anatomy textbooks include detailed renditions of the structures of the penis, with the *corpus cavernosum* and the *corpus spongiosum,* important sites of male engorgement, carefully drawn and labeled, while offering only the merest bit of a nub as a sufficient representation of the clitoris.[10]

## FINGERING TRUTH

So how do we put our finger on the truth of women's clitoral structures? Whose cartographies do we believe? For those of us who follow

Bailey–Cuomo: The
Feminist Philosophy
Reader

9. Feminist Epistemologies    Text

© The McGraw–Hill
Companies, 2008

239

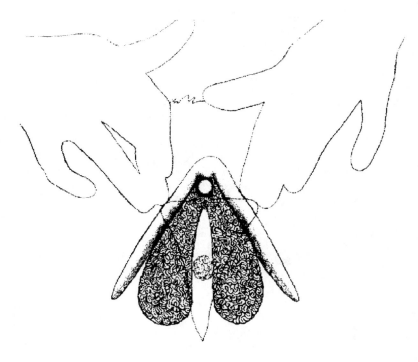

**Illustration 10**

Figure 3.23, An inner view of the clitoris during the plateau phase (Federation of Feminist Women's Health Centers 1981, 51).

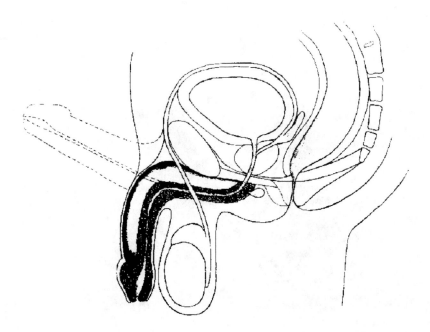

**Illustration 11**

Figure 3.17, Side view of the penis (Federation of Feminist Women's Health Centers 1981, 49).

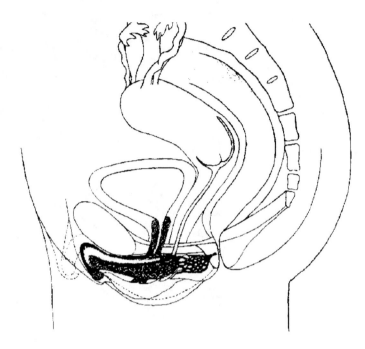

**Illustration 12**
Figure 3–16, Side view of the clitoris (Federation of Feminist Women's Health Centers 1981, 48).

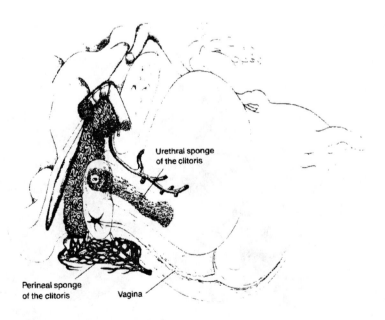

**Illustration 13**
Figure 3.12, Urethral sponge (Federation of Feminist Women's Health Centers 1981, 43).

Bailey–Cuomo: The
Feminist Philosophy
Reader

9. Feminist Epistemologies | Text

© The McGraw–Hill
Companies, 2008

241

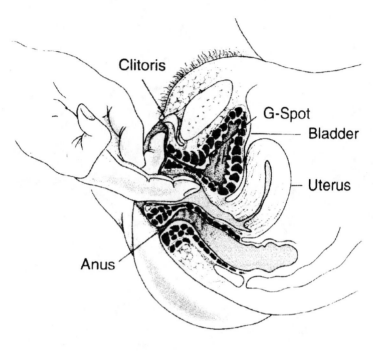

**Illustration 14**

Figure 5.7, The Grafenberg spot (Rathus, Nevid, and Fichner-Rathus 2002, 167).

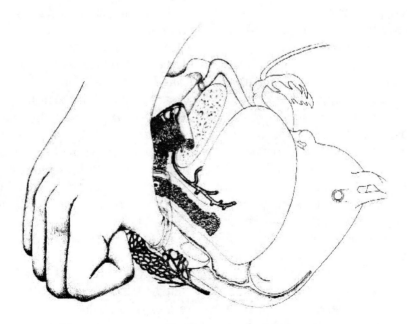

**Illustration 15**

Figure 3.14, Self-examination of the perineal sponge (Federation of Feminist Women's Health Centers 1981, 45).

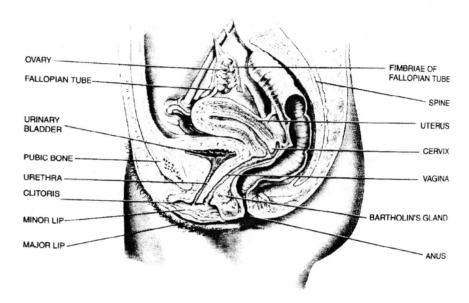

**Illustration 16**
Figure 2.4, Female sexual and reproductive organs (Kelly 1994, 44).

the speculum, the feminist influenced model of the three-fold clitoral structures have become scripture, with each detail ever more lovingly drawn. But rather than follow desire and insist that the feminist depictions of the clitoris are the truth, let me rather trace the ebbs and flows of this knowledge/ignorance.

Despite fifteen years of clear illustrations of this new view of clitoral structures, our impact has been surprisingly minimal, at least so far. A review of anatomical illustrations in standard college human sexuality textbooks reveals a surprising lack of attention to the functions and structures of the clitoris (see Illustration 16).[11] No surprise, then, that my students have, at best, a passing knowledge of the depths and complexity of its structures. These are the very same students, I remind you, who have relatively detailed knowledge of the structures of female reproductive organs and of the structures of male genitalia, though the terminology they use to label those parts often turns to street talk rather than the high Latin of medical textbooks. The human sexuality textbook writers have clearly bought the line that "size doesn't matter," and continue

to depict the clitoris as a modest, undifferentiated nub of flesh.

A politics of ignorance is at work here, one linked to the politics of sex and reproduction. Whether female and male genitalia are seen as homologous or analogous (or somewhere in between), centuries of scientific theories and lay beliefs have treated their pleasures differently. The importance of male pleasure and ejaculation for conception has been little disputed from the Greeks to the present. In contrast, the question of female seed and the link between it and female pleasure was always a point of controversy. Many scientists from the Greeks and well into the sixteenth century disputed the very existence of female seed or semen, though those in the earlier centuries who did ascribe to the existence of female seed often argued for the importance of female pleasure as the vehicle for its release (see Tuana 1988 and 1993). The infertility of prostitutes, for example, was often explained as due to a lack of pleasure in intercourse (Cadden 1993, 142–43). But by the thirteenth century and onward, the link between conception and female pleasure in sex was typically denied even by

Bailey–Cuomo: The
Feminist Philosophy
Reader

9. Feminist Epistemologies

Text

© The McGraw–Hill
Companies, 2008

243

those who allowed for the existence of female seed. Women's sexual pleasure came to be seen as inessential to reproduction, although many scholars admitted that it might be useful in promoting the desire for intercourse.

Now to this view of the function (or lack thereof) of female erotic pleasure add the politics of sex, namely the view that the only or at least the main function of sex is reproduction. To this add the politics of female sexuality, namely the tenet common in scientific and popular accounts well into the nineteenth century that women were more lustful than men and that their sexuality was a danger to men,[12] and a path is cleared to an understanding of why clitoral structures get lost in the process. The logic becomes quite clear: A) There is no good reason to pay attention to the clitoris, given that it allegedly plays no role in reproduction and that sex is to be studied (only) in order to understand reproduction. B) Worse, there is good reason to not pay attention to the clitoris lest we stir up a hornet's nest of stinging desire.[13] From Pandora on, and well into the nineteenth century, women's stinging desire and limb-gnawing passion had been branded the cause of the fall of mankind. What better reason to construct and maintain an epistemology of ignorance? What better way to disqualify and perhaps even control women's sexual satisfaction.[14]

But I simplify here to make my point. It is not true that history records no moments in the contemporary period when scientists focused their speculums on clitoral structures. Leaving Sigmund Freud aside for the moment, genitals came under scrutiny during the end of the nineteenth century as science constructed the category of the "invert," namely, those who mixed with members of their own sex. Evolutionary theory linked the newly "uncovered" sexual identity of the homosexual to degeneracy, and widespread societal fears of the degeneration of the race (that is, the white race), led to broadened support for eugenics movements. Scientists, now more intent than ever before on social control, began to examine bodies for signs of degeneration to provide

support for proper "matings" and to discourage the dangerous mixing of people across racial or sexual boundaries. Belief in the degeneration of the race led many to believe that so-called "inverts" were proliferating. Anxiety led to a desire to be able to track such undesirables and an equally strong desire to believe that their perversity and devolution would be clearly marked on their bodies. Given the desire for such knowledge, it did not take long before genitals, or at least deviant genitals, would become a focus of the scientific gaze, hornet's nest or not. Although through images to be kept only for the eyes of professionals, whose objectivity and dispassionate nature would protect them from corruption, science began to turn its gaze on the structures of the clitoris to seek out and control deviancy.

The Sex Variant study, conducted in New York City from 1935–1941, was one example of scientific investigations launched to interrogate the marks of deviance that had been imprinted onto the structures of the body. The professed goal of the study was to identify inverts so that physicians could then try to stop them from reproducing and further contaminating the race. Gynecologist Robert Latou Dickinson, the principle investigator of the Sex Variant study, believed that deviance and degeneration would be mapped on women's genitals. Clitorises were examined, measured, and sketched, along with the various contours of vulva, breast, and nipple sizes. Dickinson concluded that, indeed, the genitals of inverts were a symbol of their deviance, arguing that their genitals were different from those of "normal" women—their vulvae, larger; their clitorises, notably erectile; their labium, longer and more protruding; their vaginas, distensible; their hymens, insensitive; and their uteruses, smaller (see Illustration 17). As an aside, it should be noted here that Dickinson's gynecological studies included *only* so-called inverts (the "normal" vulva, he apparently drew from memory.) This was also a period when the genitals of "inferior" races, particularly those of African descent, were examined and measured,

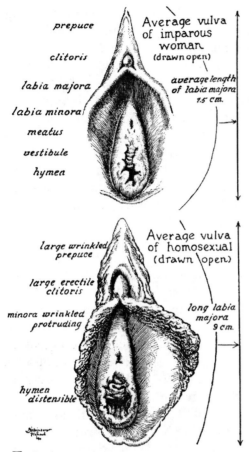

prepuce
clitoris
labia majora
labia minora
meatus
vestibule
hymen

Average vulva of imparous woman (drawn open)

average length of labia majora 7.5 cm.

large wrinkled prepuce
large erectile clitoris
minora wrinkled protruding
hymen distensible

Average vulva of homosexual (drawn open)

long labia majora 9 cm.

Typical sex variant vulva and average

**Illustration 17**
Figure 3, Typical sex variant vulva and average (Dickinson 1941, 1102).

with investigators once again believing that proof of inferiority would be marked on their genitals.[15]

The point here is that this epistemology is not about truth. I am not arguing that the feminist model of the three-fold structures of the clitoris finally uncovered the long submerged truth of the clitoris. Nor am I arguing that feminists were, finally, practicing good science and being objective. These cartographies were and are fueled by our desire to transform normative heterosexuality's vagina-only attention to pleasure. Nor am I claiming that there were no discourses on the clitoris as a source

of sexual pleasure in medical and popular literature until feminists and their speculums entered the scene. Indeed, one can find dozens, if not hundreds, of accounts of female orgasm resulting from this feminine seat of pleasure in texts as disparate as those written by midwives and penned by pornographers. Nor am I arguing that the speculum was never focused on the female vulva. However, a complex absence exists, a gap that I find important, one often repeated today. What is missing or only sketchily attended to in nonfeminist anatomies, at least when the focus is on the "normal" rather than the "deviant," is the desire to map the geographies and functions of the clitoris and our other pleasurable bits. What nonfeminist anatomists sketch seldom goes beyond the identification of this pleasurable (or dangerous) lump of flesh. What I am arguing is that the history of our knowledges-ignorances of the clitoris—indeed, our lived experiences of its beginnings and ends—is part of an embodied discourse and history of bodies and pleasures. It is a chapter in the tale of power/knowledge-ignorance.

## THE ISSUE OF PLEASURE

*Who would want a shotgun when you can have a semiautomatic?*
—NATALIE ANGIER
*WOMAN: AN INTIMATE GEOGRAPHY*

Let me remain a moment at this site of pleasure. Remember with me that until the nineteenth century not only women's desire for sex but the very pleasures they received from it were seen as far greater than those of men. In the words of Tiresias, he who had lived both as a woman and as a man, when it comes to the issue of pleasure:

If the parts of love's pleasures be divided by ten, Thrice three go to women, one only to men. (Apollodorus 3.6.7)

Bailey–Cuomo: The
Feminist Philosophy
Reader

9. Feminist Epistemologies    Text

© The McGraw–Hill
Companies, 2008

245

This image of women's sexuality shifts, at least for certain women, as we move into the nineteenth century, and with this move, we can locate a shift of knowledge-ignorance.

> *My lord Dumuzi is ready for the holy loins.*
> *The plants and herbs in his field are ripe.*
> *"O Dumuzi! Your fullness is my delight."*
>
> *. . . . He shaped my loins with his fair hands,*
> *The shepherd Dumuzi filled my lap with cream*
>     *and milk,*
> *He stroked my pubic hair,*
> *He watered my womb.*
> *He laid his hands on my holy vulva,*
> *He smoothed my black boat with cream,*
> *He quickened my narrow boat with milk.*
>     *(Inanna 1983, 41, 43)*

Many of our sociological surveys of sexuality, though not all, figure sex as it is figured in the story of Inanna, between a woman and a man. Although this is far too narrow a story to tell if what we want is an account of bodies and pleasures, let me focus on the differences between this ancient account and contemporary embodiments of heterosexual female sexuality.

A 1994 survey of heterosexual women and men in the United States between the ages of 18 and 59 reveals that one out of every three women surveyed reported that they were uninterested in sex and one out of every five women reported that sex provided little pleasure, in both cases double the number of men reporting a lack of interest or pleasure in sex (Laumann, Gagnon, Michael, and Michaels 1994). Add to this the fact that almost 25 percent of the women surveyed reported being unable to reach orgasm, in comparison with 8 percent of men, and we begin to see an impact of knowledge-ignorance on bodies and pleasures. The pleasure gap surrounding heterosexual women's and men's first coital experiences is even more startling: 79 percent of men reported that they were certain they had an orgasm during their first sexual experience, while only 7 percent

of the women could so report (Sprecher, Barbee, and Schwartz 2001).

These are astonishing figures in themselves, but they become all the more startling when set alongside of women's multi-orgasmic capacities. Women's capacity for multiple orgasm, though taken to be a revelation by contemporary scientists, was a commonplace in many scientific and popular circles in the past.

> *He caressed me on the . . . fragrant honey-bed:*
> *My sweet love, lying by my heart,*
> *Tongue-playing, one by one,*
> *My fair Dumuzi did so fifty times.*
>
> *Now my sweet love is sated. (Inanna 1983, 48)*

What was once taken to be ordinary knowledge of women's more robust sexuality and her greater orgasmic capacity submerged into the mire of ignorance sometime during the turn of the last century, where it went dormant (or perhaps just pornographic) for about fifty years and then resurfaced in the new science of sexuality.

Woman's multi-orgasmic capacity became a subject for contemporary scientific study when Kinsey's 1953 study, *Sexual Behavior in the Human Female,* revealed that almost half of the women studied reported the ability to experience multiple orgasms. Shere Hite's 1976 report on female sexuality confirmed Kinsey's results. 48 percent of the women in Hite's survey reported that they often required more than one orgasm to be sexually satisfied (1976, 602–603). William H. Masters and Virginia G. Johnson (1966) similarly documented women's ability to have more than one orgasm without a significant break. They noted that if proper stimulation continues after a woman's first climax, she will in most cases be capable of having additional orgasms—they report between five and six—within a matter of minutes. Masters and Johnson also report that with direct clitoral stimulation, such as an electric vibrator, many women have from twenty to fifty orgasms.

Despite having science and all those measuring tools on our side, efforts continue to suppress this bit of knowledge. As just one example, Donald Symons in *The Evolution of Human Sexuality* (1979), strikes a typical pose when he assures his readers that the multiply orgasmic woman "… is to be found primarily, if not exclusively, in the ideology of feminism, the hopes of boys, and the fears of men" (1979, 92).

Foucault warned us away from desire as a category implicated in the construction of human identities and cultures, but urged a greater attention to pleasure. His *History of Sexuality* (1990) documents the uses of pleasure in the practices of normalizing power and includes pleasure, not just desire, as fundamental to understanding the genealogy of sexuality. But Foucault's account also includes a creative, indeed resistant, aspect of pleasure, in which pleasure could be a site for resisting sexual normalization and a wellspring for enriching the art of living.[16]

At a time when popular culture and science alike are convinced of men's greater sexual drives, when a long entrenched fear of the power of women's sexuality is still in the background, when a clear double standard of sexuality disciplines women and men alike, and when heterosexuality remains the normalized sexuality, it is perhaps no surprise that far more women than men are dissatisfied when it comes to the issue of pleasure. But I desire to flesh out pleasure in ways that have the potential to resist this type of normalization. As a first step, I stand Inanna and Tiresias alongside the nineteenth century's passionless woman and the twentieth century's preorgasmic but sexually active woman, and by coming to understand the politics of knowledge-ignorance behind their presence, invoke the female orgasm.

## THE EITHER/OR OF WOMEN'S ORGASMS

Let me return to my history of the clitoris. In this section I will complicate this study of the epistemology of ignorance-knowledge regarding female sexuality by bringing function to form, turning my attention to accounts of the role of the clitoris in female orgasm. To understand the almost complete circumcision of female orgasmic potentiality affected by labeling practically any clitoral "excitability" deviant during the first half of the twentieth century, we must turn to Freud. The longest playing of the orgasm debates in the twentieth century began with Freud's declaration of not one but two types of orgasm: the vaginally adult kind and her immature kid sister, the clitoral orgasm (1962, 124). From this one little act of counting to two erupted a huge, now almost centuries-long debate.

Let me begin my account by returning to Columbus. While Columbus's clitoris and mine are not located in the same place, the link he makes between it and sexual pleasure marks a movement I would like us to remember. His account bears repeating. He tells us that he discovered "protuberances, emerging from the uterus near that opening which is called the mouth of the womb" that were, in his words, "the seat of women's delight," which when rubbed or touched "semen swifter than air flows this way and that on account of the pleasure even with them unwilling" (1559, 11.16.447–48; Laqueur 1989, 103). Columbus functions according to an older economy in which women's pleasure in sex mattered because it was needed for conception.

While still marked by a male economy—both in representation ("it shows itself a sort of male member") and in function ("even with them unwilling")—Columbus's depiction of the clitoris evinces another economy that dissolves the boundary between inside and out, between the so-called "external" and the "internal" genitalia. It also provides an interesting example of how knowledge once found can be lost. Columbus, a man of his time, viewed female genitalia as homologous to male genitalia but marked by a lack of heat that resulted in them remaining, for the most part, inside the body. In identifying a "protuberance" that emerges from the uterus, Columbus acknowledged that it, like the penis, grew in size

Bailey–Cuomo: The
Feminist Philosophy
Reader

9. Feminist Epistemologies | Text

© The McGraw–Hill
Companies, 2008

247

when aroused, but he did not limit female pleasure to it. He acknowledged other sites of pleasure, such as the circular folds of the cervix that cause a friction from which lovers experience wonderful pleasure and the various bits of flesh closer to the vulva by which "pleasure or delight in intercourse is not a little increased" (1559, 11.16.445; Laqueur 1989, 105). Columbus's geography described various linked structures as contributing to woman's pleasure, but he had no desire to determine where one part or orgasm stops and another begins. Nor was there a desire to locate pleasure in a clearly defined site. Protuberances, folds, and bits of flesh alike are, for Columbus, that from which pleasure flows.

What Columbus had put together, Freud would cast asunder. While Freud retained a remnant of the one-sex model, arguing that "portions of the male sexual apparatus also appear in women's bodies, though in an atrophied state" (1964, 114), he argues for an important psychical difference between the pleasures of men and those of women. In boys there is a relatively unproblematic "accession of libido" during puberty. In girls, however, he tells us that there is "a fresh wave of repression in which it is precisely clitoroidal sexuality that is effected" (1962, 123). That is, to become a woman the girl must abandon the pleasures of the clitoris and discover those of the vagina. "When erotogenic susceptibility to stimulation has been successfully transferred by a woman from the clitoris to the vaginal orifice, it implies that she has adopted a new leading zone for the purposes of her later sexual activity" (1962, 124). This is an economy that requires a level of differentiation not found in Columbus. Freud's is a map of the female genitals that requires that we can, and do, distinguish between the clitoris and all its bits, on the one hand, and the vagina and its bits of flesh on the other. And it is here, despite the trace of the one-sex model, that Freud imposes a two-sex economy that divides the clitoris from the other bits. But he does so to perpetuate an even older economy that perceives the purpose of female

pleasure, when properly channeled, to be heterosexual reproduction. Indeed, "the intensification of the brake upon sexuality brought about by pubertal repression in women serves as a stimulus to the libido of men and causes an increase in its activity" (1962, 123). In other words, repressed female sexuality increases male desire—quite a modern trope.

The story, of course, shifts in the 1960s with the tools of Masters and Johnson and the politics of feminism. Masters and Johnson (1966) rejected the purported distinction between clitoral and vaginal orgasm, arguing physiologically speaking for only one kind of orgasm. Peering through their speculums, they concluded that allegedly vaginal orgasms, which they revealingly identified as those experienced during intercourse (notice the functionality of the definition), were no different than allegedly clitoral orgasms, for both resulted from the same phenomena, namely clitoral stimulation. We are told that penile coital thrusting draws the clitoral hood back and forth against the clitoris and vaginal pressure heightens blood flow in the clitoris, further setting the stage for orgasm.

These findings were, and still are, met with skepticism in the scientific community, but not in the feminist community. Following closely on the heels of Masters and Johnson's pronouncements and the second wave of feminism that hit in the late 1960s, feminist theorists such as Ann Koedt (1970) and Alix Shulman (1971) insisted that we women should all "think clitoris" and reject the myth of the vaginal orgasm. Their concern was to discredit the vaginal orgasm and the years of pressure placed on women who did not have the "right kind." But to make the case, a frustrating reversal occurred where *only* the clitoris was *the* source of sensation—and remember we do not yet have the enlarged *Our Bodies, Ourselves* (1984) conception of the clitoris to turn to. Shulman tells us that the vagina has so little sensation that "women commonly wear a diaphragm or tampon in it, and even undergo surgery on it, without feeling any sensation at all" (1971, 294).

And although Shulman does not deny that some women might sometimes experience orgasm through intercourse, for after all some women, she tells us, sometimes experience orgasm through breast stimulation or mental stimulation or even through dreams, she does disparage the level of pleasure intercourse can provide: "Masters and Johnson observe that the clitoris is automatically 'stimulated' in intercourse since the hood covering the clitoris is pulled over the clitoris with each thrust of the penis in the vagina—much, I suppose, as a penis is automatically 'stimulated' by a man's underwear whenever he takes a step. I wonder, however, if either is erotically stimulating by itself" (1971, 296).

Despite Masters and Johnson and feminist slogans, the days of vaginal orgasm are not (yet) numbered. Josephine Singer and Irving Singer (1972), for example, argue still for two types of orgasms, the vulval and the uterine. They contend that what Masters and Johnson observed were vulval orgasms, which remain the same despite the source of stimulation, clitoral or vaginal. But they argue that the uterine orgasm occurs only in response to deep thrusting against the cervix that slightly displaces the uterus and stimulates the tissues that cover the abdominal organs. This view of two types of orgasm has received additional support from scientists who argue that orgasms that result from deep cervical or uterine stimulation are controlled by a different neural pathway and produce different subjective experiences than do those generated through clitoral stimulation (for example, see Alzate 1985; Perry and Whipple 1981; and Whipple 1995).

One response to the orgasm debates is to ask what keeps them so entrenched? As breasts and other non-genital bits attest to, the origins of orgasms are a complex matter. Why the persistence in counting even when we are reassured (repeatedly) that they are all equally "good" (see McAnulty and Burnette 2001, 119)? Though I have no doubt that the answer to this question is complex, let me explore two of its components: the geography of

the genitals, and the persistence of the belief that the function of sex is reproduction.

Those who sketch anatomical renditions of male and female genitals insist on making a distinction between internal and external genitalia. A factor of arbitrariness is clearly marked on this distinction. For males the penis is wholly an external genital, but testicles get divided in two, with the scrotum being listed as an external sex organ and the testes as internal. Since lots of bits of the penis are internal, one wonders why we even bother to make this distinction. But when it comes to the analogous division of female genitals, more than arbitrariness is at play. The politics of reproduction gets written explicitly into this division, for in the female another descriptive phrase for the internal female sex organs is "the female reproductive system" (Rathus 2002, 106). This division reinforces the orgasm debates and provides a way to "make sense" of the claim for different kinds of orgasms, those that originate from outside and those from inside.

What we have here is an instance of the politics of knowledge-ignorance. This division of female genitals evinces the persistence of a politics of viewing reproduction as central to sexuality, so that it becomes a defining element in the demarcation of female genitalia. If you set sail by Columbus's map, you would not arrive at the planned destination. Still, like his earlier navigator namesake, where you do arrive is interesting too. Seeing orgasm and reproduction as a piece of a whole cloth, Columbus had no desire to demarcate the clitoris as "external" and hence not part of the female reproductive system. But once the clitoris and its orgasmic pleasures were seen as inessential to reproduction, few anatomists saw any value in charting its contours and it was relegated into that little undifferentiated nub that could easily be deemed "external" and "nonreproductive," with the "true" genitals, those that matter, being the internal genitalia.[17]

This politics of knowledge-ignorance is in turn marked by a persistent refusal to admit that the new feminist-inspired view of female genitals

Bailey–Cuomo: The
Feminist Philosophy
Reader

9. Feminist Epistemologies | Text

© The McGraw–Hill
Companies, 2008

249

dissolves the basis for the internal/external divide, for, on its view, the clitoris is always already both. And once one has this richer understanding of all the bits involved in female orgasm, and little political commitment to retaining a teleology of reproduction in accounts of pleasure, then nothing turns on demarcating types of orgasm based on physiological location. In *Women's Experience of Sex,* Sheila Kitzinger sums up this view thusly: "Asking whether orgasm is in the clitoris or in the vagina is really the wrong question" (1985, 76). But here, despite feminist insistence that their accounts were about truth—"I think that we were revealing the truth. And how can you argue with anatomy?"[18]— we find ourselves in that complex intersection between knowledge-ignorance and power-politics. The desire to "cut nature at its joints" often requires value-laden, strategic decisions. Feminists cut nature at different joints than do others who represent the clitoris because their values concerning the politics of sex differ from the values of non-feminist anatomists. Perhaps the body speaks, but understanding what it says requires interpretation.

What we learn from feminist explorations of our genital geography is twofold. First, if you view the clitoris as an important knowledge project, whether because you are convinced that orgasm is primarily clitoral and your geographies aim to understand pleasure or because, like Columbus, you think orgasm is central to reproduction and you aim to understand reproduction, then you will focus far more attention on the structures of the clitoris than if you see it as an uninteresting though pleasant nub. What we attend to and what we ignore are often complexly interwoven with values and politics. Second, if you discover new knowledge about something others do not take seriously, do not expect your knowledge projects to have much effect. The veil of ignorance is not so easily lifted.

## BODIES AND PLEASURES

I return to my tropes, Inanna and Tiresias, and add a third to this gathering, Annie Sprinkle, porn-star-turned-performance-artist/sex educator.

If bodies and pleasures are to be seen as a resource, it is important not to think that our goal is to find those pleasures free from sexual normalization, free from disciplinary practices. Here I follow LaDelle McWhorter, who claims that "instead of refusing normalization outright, we need to learn ways to use the power of its disciplines to propel us in new directions" (1999, 181). Though we cannot simply remove ourselves from disciplinary practices, she argues that it is possible to affirm "development without affirming docility, [through] affirming the free, open playfulness of human possibility within regimes of sexuality without getting stuck in or succumbing to any one sexual discourse or formation" (1999, 181). McWhorter, following Foucault, suggests that one path to this playfulness is to deliberately separate practice from goal and simply engage in disciplinary practices for their own sake, for the pleasures they bring, rather than for some purpose beyond them. "What if we used our capacities for temporal development not for preparation for some task beyond that development but for the purpose of development itself, including the development of our capacities for pleasure? What if we used pleasure rather than pain as our primary disciplinary tool?" (1999, 182). Following Foucault, what we must work on ". . . is not so much to liberate our desires but to make ourselves infinitely more susceptible to pleasure" (Foucault 1989, 310).

Annie Sprinkle, in her one-woman show, "Herstory of Porn: Reel to Real," describes the new direction her work took in the mid-1980s when she devoted her talents to displaying the beauty of sex and the undiscovered power of orgasms. "Some people discover Jesus and want to spread the word. I discovered orgasms and want to spread the word" (Sprinkle 1999). Sprinkle's new productions attempt to refocus attention from power to pleasure. "There's a lot of people who talk about violence, rape, and abuse. But, there's not a lot of people that talk about pleasure, bliss, orgasm, and ecstasy" (Sprinkle 1999). Sprinkle's work has transformed over time. At one point her performances focused attention on female

250

Bailey–Cuomo: The
Feminist Philosophy
Reader

9. Feminist Epistemologies | Text

© The McGraw–Hill
Companies, 2008

orgasmic ejaculations, providing audiences with sights seldom before seen on stage and ones that were, as the title of her performance explains, real, not reel. She has also advocated and really performed the nongenital breath or energy orgasm in which one "can simply lie down, take a few breaths, and go into an orgasmic state."

Sprinkle is not advocating a new homologous model of female orgasm—women ejaculate too—or an ultimate radical feminist rejection of penetrative sex. Rather than setting up new disciplinary practices with clearly defined markers between "good" feminist sex and "bad" nonfeminist sex, Sprinkle explores pleasure and refers to herself as a "metamorphosexual." I am not here claiming that Sprinkle's pleasures are outside sexual normalization, but I do think she stands before us as one who explores pleasure for its own sake. I offer her pleasures as an example of how we might, in McWhorter's words, "live our bodies as who we are, to intensify our experiences of bodiliness and to think from our bodies, if we are going to push back against the narrow confines of the normalizing powers that constrict our freedom" (1999, 185).

Sprinkle's pleasures are themselves part of disciplinary practices. It is important if we go the way of pleasure that we not desire pleasures that escape power. For Sprinkle's body and pleasures are situated in economies partially shaped by the feminist speculum. A more complete story would situate Sprinkle in the decades of practices of the feminist health movement and feminist efforts to take back our bodies and our sexualities. This pleasurable account I must leave for another time. Here I will simply tantalize by repeating Sprinkle's gospel that we return to our bodies and to our orgasms, and spread the word.

## CONCLUSION

It comes as no surprise that a correlation often exists between ignorance and pleasure. The feminist quest to enhance knowledge about women's bodies and their sexual experiences had as its goal the enhancement of women's pleasures. As should now be clear, knowledge and pleasures are complexly interrelated. Indeed the old adage that "ignorance is bliss" takes on new meanings when read through the lens of an epistemology attentive to both knowledge and ignorance. Whose pleasures were enhanced by ignorance and whose were suppressed by knowledge are complex questions that must be asked repeatedly in any study of the science of sexuality.

My goal in this essay was twofold. First, I wanted to share a genuine fascination with the study of the science of sexuality, particularly in relation to female sexuality. While much effort has gone into studying the formation of sexual *identities,* far less has been devoted to the science of sexuality. While I do not want to suggest that this aspect of sexual science or our sexual experiences are divorced from the constructions of sexual identities, I do believe that a fascination with the latter has deferred full attention from the former. While sexual identity issues will always be an aspect of any study of the science of sexuality, it is my conviction that an inclusion of sexuality will highlight other axes of power.

My second goal in writing this essay was to begin to outline the importance and power of attending to what we do not know and the power/politics of such ignorances. Although my account is preliminary and suggestive, I have presented the following claims:

- Any complete epistemology must include a study of ignorance, not just knowledge.
- Ignorance—far from being a simple, innocent lack of knowledge—is a complex phenomenon that like knowledge, is interrelated with power; for example, ignorance is frequently constructed, and it is linked to issues of cognitive authority, trust, doubt, silencing, etc.
- While many feminist science studies theorists have embraced the interrelationship of knowledge and values, we must also see the ways in which ignorance, too, is so interrelated.

Bailey–Cuomo: The
Feminist Philosophy
Reader

9. Feminist Epistemologies | Text

© The McGraw–Hill
Companies, 2008

251

- The study of ignorance can provide a lens for the values at work in our knowledge practices.
- We should not assume that the epistemic tools we have developed for the study of knowledge or the theories we have developed concerning knowledge practices will transfer to the study of ignorance.

## "IN CONCLUSION"

*Inanna went to visit Enki, the god of wisdom, who possessed the holy laws of heaven and earth. She drank beer with him. They drank beer together. They drank more and more beer together, until Enki, god of wisdom, agreed to give Inanna all the holy laws. She accepted the holy laws, gathered them together, placed them in the Boat of Heaven, and sailed back across the water. [My vulva, the horn, the Boat of Heaven, is full of eagerness like the young moon.] Upon reaching land and unloading the holy laws, Inanna discovered that she returned with more holy laws than had been given her by Enki.*

—Inanna: Queen of Heaven and Earth:
Her Stories and Hymms from Sumer

I hope by now you are laughing softly with me. Lean back against the apple tree. Feel the delicate fire running under your skin. Our vulvae are wondrous to behold. Rejoice at your wondrous vulva and applaud yourself.

## NOTES

My thanks to Lynn Hankinson Nelson, Alison Wylie, and the anonymous reviewers for their very helpful editorial suggestions.

1. I choose to employ the phrase "epistemologies of ignorance" despite its potential awkwardness (theories of knowledge of ignorance) for a number of reasons. The alternative term, agnoiology, has histories I have no desire to invoke. First employed by James Frederick Ferrier (1854) to refute William Hamilton's (1858–60) thesis of the unknowableness of the Absolute Reality, Ferrier posits ignorance as properly attributable only to an *absence or lack* of knowledge of that which it is possible for us to know and precludes the term "ignorance" from being applied to anything that is unintelligible or self-contradictory. Ferrier used the term agnoiology to distinguish what was truly knowable—and thus the proper subject matter of epistemology—from that which was unknowable (1854, 536). The term agnoiology has been resuscitated by Keith Lehrer (1990) as part of an argument demonstrating that skepticism has not been philosophically refuted; he argues that the possible truth of the skeptical hypothesis entails that we can never achieve completely justified true belief. Hence, Lehrer concludes that we do not know anything, even that we do not know anything. His point is that rational belief and action do not require refuting the skeptical hypothesis, nor do they need the validating stamp of "knowledge."

2. Perhaps more important, I wish to retain the rhetorical strength of "epistemology" when investigating ignorance. Too often, as evidenced by both Ferrier and Lehrer, ignorance is only a vehicle to reveal the proper workings of knowledge or, in the case of Lehrer, rational belief and action. Ignorance itself is not interrogated but is set up as the background against which one unfurls enriched knowledge. It is my desire to retain a focus on ignorance, to foreground ignorance as a location for understanding the workings of power. Just as we have epistemology/ies of science, of religion, and so on, I wish to argue for an epistemology of the complex phenomenon of ignorance as well as to suggest that no theory of knowledge is complete that ignores ignorance.

3. I will use this particular rhetorical form to both visually remind readers of Foucault's notion of power/knowledge (1980) and to add to it my emphasis on ignorance. I am not here claiming that Foucault did not understand how the workings of power/knowledge served to suppress knowledge practices, but with our contemporary philosophical emphasis on what we do know, I think the constant reminder to attend to what we do not know is crucial. Without the reminder, the politics of ignorance are too often erased.

4. The story of Inanna and the translations that I quote are part of a large body of Sumerian tales, legends, and poems about the Queen of Heaven and Earth inscribed on various clay tablets dating back to 2000 B.C.E.

5. For an interesting discussion of Haraway's use of such rhetorical signs, see her *How Like a Leaf* (2000).

6. This conception of bodily being is developed extensively in Tuana 1996a and 2001.

7. McWhorter, in her recent *Bodies & Pleasures* (1999), convincingly (and pleasurably) argues that a neglected aspect of Foucault's philosophy is his account of pleasure as creative and as a resource for political resistance. My use of Foucault in this essay owes much to her reading.

8. It is important to emphasize that what we do and do not know is often "local" to a particular group or a particular culture. I locate my "we" in this section as the common knowledge of laypeople in the United States both because the studies and surveys that I will employ were limited to this group and in recognition of the fact that knowledge-ignorance about women's sexuality varies tremendously from one culture/country to another.

9. Richard D. McAnulty and M. Michele Burnette (2001, 67) describe the clitoris as composed of shaft and glans, but make no effort to provide an illustration. Spencer A. Rathus, Nevid, and Fichner-Rathus (2002) is the first textbook designed for college human sexuality classrooms that includes an illustration of what they label the "whole clitoris," namely, the shaft, glans, and crura.

10. McAnulty and Burnette, for example, while admitting a more complex structure for the clitoris, simply indicate that "the glans of the clitoris has a high concentration of touch and temperature receptors and should be the primary center of sexual stimulation and sensation in the female" (2001, 67). Later, when discussing the female sexual response cycle, they simply note that the diameter of the clitoral shaft increases (2001, 114).

11. For an interesting discussion of anatomical conventions in depicting female genitalia see Moore and Clarke 1995.

12. I've examined the various editions of Albert Richard Allgeier and Elizabeth Rice Allgeier (1984,

1988, 1998), Curtis O. Byer and Louis W. Shainberg (1985, 1988, 1991, 1998, 2001), Gary Kelly (1988, 1994, 1998, 2001), McAnulty and Burnette (2001), and Rathus, Nevin, and Fichner-Rathus (1993, 2000, 2002). Only Rathus, Nevin, and Fichner-Rathus include this expanded model of the clitoris. But while they provide the most detailed discussion of women's multi-orgasmic capacity, their images and discussion of the female response phases are surprisingly traditional, with the clitoris once again relegated to a mere nub.

13. I support these claims in my book, *The Less Noble Sex* (1993).

14. The reference here is to Hesiod's depiction of the creation of the first woman, Pandora. After she was molded in the shape of a goddess by Hephaistos, Zeus ordered Aphrodite to bequeath to her "stinging desire and limb-gnawing passion" (Hesiod 1983, line 66–67).

15. As just one of literally thousands of examples of the view that women's greater susceptibility to sexual temptation required control, I refer the reader to David Hume's (1978) discussion of chastity and modesty. Hume argues that women have such a strong temptation to infidelity that the only way to reassure men that the children their wives bear are their own biological offspring is for society to "attach a peculiar degree of shame to their infidelity, above what arises merely from its injustice"; also, because women are particularly apt to overlook remote motives in favor of present temptations, he argues " 'tis necessary, therefore, that, beside the infamy attending such licenses, there should be some preceding backwardness or dread, which may prevent their first approaches, and may give the female sex a repugnance to all expressions, and postures, and liberties, that have an immediate relation to that enjoyment" (1978, Bk. 3, Pt. 2, Sec. 12, Para. 6/9, 571–72).

16. Scientists believed that enlarged clitorises were both a result of and a reason for hypersexuality, and both sex deviants and racially "inferior" women were viewed as sexually deviant because of heightened sexual "excitability." For further discussion of these themes see Fausto-Sterling 1995 and Terry 1995 and 1999.

17. See McWhorter 1999 for an insightful analysis of the difference between desire and pleasure.

Bailey–Cuomo: The
Feminist Philosophy
Reader

9. Feminist Epistemologies | Text

© The McGraw–Hill
Companies, 2008

253

"The art of living" is, of course, Beauvoir's phrase.

18. This view of female genitals is surprisingly resilient. A recent story in my local State College, Pennsylvania newspaper, *The Center Daily Times,* reported that two women who were running nude were acquitted of charges of streaking. The story explains that the streaking law requires that the genitalia be exposed, something that the judge in this case decided is nearly impossible for women, since, in the judge's view, female genitalia are all internal! My thanks to David O'Hara for calling this story to my attention.

## REFERENCES

Allgeier, Albert Richard, and Elizabeth Rice Allgeier. 1984, 1988, 1998. *Sexual Interactions.* Lexington, Mass.: D. C. Heath and Co.

Alzate, Heli. 1985. "Vaginal Eroticism: A Replication study." *Archives of Sexual Behavior* 14 (6): 529–37.

*Annie Sprinkle's Herstory of Porn.* 1999. Produced and directed by Annie Sprinkle and Carol Leigh (Scarlot Harlot). 69 min. Hardcore Documentary. Videocassette.

Apollodorus. 1976. *The Gods and Heroes of the Greeks: The Library of Apollodorus.* Trans. Michael Simpson. Amherst: University of Massachusetts Press.

Baker, R. Robin, and Mark A. Bellis. 1995. *Human Sperm Competition: Copulation, Masturbation, and Infidelity.* London: Chapman and Hall.

Barash, David. 1977. *Sociobiology and Behavior.* New York: Elsevier North-Holland.

Bloor, David. 1976. *Knowledge and Social Imagery.* London: Routledge and Kegan Paul.

Boston Woman's Health Book Collective. 1984. *The New Our Bodies, Ourselves: A Book by and for Women.* New York: Simon and Schuster.

Byer, Curtis O., and Louis W. Shainberg. 1985, 1988, 1991, 1998, 2001. *Dimensions of Human Sexuality.* Boston: McGraw Hill.

Cadden, Joan. 1993. *Meanings of Sex Difference in the Middle Ages: Medicine, Science and Culture.* Cambridge: Cambridge University Press.

Christensen, John B., and Ira Telford. 1978. *Synopsis of Gross Anatomy 3rd ed.* New York: Harper and Row.

Columbus, Renaldus. 1559. *De re anatomica.* Venice.

Daly, Mary. 1978. *Gyn/ecology: The Metaethics of Radical Feminism.* Boston: Beacon Press.

Dickinson, Robert Latou. 1941. The Gynecology of Homosexuality, Appendix VI. In *Sex Variants: A Study of Homosexual Patterns,* ed. George W. Henry. New York, London: Paul B. Hoeber.

Dixson, Alan. 1998. *Primate Sexuality: Comparative Studies of the Prosimians, Monkeys, Apes, and Human Beings.* Oxford: Oxford University Press.

Fausto-Sterling, Anne. 1995. Gender, race, and nation: The comparative anatomy of "Hottentot" women in Europe, 1815–1817. In *Deviant Bodies: Critical Perspectives on Difference in Science and Popular Culture,* ed. Jennifer Terry and Jacqueline Urla. Bloomington: Indiana University Press.

Federation of Feminist Women's Health Centers. 1981. *A New View of a Woman's Body: A Fully Illustrated guide; illustrations by Suzann Gage; photographs by Sylvia Morales.* New York: Simon and Schuster.

Ferrier, James F. 1854. *Institutes of Metaphysic.* Edinburgh: Blackwood.

Foucault, Michel. 1980. *Power/knowledge: Selected Interviews and other Writings. 1972–1977.* Ed. and trans. Colin Gordon. New York: Pantheon Books.

———. 1989. Friendship as a way of life. In *Foucault Live.* Trans. John Johnston. Ed. Sylvere Lotringer. New York: Semiotext(e).

———.1990. *The History of Sexuality, Volume I: An Introduction.* Trans. Robert Hurley. New York: Random House.

Freud, Sigmund. 1962. *Three Essays on the Theory of Sexuality.* Trans. and Ed. James Strachey. New York: Avon.

———. 1964. Femininity. In *Standard Edition of the Complete Psychological Works.* Volume 22. Trans. and Ed. James Strachey. London: Hogarth Press.

Gallagher, Catherine and Thomas Laqueur, eds. 1987. *The Making of the Modern Body: Sexuality and society in the nineteenth century.* Berkeley: University of California Press.

Goodall, Jane. 1988. *In the Shadow of Man.* Boston: Houghton Mifflin.

Grafenburg, Ernst. 1950. The role of the urethra in female orgasm. *The International Journal of Sexology* 3: 145–48.

Hamilton, William. 1858–60/2001. Lectures on metaphysics and logic. In *Works of William Hamilton,* ed. Savina Tropea. Bristol: Thoemmes Press.

Haraway, Donna J. 2000. *How like a Leaf: An interview with Thyrza Nichols Goodeve.* New York, London: Routledge.

Harding, Sandra. 1998. *Is Science Multi-Cultural? Postcolonialisms, Feminisms, and Epistemologies.* Bloomington: Indiana University Press.

Hesiod. 1983. *Theogony, Works and Days, and the Shield.* Trans. Apostolos Athanassakis. Baltimore: Johns Hopkins Press.

Hite, Shere. 1976. *The Hite report: A Nationwide Study of Female Sexuality.* New York: Dell.

Hume, David. 1978. *A Treatise of Human Nature.* Ed. Lewis Amherst Selby-Bigge. New York: Oxford University Press.

*Inanna: Queen of Heaven and Earth, her Stories and Hymns from Sumer.* 1983. Trans. Diane Wolkstein and Samuel Noah Kramer. New York: Harper and Row.

Irigaray, Luce. 1985. *Speculum of the Other Woman.* Trans. Gillian C. Gill. Ithaca: Cornell University Press.

Kelly, Gary F. 1988, 1994, 1998, 2001. *Sexuality Today: The Human Perspective.* Boston: McGraw Hill.

Kimber, Diana Clifford, Carolyn E. Gray, Caroline E. Stackpole, Lutie C. Leavell, Marjorie A. Miller. 1966. *Anatomy and Physiology* 15th ed. New York: Macmillian.

Kinsey, Alfred C., and the staff of the Institute for Sex Research, Indiana University. 1953. *Sexual Behavior in the Human Female.* Philadelphia: Saunders.

Kitzinger, Sheila. 1985. *Women's Experience of Sex: The Facts and Feelings of Female Sexuality at every Stage of Life.* New York: Penguin Books.

Koedt, Ann. 1970. The myth of the vaginal orgasm. In *Notes from the Second Year: Women's Liberation,* ed. Shulamith Firestone and Ann Koedt. New York: Radical Feminism.

Laqueur, Thomas. 1986. Orgasm, generation, and the politics of reproductive biology. *Representations* 14: 1–41.

———. 1989. 'Amor Veneris, vel Dulcedo Appeleur.' In *Fragments for a History of the Human Body,* ed. Michel Feher. New York: Zone.

———. 1990. *Making Sex: Body and Gender from the Greeks to Freud.* Cambridge: Harvard University Press.

Laumann, Edward O., John H. Gagnon, Robert T. Michael, and Stewart Michaels. 1994. *The Social Organization of Sexuality: Sexual Practices in the United States.* Chicago: University of Chicago Press.

Lehrer, Keith. 1990. *Theory of Knowledge.* Boulder: Westview Press.

Lloyd, Elisabeth A. 1993. "Pre-theoretical assumptions in evolutionary explanations of female sexuality." *Philosophical Studies* 69:139–53.

Margulis, Lynn, and Dorion Sagan. 1991. *Mystery Dance: On the Evolution of Human Sexuality.* New York: Summit Books.

Masters, William H., and Virginia E. Johnson. 1966. *Human Sexual Response.* Boston: Little, Brown.

McAnulty, Richard D., and M. Michele Burnette. 2001. *Exploring Human Sexuality: Making Healthy Decisions.* Boston: Allyn and Bacon.

McWhorter, LaDelle. 1999. *Bodies & Pleasures: Foucault and the Politics of Sexual Normalization.* Bloomington: Indiana University Press.

Mills, Charles S. 1997. *The Racial Contract.* Ithaca, N.Y.: Cornell University Press.

Moore, Lisa Jean, and Adele E. Clarke. 1995. Clitoral conventions and transgressions: Graphic representations in anatomy texts, c1900–1991. *Feminist Studies* 21(2): 255–301.

Paré, Ambroise. 1968. *The Collected Works of Ambroise Paré.* Trans. Thomas Johnson. New York: Milford House.

Perry, John Delbert, and Beverly Whipple. 1981. Pelvic muscle strength of female ejaculators: Evidence in support of a new theory of orgasm. *Journal of Sex Research* 17(1): 22–39.

Proctor, Robert N. 1995. *Cancer Wars: How Politics Shapes What We Know and Don't Know About Cancer.* New York: Basic Books.

Rathus, Spencer A., Jeffrey S. Nevid, and Lois Fichner-Rathus. 1993, 2000, 2002. *Human Sexuality in a World of Diversity.* 5th Ed. Boston: Allyn and Bacon.

Rosen, Raymond, and Linda Reich Rosen. 1981. *Human Sexuality.* New York: Alfred A. Knopf.

Schiebinger, Londa L. 1989. *The Mind Has No Sex? Women in the Origins of Modern Science,* Cambridge: Harvard University Press.

Sedgwick, Eve Kosofsky. 1990. *Epistemology of the Closet.* Berkeley, Los Angeles: University of California Press.

Shulman, Alix. 1971. Organs and orgasms. In *Women in Sexist Society,* ed. Vivian Gornick and Barbara K. Moran. New York: New American Library.

Bailey–Cuomo: The
Feminist Philosophy
Reader

9. Feminist Epistemologies | Text

© The McGraw–Hill
Companies, 2008

255

Singer, Josephine, and Irving Singer. 1972. Types of female orgasm *Journal of Sex Research* 8 (4): 2550–267.

Small, Meredith F. 1995. *What's Love Got to do with it? The Evolution of Human Mating.* New York: Anchor Books.

Sprecher, Susan, Anita Barbee, and Pepper Schwartz. 2001. "Was it good for you, too?": Gender differences in first sexual intercourse experience. In *Social Psychology and Human Sexuality,* ed. Roy F. Baumeister. Philadelphia: Taylor and Francis.

Symons, Donald. 1979. *The Evolution of Human Sexuality.* New York: Oxford University Press.

Terry, Jennifer. 1995. Anxious slippages between "us" and "them": A brief history of the scientific search for homosexual bodies. In *Deviant bodies: Critical Perspectives on Difference in Science and Popular culture,* ed. Jennifer Terry and Jacqueline Urla. Bloomington: Indiana University Press.

———. 1999. *An American Obsession: Science, Medicine, and Homosexuality in Modern Society.* Chicago: University of Chicago Press.

Tuana, Nancy. 1988. "The Weaker Seed: The Sexist Bias of Reproductive Theory." *Hypatia: A Journal of Feminist Philosophy,* 3 (1): 35–39.

———. 1993. *"The Less Noble Sex: Scientific, Religious and Philosophical Conceptions of Woman's Nature.* Bloomington: Indiana University Press.

———. 1996a. "Fleshing Gender, Sexing the Body: Refiguring the Sex/Gender Distinction," *Spindel Conference Proceedings. Southern Journal of Philosophy.* Vol. XXXV.

———. 1996b. "Re-valuing Science." In *Feminism, Science, and the Philosophy of Science,* ed. Lynn Hankinson Nelson and Jack Nelson. Dordrecht, Netherlands: Kluwer.

———. 2001. "Material locations: An Interactionist Alternative to Realism/Social Constructivism." In *Engendering Rationalities,* ed. Nancy Tuana and Sandra Morgen. Bloomington: Indiana University Press.

Whipple, Beverly. 1995. "Research Concerning Sexual Response in Women." *The Health Psychologist* 17 (1): 16–18.

## FOR FURTHER READING

Alcoff, Linda Martín, and Elizabeth Potter, eds. *Feminist Epistemologies.* New York: Routledge, 1993.

Antony, Louise M., and Charlotte E. Witt, eds. *A Mind of One's Own: Feminist Essays on Reason and Objectivity.* 2nd ed. Boulder: Westview Press, 2002.

Belenky, Mary Field, Blyth M. Clinchy, Nancy R. Goldberger, and Jill M. Tarutle. *Women's Ways of Knowing: The Development of Self, Voice and Mind.* New York: Basic Books, 1986.

Bleier, Ruth. *Science and Gender: A Critique of Biology and Its Theories on Women.* London: Pergamon Press, 1984.

Chodorow, Nancy. *The Reproduction of Mothering.* Berkeley: University of California Press, 1978.

Code, Lorraine. *What Can She Know? Feminist Theory and the Construction of Knowledge.* Ithaca, NY: Cornell University Press, 1981.

Code, Lorraine. *Rhetorical Spaces: Essays on Gendered Locations.* New York: Routledge, 1995.

Collins, Patricia Hill. *Black Feminist Thought.* New York: Routledge, 1990.

Duran, Jane. *Toward a Feminist Epistemology.* Savage, MD: Rowman and Littlefield, 1991.

Haraway, Donna. *Simians, Cyborgs, and Women: The Reinvention of Nature.* New York: Routledge, 1991.

Harding, Sandra, and Merrill Hintikka, eds. *Discovering Reality: Perspectives on Epistemology, Metaphysics, Methodology, and Philosophy of Science.* Dordrecht, Holland: D. Reidel, 1983.

Harding, Sandra. *Whose Science? Whose Knowledge?* Ithaca, NY: Cornell University Press, 1991.

Harding, Sandra, ed. *The "Racial" Economy of Science: Toward a Democratic Future.* Bloomington, IN: Indiana University Press, 1993.

Hartsock, Nancy. "The Feminist Standpoint: Developing the Ground for a Specifically Feminist Historical Materialism." In *Discovering Reality: Perspectives on Epistemology, Metaphysics, Methodology, and Philosophy of Science,* edited by Harding and Hintikka. Dordrecht, Holland: D. Reidel, 1983.

Hartsock, Nancy. *The Feminist Standpoint Revisited and Other Essays.* Boulder: Westview Press, 1998.

Chapter 9 / Feminist Epistemologies

Heckman, Susan. *Gender and Knowledge*. Boston: Northeastern University Press, 1990.

Keller, Evelyn Fox. *A Feeling for the Organism: The Life and Work of Barbara McClintock*. San Francisco: W. H. Freeman, 1983.

Keller, Evelyn Fox. *Reflections on Gender and Science*. New Haven: Yale University Press, 1985.

Lloyd, Genevieve. *The Man of Reason: "Male" and "Female" in Western Philosophy*. Minneapolis: University of Minnesota Press, 1984.

Longino, Helen. *Science as Social Knowledge*. Princeton, NJ: Princeton University Press, 1990.

Mills, Charles. *The Racial Contract*. Ithaca, NY: Cornell University Press, 1997.

Nelson. Lynn Hankinson. *Who Knows?: From Quine to Feminist Empiricism*. Philadelphia: Temple, 1990.

Nelson, Lynn Hankinson. "The Very Idea of Feminist Epistemology." *Hypatia* 10(3) (1995): 31–50.

Rooney, Phyllis. "Gendered Reason: Sex Metaphor and Conceptions of Reason." *Hypatia* 6(2) (1991): 77–103.

Rooney, Phyllis. *Feminism and Epistemology*. New York: Routledge, 2006.

Rose, Hilary. "Hand, Brain, and Heart: A Feminist Epistemology of the Natural Sciences." *Signs* 9(1) (1983): 73–90.

Scheman, Naomi. *Engenderings: Constructions of Knowledge, Authority, and Privilege*. New York: Routledge, 1993.

Smith, Dorothy. *The Everyday World as Problematic*. Toronto: University of Toronto Press, 1987.

Tanesini, Alessandra. *An Introduction to Feminist Epistemologies*. Malden, MA: Blackwell Publishers, 1999.

Tuana, Nancy. *The Less Noble Sex: Scientific, Religious, and Philosophical Conceptions of Human Nature*. Bloomington, IN: Indiana University Press, 1993.

Tuana, Nancy, and Sandra Morgan. *Engendering Rationalities*. Albany, NY: SUNY Press, 2001.

## MEDIA RESOURCES

***Evelyn Fox Keller: Science and Gender.*** VHS. Produced by Leslie Clark (US, 1994). PBS World of Ideas Video Series, Public Affairs Television, Inc. In this 30-minute interview with Bill Moyers, Evelyn Fox Keller discusses how gender plays a significant role in the language that scientists use to describe their work. Available: Films Media Group at http://www.films.com/Home.aspx?BrandType=F or by calling 1–800–257–5126.

***Epistemology: What Can We Know?*** DVD. (US, 2004). This 46-minute program travels from Plato's cave to Gettier's papier-mâché barns as a way of addressing questions such as: What does it mean to really know something? How do I know what I know? And is seeing the same thing as believing? Rutgers University's Alvin Goldman and Peter Klein and Princeton University's Alexander Nehamas and Daniel Garber deconstruct the basic principles of epistemology. A good background for students unfamiliar with basics of traditional epistemology, and a good way of illustrating how epistemology is done in "apolitical" ways. Available: Films for the Humanities and Sciences, http://www.films.com/, or 1–800–257–5126.

Charles Lemert is Professor of Sociology at Wesleyan University. He has written widely on social theory, politics, race, and culture. His books include *Sociology After the Crisis* (HarperCollins, 1995); *Social Theory: The Classic and Multicultural Readings* (HarperCollins, 1993); *The Goffman Reader* (Basil Blackwell, 1996, with Ann Branaman); *Michel Foucault: Social Theory and Transgression* (Columbia University Press, 1982, with Garth Gillan); and *Postmodernism Is Not What You Think* (Basil Blackwell, 1997). Lemert is a past chair of the Theory Section of *The American Sociological Association*.

*chapter*
# Postmodernism and Social Theory

Charles Lemert

## ► CHAPTER OUTLINE

## ► INTRODUCTION

Just weeks before sitting down to write this chapter, I was in Kyongju, South Korea, a small provincial city about 250 kilometers southeast of Seoul. Kyongju was once the center of the ancient Silla Kingdom that dominated the Korean peninsula significantly from the sixth century (A.D.) until the rise of the Koryo dynasty in the tenth century. Crafts, culture, and Buddhism flourished under Silla's medieval culture. UNESCO considers ancient Kyongju one of the world's ten most important ancient cities.

Today, however, Kyongju is a tourist city served by a modern interstate expressway and ringed by newly developed ultra-modern hotels. Through the miracle of satellite television I watched the third game of the 1995 Houston-Orlando NBA championship series in my hotel room. Later that evening, I walked along a small lake with my Korean host, Hong-Woo Kim. The night was calm, a slight breeze cooled the air. We talked quietly of sociology and other common interests. In a café across the lake, a singer crooned American popular love songs in perfect English. I tried to tell Professor Kim of the many other times I had strolled on summer evenings by the lakes and seasides of my youth listening to songs like these. But I was not quite able to convey the exact sense of summers in Maine and American teenage romance. Cultures are just too different on the fine points of feelings and memories.

Early the next day, I prayed somewhat self-consciously in a Buddhist temple high in the mountains above Kyongju. The main temple at Kirim-sa was already packed with monks and other devotees sitting, bowing, and joining in the ancient chants that were broadcast, in highest fidelity sound, across the monastery grounds. Buddhist monks like those chanting that morning had chanted similarly in that same place since the temples were first built in 643 A.D. Save for electricity and plumbing, nothing was different, though I did notice one of those TV satellite dishes discreetly mounted just off the perimeter of the monastery compound. On the way out, I bought a compact disc recording of those monks chanting. The ancient live on with, and through, modern technology!

Postmodernism has something to do with experiences of this kind. But, in saying this, I refer not as much as you might suppose to the miracles of technology and transport that put different people in surprisingly close contact with each other and their different cultures. This is only part of what makes the world today peculiar and a bit shocking. At a deeper level, experiences such as the one I had in Kyongju are an increasingly normal feature of daily life among people of widely different social positions and geographic places. It is not just that technology *allows* people closer communication with each other, creating a global village (as Marshall MacLuhan put it[1]), but that the globalizing processes are of such a nature as to have fundamentally changed the way the world is experienced. Human contact today is not just intensified, it is also reorganized, strangely—and not always for the better.

In the simplest of terms, some say that **postmodernism**, though it is a very complicated thing to understand, is about this odd fact that historical aspects of the world that do not belong together are, today, jumbled up with each other. Accordingly, postmodernists believe the world has changed in a hard-to-describe, but unmistakable, way in which things are out of kilter, though meaningfully so. The reasonable kilters of modern life are somehow rearranged in odd, incongruent ways that, nonetheless, seem normal in spite of their abnormality. Just how odd these new arrangements are will become apparent from our discussion that shows it is impossible to talk about "postmodernism and social theory" without also talking about "modernism" and its social theories. So strongly do I believe this that when I turn to a direct exposition of the social theories themselves, I include a discussion of *radical modernism* as well as presentations of *two* different views of postmodernisms—one considers that modernism is done with (*radical postmodernism*) and another considers that modernity is at least in need of a thorough remaking (*strategic postmodernism*). I mention them here merely to establish the idea that postmodernism, including the theories it has spawned, is no simple matter, and certainly not one which can be treated as though any one theory of it could render others, even the strongest theories of the modernism, somehow defunct.

There is no easy way to begin a discussion of postmodernism. Such a discussion must include an attempt to dispel the most common misconceptions about it; this I do in the section "Postmodernism Is Not What You Think." Postmodernism being hard to understand, it is easily misunderstood. But this does not mean that one should not attempt, from the first, to say as clearly as possible where in the world those interested in it might look for it.

## ▶ POSTMODERNISM: WHERE DOES ONE LOOK FOR IT?

Postmodernism has something to do with what is allegedly happening to modernism. So, if **modernism** is the culture of the modern age (or, simply, of **modernity**), then **postmodernism** has something to do with the breaking apart of modernism. Thus, if one wants to find postmodernism, it is necessary first of all to look at culture—not because culture is the only important thing in the world, but because culture is a particularly sensitive aspect of social life. Cultures are sensitive enough that when one suspects that the world is changing, including its economic and political arrangements, cultures are where one might first find signs of the purported change. This is especially the case when the change is so great as to entail the breaking up of modernity.

What then is **culture**? A reasonably simple way of describing culture is to say that it is the complex of socially produced values, rules, beliefs, literatures, arts, media, penal codes, laws, political ideas, and other such diversions by which a society, or any social group, represents its view of the world—as its members (or at least the members in charge) believe it is or

ought to be. Madonna, like it or not, is part of culture. As are your local mosque and temple, the rhetoric of all the political parties, the finest poetry, John Updike's latest novel, TV ads for Air Jordan shoes as well as Michael Jordan himself, and much more. Though itself a complicated thing, culture possesses one attribute which is relatively straightforward, even though it is seldom discussed. Any collective attempt to represent, or express, what a group of people think the social world ideally is must, necessarily, exclude those worlds that people disapprove of. Madonna is the expression of a cultural view that invites all sorts of outrageous sexual experiences. The culture that has produced Madonna—and a good bit of today's popular culture—is a culture that frowns upon the more traditional and puritan sexual values, just as certain religious conservatives produce a culture that intends to exclude Madonna. Simply, cultures are means for a social group to say what it likes and what it hates. Though the former is easier to spot than the latter, it too can be found with a little investigating.

We might say that postmodernism is a culture that believes there is a better world than the modern one. In particular it disapproves of moderism's uncritical assumption that European culture (including its diaspora versions in such places as South Africa, the United States, Australia, and Argentina) is an authentic, self-evident, and true universal culture in which all the world's people ought to believe. Postmodernism is a culture that prefers to break things up, to respect the several parts of the social world. When it speaks of culture it prefers to speak of culture**s**.

This is readily seen when one looks at those aspects of culture most famously associated with postmodernism—architecture, for example. One of the most frequently cited representations of the postmodern is the famous AT&T (now SONY) building at Madison Avenue and Fifty-fifth Street in New York City.

This midtown Manhattan building, like most in that section of the world's most famous city of skyscrapers, is a tall imposing structure. In this sense it is purely and classically modern. The skyscraper is said to be the architectural symbol of modernity's brash self-confidence—rising above common things to dominate the urban world. Yet, this same building is evidently weird. There is, for one thing, a Chippendale flourish at the pediment, or top-most part. Chippendale is a seventeenth-century furniture design which includes two rising angles that, at their apex, are broken by a wide circular opening. Many have seen such furniture in their grandmothers' houses. But for those unfamiliar with this emblem, the top of the AT&T building could just as well appear to be an old-fashioned, telephone cradle. Either way, this surprising design feature makes those who view the building wonder at its oddity. More odd still, at the base of the building, there are columns reminiscent of classical Greco-Roman temples and an entrance with a prominent semicircular, Byzantine arch that recalls still another culture from anther time. What exactly are these ironic design features doing on such a modernist structure? Was the building's architect, Philip Johnson, playing a joke on the city of New York?

Even if you have never seen this building, there are few American cities where there is not some postmodern building adorned with figures of architectural speech from differing eras and contrasting forms—copper flashing typical of small-town farm houses askance modernist corporate headquarters, triangulated cupolas protruding in surprising directions atop tall buildings. Thus, just like the odd mixture of the ancient and modern that I experienced in Kyongju, Korea, most Americans live with something similar in their local malls or downtown centers.

Or, to suggest still another category, think of the most striking personalities of popular entertainment. What do Michael Jackson, Madonna, Snoop Doggy Dogg, and the-artist-formerly-known-as-Prince have in common? Each has a uniquely composed public persona. True, many entertainment personalities assume stage names and identities. But with these four something different is going on. The personae they have invented are made out of absurdly contradictory elements juxtaposed to each other to create, not just shock, but irony. Michael Jackson has remade his body into a sexually ambiguous form through which he expresses powerful, but confusing, erotic messages. At one moment his face is girlish, coy. At another he demonstratively grabs his crotch in the most masculine of gestures. Yet, in the end we hear a child's voice. Madonna presses the very limits of heterosexual provocation, while frequently blurring the visual and sensual line between heteronormative and lesbian sexual desire. Snoop Doggy Dogg is a play on names in which a child's cartoon figure names a music that samples the most extreme forms of political and sexual expression. In fact, Hip-hop music's use of sampling is a near-perfect illustration of the postmodern form. Here elements from differing musics, from political discourse and TV sitcoms, from artificial street sounds and the manipulation of the recording discs themselves are packed into a dense, mixed-up sound effect through which a nonetheless clear message line is conveyed.

Whether one is looking at public architecture or these invented personalities and musical forms, such cultural forms are the kinds of things examined by students of postmodernism. Each of these examples suggests that the postmodern entails a playful aggression of the modernist ideal that the world we live in is reasonable and responsive to the natural human desire for progress and a better world. To be sure, postmodernism involves jokes of various kinds like the AT&T building, but it is also

Calhoun & Ritzer:
Social Problems

Chapter on
Culture

Lemert
Postmodernism & Social
Theory

© The McGraw–Hill
Companies, 1996

261

an entirely serious criticism of any innocent modernist ideal that all things work together for the common good.

*KANT*

At the same time, the postmodern also uses the modern alongside other cultural forms. Whatever Madonna and Michael Jackson are doing, they are unmistakably still highly successful popular music performers, just as the AT&T, or SONY, building is still a very tall and very modern building with all the efficiencies required to satisfy its corporate clients. Whatever may be the relation of the postmodern to the modern, that relation is not one of simple progression and criticism. Common sense alone suggests that the world in all its major structural features is still very much the same—if not exactly the same—world that emerged politically, culturally, and economically over the last half-millennium since Europeans first set out to explore and conquer the new world. If the world is postmodern (and many think it is), then it is also somehow still modern.

*WHAT'S POSTMODERN TO US, WILL BE MODERN TO OUR KIDS?*

▶ SOCIAL THEORY: WHAT IS IT?

**Social theory** is any theory of society or social life that distinguishes itself from scientific theories by its willingness to be critical as well as factual. Though the distinction between social theory and, say, "sociological theory" is often blurred today, there is a difference. Many sociologists, for example, believe that sociology is a science and must, therefore, obey strict rules and protocols. They want to obey rules so that they, in their opinion, are able to assure *objectivity* (the idea that facts, once analyzed, can be considered valid indications of the objective nature of the things they represent). A sociological theorist (that is, a sociologist who thinks of himself as a scientist) might, for example, look for objective measures of the number of individuals who espouse favorable attitudes toward the work ethic—the idea

that the economic world encourages a progressive improvement in the social prospects of those who work hard. If a measurably significant number of persons interviewed in the Republic of Korea admit that they hold this attitude, then (if there is similar confirming data) a sociological theorist might be willing to assert that Korea *is* a modern society. A social theorist, by contrast, would be very interested in what a sociological theorist claims as objective fact, but he or she would tend to be more skeptical, even critical of the idea that objective measures can be found. A social theorist is inclined to say that the attitudes people claim to hold, and report to interviewers, are themselves mediated as much by what people are taught (perhaps by television and other media) about their social situation as by any certifiable prospect that the world they live in is hospitable to their attitudes. This is just one example of the way social theorists are, usually, respectful of scientific description, but wish to add to it a more critical, or imaginative, dimension that cannot be fully verified. Social theorists are, in short, more relaxed in their science and more intense in their politics.

The tradition of social theory is, if anything, even longer than that of the more scientific sociological theories. It is reasonable, for example, to say that the great nineteenth-century radical thinker Karl Marx was an important social theorist. His monumental study, *Capital*, was based on the most current evidence and concepts available in his day. It was, in this sense, scientific. But Marx made no secret of his intention of writing this book in order to produce what many have considered a devastating criticism of the social effects of capitalism. Marx made no pretense of objectivity, even though much of what he said is indeed a reliable description of the capitalist world. On the other hand, early sociological theorists like Émile Durkheim, who wrote in France in the late nineteenth and early twentieth centuries, believed that sociology could be, and must be, a science of social things. His scientific procedures were among the most rigorous of his day. His study, *Suicide*, for example, was based on careful empirical analysis that led to a theory of suicide which holds up pretty well today. Yet, even though he considered himself a scientist, Durkheim pursued his science because he was critical of a society that seemed to leave so many people at a loss as to the rules they should follow in daily life. He was as deeply concerned about people who committed suicide as Marx was about those exploited by the early factory system. Scientific sociological theories are not uncaring, even though they are more cautious. Conversely, social theories are less cautious with respect to facts in order that they may be more bold with respect to human values. This should explain why those who attempt to interpret, promote, or attack postmodernism are more likely to be social theorists. The more scientific sociologists consider the argument, at best, hogwash; at worst, dirty business.

You can see why social theorists are interested in a phenomenon like postmodernism. It is their business to be concerned with anything that suggests that something is wrong with the world. And this is why there are at least two different groups of postmodern social theorists, and one large group of modernist social theorists who worry about the postmodern even while believing it is a terrible thing. Social theorists gravitate toward controversy. They do not agree with each other because they deal with subjects, like postmodernism, that are beyond hard factual proof but are of evident importance to an understanding of the world we live in.

► POSTMODERNISM IS NOT WHAT YOU THINK

The title of this section has two meanings. Postmodernism is not what you think. Not only is it not what you might suppose it is, but it is not *primarily* something one thinks. It is not *principally* (and certainly not exclusively) a form of social thought. True, it has spawned a great deal of important social theory. But this fact alone must be interpreted with respect to the more interesting question: What does the remarkable appearance of postmodernism in fields as seemingly different from each other as social theory, architecture, and popular music say about the world?

It is important to distinguish between a theory or cultural attitude *about* the world and the facts of world reality themselves. This distinction is inherent in the difference between speaking of *postmodernity*, a purportedly new state of world affairs, and postmodernism, a theory or cultural attitude toward those affairs. This is not an uncommon distinction. We are well accustomed to speaking about modernism as the culture of modernity, and there is very little reason to doubt that such a state of world affairs as modernity, or the modern age, has existed for the better part of the last half-millennium. Modernity, thus, is the dominant reality in the worldly affairs of Europe and North America and their vast imperial systems across the globe from the first age of explorations in the late fifteenth century through at least the two decades following World War II. Thus, just as modernism would be the culture of that age, so postmodernism is the culture (including the social theories) of an age that is alleged to be after, against, but still mixed up with modernity. Thus, postmodern social theorists are usually preoccupied with events that occurred in the last half-century and especially those that made the 1960s such a notorious time. It was then, postmodernists believe, that the world began to change. It was then that modernity, they think, started visibly to come apart.

It is important to keep in mind the distinction between theories about the world and events in the world when studying postmodernism. One ought first to inquire into the nature of the world itself before taking the theories of that world too much at their face value. This is the fundamental sense in which postmodernism is not what you think. Postmodernism has spawned many social and cultural theories about the world, but their plausibility should be tested against the "facts" of the world. To be sure, this is tricky business because these are social theories of a subject that is beyond factual proof. Still there can be plausible social theories, even when the facts are not as robust (or possible) as one might like.

So, to say that postmodernism is not what you think is to challenge the idea that this could be just an idea. The reason it is so difficult to overcome the idea that postmodernism exists apart from a possible postmodern world reality is that the appearances of the idea are so alluring in and of themselves. In fact, one of the most notorious strains of postmodern cultural theory is the one associated with the French social theorist, Jean Baudrillard. Those who agree with Baudrillard believe that today the world of culture is cut loose from any necessary basis in reality. Social life, according to this school of postmodern thought, is much more a spectacle that simulates reality than reality itself. People, they say, get their reality mostly through media. There is something to this but, I should warn, it does not necessarily mean that the world does not exist—only that it exists in some strange new form.

By the time many American children enter school they will have already watched more hours of television than the total number of hours of classroom instruction they will encounter in their school careers. The media, notably television (more recently its extension and transformation in the many new forms of cyber-real technologies), are surely one of the most pervasive culture forces in most societies, worldwide. (What *do* those Buddhist monks in Kyongju watch through their satellite TV hook-up?) A simple fact such as this has been analyzed by writers like Baudrillard into a general theory of society as **hyperreality**, in which simulation of reality is more real than the thing itself. Baudrillard has actually said that Disneyworld replications of a mythical America is the real American thing—more real than any actual American village.[2]

What is it about the world itself that produces a theory like Baudrillard's and what inspires so many people to find it wholly plausible? To propose an answer, let us return to Madonna.

*What* exactly is Madonna? The Madonna we viewers of MTV know and love is so far beyond a "who" that it hardly makes sense to use the expected pronoun. Surely, we assume, there is some real, beautiful and talented, outrageous still-young woman behind the name and persona. But to those who get their sense of sex, love, gender, and sexuality from the MTV star (their number is considerable), it hardly makes any difference who the girl was out of whom Madonna has been invented. Like it or not, one of the first facts of culture today is that its influence on the shaping of one's sense of herself and her place in the world is *more*, not less, powerful to the *very* extent that culture itself is *less*, not more, real in the usual sense of the word. As we shall see, "reality" is itself very much at issue in discussions of the postmodern. But, for now, to say that culture is "less real" is to acknowledge that, like Madonna, culture itself is seldom exactly what it seems to be.

But, what does it mean to say that the world is "less real" because it is hyperreal, or "super-real"? This strange notion can be so because, today, as cultural theorists would put it, culture is **mediated**.[3] The media, notably television, are literally tools through which we gain a "sense of the world." That sense may be expanded, displaced, distorted, perverted, intensified, and more. It may be, in our view, good or bad. But the important fact is that when we live in a culture where culture is mediated, our sense of reality is, to some important degree, mediated, hence indirect, hence (further) susceptible to intrusions and perhaps corruptions through the process of mediation. Several times I watched an NBA basketball game in person at the old Boston Garden. The seats were in the first balcony. As a result, the players (most near seven feet) actually appeared very small indeed. But I knew who the stars were, and what to expect of them. When Larry Bird hit an impossible three-pointer while falling behind the baseline I *knew* what was going on. But I knew it in spite of the fact that, at such a distance in the first balcony, I could hardly make out the details. How did I know what I knew? I knew because I had seen them close up many times on television. I knew these men as others know Madonna because I saw them through a very articulate medium. So powerful is that medium that, one supposes, the real person hardly matters. What matters is the show and I know the show because I saw it on television, mediated.

I have never met Larry Bird though I once visited French Lick, Indiana, where he grew up and still has a home. There is little about this faded, once-grand tourist town that helps me explain who Larry Bird really is. For those who don't know basketball one of the best-known "facts" about the real Larry Bird is that he is said to have been the hardest-working white guy in basketball history. He practiced and practiced, long after he had become one of the game's immortals. In sports culture, the legend is that this is what made him great and that it was the values of small-town Midwestern life that accounted for Bird's basketball genius. Perhaps, but not likely. This is just another mediated story, one that gains currency through the avaricious talk of the sports media (again the word). Whatever made Larry Bird great almost surely had only the most accidental relation to that small town. I have lived in small Midwestern towns. Most of the white

guys are like young white guys everywhere. They don't practice much of anything. In fact they spend much of their time drinking beer and talking about how small-town life made men like Bird different. When we know what we know about culture, even the heroes of sports culture come to us in mediated form, behind which it is awfully hard to find the real thing.

The same is true, more true, of characters like Madonna who are almost purely an artifact of televisual culture. Televisual media are unlike others. Radio, by contrast, is considered to be a medium that invites the listener to expand his or her imagination. I am old enough to have listened as a boy to the Cincinnati Reds games on radio broadcast in the days when broadcasters seldom traveled with the team. When the Reds were in St. Louis, the account of the game was transmitted from somewhere in Cincinnati by a broadcaster who literally made up the action he described from teletype facts. From a telegraphic code something like: "2out/2:1/29StL at bat, K," we heard "Blackwell winds, holds the runner at first, throws. Another blazing fastball, inside corner. Strike. He's got his stuff tonight." Radio (before today's top forty and talk-a-thon formats) was like that. One had to imagine to get it.

Movies are more different still. One "goes to" the movies, and there enters into a darkened environment in which a story is projected from behind onto a huge screen, so huge that one loses oneself in the images and sounds. Have you seen *Bridges of Madison County*? Did you cry? I did, and I can't say why. The film is about longing and lost loves. But I saw the film with the love of my life who was right there crying with me. We passed the same popcorn napkin back and forth. What is the power of the movies to evoke deep feelings in such an artificial environment, bad popcorn and all? Somehow this is a medium that, by projecting images before us, causes us to project ourselves into those images, drawing out feeling from our unconscious. But the movies, like radio, are not, for the most part, the least postmodern. When a movie is over we leave, and we leave behind the feelings. I can remember still crying a little two miles out from town back home. But when we got home, I am embarrassed to say, we flipped on the TV to check the Yankees game, and all we had felt ten minutes earlier was gone, completely.

Televisual media are different because they are in our lives. I once saw Madonna's memoir film, *Truth or Dare,* two nights after its release in a remote vacation village. It was a Sunday night. In the sparse crowd, I recognized the famous feminist journalist, writer, and organizer, Betty Friedan, author of the classic work of American feminism, *The Feminine Mystique.* But I never got up the nerve to ask her what she thought of Madonna's gender politics. Her presence made the setting and the film itself all the more bizarre. There was Betty Friedan, an icon of modern feminism, watching Madonna, an icon of postmodern, postfeminism. Madonna plays so wildly with images of female sexuality that the issues that feminists care about are at once oddly accentuated and blurred. The movie was a documentary. Its portrayal of Madonna's behind-the-scenes activities revealed a style that was what seemed to me little different from the concert performances or the videos. She had no particular "real life" story to tell. Movies are meant to tell stories with beginnings and endings. Television, by contrast, immerses the viewer in a sea of loosely organized, provocative images. Madonna is a product of television. She enters our lives and hearts as we channel-surf from this to that, make trips to the john or the fridge, or tape stuff so we can occasionally go out into the "real" world to do whatever—attend a class, rake a few leaves, shop.

This is the nature of televisual culture. It is composed in large part by us *in the very course of*

*the life* in which we are composing our daily lives. Thus, an MTV video lasts, at the most, a few minutes, because televisual "events" must be fitted in, by the channel-surfing viewers, among other tubal attractions and events occurring without interruption around the house—cats or babies crying, thunderstorms, gun shots in the hallway, etc. You cannot make a movie of Madonna because there is no story there. She's a TV thing, about five minutes at the most. She's good enough to get us to stop for those minutes, but there is not much there, after or before. This is what makes televisual and advanced televisual culture, like video games and the Internet, different from other media and so effective in the course of world affairs. They are not *unreal* or even *irreal* (that is, extreme distortions of the real). Hyperreality is some other dimension of reality that borrows its images and contents from a purported real world which then remakes them in vastly more complex mediated forms than one ever experiences in the so-called real world. The *hyperreal* is, literally, more real than reality itself. It is highly unlikely, for example, that there is a real family anywhere as "super-real" as that of Ozzie and Harriet or of the Cosbys.

It is pervasive experiences such as those we have had through exposure to televisual culture that lend plausibility to the idea of postmodernism, and they lend it even when we are unable to provide a proper theory of the culture's effect on us. Note that I said "the plausibility" of the postmodern. The postmodern cannot be proven because, if it exists, it exists as a world order that exaggerates the world of real facts and evidence. As a result, social theories of the postmodern are not so much arguments from undisputed facts as representations of a way of understanding the world. This does not mean, however, that postmodern social theories are uninterested in the real world. On the contrary, they take "reality" with extreme seriousness because they begin from the assumption that in a televisual culture the reality of the world is always *mediated*—that is, not directly present to those who live in the world.

This, then, is the sense in which the world is seen as *post*modern. Postmodernism is the culture that takes seriously the breaking apart of the world, which, if this is what is happening, is clearly a question of just how hyperreal is reality. It is thereby a question to which evidence of a sort can be brought, if only to provoke one's thinking about what is going on.

### ► THE CLAIM THAT THE WORLD MIGHT BE POSTMODERN

It cannot be proven that the world has become postmodern. In fact, one of the central tenets of postmodern philosophies is that nothing can be *proven*, everything is open to argument, everything is more a truth-claim than a stable argument.[4]

It is all too easy to forget that whenever one is talking about massive changes in world structures it takes several hundred years before a considerable number of people will agree that the change has indeed taken place.[5] Consider, for a moment, just how long it must have taken for moderns to realize that the traditional feudal world was irretrievably gone. Even today people are searching for some way to return to the simpler times of agrarian, village life. Vermont and Montana are, as you read, filling up with urban migrants doing just that. And no one would visit the world's ancient sites, like Kyongju, were the traveler not enchanted by the past before the world had changed. So, one does not have to be a determined modernist to be cautious before the claim that the world has changed.

Thus, if postmodernism is not what one thinks, it is important to state the evidence for its reality, even if that evidence will not do much more than explain the prior, and in-

triguing question: Why are so many people, often against their wills, concerned about postmodernism? It is impossible to go anywhere in the world without encountering intellectuals, artists, or politicians wondering about postmodernity. I have some thirty-five books on postmodernism. This is an interesting number because, to the best of my recollection, I have purchased no more than two of them. All the rest were sent as unsolicited copies by various publishers. If so many appear without asking how many others must there be? More interesting yet, two of the most frequently cited books on the subject are by authors who take a decidedly negative attitude toward postmodernism.[6] If the subject occasions such feeling, and causes people who are not postmodernists to write about postmodernism, then we know, virtually for certain, that something real is going on out there. But what might be the evidence for it?

One does not have to be a postmodernist to grant that the world is changing. At the least it is obvious that the world which for a long time has been thought of as "modern" is experiencing a crisis of grave and global proportions. What the changes mean exactly we cannot know, but it is clear that they are disrupting the most fundamental structures that underlie the modern world—structures that were built up and have endured for nearly half a millennium. Though one could describe the changes in various ways, I suggest just the three most obvious and serious:

1. The Euro-American colonial sytsem has collapsed, suddenly and completely, within the very short world time of a third of a century or so. The collapse began with the successful decolonizing movements in the late 1940s and 1950s in which, first, India, then, China, were liberated from direct or indirect colonial rule. Through the 1950s most of Europe's African colonies were struggling toward liberation. By 1959, Cuba threw off

META NARRATIVES:
STORIES ABOUT OTHER
STORIES.
OUR STORY IS RIGHT. YOURS WRONG

American rule and, by the end of the 1960s, most of the Caribbean, Asia, and Africa were free of European political control, however much many continued to rely on economic relations with the West. Most notably, the defeat of the Americans in Vietnam marked the most impressive decolonizing event of the 1970s. But the similar defeat of the Soviets in Afghanistan somewhat later was, though less noisy, more important because it seems the Soviet failure in this colonizing war sapped too much moral and economic capital from an already weak Soviet system. Here was a notable instance in which failure to colonize led directly to a collapse of the colonizing regime itself. By 1990, it was not just the Cold War that had ended. Far more important is that the colonial system that had begun half a millennium earlier in the 1490s was at its end, at least as a formal world political system.

In the simplest of terms, the collapse of the colonial system has destroyed the foundational economic base for the so-called modern world. Obviously, this does not mean that all that went before has disappeared. In fact, a newly structured world system has come fast on the heels of the original modern one. But the fact remains (even if we do not agree on what it means) that the classic modern world system, one based on a half-millennium of colonization, has collapsed.

**2.** One of the most enduring features of that classic system was that there was always one, unrivaled, imperial center.[7] In the sixteenth century it was the Iberian powers, in the seventeenth it was the Dutch, by the nineteenth it had become the British, by mid-twentieth century it had become the United States. References to Pax Britannica or the American Century were, respectively, references to the days when Great Britain and the United States were the guarantors of the world order such as it was. It hardly needs to be said that such imperial power (even when the term *empire* was

studiously avoided) meant also that these great nation-states were as much the center of world culture as of world economic and political systems. But not any more.

The so-called defeat of communism and the triumph of the capitalist societies in 1990 have left the world without an unchallenged center. The United States is still the world's most powerful economy by volume and U.S. military might is without peer. But U.S. power is a qualified power. The size of its economy is limited by its economic and social debts—debts so severe that no one quite knows how to settle them. Shortly after the turn of the millennium, Japan will likely pass the U.S. in GNP. Still, to be sure, no other nation rivals America's military capability. But what use is all that technological finesse in wars like the one against Iraq in which, afterward, Kuwait was "liberated" but the real target, Sadam Hussein, remained securely in power? And what can military sophistication do in a world where a chemically treated pile of manure is sufficient to destroy a federal building in Oklahoma City?

Today the world lacks the center it always had in the modern, colony-based world economy. The new arrangement for world domination (or world order) is at best one in which a group of North American and European states plus Japan, consulting guardedly with Russia and China, rule the world economy. They do not agree with each other and are seldom able to impose their political will where regional interests are sharply defined—in places like Bosnia, Somalia, or the Middle East. The most pervasive fact of the world order today is that the plight of the hungry and the poor is so much worse than anyone would have imagined and that there is no world center of power willing or able to do anything about it. At least, under the colonial system, the great power centers claimed to care about their subjects and believed they could do something about their supposedly inferior states of learn-

*[handwritten note in top margin: U.S. was center. Now leaving. we are — ]*

ing and well-being. Today, fewer care, and hardly anyone believes that good can really get done.

The absence of an unchallenged political and economic center in world affairs since the collapse of the American post-World War II hegemony is the most striking fact of today's world order. It is indeed a new world order, but not a very promising one and, without much doubt, it is *not* very similar to the system that ruled the world during the modern era. In the absence of a dominant core state, the definitive structure of the modern world has lost its classic form.

**3.** Along with the collapse of the center, the world has experienced the rise of dramatic, vital, and persuasive opposition to the very idea of a unified and universal world culture based on Euro-American values. The modern world is itself a pervasive culture based on a compelling theory of the world. In the simplest terms, that theory was that the West was best and that the culture that took definite shape in Europe and North America in the eighteenth century was, in the words of the American Declaration of Independence, the self-evident truth of "all men." Life, liberty, and the pursuit of happiness are fine values. Though I would personally like to see more assurance of equal distribution built into the happiness ideal, this is a good list of virtues to which indeed all men and women might aspire. But the culture of the modern world was one in which it was assumed that these truths were not just "self-evident," but were the hard-and-fast universal ideals to which all *must* aspire. What else could explain the naïve self-confidence with which Europeans and Americans felt they could and should descend anywhere in the world both to teach their ways to the natives and take home whatever they found to be of economic worth? The universal right of self-evident truth was so closely mixed up with the presumptive right to extract ("steal," if you prefer) wealth from other peo-

*[handwritten margin note: NOT ALLOWED ANYMORE (multi cultural)]*

ple of other cultures that one hardly questioned it. Leaving aside for the moment the slave trade and related means of stealing other peoples' lives and labor, the modern world system was (or is) one whose principle was that truth was so obvious that the stealing could not really be stealing. There is little reason to believe that the Romans were interested in their colonies for anything other than pure imperial motive. They left behind aqueducts, civil codes, and administrative practices because colonizers always leave something behind, not because it had been the Roman moral mission to redeem the world. But the British in India and the Americans in Vietnam actually thought they were doing good by right and responsibility of the superiority of their culture. That is the way of modern culture.

And all that is changed, as a short list of all-too-real events will demonstrate:

- the resistances by New Social Movements (such as feminist, race-based, or gay rights movements) within the North American and European nations;
- the reemergence of ethnicities, as opposed to nationalities, as a primary basis of social identification, particularly in the collapsed sphere of influence of the former Soviet Union (Chechnya, for example);
- the reappearance of traditionalist cultures as a basis for opposition to American and other modernist cultures in the form of various religious fundamentalisms (Christian in the United States, Muslim in the Middle East and parts of Asia and Africa).

Modernity's longstanding claim to be *the* universal culture of human progress lacks the global legitimacy it once demanded and, to a surprising extent, was granted.

This list could be much longer, or arranged differently, but it is sufficient for present purposes. There is more than enough reason to suspect that the so-called modern world has changed, or is changing, with respect to three of its most fundamental features: the colonial system from which core states extracted natural and labor resources[8]; the organizing centers from which the colonizers administered world politics and exploited world markets; the presumptive culture on the basis of which the Euro-American centers successively and collectively constructed interpretive principles to account for world dynamics or "world history."

In other words, three of the most essential characteristics of the global system that emerged in the late fifteenth century with the first systematic and continuing European intrusions into Africa, the Americas, and Asia are in a state of flux, if not outright collapse. One might even speculate that the change is in the direction of a reversion to what were once called "primate social orders." But whichever the direction and nature of the change, something is changing, and the world thus changing is the world that was once called, without serious controversy, "the modern world." That it is changing accounts for the fact that the question is asked everywhere one goes, even by those who still believe in and seek to defend modernity. That it is changing in ways that involve the breaking apart of the five-hundred-year-old structure based in a colonial system (or its analogues) controlled by one or another Euro-American state creates the distinctive impressions that are associated with postmodern theories of the world.

It would be hard to ignore the coincidence between the world's actual structure as it is changing and the main features of postmodern theories. As we will see in the next section, most postmodern theories argue that a once linear and well-defined world has given way to one that can be characterized by such terms as fragmented, decentered, playful, anarchical, ironic, indeterminate. Where the modern world was allegedly well-organized along a linear history yielding straightforward meanings, the postmodern world is thought to

be poorly organized in the absence of a clear, predictable historical future without which there are, at best, uncertain, playful, or ironic meanings.

## ▶ POSTMODERN SOCIAL THEORIES TODAY

There are, as I said, three compelling, and inherently important, positions with respect to the postmodernism question. They are: **radical postmodernism,** of which Jean Baudrillard's theory discussed above is a good example; **radical modernism,** which objects to theories like Baudrillard's while granting that something has changed but not enough to consider modernity dead; and **strategic postmodernism,** which in its way shares aspects of the former two—a postmodern readiness to think of the world as transformed by a strategic and appreciative reconsideration of modernist culture.

### Radical Postmodernism

**Radical postmodernism** considers modernity a thing of the past because it believes the present situation is, again, hyperreal. This, then, the first of three positions in the debate, has already been introduced earlier in this chapter where Jean Baudrillard was first discussed. To understand postmodernism one must understand why a serious social theorist like Baudrillard would come to the ideas he holds about the mediated, spectacular nature of today's social world.

Without going into the details, it is easiest to suggest the reasons by noting that in 1968 Baudrillard was professor of sociology at the Nanterre campus of the University of Paris. It was on this campus, in the spring of 1968, that the famous student rebellions broke out, soon spreading across Paris and eventually to most of the urban centers of France. Of all the student rebellions worldwide in the 1960s, few had a more paralyzing effect on their society as a whole. There was a moment that spring when, quite literally, all of Paris was consumed by the spectacle of pitched battles between police and students and workers, by public demonstrations and debates about the quality of life in France, and eventually by the remarkable drama of the President of France, Charles de Gaulle, quitting the homeland in order to rally the French foreign legion to retake Paris just as, almost a quarter of century before, he had led the Allied troops as the Nazis fled France. De Gaulle's 1968 heroics turned out to be laughably unnecessary. The whole drama of *Mai '68* was a replaying of France's historic dramas. For the young radicals it was in part a renewal fantasy of the storming of the Bastille in 1789 and the revitalization of the dream of a new society.

At about the same time many thousands of my generation in the United States participated in civil rights and antiwar demonstrations, often recalling the sacred texts of the American revolution of 1776. These movements were deadly serious business. Hundreds were injured and some died. But they also had the aspect of a huge national drama—if not a game, at least a public theater. This effect was heightened in two ways: first, by the ever-present television cameras which altered the events themselves as a consequence of their being watched[9]; second, by the ultimate failure of most of the actions which at the time seemed certain to be true revolutions. Both of these secondary effects lent to social participation an aura of what later came to be called *hyperreality*—social experience was incredibly intensified, making it seem all too real, yet in the end not tangibly real at all. Many of those active in politics in the 1960s came away from it with a qualified sense of accomplishment. There were some real changes, but many of them faded into caricatures of the original dream. Civil rights gains are today being reversed. The war in Vietnam was ended, but the

militarism continues. Poverty in America was discovered anew, but the number of hungry and homeless has grown. Far from being producers of a new social order, we were destined to become consumers of a culture that was subjected to an ever-intensified recommodification. The very culture of the 1960s is today repackaged and resold for a generation of youth born well after the sixties. Sixties happenings like *The Grateful Dead* and *The Rolling Stones*—for that matter the very form of the rock concert itself—linger on as bizarre simulations behind which all the original political and cultural ideals are barely intelligible, if at all.

You can see the likely correspondence between the events Baudrillard experienced in his youth and the ideas he came to articulate with greater and greater intensity in subsequent years. He was far from alone. In 1967, just before Baudrillard published his first book, Guy Debord published what has since become a kind of radical postmodernist manifesto, *Society as Spectacle,* which began:

> In societies where modern conditions of production prevail, all life presents itself as an immense accumulation of *spectacles*. Everything that was directly lived has moved away into a representation. . . . The spectacle is not a collection of images, but a social relation among people mediated by images.[10]

If you find these remarks a bit obscure, just reread them with the following questions in mind: In your opinion, how often do most people get their information about "what's really happening" from representations and images produced by televisual media rather than from direct experience? How much do the people you know live directly? What role does the culture represented in their **media** (television, Internet, CD-ROM, VCR) play in their lives? You do not have to believe this is a good thing (as some naïve radical postmodernists seem to suggest) to see that it captures a compelling truth about the world we live in.

Radical postmodernists such as Baudrillard and Debord are the ones that opponents of postmodernism like to hate. Unfortunately, even such a radical position is not as simple as it may seem. This discomforting fact is illustrated by reference to a writer whose ideas are taken seriously by radical postmodernists and some less radical ones, even by some modernists. It is possible that the most frequently quoted of all philosophical discussions of postmodernism is a book by Jean François Lyotard. In his essay *The Postmodern Condition: A Report on Knowledge* (first published in French in 1979), Lyotard provided an influential summary of radical postmodernism. Two statements from an otherwise complicated argument are: "Scientific knowledge is a kind of discourse" (p. 3), and: "I define *postmodern* as incredulity toward metanarratives" (p. xxiv).[11] The argument that connects these two statements is this: All knowledge, including science, has a social basis and is supported by the shared culture of the society in which the knowledge is produced. "$E=mc^2$" may be true scientifically, but it is also believable to those who believe the legends about Einstein and modern science, even to those who have no idea what it means. The culture by which science itself, as well as its particular knowledges, is shared by the sharing of metanarratives of which the legend of Einstein is a part.

Lyotard's argument continues: Science and other forms of knowledge depend on the legitimacy in which the culture holds it. Modernity, thus, is that culture which believes certain **metanarratives,** or widely shared stories about the value and "truth" of science, and truth itself. This is an important way in which science is discourse. In short, then, postmodernity is that culture in which those metanarratives are no longer considered completely legitimate and, thus, are not universally held to be completely credible.

One of the consequences of a theory such as Lyotard's is the assumption that if what modern knowledge says about reality is no longer held to be automatically true, then in this sense "reality" itself is held in some doubt. Postmodernism is about this incredulity and its effects throughout society. One could say that Madonna and Michael Jackson exhibit a certain inexpressible incredulity toward modern sexual morality—by making themselves the be-all and end-all of sexual and gender possibilities, they point beyond themselves to something more real than reality. Baudrillard, for example, said the following of Michael Jackson:

> He has constructed himself in every tiny detail. It is this which makes him a pure, innocent child—the artificial androgyne of the fable, who, better than Christ, can reign over the world and bring reconciliation, because he is better than the child-god: he is a prosthesis-child, an embryo of all the forms of mutation we have imagined to deliver us from race and sex.[12]

When it comes to doubting reality Lyotard and Baudrillard are not far apart. Indeed, Lyotard is often seen as a radical postmodernist. But Lyotard's postmodernism is in fact more complicated and cautious than Baudrillard's.

The English edition of Lyotard's *The Postmodern Condition* ends with the cryptic statement: "Let us wage a war on totality; . . . let us activate the differences and save the honor of the name."[13] What he means is that in modernity the power of those metanarratives created the illusion that the world was itself whole or, in the language of philosophy, a **totality**—a myth that had the effect of suppressing differences. Though postmodernists of both kinds wage war on totality—on cultures that want to unify the human race around grand, but artificial ideas and, in some instances, fascist politics—so too do many modernisms. This is why one cannot understand postmodernism without studying the more radical modernism as well.

Just to show how complicated this debate is, Lyotard's statement is one that could be supported by prominent representatives of

Calhoun & Ritzer:
Social Problems

Chapter on
Culture

Lemert
Postmodernism & Social
Theory

© The McGraw–Hill
Companies, 1996

*both* radical modernism and strategic postmodernism, as we shall now see.

### Radical Modernism

"Let us wage war on totality" is a slogan whose meaning depends mostly on what one thinks about the world itself. For most postmodernists (radical and strategic alike) it refers to the deceptions of modern culture by which the dream of a universal humanity based on Western ideals imposes itself and thus restricts human freedom. Behind all the humanistic idealism of modern culture, postmodernists find a deeper desire to suppress the unspeakable social differences that disrupt the ideal. This is known as the critique of **essentialism**, or the critique of the cultural ideal which holds that social differences are at best incidental variances on one, universal, true, and essential human nature.

Radical modernists, on the other hand, believe that this critique, while sensitive to important political and moral issues, is itself dangerous. Instead, they view the sad effects of totalization as a *social* failure under certain historical conditions, but not as an inherent flaw of modernity itself. Today, the single most important tradition of radical modernism is the German school of **critical theory**, often known as the "Frankfurt School" after the city in which its original institute was located in the 1930s. One need only reflect on the time and place of this school's founding to imagine what its most formative historical experience was. The Nazi reign of terror in Germany and Western Europe imposed a totalizing system of culture and politics. The Frankfurt theorists were among the first to see that the Enlightenment ideal of a true, universal humanity was also at risk of being distorted into the kind of evil Hitler actually unleashed. Hitler wanted to eliminate human differences, to create a pure, universal master race.

From the beginning, the Frankfurt School

was intent upon rethinking classic texts of the Enlightenment tradition as well as the social theories of Karl Marx, Max Weber, and Sigmund Freud. The idea was (and is) to produce a social philosophy that could both draw on these sources *and* remain actively critical both of them and of modern society (hence, the appellation "critical theory"). Critical theory could just as easily be considered that school of social theory most devoted to "waging war on totality," at least as much as any postmodernism. Indeed, Lyotard's line is very nearly a rephrasing of the classic idea of Theodor Adorno, one of the founders of the Frankfurt School, who once said that "Auschwitz demonstrated that culture has failed," and who believed that the whole is always untrue.[14]

One of the consequences of the historical situation of the critical theorists was that, by the end of the 1930s, most of the original Frankfurt School members had fled Hitler's Germany, mostly to the United States. There they continued their work, often applying it to other sociological subjects in which the problem of totalization is evident. One of these was mass culture. It is well known that, among other evils, Hitler was a master manipulator of the masses. It is not surprising, therefore, that the critical theorists, once they were ensconced in the United States, turned their attention to such subjects as the mass media—radio, Hollywood movies, even jazz and other forms of popular music. It is safe to say that Adorno, were he still living, would be no fan of Madonna, Hip-hop, or Michael Jackson. His critical theory was profoundly suspicious of any form of culture with mass appeal which (because of his direct historical experience with fascism) he considered inevitably a totalizing force destructive of human freedom. "The culture industry," Adorno once said,[15] "intentionally integrates its consumers from above." In other words, Adorno would have seen a phenomenon like Madonna as anything but a liberating playing out of *popular* desires with respect to sex, sexuality, and gender. He would have been far more inclined to view her as, to use his word, the intentional manipulation of popular consciousness by a totalizing industry serving elite corporate interests for which the media, especially television, are their most important instruments for manufacturing consumer tastes for their goods and services. A more recent critical theorist, Herbert Marcuse, developed a version of this idea in his book, *One Dimensional Man* (1964).[16] This book became one of the "must reads" of 1960s cultural radicals who also believed that the dominant powers in society had made ordinary people one-dimensional, that is, lacking in the critical capacity to stand outside the cultural forces shaping them. If you wonder what this might mean, just ask yourself the next time you're hanging out watching MTV what most of those videos are really saying to you about who you are supposed to be? And how easy or difficult is it for you, on those occasions, to be critical of their effects on your life, even if the only "critique" is that, while you were hanging out you could have been reading a book or organizing a political rally?

Today the most important critical theorist is the German social theorist, Juergen Habermas. Like others in this tradition, Habermas's voluminous writings usually dwell on depth reinterpretations of the classic texts of modernity. Also like his predecessors, Habermas is critical of the Enlightenment tradition with its dangerous temptations to essentialize all humanity into a one-dimensional totality shorn of real differences. Yet, this position is a radical *modernism* because it seeks critically to discover the liberating potential in modern culture. It would be impossible here even to begin to demonstrate the details of how Habermas does this. But it can be illustrated by quoting from one of his most straightforward definitional statements of the basic concepts of social thought:

I call *culture* the store of knowledge from which those engaged in communicative action draw interpretations susceptible of consensus as they come to an understanding about something in the world. I call *society* (in the narrower sense of a component of the lifeworld) the legitimate orders from which those engaged in communicative action gather a solidarity, based on belonging to groups, as they enter into interpersonal relationships with one another. *Personality* serves as a term of art for acquired competences that render a subject capable of speech and action and hence able to participate in processes of mutual understanding in a given context and to maintain his own identity in the shifting contexts of interaction.[17]

If you have not read Habermas, this may seem a little abstract (and, indeed, his writing is abstract in the sense of being highly theoretical). But even so, you can see that behind the concepts is a deep, abiding respect for the liberating and community-building potential of human beings. Culture, far from being merely an imposed integration (as Adorno put it), allows people to communicate in ways that can build consensus. Society, far from being a totalizing abstraction, is rooted in the life world of ordinary people coming into relations with each other. Personality, far from being a passive vehicle of the subjugating force of totalities, refers to the art of participation and of keeping true to one's identity. You can see, at least, that Habermas's radical critique of modernity serves the purpose of radically rethinking modernity to serve the ideal of human freedom and community.

If you still find this abstract, remember that this tradition of radical modernism was originally forged in the terrible furnaces of the Holocaust from whence comes its steadfast commitment to protecting the human spirit. This also is one of the reasons radical modernists hold to the grand humanistic principles of the modern age. Their purpose is far too serious, in their experience, to sacrifice known principles of emancipation for the whim of fractious postmodernism that presents itself too often in the spectacle of popular culture. Where, really, is the common humanity you or I share with the artist-formerly-known-as-Prince or Michael Jackson? It must be there behind the show, but radical modernists are too sober to play. One must respect their reasons.

There are quite a number of radical post-modernists today.[18] At their best, they share this sense of sober regard for the human values of the modern age. Among them is a line of contemporary feminism which, like the earliest critical theorists, writes social theory out of a very clear sense of the oppressions women have suffered and the urgent need to protect some universal principles of ideal humanity with which to wage war on totalizing attempts to ignore the differences sexism has imposed on women's lives.[19] Some consider this position still too essentialist. But the important fact about radical modernism is that, far from dismissing postmodernism, it is engaged with it in order to redefine the modernist ideal.

## Strategic Postmodernism

There is a category of thinkers who are commonly lumped together with the radical post-modernists even though there is little evidence they would (or would have) accepted the designation for themselves. This is because when social theorists try to understand post-modernism they quite naturally gravitate to the writings of figures who have justifiably strong reputations and whose thinking *seems* to be postmodern. The most famous of these are two French social thinkers: Michel Foucault and Jacques Derrida.

Foucault and Derrida share the following general theoretical views: (1) a commitment to reinterpreting the modern classic social thinkers (Nietzsche, Husserl, and Freud, respectively, among many others); (2) a conviction that language, or discourse, is fundamental to any science of the human; (3) a rejection of any version of the ideal of a universal essence, totality, or center as a basis for social

thought. You can see immediately that the first two of these three points fail to distinguish them from either of the two groups of radicals. All three of the groups are devoted to rewriting the classics in one fashion or another. And all three are involved in what Habermas and others have called the "linguistic turn" in social theory. Only the third of the three general attributes of the strategic postmodernists can be said to be a distinctively postmodern social idea. This is, in fact, the principle that most strongly separates postmodernists of both kinds from modernists of all kinds. Yet, when this principle is examined closely enough, it is plain that it is also a point of demarcation between the two kinds of postmodernism.

Strategic postmodernists differ from radical ones in the way they attack the totalizing aspects of modernist essentialism—that is, in the way they wage war on totality. They are far less inclined to take for granted that the world has yet changed. They might, in fact, be properly accused of wishing the world were changed or acting as though it had. But in their writings, they take a more modest attitude toward culture and world reality than the radical post-modernists. Like the radical modernists, strategic postmodernists are less concerned with imagining the new world, than with rethinking and rewriting modernity itself. In this sense they too are critical theorists of a special kind.

Here is where the most famous of the words associated with postmodernism must be mentioned: **deconstruction.** This is a more difficult term to use correctly than many realize. Notice that the word is not "deconstruction-*ism.*" Strategic postmodernism is most emphatically opposed to any "ism" because it considers ideology one of the most tricky and debilitating features of modern culture. Nor is the word meant to be a sly cognate for "*des*truction"—though some of the word's abusers jump to this conclusion because they view deconstruction all too simply as a "taking apart" of modern culture. There is nothing destructive or, as it is sometimes said, "nihilistic" about strategic postmodernism (though this might be said more accurately of some radical postmodernists). Nor should the word be used casually in the infinitive form, "to deconstruct," which suggests a transitive action, as in "Madonna deconstructs sexuality." Deconstruction is not a new method, though it is taken as such by those with a loose understanding of Jacques Derrida, the originator of the idea. Deconstruction is more an attitude, a way of working with culture in order to reconstrue it.

Derrida's basic ideas were first presented in two early and very difficult books (both originally published in 1967, just before the student and worker rebellions in France): *Of Grammatology* and *Writing and Difference*. One of the reasons Derrida's writings are so difficult for the first-time reader is that he writes in an unusual manner, but for a purpose. Derrida believes it is impossible even for the critics of modernity to abandon the culture and the language of modernity. Thus, the only way to be critical of modernity is to subvert it by using its own language and ideas against it. In his early writings, therefore, Derrida often spoke of putting language under erasure—literally of using the words and concepts one *must* use, but to put an "X" through them, literally in some cases, figuratively in most.

An irony used in deconstruction that is somewhat easier to understand is the *double entendre*, or "double meaning." The most famous of those used by Derrida is also the one that best illustrates his basic theory of modernity. In the French language, the words **différence** and **différance** sound exactly the same when spoken. But, in writing, their meanings are distinct. The former means what it means in English, but the latter, *différance* with an "a," means "the act of deferring," or "of putting off for a later time." Now you might wonder what in the world do "differences" have to do with the act of "deferring"? The answer is quite surprising.

The two terms (and the cultural concepts they convey) refer to the most fundamental facts of modern society and culture. To explain this, I will use ideas that are faithful to Derrida but are a somewhat free interpretation of his thinking. As we have seen, the postmodern critique of modernity's essentialism is an attack on modern culture's inability to tolerate or even to recognize the importance of actual social differences. Social theories that rely on Derrida would say that the fact of differences is so fundamental that it appears even in the most subtle aspects of culture, most especially in the very language that we speak.[20]

According to Derrida, one of the ways in which the fact of differences is masked and ignored is by the privilege modern culture accords to speech over writing. By this he does not mean that Western culture has no appreciation of great writing. Rather he is referring to the assumption made in Western culture that speaking is presumed to be the "most original" and "most basic" form of communication. Our culture does indeed place a very heavy emphasis on "direct" talk, which is taken as the "more honest" and "more human" type of communication. For example, we are suspicious of relationships and communications that are not "face to face." One of the reasons we are suspicious of lawyers is that they reduce everything to writing. Conversely, perhaps one of the reasons we are seduced by televisual media is that they create the illusion of "being there" in some primary way (which of course we know not to be so). Visual media allow us to "see" and "hear" what people are "really" saying. Lincoln's Gettysburg Address would have been a flop on TV. In fact, it was a flop at Gettysburg when spoken. But it was a brilliant success when published. Why? What is at issue is the difference between speech and writing.

Derrida believes that the difference between speech and writing is that in writing the meaning of what is being said is "deferred." Americans really did not get the meaning of the Gettysburg Address until long after it was spoken. Most of those present on November 19, 1863, could not even hear Lincoln. And it is important to note that the meaning of the address itself was dependent on its reference, most of all, to the horrible battle in which 51,000 men were killed. The Civil War was, and still is, the worst nightmare in American history—worse even than Vietnam. At Gettysburg, as we know, the tide had turned—the Union would be preserved, the slaves emancipated. A follower of Derrida, thus, might say that Lincoln's address was actually a piece of writing that called forth at a later time the "historical writing" or "inscription" of the moral meaning of the Civil War and its most famous battle in the American psyche. If you doubt this, visit the battlefield and see whether or not something is not inscribed there, even now in the quiet hills and monuments. In other words, Derrida argues that human culture and history are the primary "inscriptions" of human meaning—written, if you will, in the monuments, battlefields, village and urban plans, on literally the whole of culture which always imposes its visible markings on the landscape of a nation. But, these meanings are *deferred*. We get them after the fact, with some work, if at all.

Against this, compare the illusion of the "primary meanings" associated with speech. Of course, they are very slippery. A speaker can always say (as politicians do), "Oh, but I didn't mean it." But when something is written—whether on the back of an envelope, or on a battlefield—its marks remain, and its truth is definite. Writing, in effect, cannot ever be completely erased. Thus (again treating Derrida somewhat loosely), we can say that a strategic postmodernism would be based on a critique of Western culture's privileging of "primary speech" as an illusion that broadcasts

true meanings as though their truth were derived from their immediacy. It is the illusion that social meanings are immediately available which, among much else, masks the fact of differences.

Likewise, the spoken words *différence/différance* are indistinguishable in speech, while in writing their important differences are evident. Modernity, therefore, could be said to work its cultural effects by centering culture on the ideal of primary, essential meaning (idealized in the face-to-face speaker, the truth giver). In this, modern culture has hidden all the many subtle, complicated, and embarrassing meanings of its history, not the least of which is the fact that modernity struggles with the reality of social differences just as it seeks to bring all meanings into the present moment. The problem is that if social differences such as those of class, race, and gender are real (as they surely are), then the meaning of those differences will be "deferred" or postponed and put off in the pious platitudes of the politicians. But, to anyone who "reads" the writing of urban ghettos torn by economic misery, of women bruised by violence, of neighborhoods pocked by dilapidation, or of monuments to dead young warriors, the painful reality of differences could not be more evident.

This is why, in the spirit of Derrida, strategic postmodernism can be understood as more cautious than radical postmodernism but more critical even than radical modernism. Thus, one could say that a great deal of this line of postmodernism is engaged in the process of rewriting the history of modernity. Derrida himself is a philosopher, so his rewriting is directed at philosophers (from Husserl, the subject of his first book, to Marx, the subject of one of his latest). Beyond Derrida, this kind of postmodernism has had an important influence on feminism, gay-lesbian, African-American and other new forms of social knowledge. While not all African-Americanists consider themselves postmodernists of any kind, nor followers of Derrida, they do enjoy a certain similarity of purpose. African-American studies, like feminism and queer studies, are in large part attempts to rewrite the history of society in ways that are explicitly critical of the culture's exclusion of blacks, women, and gays or lesbians.

This reconstructive style appears in other of the strategic postmodernists. Michel Foucault is perhaps somewhat easier to understand than Derrida because his subject matter is more historical and within the range of common experience. Foucault, who died in 1984 of AIDS, wrote books on an amazing range of topics—on madness and the rise of modern psychology (for example, *Madness and Civilization* [1961]), on the emergence of modern medical practice (*Birth of the Clinic* [1963]), on the history of the social and human sciences (*The Order of Things* [1966]), and on the early modern penitentiary (*Discipline and Punish* [1975]). What these studies have in common is that all are about the histories of the most distinctive institutions of modern society. Many scholars agree that one of the most unusual features of modernity is its attempt, and claim, to treat all persons in a more humane way by doing away with the terrors often associated with feudal societies. This is one of the reasons we associate the culture of "humanism" with modernity itself. All of the institutions Foucault wrote about were notable for their apparent commitment to using gentle, humane, and liberal (another word associated with modern culture) means to heal the ill, understand social life, and rehabilitate the criminal. Like Marx long before him (though Foucault was not a Marxist), and his contemporary Derrida, Foucault's social theory of modernity refuses to take modernity at face value. Appearances are in fact the very opposite of reality.

Let us consider an example from Foucault's last and very controversial project, *The History of Sexuality* (1976). In this book, the introductory volume to a series of studies on sex in the West, Foucault provides a succinct summary of *his* most famous concept, **power/knowledge.** Before going into the concept, however, let me first explain his method and how he proposed to apply it to the history of sex and sexuality in the modern age. Many historians are infuriated by Foucault's studies because he presents his ideas without the usual heavy footnoting of his sources and facts. Though he did his own archival research on original documents in France's national library, his literary style and his ideas are filled with surprises. Often he begins with a shocking claim that runs entirely contrary to what most people think (like Derrida, Foucault also deals in irony and literary tricks—though not in so obscure a manner).

In the beginning of his book on sexuality, Foucault immediately attacks (in an understated way) two general concepts that are typical of modern thinking: that power is the effect of strong elites consciously and overtly crushing ordinary people; and, that Christian morality and its secular successors were determined to repress all talk of sex, not to mention sex itself. Most of us are inclined to believe, for example, that the fabled prudishness of the Victorian age in the late nineteenth century is, simply, a fact—plain and simple. Foucault disagrees. In his view, if one looks more skeptically at the facts, it appears that the Victorians talked a great deal about sex. Foucault points to a number of documents that were widely read in the Victorian era. If you doubt this, just think of the romance novels that became popular in the mid-nineteenth century and continue to be popular today. Charlotte Brontë's *Jane Eyre* is a classic example of a book on romantic longing. In this novel, true sex is not described as it would be today but the book is very much about sexual desire, sexual tragedy, sexual conquest, and abandonment. Or, in an early era, consider Jean-Jacques Rousseau's *Confessions* from the eighteenth century. Though written in very high language, the book is very hot indeed. Rousseau liked sex and had a lot of it. These, of course, are just two famous classic writings of modern culture. Foucault refers to lesser-known writings, often ones he discovered hidden away in the French archives.

Take as an example one of the stories he reports in *The History of Sexuality* from a lost document he found somewhere on a dusty library shelf: In 1867, Juoy, apparently a retarded person (perhaps the village idiot), was arrested for what we would consider the sexual abuse of a young girl. What he had done, apparently, was to persuade her to exchange sexual touches under the guise of a game he had seen children play in the village. Children everywhere play with sex in this way. The man did not realize he was not a child. Today, Juoy would have been thrown in jail and severely punished, as he might have been prior to modern times. But in this small, still rural nineteenth-century village, he was sentenced, in effect, to become a subject of study and investigation. The man had his brain pan measured, his facial anatomy examined, his personal history taken down, and more. He was studied in the most minute detail. The then-new methods of the medical and social sciences were applied to the end of "understanding" this man. The basic fact was that he *was* indeed punished but by the extraordinarily gentle means of being subjected to examination—just as today mental patients and criminals are, first of all, processed through diagnostic procedures that classify their exact illness according to carefully defined rules of medical or criminological evidence. By contrast, in the feudal age, the insane, the confused, the poor, *and* the criminal were locked up without distinction, often thrown into the same prison cell as though there were no differences between the criminal and the ill.

Foucault's idea is that in the modern age the knowledge of the new human sciences was used to control individuals, including those like the simpleton Juoy who deviated from accepted adult sexual norms. In this case, Foucault drew his conclusions from an archive, originally a very public document taken from much discussed legal and medical hearings. In other words, in that small village the sexual offense of the man was talked up all over town. Not very prudish. Foucault's larger argument is that throughout the history of the West the Christian prohibition against sex, and talk of sex, was actually quite contrary to the practices of daily life. Even in feudal Christendom, the Roman Catholic confessional was, in fact, a place in which the penitent were (as today) *encouraged* to talk about sex, just as at a later time in the twentieth century junior high school manuals about "dating" encourage sex talk and giggles, or, for the more sophisticated, psychotherapeutic counseling sessions today induce people to talk about their sexual feelings and activities, among other things. Remote as it is from our day where every part of culture is saturated by sex talk, these seemingly more innocent occasions for talk of sex were actually precursors of today's situation. Foucault suggests that the confessional was actually the origin of the West's preoccupation with sex—a preoccupation that grew more and more (*not* less and less) intense through the Victorian and post-Victorian eras.

How does Foucault link sex to power? Here you can again see the irony in strategic postmodernism's method. Modernity appears to be prudish, when in fact it is very sexy. Why this encouragement of sex talk? Foucault says (in a more subtle argument than this) that talk about sex is the method by which modern culture teaches people to control their sex in a definite way. What the modern world had to do, in the nineteenth century, was to control a dramatically changing population of people who were migrating from rural towns to the new factories. For the factories to function in an efficient and productive way, those new workers had to be disciplined into a new form of life. Since the rules of modern culture are that people must be considered free and not forced to work or live according to imposed rules, workers had to be *taught* to organize their lives in a certain factory-like way. With respect to sex, it was a matter of some urgency that the waves of new workers from the countryside be taught, let us say, to have just enough sex to produce new generations of baby workers but not so much sex that the population would overwhelm the social system's ability to provide.

Obviously, such a system must accomplish two tasks: produce a reasonable number of workers; but do so by reasonable, gentle, and human means. Thus, argues Foucault, modernity is interested in teaching people about sex and everything else, hence its interest in knowledge and education. It must use moral and formal instruction to discipline because its own cultural values prohibit force. These methods were so successful that ordinary people were, and are, among the most fervent believers in the teachings by which they were disciplined. This is one reason why the working class is often the most patriotic in industrial societies.

You now can see the importance of Foucault's concept *power/knowledge* and his surprising criticism of the usual assumption about power as a force that works from the top down. Power in modernity mostly operates through knowledge—through the teachings of judging priests, prudish school marms, prying guidance counselors, officious boy scout leaders, ambitious authors of dating guides, probing therapists, and so on. Modernity must use knowledge to discipline; and, discipline is an exercise of power that works through the (seemingly) gentle means of teaching. This is why, according to Foucault, the invention of new forms of knowledge in medicine, mental

health, criminology, sociology, and sexology were fundamental to the establishment of modern culture.

Once again, you can see why this is a strategic postmodernism, one parallel to, if not the same as, Derrida's. Foucault's main work was to rewrite the history of modernity in order to expose the ways power worked, not overtly or from the top down, but through the popular effects of *knowledge*—through the (apparently) benign means of education for the masses. Though Foucault upset a lot of people by his daring and unconventional methods and ideas, he has served as a model and, in many ways, an inspiration to social theorists who seek to rewrite the histories of oppressed people with whom they identify.

Foucault himself was openly gay in later life, and is considered one of the classic figures in what today is known as **queer theory:** the politically radical but intellectually demanding social theories of gay, lesbian, or bisexual people who take "queer" as a sign of their refusal to be disciplined by the standards of heterosexual society. Once a stigmatizing term, "queer" is used by queer theorists to challenge modernity's sacred beliefs about them. Foucault, so far as I know, did not use the term "queer" for his own politics, even though his ironic method was clearly a forerunner of this and other radical social theories. You might also be able to imagine the parallels of the strategic use of "queer" with Derrida's own play on words.

## ▶ CONCLUSION

The differences among the three types of postmodern social theory are perhaps clearer now. *Radical postmodernism* tends to believe that modernity is utterly overthrown by a new social arrangement in which reality is a virtual reality, in which the differences between fact and fiction no longer apply, and in which there is little basis for defending any specific idea or ideal as more real than any other. *Radical modernism* believes that, though modernity has produced social evil, modern culture remains the only discernible basis for human liberation from those evils. It holds fast to the principle that to give up on the modern world is to give up any hope of finding values and principles able to criticize and correct social evil. *Strategic postmodernism* believes that modernity is too clever, too subtle in its workings, for anyone to be able to criticize it from the point of view of its own ideas. Yet, this third position also believes that we have no sensible choice but to use modern culture, that is, to subvert the culture, to overcome its denial of differences, its deceptive deployment of *power/knowledge,* its self-denying ideologies.

Or, one might summarize by returning to Lyotard's line about totality. *Radical postmodernism* wages war on totality by moving beyond the real to the hyperreal. *Radical modernism* wages this war by radicalizing the most powerful critical weapons of modern culture to attack real totalizing effects. *Strategic postmodernism* neither gives up on nor overrates modernity's power. It wages war on totality by working within the modern, as modernity works within us. As modernity deceives us into ignoring painful differences, this last postmodernism seeks to subvert those deceptions by its own tricks.

Whichever position you prefer in the postmodernism debate will depend to a large extent on your historical interpretation of the present age. In the end, postmodernism is about the extent to which our world has changed. Social theories of the postmodern are interpretations of that world, the reality (or hyperreality) of which is much more in the experiences of living in it.

▶ SUMMARY

1. Postmodernism attempts to come to terms with the odd fact that historical aspects of the world that do not belong together are, today, jumbled up with each other—Hip-hop culture, for example.

2. Postmodern social theories are those that take seriously cultural and historical evidence that the world today is more and more different from the modern world. Postmodern social theories are, therefore, critical theories that draw their conclusions about current world history from differing interpretations of the evidence.

3. Postmodernism, however, should be thought of less as a theory of the world than as an attempt to account for the way the world is. One example of an important change that encourages some postmodern social theorists is the widespread influence of mediated cultures, like television, in which reality is experienced indirectly while seeming to be real and direct.

4. One of the reasons postmodernism has drawn so much attention is that there is reasonable historical evidence to suppose that the modern world is undergoing a fundamental transformation. This evidence includes: the collapse of the colonial system, the absence of an organizing center to world politics, the appearance of so many different movements that resist the cultural ideals of modernity.

5. There are three groups of social theorists involved in the postmodernism debate: radical postmodernists, radical modernists, and strategic postmodernists. Each of them is critical of the modern and, in different ways, believes that the modern world is either at its end, *or* in some serious difficulty, *or* both.

6. Radical postmodernism takes the fact of mediated culture with ultimate seriousness. Jean Baudrillard, for example, believes that the world is now characterized by hyperreality in which the most real experiences are very

often simulations, or imitations of reality such as Disneyworld or Michael Jackson. The hyperreal is considered more real than reality itself, just as the simulation is more real than the thing copied. The only American frontier towns idealized by people are to be found in movies or Disneyworld. In Wyoming itself people drive air-conditioned Jeeps and shop at Walmart.

7. Radical modernists grant that the world, especially over the last century, is troubled by social evil. The most important radical modernists are those in the tradition of the German school of critical theory, a perspective that developed in response to the evil of the Holocaust during Hitler's rule. Yet, radical modernists believe that to abandon the values of the modern world is to abandon the only political and social values clearly able to explain and encourage human liberation from social evil.

8. Strategic postmodernists agree only partly with the other two schools of thought. Like radical postmodernists, they tend to believe that the modern world is no longer real as it once was. Yet, like radical modernists, they are cautious about rejecting modernity itself before it is fully understood. Writers like Jacques Derrida and Michel Foucault recommend that we rethink and rewrite the ideas, cultures, and practices of the modern age in order to expose modernity's deceptions.

9. Which, if any, of the three schools of thought one trusts the most should be determined not by the appeal of the theorists but by one's own assessment of the world one lives in. Postmodernists can be very alluring, but ultimately postmodernism is not about what anyone thinks so much as what the world is.

► SUGGESTED READINGS

Calhoun, Craig: *Critical Social Theory: Culture, History and the Challenge of Difference*, Cambridge, Mass., and Oxford, UK, Basil Blackwell, 1995. A summary of the radical modernist position that comments critically, but responsibly, on various postmodernisms.

Clough, Patricia Ticineto: *Feminist Thought: Desire, Power, and Academic Discourse*, Cambridge, Mass., and Oxford, UK, Basil Blackwell, 1994. A presentation of various aspects of feminist social theory, including: African-American, queer, postcolonial. These are the traditions of social thought that, while not always explicitly postmodernist, share a considerable affinity with strategic postmodernism.

Lemert, Charles (ed.): *Social Theory: The Multicultural and Classical Readings*, Boulder, Colo., and New York, Westview/HarperCollins, 1993. A comprehensive collection of readings by authors representing all three groups in the postmodernism controversy (especially in the final section).

Nicholson, Linda (ed.): *Feminism/Psotmodernism*, New York, Routledge, 1990. Still the most important collection of original essays on postmodernism in feminism.

Seidman, Steven: *Contested Knowledge: Social Theory in the Postmodern Era*, Cambridge, Mass., and Oxford, UK, Basil Blackwell, 1994. A reinterpretation of the history of sociological social theory from a postmodernist point of view.

► GLOSSARY

**critical theory:** a feature of all social theories whereby they are distinguished from theories of the "pure" sciences which vainly attempt to avoid value judgments; the tradition of radical modernist social theory associated with the German school of critical theory or the Frankfurt School.

**culture:** the complex of socially produced values, rules, beliefs, literatures, arts, media, penal codes, laws, political ideals, and other diversions by which a society, or social group, represents its view of the world as it is and ought to be; the complex of mechanisms by which societies, or social groups, justify their exclusions of realities they find intolerable.

**deconstruction:** a social theoretical attitude that has led to the use of irony to rethink, rewrite, and reconstrue the basic features of modernity and modernism; the most misunderstood and misused term in postmodernism; a term associated with Jacques Derrida and his followers; not an "ism," nor a method, nor a "destruction."

**différence/différance:** French language words that sound the same but do not have the same meaning in writing; ironic terms used by social theorists associated with deconstruction to critique the modernist (and essentialist) ideal of primary and universal cultural meanings.

**essentialism:** a social theoretical term used to describe modernism's cultural ideal by which social differences are considered secondary and nonessential variances on the nature of universal human nature, as in: "We hold these truths to be self-evident, that *all men* are created equal . . . "

**hyperreality:** a radical postmodernist concept that describes the world as being so much under the sway of mediated cultures that the sense of reality is intensified such that simulations of reality (e.g., Disneyland or television) are experienced as *more real* than the realities they simulate.

**ideology:** an ironic concept whereby modernism both expresses its belief that truth must be free of distortion and recognizes (though indirectly) that its own claim to truth is itself a distortion; related to modernism's faith in reality, as in the belief that truth reflects the real order of things, while ideology is a motivated distortion of reality.

**irony/ironic:** a literary device (or, trope) used to call surprising attention to usually ignored traits by means of reversal or negation, as in Foucault's oxymoronic ideas: sexy Victorians, gentle power; a typical literary and theoretical device of strategic postmodernists.

**linguistic turn in social theory:** refers to the remarkable fact that, since the 1960s, a very large number of social theories, of very different origins (France, Germany, Russia, the United States, Finland, notably) rethought social theory by placing a surprisingly strong emphasis on the role of language, or discourse, in social life.

**metanarratives:** widely shared cultural stories by which a society, or social group, sometimes expresses the most fundamental ideals, or "truths," of its culture; as in the metanarratives of modernism whereby scientific truth is considered to be objective and, simply, "true."

**media:** any socially or technologically produced means by which reality is communicated indirectly; see *mediated cultures*.

**mediated cultures:** any cultural form that communicates representations of reality by indirect means, as in the culture produced by prolonged, mass exposure to television and other televisual media.

**modernism:** the culture, including the theories, of modernity; compare *modernity*.

**modernity/the modern age:** the historical period that arose around 1500 with the era of European exploration and colonization of the world, the high culture of which was formulated in the eighteenth and nineteenth centuries, beginning with the Enlightenment.

**postmodernity:** a historical period that is believed by some to mark the end of modernity; the complex whole of a real social historical period; compare *postmodernism*.

**postmodernism:** the culture, including the theories, of postmodernity; any culture or theory that celebrates or otherwise takes seriously the breaking apart of modernity.

**power/knowledge:** a concept formed by bringing together two others as though they were one in order to express the social theoretical idea that, in modernity, power actually works indirectly *through* knowledge, rather than directly as overt abuse, domination, and control; the best-known concept of Michel Foucault.

**queer theory:** social theories that subvert the epithet often hurled at gay, lesbian, or bisexual people in order to call attention to the queer nature of modernity's abuse of queer and other people whose differences many modernisms consider deviant; a variant, if not self-conscious, form of strategic postmodernism.

**radical modernism:** a group of social theories that strive to be simultaneously critical of and loyal to modernism and modernity itself.

**radical postmodernism:** a group of social theories that consider modernity a thing of the past (or, at least, in its last historical moments); social theories that consider the present situation to be characterized more by hyperreality than reality.

**reality:** a modernist concept representing modernity's willingness to suspend disbelief in the originality of the things of the world.

**social theory:** any theory of society or social life that distinguishes itself from scientific theories in sociology by a willingness to be critical as well as factual.

**strategic postmodernism:** a group of social theories that seek to reconstruct the cultural, social, and political history of modernity in order to expose the deceptions of the modern age; neither hyperrealists, nor realists.

**totality:** a concept used by social theorists to describe one of the most essential characteristics of modern culture, namely: the cultural urge to think of social life and world reality as being (and needing to be) complete, whole, and constant; frequently, and notoriously, converted into a political idea, as in Hitler's intent to purify Western culture by eliminating Jewish people; one of the most common objects of criticism by radical modernist and postmodernist social theories.

► ENDNOTES

1. Marshall McLuhan, *Understanding Media*, New York, McGraw-Hill, 1964.

2. "The Disneyland imaginery is neither true nor false. It is a determined set-up to rejuvenate in reverse the fiction of the real." Jean Baudrillard, "Simulacra and Simulation," in Mark Poster, ed., *Jean Baudrillard: Selected Writings*, Palo Alto, Calif., Stanford University Press, 1988, p. 172.

3. Though she would not put things as I have, most of the following section is influenced by the thinking and writing of Patricia Clough. Most of her writing about television is in recent unpublished essays. But her line of argument is outlined in *End(s) of Ethnography*, Newbury Park, Calif., Sage, 1989.

4. For examples, see Jean François Lyotard, *The Postmodern Condition: A Report on Knowledge*, Minneapolis, University of Minnesota Press, 1984/1979; Richard Rorty, *Contingency, Irony, and Solidarity*, Cambridge, UK, Cambridge University Press, 1989.

5. It is too easy to forget that Max Weber wrote his famous and persuasive book, *The Protestant Ethic and the Spirit of Capitalism*, nearly three centuries after the events whose causes the book examined. It takes about that long to really see historical change. Even then he could not prove his point.

6. Fredric Jameson, *Postmodernism, or The Cultural Logic of Postmodernity*, Durham, N.C., Duke University Press, 1991; and David Harvey, *The Condition of Postmodernity*, Oxford, Basil Blackwell, 1989.

7. For the principal example see Immanuel Wallerstein, *The Modern World System*, Vol. I, New York, Academic Press, 1974.

8. "Core state" is from Wallerstein, ibid.

9. See Todd Gitlin, *The Whole World Is Watching*, Berkeley, University of California Press, 1980.

10. Guy Debord, *Society as Spectacle*, Detroit, Mich., Black and Red Press, 1984, paras. 1 and 2.

11. Lyotard, op. cit.

12. Jean Baudrillard, *Cool Memories,* London, Verso, 1990, p. 147.

13. Lyotard, op. cit., p. 82.

14. Theodor Adorno, *Negative Dialectics,* New York, Seabury Press, 1973, p. 366.

15. Theodor Adorno, "The Culture Industry Reconsidered," in Stephen Bonner and Douglas Kellner, eds., *Critical Theory and Society: A Reader,* New York, Routledge, 1989, p. 128.

16. Herbert Marcuse, *One Dimensional Man,* Boston, Beacon Press, 1964.

17. Juergen Habermas, *The Philosophical Discourse of Modernity,* Cambridge, Mass., MIT Press, 1987, p. 343.

18. Among sociologists, the most important radical modernists are Anthony Giddens and Pierre Bourdieu. For a discussion see Charles Lemert, *Sociology after the Crisis,* HarperCollins, 1995, Chap. 7.

19. See Linda Nicholson, *Feminism/Postmodernism,* New York, Routledge, 1990; and Patricia Clough, *Feminist Thought,* Oxford, Basil Blackwell, 1994.

20. Though I cannot go into it here, this idea also involves an extraordinarily technical argument about the effect of phonetic and semantic differences in the functioning of language; the classic source is Ferdinand de Saussure, *Course in General Linguistics,* New York, McGraw-Hill, 1959/1911.

# 3

# A WALK ON THE WILD SIDE

## *Social Constructivism, Postmodernism, Feminism, and That Old-Time Religion*

## THE CONSTRUCTIVIST CHALLENGE

IF THERE EVER HAS BEEN a "hero of science," it was Louis Pasteur. He is famous all over the world, commemorated on every milk carton with the word "pasteurized." In his native France Pasteur was honored almost as a living saint during his lifetime. Now, well more than a century after his death, the Pasteur Institute in Paris remains a leading center for bio-medical research. Though he had many brilliant accomplishments, he was most honored for developing vaccines, especially the vaccine against the dreadful disease rabies. Rabies had never been a great killer, like smallpox or cholera, but fear of the disease had always been far out of proportion to the number of its victims. Paul De Kruif's classic *The Microbe Hunters* contains an unabashedly heroic account of Pasteur's conquest of rabies. Here is De Kruif's description of Pasteur fearlessly risking his own life to combat disease:

> And now Pasteur began—God knows why—to stick little hollow glass tubes into the gaping mouths of dogs writhing mad with rabies. While two servants pried apart and held open the jowls of a powerful bulldog, Pasteur stuck his beard within a couple of inches of those fangs whose snap meant the worst of deaths, and, sprinkled sometimes with a maybe fatal spray, he sucked up the froth into his tube—to get a specimen in which to hunt for the microbe of hydrophobia. (De Kruif, 1926, 169)

After a long series of excruciatingly difficult experiments, Pasteur found a way to weaken the infectious agent of rabies, now known to be a virus. He concocted a vaccine that was administered in a series of four-

The Constructivist Challenge   **61**

teen injections, starting with the most weakened virus and proceeding to the most virulent. The vaccine worked perfectly on dogs, but would it work on humans? Pasteur was reluctant to try, but the story of how he did is one of the most famous in the history of medicine. In July 1885, Joseph Meister, a nine-year-old boy from the Alsace region, was mauled by a mad dog. His mother brought him to Paris and begged Pasteur to save her child. Moved by the plight of the terrified boy and his desperate mother, Pasteur agreed to try. De Kruif tells the story:

> And that night of July 6, 1885, they made the first injection of the weak-ened microbes of hydrophobia into a human being. Then, day after day, the boy Meister went without a hitch through his fourteen injections— which were only slight pricks of the hypodermic needle into his skin. . . . And the boy went home to Alsace and never had a sign of that dreadful disease. (179–180)

Pasteur's greatest triumph occurred when nineteen Russian peasants who had been bitten by a rabid wolf nearly three weeks before were brought for his treatment. So long a time had passed since they had been attacked that few believed that Pasteur could save them. He took a ter-rible risk in trying; had he failed his vaccine would have been blamed. Usually eight out of ten people bitten by rabid wolves got rabies, and once the disease strikes death is inevitable. De Kruif records the result:

> And at last a great shout of pride went up for this man Pasteur, went up from the Parisians, and all of France and all the world raised a paean of thanks to him—for the vaccine marvelously saved all but three of the doomed peasants. . . . And the Tsar of All the Russias sent Pasteur the dia-mond cross of Ste. Anne, and a hundred thousand francs to start the building of that house of microbe hunters in the Rue Dutot in Paris—that laboratory now called the Institut Pasteur. (181)

De Kruif is unabashed in his hero worship, and the same sort of awed gratitude has been expressed by many of Pasteur's biographers. Then, in 1988, Bruno Latour—a Frenchman, no less—decided to take Pasteur down a few pegs. Latour's book *The Pasteurization of France* is anything but hero worship. In fact, it is a direct assault upon the whole notion of scientist-as-hero. The Pasteur that emerges from Latour's work is not exactly a ras-cal, but he is certainly an opportunist and a grandstanding self-promoter whose successes were more theater than science.

Why does Latour want to expose Pasteur as a clay-footed giant? La-tour is not motivated by envy or mean-spiritedness; he just does not see science as the noble, selfless, pursuit of truth carried on by a few "great men" as De Kruif and other popular writers have depicted it. For Latour  science is war. Scientists may give lip service to the ideals of method and

**62**     Chapter 3  •  *A Walk on the Wild Side*

objectivity, but, just as the chaos of battle nullifies the generals' beautiful plans, so scientific battles make nonsense of such fine talk. For Latour, preaching standards and values in the middle of a scientific squabble would be like reciting the Ten Commandments in a barroom brawl.

Latour has a point. Anyone who thinks of scientists as serene truth-seekers or emotionless Mr. Spock types has another thing coming. We have already mentioned in previous chapters the vicious fight that broke out over the impact theory of mass extinction. Scientists sometimes harbor personal animosities that border on mania, and pursue vendettas with such tenacity that they harm science itself. The feud between Edward Drinker Cope and Othniel Charles Marsh, the two leading American paleontologists of the nineteenth century, is a case in point. They hated each other with a reckless intensity that tarnished their reputations and corrupted their science. According to reliable reports, Marsh ordered his workers to destroy fossil specimens rather than have them fall into Cope's hands. Cope launched a yellow-press newspaper attack on Marsh, leading to highly public mudslinging that dishonored both parties. In an effort to better his highly prolific rival, Marsh often rushed his findings into print, leading to errors that took the better part of a century to sort out.

The rancor between Marsh and Cope may have been exceptionally bitter, but in the history of science there has been no lack of conflict. Also, there is no question that some of the greatest scientists have been involved in some of the loudest disputes. But hardly any great achievement in any field has ever been accomplished without bitter, intransigent, and sometimes violent opposition. So, is science really less noble, or scientists any less worthy, because controversy always accompanies discovery? Latour puts his case this way:

> We would like science to be free of war and politics. At least, we would like to make decisions other than through compromise, drift, and uncertainty. We would like to feel that somewhere, in addition to the chaotic confusion of power relations, there are rational relations. . . . Surrounded by violence and disputation, we would like to see clearings—whether isolated or connected—from which would emerge incontrovertible, effective actions. To this end we have created, in a single movement, politics on one side and science or technoscience on the other. The Enlightenment is about extending these clearings until they cover the world. . . . Few people still believe in such an Enlightenment, for at least one reason. Within these clearings we have seen developing the whole arsenal of argumentation, violence, and politics. Instead of diminishing, this arsenal has been vastly enlarged. Wars of science, coming on top of wars of religion, are now the rage. (Latour, 1988, p. 5)

Parsons: Copernican
Questions: A Concise
Invitation to the Philosophy
of Science

3. A Walk on the Wild Side:
Social Constructivism,
Postmodernism, Feminism,
and that Old–Time Religion

Text

© The McGraw–Hill
Companies, 2006

289

The Constructivist Challenge    **63**

The dream of the leading thinkers of the European Enlightenment of the eighteenth century, a dream inspired by the enormous achievements of modern science as epitomized by Newton, was that the rise of modern science had, at long last, brought truly objective knowledge and the one sure method for discovery. In the minds of Enlightenment thinkers, science had ushered in the Age of Reason that would displace the ages of dogma and superstition that had gone before. Humanity could finally outgrow the endless and divisive theological disputes, and the concomitant persecutions, inquisitions, and holy wars. Freed from the ever-finer hairsplitting of metaphysical speculation, the finest human minds could now turn to the production of useful knowledge. Some of the founders of modern science, like Francis Bacon and René Descartes, believed that the discovery of the scientific method meant that such pointless controversy could end. Once we have the true method, our disagreements no longer will lead to bickering; rather, we will simply calculate. Scientific questions will be solved by appeal to universally accepted procedures and will be as calm, dispassionate, and as certain as doing sums in arithmetic. It hasn't worked out like this. On the contrary, Latour argues, in science things are settled by rhetoric, negotiation, power politics, wheeling and dealing, grandstanding, *ad hominem* attacks, and intimidation, the same as everywhere else. The most successful scientists were those who were best at forming powerful alliances, appropriating grants or scarce resources, browbeating opponents, or propagandizing their views.

There is considerable truth in Latour's gruesome depiction of scientific warfare. Scientists can play political hardball. Some, like Cope and Marsh, stoop to character assassination to deal with scientific opponents. The old saying about who you know being more important that what you know does often apply in science. Scientists are merely human and they are subject to all the weaknesses and foibles—egotism, petty jealousies, spite, and narrow-mindedness—that prey upon everyone else. Also, the hope that humanity has found a single, universal, scientific method is a pipe dream. Instead, there are many different methods for many different scientific disciplines; geology and particle physics just cannot be done the same way. In addition, within each discipline methods are changing and developing all the time. But surely Latour's view is too cynical, most would still say. Science has made some incontrovertible discoveries that have revealed much about the components and workings of nature, e.g., the blood circulates, DNA is the genetic material and it has a double helix structure, the solar system is part of a giant spiral galaxy we call the Milky Way, things are made of atoms, which are themselves composed of even smaller parts called electrons and quarks.

**64**    Chapter 3 • *A Walk on the Wild Side*

Latour is not impressed by such litanies of scientific achievement. In 1979 he coauthored, with Steve Woolgar, a book titled *Laboratory Life: The Construction of Scientific Facts.* Latour prepared to write this book by taking a menial job at the Salk Institute, a leading laboratory for biomedical research. This job gave him the opportunity to observe scientists at work in their native habitat, like an anthropologist who lives with a rainforest tribe to observe their customs and practices. In particular, he followed scientists through the laborious, tortuous process of trying to identify and isolate a highly elusive bodily substance called TRF for short. Latour charted the complex discussion and debate as scientists initially proposed the existence of TRF, encountered skepticism and opposition, responded to criticisms, engaged in a series of rebuttals and rejoinders, and finally succeeded in convincing their colleagues that TRF is real. Like a good anthropologist, Latour studied his subjects without accepting their worldview. Just as the anthropologist does not accept at face value the tribal shaman's claims about gods and magic spells, so Latour did not take for granted the truth of scientific claims.

In *Laboratory Life,* however, Latour and Woolgar do not simply give a detached anthropological description of the customs and beliefs of the scientific tribe. Rather they offer an analysis and interpretation that radically undercuts the claims of science to discover objective facts about the natural world. Put bluntly, their aim seems to be to debunk science. For Latour and Woolgar, scientific "facts" are not discovered; they are constructed. According to this "social constructivist" view, the so-called facts of science are mere artifacts of scientific culture, just as beliefs in gods, demons, and magical powers are artifacts of tribal cultures. According to *Laboratory Life,* scientists are in the business of generating fact-statements, but nature—conceived as something that exists "out there" independently of our concepts—has virtually nothing to do with the generation of such fact-statements. Such fact-statements emerge when a given scientific community reaches consensus on the issue, and consensus is a *rhetorical* achievement (rhetorical in the sense of "mere rhetoric," where the goal is persuasion by any means necessary). In other words, all of the methods and techniques deployed in scientific debate are really just elaborate rhetorical devices, not, as scientists like to think, reliable means of testing theory against empirical reality. Consensus emerges, and so new "facts" are established, when some group of scientists employs such rhetorical devices skillfully enough to convince, or at least silence, all opponents.

For Latour and Woolgar, the means whereby scientists generate fact-statements is really quite insidious. Every new "fact" begins as an innocent hypothesis. Everyone admits its tentative and speculative nature. But as the debate proceeds, proponents of the new "fact" use all the rhetorical

The Constructivist Challenge    **65**

means at their disposal to get skeptics to drop their opposition and accept the "fact." Once this has occurred, once consensus emerges in a scientific community, a curious process that Latour and Woolgar call "inversion" allegedly takes place. An "inversion" supposedly occurs when a scientific community forgets that its agreement on the new "fact" was achieved by rhetorical means, and starts to think of the "fact" as "out there," i.e., something that really has all along existed in the natural world. However, this is merely self-deception, Latour and Woolgar contend. The "out there"-ness is just a figment of the scientific imagination induced by a sort of collective amnesia whereby scientists conveniently forget the real process of rhetorical manipulation that got everyone to accept the new "fact." I say "conveniently" because it is greatly in scientists' interests to portray themselves as discoverers of objective reality rather than, as Latour and Woolgar think they really are, just another set of tribal shamans pursuing their own myths and rituals. Biologist Matt Cartmill provides an unfriendly but accurate summary of the social constructivist view:

> The philosophy of social constructivism claims that the "nature" that scientists pretend to study is a fiction cooked up by the scientists themselves— that, as Bruno Latour puts it, natural objects are the *consequences* of scientific work rather than its *cause*. In this case, the ultimate purpose of scientists' thoughts and experiments is not to understand or control an imagined "nature," but to provide objective-sounding justifications for exerting power over other people. As social constructivists see it, science is an imposing but hollow Trojan horse that conceals some rather nasty storm troopers in its belly. (Cartmill, 1999, pp. 49–50; emphasis in original)

In his more recent writings Latour claims to have abandoned strict social constructivism. In *We Have Never Been Modern* (1992), he argues that scientific objects should be regarded as hybrid entities, neither as wholly natural, as scientists view them, nor as mere artifacts, as social constructivism holds. Rather, scientific objects, a virus, say, should be thought of as more or less natural or more or less constructed, depending on the context. Unfortunately, he never really clarifies just what it would mean to regard a virus as such a hybrid. Some commentators claim to have detected a "creeping realism" in Latour's later writings. They think that he begins to admit (sort of) that—just maybe—things like microbes really exist and have *some* bearing on the course of science. Whether or not this is so, with Latour, as with Kuhn, it was the earlier, more radical views that most impressed Latour's friends and critics.

Anyone imbued with a more traditional view of science might be tempted to dismiss social constructivism as a farrago of fuzzy thinking and exaggeration. The problem with such pat dismissal is that there are

292 | Parsons: Copernican
Questions: A Concise
Invitation to the Philosophy
of Science

3. A Walk on the Wild Side:
Social Constructivism,
Postmodernism, Feminism,
and that Old–Time Religion

Text

© The McGraw–Hill
Companies, 2006

**66**   Chapter 3 • *A Walk on the Wild Side*

so many episodes in the history of science that do make us wonder how effective science really is at separating the real from the chimerical. How much of what we take to be facts about the natural world are really artifacts of our own making? One episode that raises this question is the famous wrongheaded dinosaur scandal.

The Carnegie Museum of Natural History in Pittsburgh houses one of the world's foremost exhibits of dinosaur fossils. For forty-five years the Carnegie Museum displayed one of its prize specimens, the gigantic *Apatosaurus louisae,* with the wrong head. The head was not a little bit wrong, but way off, like a paleontologist of the distant future putting a giraffe's head on a horse's body. Worse, other paleontologists accepted the chimera as real. All the top authorities accepted the wrongheaded creation as the real *Apatosaurus.* How did this happen?

Briefly, the problem had its roots in the feud between Marsh and Cope. Marsh published a reconstruction of *Apatosaurus* in 1883, which, to add to the confusion, he called by the familiar name *Brontosaurus,* mistakenly thinking it was a different kind of dinosaur than *Apatosaurus.* The problem was that *Apatosaurus/Brontosaurus* had been found without a head, and it just would not do to have a reconstruction without a head. So, Marsh improvised and stuck on a cranium that he had found at a completely different site. It eventually turned out that the head he found belonged to *Camarasaurus,* a creature not closely related to *Apatosaurus.* When the Carnegie Museum mounted its prize *Apatosaurus* specimen in 1915, the museum's director, W. J. Holland, an outstanding paleontologist in his own right, had deep reservations about the head Marsh had given the creature. Unfortunately, when the Carnegie Museum's specimen was found, it also lacked a head, so Holland had no definitive evidence against Marsh's reconstruction. Holland simply mounted the skeleton with no head.

Holland died in 1932 and in 1934 the new director of the museum decided that *Apatosaurus* needed a head. Just who made the decision and on what grounds is not clear. Probably, since museums are not only research institutions, but are there for the edification and entertainment of the public, everyone felt that a headless *Apatosaurus* just made a terrible impression. So, following Marsh's precedent, a very robust *Camarasaurus* skull was attached to the *Apatosaurus* skeleton. The big skull looked great on the massive skeleton and for over forty years everybody was satisfied, everybody except John S. McIntosh, perhaps the world's leading authority on sauropod dinosaurs like *Apatosaurus.* McIntosh began to suspect that another skull, one already in the Carnegie Museum's possession, was the right one. That other skull, designated as CM 11162, was found with the *Apatosaurus* specimen, but not in position at the end of its neck. Skull

Parsons: Copernican
Questions: A Concise
Invitation to the Philosophy
of Science

3. A Walk on the Wild Side:
Social Constructivism,
Postmodernism, Feminism,
and that Old–Time Religion

Text

© The McGraw–Hill
Companies, 2006

293

The Constructivist Challenge     **67**

CM 11162 looked too small to belong to so massive a creature as *Apatosaurus*. It looked like a somewhat larger version of a *Diplodocus* skull, and *Diplodocus* was a much slimmer animal than the ponderous *Apatosaurus*. However, after a thorough review of the records of the discovery of the Carnegie Museum's *Apatosaurus,* and a careful examination of skull CM 11162, McIntosh decided that it had to be the right one. He published his conclusions with coauthor David Berman in 1978. Their argument was so convincing that the Carnegie Museum agreed to remove the *Camarasaurus* head. Finally, in 1979, after forty-five years of displaying *Apatosaurus* with the wrong head, the Carnegie Museum held a ceremony to remove the old skull and attach a cast of CM 11162.

It is really quite shocking that one of the world's leading museums would display a prize specimen with the wrong head for so long. What if the Louvre had displayed a painting upside down for so long? Don't incidents like this make us wonder whether what we take to be scientific fact might not be artifact? Worse, there seemed to be no very good scientific reason for the Carnegie Museum's decision to mount the bogus head. It seems to have been a response to the demand to present a whole specimen for public viewing. Unlike the Venus di Milo, missing parts did not make *Apatosaurus* more appealing. Incidents like this lend credence to the claim that scientific decisions are often (strict constructivists would say *always*) made in response to social pressures, and not based on objective evidence.

Even if we admit, as we must, that science is often deeply influenced by social, political, and ideological pressures, must we accept the constructivist claim that, as Latour contends, the course of science is determined by power politics and rhetorical manipulation? Again, the issue of social and political influence on science is a very real and a very serious concern. It is indeed a serious matter when wealthy corporations aided by political ideologues manipulate or suppress legitimate scientific findings. But can the social constructivist theory be the *whole* story about science?

A problem with assessing the claim that facts are social constructs is that the word "fact" itself is ambiguous. According to *The American Heritage College Dictionary,* one sense of fact is "Information presented as objectively real." In another sense "fact" can mean "something having real, demonstrable existence." In other words, "fact" can refer to a *claim,* the assertion that something is really so, or it can refer to the *reality* that our factual claims are about. So, when one claims that scientific facts are constructed, this could mean either of two things: (a) our supposedly factual statements do not correspond to anything real (or if they do, it is a sheer accident), but are mere artifacts of the scientific process, or (b) there is no objective, "out there" reality consisting of states of affairs that exist

**68**    Chapter 3  •  *A Walk on the Wild Side*

independently of our beliefs or concepts. Sometimes Latour speaks as if he means to assert (a) and sometimes as if he means (b). So far, I have assumed that he means (a), since it seems a more plausible claim. That is, I have taken Latour to claim that, whether or not there is a real physical universe, such a putative natural world has no influence upon the "nature" conceived by scientists. The "nature" scientists study is therefore just an artifact, or, more bluntly, just a figment of the scientific imagination. Assuming that this is Latour and Woolgar's claim in *Laboratory Life*, how sound is it?

Latour and Woolgar present their conclusions as grounded upon empirical (i.e., scientific) evidence. Latour based his conclusions in *Laboratory Life* upon his research as an anthropologist of the laboratory. Anthropology is a science. If all scientific conclusions are social constructs, as *Laboratory Life* asserts, so are those of anthropologists like Latour. Practitioners of social constructivist anthropology or sociology of science have only two choices when they confront this problem of self-reference or "reflexivity" as it is called: They can bite the bullet and frankly admit that their "facts" are just as socially constructed as those of the natural sciences are alleged to be. In this case they have the burden of explaining why their so-called findings about the practice of science should be taken seriously by anyone skeptical of those alleged findings. The alternative is for social constructivists to argue, very implausibly, that social sciences like anthropology or sociology *do* draw upon reliable methods and objective evidence while the natural sciences, like organic chemistry or particle physics, do not. In other words, Latour's science was legitimate and Einstein's was not. Social constructivists have vigorously debated among themselves which horn of this dilemma to grasp, but neither option seems very appealing. The upshot is that if the social constructivist thesis is taken in the above sense (a), it is hard to see how constructivism can debunk science without debunking itself.

Sometimes, however, Latour seems to be making the above assertion (b)—that there is nothing that just *is* so, but that reality is, in some sense, created by the beliefs or concepts we form. That is, he sometimes seems to be implying a metaphysical claim about the nature of reality. For instance, in his book *Science in Action* (1987), he considers the famous case of the French scientist Rene-Prosper Blondlot, who, in the early twentieth century, claimed to have discovered a new type of radiation he called N-rays. The way the story is usually told, Blondlot thought he could observe a previously undetected sort of radiation emitted by metal under strain. Other physicists were skeptical because they could not reproduce Blondlot's claimed observations. An American physicist, Robert W. Wood, visited Blondlot's lab to see the procedure whereby N-rays supposedly

Parsons: Copernican
Questions: A Concise
Invitation to the Philosophy
of Science

3. A Walk on the Wild Side:
Social Constructivism,
Postmodernism, Feminism,
and that Old–Time Religion

Text

© The McGraw–Hill
Companies, 2006

295

The Constructivist Challenge    **69**

were detected. At one point in his visit, while Blondlot was engaged with his experimental apparatus, Wood quietly removed an essential piece of the equipment. Yet Blondlot continued to proclaim that he could observe the N-rays as they were being generated. For Wood, and soon the whole physics community, this was proof that Blondlot's N-rays did not actually exist and that the reported "observations" of them were delusions.

Latour indignantly insists that we should not interpret this incident as implying that Wood was right and Blondlot wrong:

> It would be easy enough for scientists to say that Blondlot failed because there was "nothing really behind his N-rays" to support his claim. This way of analyzing the past . . . crowns the winners, calling them the best and the brightest and . . . says that the losers like Blondlot lost simply *because* they were wrong. . . . Nature herself discriminates between the bad guys and the good guys. But is it possible to use this as a reason why in Paris, in London, in the United States, people slowly turned N-rays into an artefact? Of course not, since at that time today's physics obviously could not be used as the touchstone, or more exactly since today's state is, in part, the *consequence* of settling many controversies such as the N-rays. (Latour, 1987, p. 100, emphasis in original)

That is, since the opinions of present physicists about the (non)reality of N-rays were shaped by the outcome of the N-ray controversy, those opinions cannot explain the outcome itself.

Well why not? Of course, it was, in part, Wood's fine job of debunking that convinced everyone at the time that Blondlot's claims were false. But once we are convinced that there was nothing there for Blondlot to detect, doesn't this explain why he failed to see them (given that his equipment *would* have detected them had they been there)? Why did people in April 1912 fail to see the *Titanic* docking in New York? Because it never arrived. As for why Blondlot *thought* he saw N-rays, this is given a psychological explanation in terms of how wishful thinking and the inherent limitations of human perceptual abilities can make us "see" things that are not there.

For Latour, such a common-sense account of the outcome of the N-ray episode just will not do. Notice his language. He says that people "turned" N-rays into artifacts. This seems to imply that for Latour, there was no fact of the matter, no way that things really were, before the controversy over N-rays was settled. It is not that Blondlot was deluded all along, and that Wood proved this to everyone else's satisfaction. Rather, Wood and others *turned* N-rays into artifacts. Does Latour think that N-rays could just as easily have been turned into real phenomena? It is hard to know just what Latour means here, but he seems to be saying that

**70**    Chapter 3  •  *A Walk on the Wild Side*

there simply was no fact of the matter about N-rays; they were neither real nor a mere artifact, until physicists *decided* the case. It is not just that nobody knew that Blondlot's purported observations were not real until Wood did his debunking; such a claim would be boring even if true (and Latour is never boring). Rather, there was NO fact of the matter—nothing there to know—until the physics community agreed on its story!

Now such a claim may strike many as bizarre, but it is not obviously incoherent or self-defeating. It is reminiscent of the metaphysical idealism of British philosophy in the nineteenth century, which held that physical reality is a creation of the mind. I'm sure, though, that Latour would abjure any "idealist" label and certainly would disclaim any metaphysical agenda. Yet he seems to have fallen for an all-too-common fallacy of the sort that afflicted much idealist philosophy. This fallacious way of thinking begins with the innocent observation that we can only think with our ideas, but then leaps to the conclusion that all that we can know are our ideas. Michele Marsonet explains this fallacy and points out its obvious flaw:

> We do not know reality *directly*, but only through representations such as ideas and mental images. If this is true, it follows [so the fallacious argument goes] that we only know our representations, while it is impossible to know an alleged reality in itself. However, it should be easy to realize that from the fact that we know *through* representations, it does not follow that we can only know representations and nothing else. . . . (Marsonet, 1995, p. 59)

Of course, the philosophical debate about the relation of ideas to reality is extremely long and complex, and we cannot enter it here even in the most superficial way. So, let us assume that Latour does hold, as he certainly seems to, that all that we can know are our own ideas, and cannot infer anything about any putative reality behind those ideas. He then has two options about how he thinks about any alleged mind-independent physical world: He can be agnostic about the existence of an objective physical universe, perhaps giving the stereotypical Gallic shrug when asked about it, or he can take the stronger position that there is no such world. We saw above that he sometimes speaks as though he takes the stronger line.

The problem with agnosticism about the existence of the physical world is that it is not clear how we are to explain the existence and the contents of our ideas unless we postulate physical objects as their causes. Surely René Descartes was right that our ideas have to be caused *somehow*, and do not just pop into existence *ex nihilo*. Immanuel Kant postulated the existence of unknowable "*Dinge an sich*" (things in themselves), as the cause of our perceptions. Later philosophers complained, reasonably

Parsons: Copernican
Questions: A Concise
Invitation to the Philosophy
of Science

3. A Walk on the Wild Side:
Social Constructivism,
Postmodernism, Feminism,
and that Old–Time Religion

Text

© The McGraw–Hill
Companies, 2006

297

The Constructivist Challenge     **71**

enough, that we cannot meaningfully say that something exists—and much less that it causes all our perceptions—unless we attribute some sort of nature or character to it. So, it cannot be satisfactory to postulate physical objects as the unknowable "things in themselves" that cause our ideas. In *Laboratory Life*, physical objects do not even function as *Dinge an sich*. Instead, Latour and Woolgar invoke social and political factors as the sole and sufficient causes of scientific ideas. The problem with this option, as we have seen, is that it runs into the problem of reflexivity, that is, it undermines itself because if all truth claims are social constructs, so are those made by social constructivists.

Well, just what is wrong with denying the existence of the physical world? It is hard to say precisely how one could argue that there *is* an external, mind-independent physical world since any evidence you could mention would presuppose the existence of such a world. Could you convince someone like Latour of the reality of the external world by pointing to physical objects or waving them in his face? Should we attempt to prove the existence of an external world as British philosopher G. E. Moore famously did, by pointing to a hand and saying, "Here is a hand"? Steve Woolgar, Latour's collaborator on *Laboratory Life*, challenged his students to reveal a physical object to him without employing a representation of some sort. When students would point to a book or table, Woolgar would reply that pointing is itself a kind of representation. Maybe Woolgar was trying to make a point like the one artist Rene Magritte made when he painted a picture of a pipe and wrote under the depiction "*Ceci n'est pas une pipe*" ("This is not a pipe"). Just as the picture of a pipe is not a pipe, so pointing to a pipe is a representation, not a pipe. Woolgar was (I think) trying to show that we live in a world of representations, signs, symbols, images, and ideas—not objects.

What the students should have done is to point out that Woolgar has set them a task that is by definition impossible. You cannot indicate an object without indicating it, and Woolgar will say that any such act of indicating is a representation. But while it is certainly true that you cannot indicate something without indicating it, it does not follow that indicateable objects do not exist independently of our representations. Neither does it follow that we can never know objects, but only our representations.

The approach to take with questions like the existence of an external world is to begin by noting that, as the philosopher John Searle puts it, the human mind comes with certain default settings. When you first boot up a personal computer, in order to function at all it must come with certain default settings that it will keep until you change them. Likewise, the human mind seems just naturally pre-set to take certain things for granted. One of those things we just take for granted is that there is an

**72**    Chapter 3 • *A Walk on the Wild Side*

external physical world that exists "out there" independently of our consciousness. Now default settings can be changed on your computer and in your mind, but we humans have every right to demand *very* good reason before we abandon a belief that is so spontaneous, natural, and (nearly) universal as belief in an external physical reality. In other words, to say the very least, a very heavy burden of proof is on those who would deny the existence of an external world. How could one make such an argument? Merely pointing out that we cannot think about things without using concepts, or indicate objects without somehow representing them, or make observations without appealing to some theory, will not prove this at all. All of these claims may well be true (even truisms), but it just does not follow from any of them that there is no mind-independent reality or that we cannot know a great deal about it. At this point I shall simply cut to the chase and assert that, in my opinion, nowhere does Latour, Woolgar, or any other social constructivist offer arguments anywhere near strong enough to support so sweeping a claim as the nonexistence of a mind-independent physical reality. Nor do they show that we fail to have cognitive access—*through* our perceptions and concepts—to that reality. So, Latour and Woolgar's version of social constructivism fails in its effort to debunk science.

## POSTMODERNISM ATTACKS!

However, social constructivism is not the only recent program of radical science critique. There are also the postmodernists. "Postmodernism" is a term that defies precise definition. A variety of movements or styles in literature, art, and architecture may be called "postmodern." The "postmodernist" label has been attached to a wide variety of writers, including the philosopher Gilles Deleuze, his frequent collaborator the psychoanalyst Felix Guattari, sociologist Jean Baudrillard, psychoanalyst Jacques Lacan, and Luce Irigaray, whose writings deal with topics in many fields. So multifarious are these various manifestations of the postmodernist spirit that I can only give a very broad and impressionistic characterization of the attitudes and outlooks that tie them together. Anyway, postmodernist theorists themselves would probably reject any proffered canonical definition of "postmodernism," since one thing postmodernists share is a distaste for canonical statements of anything. For them, anything that presents itself as canonical, authoritative, or definitive is something to be abused, ridiculed, or otherwise subverted. For the postmodernists, it is a dangerous delusion to think that we ever have the complete story or final answer about anything. We are all ". . . on a darkling plain; swept with confused alarms of struggle and flight; where ignorant armies clash by night" (to quote Matthew Arnold, one of the canonical "great poets" postmodernists love to hate).

To avoid confusion, let me make an important distinction: Practically all philosophers these days are fallibilists. That is, they recognize that even our best-supported theories and factual claims are fallible and may turn out wrong—as, indeed, they so often have in the past. But fallibilism does not entail relativism. Even a thorough fallibilist can say that, so far as we can tell, some things just are so, some questions really have been settled, and some norms have at least *prima facie* validity. Not so for the postmodernists. For them all norms—whether ethical, aesthetic, or epistemological—have merely local authority and applicability and are radically contingent upon such factors as gender and social class. Postmodernists are hostile to any claim that a standard is more than merely parochial, viewing all claims to objectivity as attempts by one group to impose its values on others. Hence, in all fields postmodernists celebrate a promiscuous eclecticism of standards, values, and norms.

Postmodernism often comes across more of a style than a stance, more of a pose than a position. Sometimes postmodernists seem to take pride in outraging more traditional thinkers. They scorn even ordinary speech, which they regard as polluted by oppressive standards of clarity and truth. For them, the requirement that words should have definite meanings is just another tool of oppression. Their prose style therefore is often verbose, paradoxical, allusive, convoluted, and, in general, intended to disrupt and frustrate our ordinary ways of thinking. The downside is that much of what they say sounds like gibberish to outsiders. Postmodernists typically also reject the idea that it is a legitimate function of language to *represent* a language-independent reality. Baudrillard argues that an image should no longer be regarded as a simulation of reality, but that our media-drenched world *is* now a world of rootless, free-floating signs.

From what I've said so far, you may have gotten the impression that postmodernists are a bunch of zanies who lack seriousness of purpose and whose views have no intellectual motivation. Such an impression would be mistaken; postmodernists are entirely serious in their aims and their inspiration comes from thinkers who unquestionably were intellectual superstars. One such luminary was Friedrich Nietzsche (1844–1900). One aspect of Nietzsche's thought that the postmodernists have particularly emphasized is his view on the relation between knowledge and power. Nietzsche said that knowledge is an instrument of power, that is, that the motivation to acquire knowledge is to acquire more power. We want to "master" certain fields, thereby making that field of knowledge into a servant to promote our interests. For Nietzsche, as for the pre-Socratic

74    Chapter 3  •  *A Walk on the Wild Side*

philosopher Heraclitus, reality is an eternal flux that is always in a process of becoming. Knowing is not a matter of recognizing an objectively given reality; there is no such determinate, independent reality, only flux. Understanding therefore involves imposing our conceptual schemes, categories, and interpretations on the flux, thereby creating Being out of sheer Becoming. The interpretations we place on reality will reflect our vital interests and concerns, that is, the "reality" we create will be one that serves our purposes and enhances our power. Indeed, from an evolutionary perspective, only those "truths" that are useful survived. For Nietzsche, the idea that there is absolute truth, truth independent of all our interests and purposes, is a myth created by philosophers who hanker after a stable and permanent reality and are afraid to embrace endless flux. It follows that for Nietzsche, there is no one perspective, no "God's-eye view," that gives a comprehensive and authoritative view of the whole of reality.

Another, more recent, progenitor of postmodernism was philosopher Jean-Francois Lyotard (1924–1998). Lyotard argues that we should reject all "metanarratives." A "metanarrative" is any attempt to establish an absolute standard for any value or ideal—truth, rationality, goodness, or justice, for instance. Instead, we must recognize that there is an irreducible plurality of incommensurable narratives, each encompassing its own criteria for goodness, truth, etc. Lyotard expressed these views most influentially in his work *The Postmodern Condition: A Report on Knowledge* (1979).

Another notable philosophical work published in 1979, Richard Rorty's *Philosophy and the Mirror of Nature* articulated and promoted various postmodernist themes for an English-speaking audience. Rorty characterizes his philosophy as "pragmatist," i.e., in the tradition of classical American philosophers such as William James and John Dewey, but many of his ideas are typically postmodernist. For instance, he strongly advocates that philosophers abandon the attempt to establish absolute foundations for knowledge and instead dedicate themselves to the facilitation of the "conversation of mankind." According to Rorty, all of the "voices" of humanity, from Hopi philosophy to Polynesian mythology to quantum physics, deserve to be heard and no one narrative should be preeminent. When it comes to grounding our beliefs, Rorty says that we can do no better than to say what our society lets us say, that is, when in Rome, follow the epistemological practices of the Romans. This does not mean that our beliefs are not to be subject to strict critical scrutiny, but Rorty thinks that the standards we employ when we thus examine our beliefs are contingent historical products of a particular time and place and lack universal authority.

It is hardly surprising, given such an intellectual background, that postmodernists do not like science very much. After all, there are some

Postmodernism Attacks!    **75**

things that science says are just so, and others definitely not so—period. Heavy bodies in free fall in the vicinity of the earth's surface accelerate at a rate of about 9.8 meters per second squared. The sun has a mean distance from the earth of 149.5 million kilometers. The nuclei of human somatic cells contain 46 chromosomes arranged in 23 pairs. Science does not say that such things are so from a given perspective, or according to some traditions, but that they are just so. Science claims to be the authority in answering certain questions. Where did birds come from? They evolved from theropod dinosaurs in the late Jurassic, say (many) paleontologists. Science says that the story that God created them all at once during the six-day creation is simply false. Further, science claims that its methods alone are the right methods for investigating the natural world and not, for instance, consulting horoscopes, gazing into crystal balls, or invoking the authority of ancient texts.

Because science so often claims to have *the* answer, and not simply to offer one among indefinitely many perspectives, it is bound to ruffle postmodernists' feathers. What right do paleontologists have to tell Christian fundamentalists and Orthodox Jews that the Genesis creation account is false? Is it not arrogant for anthropologists to tell Native Americans, whose traditions teach that they are indigenous to North America, that their ancestors actually came across a land bridge from Asia? Following Nietzsche, postmodernists say that knowledge is power. They do not mean this the way that Francis Bacon did, as a recognition of the fact that knowledge gives us power over nature, but in the sense of one of their favorite writers Michel Foucault (1926–1984). When Foucault says that knowledge is power, he means it in the sense that the winners get to write the history books. For instance, the anthropological account of the origin of American Indians is just the story that the winning white European culture gets to impose on the losing Native American culture. Postmodernists regard the reigning standards that define rational discourse—the standards that tell us what counts as a logical inference, objective evidence, or coherent speech—as potential tools of oppression. Small wonder that postmodernists want to challenge what they see as the intellectual hegemony of science. Though their jargon may be opaque, their intentions are clear. They aim to cut science down to size, to display it as just another form of discourse, and as no more "rational" or "objective" than any other. Postmodernist literature is vast and highly diverse. From these many writings I have selected two books to examine here: Donna Haraway's *Primate Visions* (1989) and W. J. T. Mitchell's *The Last Dinosaur Book* (1998). These two books offer postmodernist analyses of two fields of science that have much popular appeal, primatology and dinosaur paleontology.

**76**    Chapter 3 • *A Walk on the Wild Side*

Reading postmodernist literature, you can get the impression that they are obsessed with the electronic media. Because they reject the distinction between "high" and "low" culture, postmodernists repudiate the traditional academic disdain for popular entertainment. Papers by academic postmodernists will often have titles like *From Homer to Homer Simpson* where canonical texts like the *Iliad* and popular TV comedy get equal (and equally obscure) treatment. Not only do they collapse the distinction between popular and highbrow entertainment, they go even deeper, questioning the very distinction between a symbolic representation and the reality that it represents. Typically, postmodernists oppose what Haraway calls "binarisms"—paired concepts that, in their view, channel our thinking into narrow and misleading dichotomies. They say that rigid distinctions like subject/object, fact/fiction, same/other, and image/reality are embedded in our language, and so lead us to box things into overly restrictive categories. Invidious value judgments go with such labeling, postmodernists argue, so that, for instance, people the "same" as us are good and those "other" than us are not.

Haraway attempts to subvert the distinction between science fact and science fiction. Likewise, Mitchell argues that it is impossible to maintain the distinction between the popular image of dinosaurs and what paleontologists think they really know. For Haraway, science is just another kind of narrative. True, primatologists have their story to tell, but it is just one of many and has no special authority over any other account. Similarly, Mitchell certainly feels that paleontologists should lend their "testimony" to our understanding of dinosaurs, but such "testimony" must be supplemented by the work of humanities scholars who are experts at the analysis of symbols and images. After all, echoing some of Latour's talk about hybrid objects, Mitchell says the dinosaur is not merely a natural object nor is it a pure fantasy, but is an irreducible composite. Mitchell holds that there is no way to make a workable demarcation between the extinct animal and the cultural icon.

For Haraway, the idea that science can be done in a neutral, disinterested, and impartial way is a pernicious myth. It is a myth because, she holds, all science is inevitably *political* science, since it always promotes the interests of some particular group. The myth of neutrality is pernicious because it obscures the fact that every scientific account, however purportedly "objective," or based on "logic," serves a hidden agenda. So far that agenda has been the promotion of the interests of scientists, and their sponsors in government and industry, who are almost always white, male, and privileged. She strongly endorses the Latour/Woolgar view that all scientific "facts" are socially constructed and adds that it is vital to see for whose benefit they are constructed. She cites a well-known story about

Parsons: Copernican
Questions: A Concise
Invitation to the Philosophy
of Science

3. A Walk on the Wild Side:
Social Constructivism,
Postmodernism, Feminism,
and that Old–Time Religion

Text

© The McGraw–Hill
Companies, 2006

303

Postmodernism Attacks!     **77**

the history of primatology. According to this story, when primatologists began to analyze the social structure of primate groups, the (predominately male) scientists focused on the dominance of the so-called alpha male. The alpha male, like the silverback leader of a gorilla troop, is the dominant male. According to those early accounts, the story goes, the dominance of the alpha male was depicted as absolute. In particular, all of the females of the group were, in effect, the harem of the dominant male since he had exclusive right to mate with them.

It is easy to see how such a representation of primate social groups could benefit males. Since primates are the closest animal relations to humans, the alleged dominance of the alpha male could be seen as the natural pattern for human society as well. That is, male dominance in human society could be justified as "natural" by pointing to the dominance of the alpha male in primate society. However, says Haraway, it fell to female primatologists to point out that the alpha male's dominance is far from absolute, and that female primates wield considerable power. For instance, among mandrills when a new alpha male takes over by defeating the previously dominant male, he finds, no doubt to his intense chagrin, that the females are not instantly his to command. The females will defiantly refuse to mate with him until he meets their approval. Of course, Haraway cannot think that the female primatologists' conclusions were any more objective than those of their male counterparts. What matters about the stories science tells is not whether they are "true" (the quotes are needed because postmodernists do not buy the notion of just plain truth). What matters is whose interests those stories serve. As we shall see below, feminist theorist Sandra Harding picks up on this theme and runs with it.

Science has always assumed that the objects it studies are determinate entities that exist objectively and independently of the merely human activity called science. Science therefore gave itself the job of discovering such entities and understanding them as fully as possible. Even the weirdness of quantum mechanics has not really altered this fundamental goal of science. Quantum mechanics, at least as it is usually interpreted, tells us that there are some properties of particles that have no definite values until we interact with those particles in some way. But once the requisite interaction occurs and the particle assumes a definite value, then that value is as objective and determinate a fact as any other. For postmodernists, scientific objects lose all such status as determinate and independent entities. In postmodernist literature, a scientific object is little more than a nexus of multiplying interpretations, a blank screen onto which interested parties may project practically any image.

For paleontologists, a dinosaur was an *animal,* a creature that roamed the Mesozoic landscape and possessed distinct anatomical, physiological,

GORILLA
STORY

Parsons: Copernican
Questions: A Concise
Invitation to the Philosophy
of Science

3. A Walk on the Wild Side:    Text
Social Constructivism,
Postmodernism, Feminism,
and that Old–Time Religion

© The McGraw–Hill
Companies, 2006

and behavioral traits that we try to discover by the framing and testing of
hypotheses. Mitchell treats dinosaurs as prefabricated metaphors, ready-
made symbols that can stand for just about anything. For instance, dinosaurs can symbolize obsolescence, backwardness, and stupidity.
Cartoonist Gary Larson picked up on this theme in his *The Far Side* strip.
He depicted a Stegosaur lecturer speaking to an audience of dinosaurs:
"The picture's pretty bleak, gentlemen. . . . The world's climates are
changing, the mammals are taking over, and we all have a brain about
the size of a walnut." On the other hand, dinosaurs can be cool and chic,
like the sleek, fast, and deadly *Velociraptor* of *Jurassic Park.* According to
Mitchell, dinosaurs can serve as the "clan sign" for just about any group.
*T. rex* could symbolize unbridled ferocity while *Apatosaurus* might represent the gentle giant. A dinosaur can even be a plush purple TV figure
who warbles saccharine ditties to preschoolers. For Mitchell, any attempt
to strip away the layers of symbolism and get down to the *real* dinosaur
would be like peeling an onion. You would never hit factual bedrock, only
layer upon layer of symbol and metaphor. The upshot is that paleontologists cannot hope to understand dinosaurs, since they are under the illusion that they are studying an unambiguously *natural* object. Mitchell
argues that to really understand dinosaurs, the researches of paleontologists must be supplemented by the work of humanities scholars, like himself, who are experts at the analysis and interpretation of symbols. Since
dinosaurs are hybrid objects, irreducible composites of the natural and
the symbolic, they must be studied by a hybrid discipline that combines
the "testimony" of paleontologists with the interpretations of practitioners of cultural studies.

For Mitchell as for Haraway, scientific objects *always* have political
overtones. For instance, he sees the paintings of battling dinosaurs done
by Charles R. Knight at the beginning of the twentieth century as symbolic of the unrestrained capitalism of the Gilded Age:

> Knight's scenes of single combat between highly armored leviathans are
> the paleontological equivalent of that other war of giants, the struggles
> among the "robber barons" in late Nineteenth-Century America. This pe-
> riod, so often called the era of "Social Darwinism," economic "survival of
> the fittest," ruthless competition and the formation of giant corporate en-
> tities headed by gigantic individuals, is aptly summarized by the Darwin-
> ian icon of giant reptiles in a fight to the death. (Mitchell, 1998, p. 143)

Postmodernists also often claim to detect a sexual subtext in contexts
where to others it seems hardly present. For instance, he comments on
Henry Fairfield Osborn's dinosaur displays at the American Museum of
Natural History in the early 1900s:

Postmodernism Attacks! **79**

Perhaps Osborn's most important contribution to the myth of the modern dinosaur was his linkage of it to questions of male potency. The connection between big bones and virility had already been established. . . . Big bones were also the trophies of the masculine ritual of the big game hunt, and the phallic overtones of "bones" need no belaboring by me. (p. 150)

Even the greenish color given to dinosaurs in most depictions is full of symbolic import for Mitchell:

So where does this leave greenness? Is it a symbol of the "colored" racial other, the savage, primitive denizen of the green world? Or is it an emblem of the white man's burden, the color of the military camouflage required for the Great White Hunter to blend in with the jungle and thus to dominate it? (pp. 147–149)

Can *everything* about dinosaurs really be bursting with political and/or sexual significance? Mitchell apparently thinks so, and he therefore recommends that Marx and Freud be invoked to analyze the political and sexual content of dinosaur images.

Any attempt at a straightforward point-by-point rebuttal of postmodern critiques of science will probably fail. This is not because those critiques are sound and therefore irrefutable. Rather, it is because almost anything a critic would take as a flaw of postmodernist analyses would be seen as a virtue by the postmodernists. Leading primatologist Matt Cartmill vents his frustration in attempting to criticize Haraway's *Primate Visions:*

This is a book that contradicts itself a hundred times; but this is not a criticism of it because its author thinks contradictions are a sign of intellectual ferment and vitality. This is a book that systematically distorts and selects historical evidence; but that is not a criticism, because its author thinks that all interpretations are biased, and she regards it as her duty to pick and choose her facts to favor her own brand of politics. . . . This is a book that clatters around in a dark closet of irrelevancies for 450 pages until it bumps accidentally into an index and stops; but that's not a criticism, either, because its author finds it gratifying and refreshing to bang unrelated facts together as a rebuke to stuffy minds. . . . In short, this book is flawless, because all its deficiencies are deliberate products of art. (Cartmill, 2003, p. 196)

Perhaps we have at last found a genuine example of incommensurable discourse: the debate between postmodernists and their critics! Seriously, though, how do you meaningfully disagree with those who have apparently repudiated the very conditions of meaningful disagreement? How do you deploy objective evidence against those who regard objectivity as a myth? Perhaps the would-be critic would try to "deconstruct" postmodernist texts. "Deconstruction" is a kind of radically skeptical

**80**    Chapter 3 • *A Walk on the Wild Side*

textual analysis frequently used by postmodernists. A deconstructive analysis turns a text against itself and attempts to show that it has no definite, distinct meaning, but lends itself to innumerable interpretations. Could we deconstruct Haraway's and Mitchell's texts? There seems to be no reason why not. That is, if we had the patience, we could no doubt go through their texts and pick out numerous passages that we could then interpret as meaning the exact opposite of what Haraway and Mitchell apparently intend. For instance, we could take Haraway's animadversions against objectivity and interpret them as ironical *defenses* of objectivity that work by showing the absurd consequences that follow when objectivity is repudiated. Likewise, we could take Mitchell's meditation on dinosaurs' greenness as a demonstration of the silliness that inevitably results when basic distinctions are systematically conflated, like the distinction between an object and its image. In short, it looks like postmodernists are vulnerable to the same problems of reflexivity that plagued the social constructivists. If all texts can be deconstructed, so can the texts of postmodernists.

But such a quick, down-and-dirty dismissal of postmodernism completely misses the point since postmodernists emphatically reject the canons of rationality that underlie any such critique. They reject all demands that texts meet standards of consistency, coherence, or truthfulness. Postmodernists have no problem with reflexivity. They would be the first to admit that their own texts can be deconstructed! Perhaps then postmodernist texts should not be regarded as rational arguments; their goal is not to arrive at truth, or even to achieve coherence; such notions are for them passé. Postmodernist writing is above all a *performance*. That is, perhaps it is best to regard postmodernist science critique as a genre of confrontational performance art; its goal is not to persuade but to provoke. Some critics of postmodernism have therefore concluded that instead of wasting rational argument on such provocateurs they should play tricks back on them.

This is precisely what physicist Alan Sokal did when he wrote a spoof of postmodernist science critique, intentionally filled it with arcane postmodernist jargon and absurd arguments, and passed it off as a serious article to *Social Text*, a periodical that prominently features postmodernist writers. Sokal gave his piece a suitably portentous title: "Transgressing the Boundaries: Towards a Transformative Hermeneutics of Quantum Gravity." The text was a farrago of ludicrous claims about the political implications of recent developments in physics spiced with particularly opaque passages from leading postmodernist writers. In 1996 *Social Text* published Sokal's parody as a serious article, and the joke was on them. Sokal revealed the hoax in the periodical *Lingua Franca,* and contended that his successful sting had exposed the ignorance and laziness of the postmod-

Parsons: Copernican
Questions: A Concise
Invitation to the Philosophy
of Science

3. A Walk on the Wild Side:
Social Constructivism,
Postmodernism, Feminism,
and that Old–Time Religion

Text

© The McGraw–Hill
Companies, 2006

307

ernist science critics. He charged that such critics had shown that they would endorse anything, no matter how incompetent, that supported their view. Needless to say, many of the postmodernists were embarrassed and outraged and responded to Sokal with considerable asperity. Stanley Fish, a noted literary scholar and onetime editor of *Social Text,* castigated Sokal and accused him of creating a spiteful Trojan Horse to embarrass colleagues. Such behavior, Fish charged, only undermined the basic trust necessary for scholarship as a cooperative enterprise. Even some philosophers of science who are sympathetic to Sokal's view feared that his hoax would only lead to polarization when bridge-building between various disciplines is sorely needed.

There are places in postmodernist writings where they do seem to be making straightforward claims backed by evidence and argument. For instance, what are we to make of Mitchell's proposal that paleontology be replaced by a hybrid discipline that combines the expertise of paleontologists and the skills of "cultural scientists," as he thinks specialists in his field should be designated? Our reaction to this proposal will depend on how we take Mitchell's claim that dinosaurs are inevitably hybrid objects and that it is impossible to scrape off the accretion of symbolism and get down to rock-solid, literal truth about dinosaurs. Now admittedly there are some things about dinosaurs we do not and very probably never will know. For instance, the colors of dinosaurs will probably remain conjectural. We just have no way of knowing whether dinosaurs were the greenish color that got Mitchell's interpretive juices flowing or whether, maybe, they really were purple. We hardly know everything about living creatures, so how could we ever know everything about extinct ones?

Yet we seem to know that some things about dinosaurs *are* so, and Mitchell never offers any good reason to doubt that we do. Just because an object has potent symbolic import for us is no reason to think that we cannot know many things that are literally true of that object. For instance, a cross naturally has deep symbolic significance for devout Christians, but Christians can still understand the cross as the instrument of torture and death that it actually was. Mitchell tells us "Nature *is* culture, science is art. We don't ever 'see nature' in the raw, but always cooked in categories and clothed in the garments of language and representation" (p. 58; emphasis in original). Of course, since it is true by definition, we must admit that we cannot think about nature without using language, categories, and representations (we cannot think about something without thinking about it). But we can admit this and still think that we do, on occasion, get things right.

How would the workaday scientist react to postmodernist writers? He or she would probably think that writers like Haraway and Mitchell, whose

**82**   Chapter 3 • *A Walk on the Wild Side*

academic careers have involved them exclusively in a world of symbols, tropes, and texts, have simply lost contact with the intractable, obstinate, downright recalcitrant world of physical fact that scientists confront daily. Even scientists who never leave their air-conditioned labs must struggle daily to square their conjectures with the hard constraints imposed by an unyielding cosmos. When it comes to telling stories about dinosaurs, Mitchell says, "There is no limit to the stories that can be made up. . . ." (p. 48). For the paleontologist, coming up with even *one* story can be devilishly difficult. The reason for this difference is that nothing constrains Mitchell's storytelling except the limits of his own imagination. Paleontologists' stories are severely constrained both by background knowledge and by physical fact. For Mitchell, the stories we tell about dinosaurs should be full of "fantasy, unbridled speculation, and utopian imagination" (p. 284). Science also thrives on speculation and imagination, but in science fancy must sometimes be allowed to crash into the hard rock of empirical reality. Because of these fundamental differences between Mitchell's cultural studies approach to dinosaurs and the paleontologist's, a hybrid discipline that yokes these two disciplines is not feasible.

## IS "OBJECTIVITY" WHAT A MAN CALLS HIS SUBJECTIVITY?

A major intellectual movement of the last three decades has been the rise of feminist scholarship. Science has drawn the attention of many feminist writers. These writers certainly found much about science that rightly concerned them. When you look at the index of any history of science, you find that scientists have been a very diverse lot. Over the past 5,000 years significant scientific discoveries have been made by Egyptians, Babylonians, Greeks, Chinese, Indians, Arabs, Jews, Mayans, Italians, Germans, English, Scots, Russians, Hungarians, French, Danes, Americans . . . and on and on. Great scientific work has been done by Pagans, Christians, Jews, Muslims, Hindus, Buddhists, Confucians, Atheists, and Agnostics. Scientists of my personal acquaintance run the gamut from conservative Republicans to Marxists. Scientific journals are published in dozens of languages. In a given year, a scientist might attend professional conferences in London, Rio de Janeiro, or Riyadh. A *Who's Who* of scientists would have representatives of almost every race or ethnicity. Truly, science seems to be a characteristically human enterprise and not the domain of just one group.

Or is it? One jarring fact about the names we find in an index of the history of science is that the overwhelming majority of those scientists

Is "Objectivity" What a Man Calls His Subjectivity?     **83**

were *male*. Of course, there have been distinguished women scientists from ancient times to the present day. The list would include such names as Hypatia, Caroline Herschel, Marie Curie (winner of Nobel Prizes in chemistry *and* physics), Irène Joliot-Curie, Lise Meitner, Ceceliu Payne-Gaposchkin, Barbara McClintock, Rosalind Franklin, Vera Rubin, and Lynn Margulis. But these were very much the exception to the rule. One reason for the lack of female names in the lists of notable past scientists is unquestionably that women in the past simply were not given due credit for their scientific work. For instance, Caroline Herschel was certainly a notable astronomer, but her work is usually mentioned as a footnote to the achievements of her more famous brother William Herschel. Still, there can be no doubt that the apparent paucity of women scientists largely reflects the historical reality of women's exclusion from science. The inescapable conclusion is that over the centuries a vast reservoir of scientific talent was hardly tapped at all. Things are better today, but still far from ideal. Some fields, like medicine, have basically achieved parity in numbers (if not in status and power); other areas, such as many engineering fields, are still over 80 percent male.

Why has science historically been, and to a large extent still is today, so predominately a male enterprise? For feminists, the answer is obvious: Science is a boy's club. It is run not only by but for men. Women are still subtly, and sometimes not so subtly, discouraged from entering science. Even when women succeed in becoming scientists, they sometimes are marginalized and relegated to lower-status jobs or just "left out of the loop" by male colleagues. A woman of my personal acquaintance, a nuclear engineer, was told by her boss that women are "weak links" who must be driven from the profession. Further, male scientists have certainly entertained some odd, even bizarre, notions that it is hard to imagine female colleagues—had there been any—taking seriously. For instance, many physicians of the nineteenth century addressed the problem of hysteria, allegedly a nearly universal ailment of women that was supposed to cause them to experience uncontrollable emotions (*hysteria* is the Greek word for "womb"). The diagnosis of a troublesome woman's behavior as hysterical was certainly a convenience for men. If a woman made a public scene (like demonstrating for the right to vote), the problem was medical; she was hysterical.

Feminists are rightly concerned about such issues. Insofar as they aim to redress past wrongs and assure that women have equal opportunities to enter and advance in scientific fields, their efforts can only be welcomed. But for more radical feminists, such efforts merely scratch the surface. The deeper problem, as they see it, lies not just with the obstacles that have been put in the way of girls and women who might enter

310

Parsons: Copernican
Questions: A Concise
Invitation to the Philosophy
of Science

3. A Walk on the Wild Side:
Social Constructivism,
Postmodernism, Feminism,
and that Old–Time Religion

Text

© The McGraw–Hill
Companies, 2006

84    Chapter 3  •  *A Walk on the Wild Side*

science, but with the very ideals and standards of science. The focus of
much radical feminist science critique is the idea, which scientists have
championed since the scientific revolution of the seventeenth century,
that science should be value free. Here we must make an important distinction between epistemic values and non-epistemic values. As we noted
in an earlier chapter, "epistemic" means "relating to knowledge," so, the
epistemic values of science are those conducive to the aim that science
produce genuine knowledge. For instance, scientists place great value on
the rigorous empirical evaluation of hypotheses since they hold that only
such stringent testing can eliminate false hypotheses and lead us towards
the true ones. Non-epistemic values are those which, although most important for human life, do not set norms for good inference or the correct evaluation of evidence. For instance, moral values can tell us that
murder is wrong, but they do not tell us the right way to conduct a homicide investigation. A homicide investigation is an empirical inquiry and is
guided by epistemic values. Non-epistemic values also include political
values, spiritual values, aesthetic values, and so forth.

Traditionally, scientists and philosophers of science have held that science should, insofar as possible, make its practice independent of non-
epistemic values. The reason why seemed obvious. People are passionate
about their moral, political, and religious values. The "hot button" issues
that enliven political campaigns and editorial pages are hot because they
involve such basic values. Budget deficits might doom our children to a
future life of hardship, but that distant prospect gets people less excited
than whether kids should say "under God" while reciting the Pledge of
Allegiance. Scientists are people too and just as likely as anyone else to
have strong feelings about political, religious, and moral issues. If, therefore, the results of science were not made independent of our strong feelings about moral, political, and religious values, scientists feared that
scientific objectivity would be badly compromised. Objectivity is the goal
of telling it like it is, even when our scientific conclusions run against
deeply entrenched convictions.

Unquestionably, science does often conflict with such entrenched
convictions. Darwinism is probably the most obvious example. There is
the famous anecdote about the aristocratic Victorian lady's reaction upon
first hearing of Darwin's theory. She cried out to her husband in horror:
"Oh, my dear! Descended from apes! Let us hope that it is not true, and
if it is that it does not become generally known!" Philosopher Daniel Dennett has rightly characterized Darwinism as "universal acid," an idea so
corrosive that it threatens to dissolve any dogma or ideology it contacts.
The only problem with Dennett's claim is that it is not broad enough.
Any scientific theory, not just Darwinism, can and often does undermine

Parsons: Copernican
Questions: A Concise
Invitation to the Philosophy
of Science

3. A Walk on the Wild Side:
Social Constructivism,
Postmodernism, Feminism,
and that Old–Time Religion

Text

© The McGraw–Hill
Companies, 2006

311

Is "Objectivity" What a Man Calls His Subjectivity?     **85**

entrenched beliefs. Inevitably, then, science will often run into entrenched ideological opposition and the inevitable pressure to modify or reject scientific conclusions when it does. To prevent such ideological obstruction, and to permit science to tell it like it is even when the truth hurts, scientists have embraced norms and methods intended to identify the polluting taint of ideology and insulate science from its influence. For instance, though scientists like everyone else often have strong political convictions, they are supposed to follow norms and practice methods that prevent their convictions from distorting their science. Thus, science is supposed to be dispassionate, disinterested, and politically neutral even though the people that practice it, being merely human, cannot be.

Many feminist writers reject the idea that science should, or can, be freed from the influence of non-epistemic values. They argue that science is inevitably and pervasively influenced by such values and that these shape both the practice and the conclusions of science. It is therefore pointless, and in fact disingenuous, for science to pretend to be value free (from now on, by "value," I'll mean non-epistemic value). Rather, it should explicitly embrace the *right* values. Science should begin to serve the interests of the down-and-out, and stop catering to the up-and-in.

Sandra Harding is one feminist writer who argues this way, and she gives this argument perhaps its most uncompromising expression. She says that science has so far claimed to follow the ideal of neutral, disinterested, and dispassionate inquiry. She calls this ideal "weak objectivity" and says that, though scientists and philosophers of science pay lip service to this ideal, in reality it never has and never will be actually practiced. She cites Kuhn and the social study of science to back her claim and concludes:

> Modern science has again and again been reconstructed by a set of interests and values—distinctively Western, bourgeois, and patriarchal. . . . Political and social interests are not "add-ons" to an otherwise transcendental science that is inherently indifferent to human society; scientific beliefs, practices, institutions, histories, and problematics are constituted in and through contemporary political and social projects and always have been. (Harding, 1991; 2003, p. 119)

In short, Harding endorses the slogan that heads this section: "Objectivity [as traditionally construed] is what a man calls his subjectivity." That is, the values that guide science have been those that men personally endorsed because they served male interests. Men tried to disguise the self-serving and subjective nature of those values by calling them "objective," "disinterested," and "impartial." Further, the influence of social and political factors on science cannot be blocked by adopting stricter methods and tighter controls. The idea of a value-free science is therefore not only

312 | Parsons: Copernican
Questions: A Concise
Invitation to the Philosophy
of Science

3. A Walk on the Wild Side:
Social Constructivism,
Postmodernism, Feminism,
and that Old-Time Religion

Text

© The McGraw-Hill
Companies, 2006

**86**    Chapter 3 • *A Walk on the Wild Side*

a myth, it is a dangerous myth since it employs the language of impartiality to obscure the hidden agendas that science has always served.

Harding recommends that science instead pursue the ideal of "strong objectivity," which science can achieve only when it starts "thinking from women's lives." That is, "women's experience," specifically as interpreted by feminist analysis, must inform all of the standards, values, and methods of science. Feminist analysis turns women's experience of sexist oppression into a source of insight by raising victims' consciousness. Men, as the beneficiaries rather than the victims of sexist oppression, will not have such insights. It is like the situation where the slave knows all of the master's moods, whims, and quirks perfectly, but the master is largely oblivious of his slaves' lives. To get the benefit of women's experience (correctly interpreted), and realize the ideal of "strong objectivity," science must explicitly adopt the feminist standpoint.

Let me emphasize here that Harding is not making the rather bland recommendation that science should be open to people from many different backgrounds so that scientific communities will contain persons with a variety of perspectives arising from differences of "life experience." The idea that there should be a diverse "web of knowers" whose different perspectives will lead to a fairer evaluation of knowledge claims seems to be a reasonable suggestion. Harding, though, wants science to adopt a *specific* perspective and set of values—hers.

Now Harding realizes that critics will point to notorious cases when people adopted doctrinaire assumptions and tried to do "politically correct" science. Perhaps the most famous incident involved Soviet pseudo-scientist Trofim Lysenko, whose attempt to introduce a Marxist/Leninist brand of genetics destroyed the legitimate practice of that science in the Soviet Union. By currying favor with Stalin, who imposed a totalitarian stranglehold on every aspect of Soviet life, Lysenko was able to get his rivals banished to the Gulag and insure that only his own views were taught. The attempt to apply Lysenko's crackpot theories to agriculture resulted in disaster, and, perhaps, ultimately contributed to the fall of the Soviet Union. Maybe equally notorious were the attempts in Nazi Germany to pursue an "Aryan Science" that repudiated "Jewish Science" such as the theories of Einstein.

Harding's reply is to reiterate her allegation that a value-free, apolitical, impartial science is a myth, and again to state that all science must be done from some political perspective and work to promote some set of values. Therefore, we must choose whether science will serve a liberating set of values or the values of an oppressive doctrine. Immediately, though, there is a problem. Just who gets to decide which doctrines are "liberating" and which are not? Why cannot evangelical Christians, for instance,

Parsons: Copernican
Questions: A Concise
Invitation to the Philosophy
of Science

3. A Walk on the Wild Side:
Social Constructivism,
Postmodernism, Feminism,
and that Old–Time Religion

Text

© The McGraw–Hill
Companies, 2006

313

Is "Objectivity" What a Man Calls His Subjectivity?     **87**

insist that *their* doctrine is the liberating one and that science should be based on *their* perspective and values? Harding says that the feminist standpoint is preferable because it leads to a science that is less "partial and distorting" than other doctrines. However, this implies that we can have some impartial means of telling which doctrines are more "partial and distorting." That is, we have to have some dependable methods for recognizing whole, undistorted truth and distinguishing it from the half-truths and distortions of ideologues. Those methods, whatever they are, of distinguishing truth from distortion cannot themselves presume the feminist standpoint. Assuming the feminist standpoint to prove the legitimacy of the feminist standpoint is obviously arguing in a circle. If Harding admits this, she must admit that we have reliable means of recognizing whole, undistorted truths, and that those means do not depend upon adopting the feminist standpoint or any other ideology. But this seems tantamount to admitting that we *can* have a disinterested, impartial, value-neutral science.

A deeper issue is what exactly it would mean for science to adopt the feminist standpoint. Most important scientific discoveries were credited to male scientists. It is a good bet that most of these men of science shared the common prejudices of their day. Some were even blatantly misogynistic. However, with many of these discoveries it is very hard to see how the incorporation of "women's experience" into the information available to scientists would have aided the discovery process or made the results less "partial and distorting." Objects fall at the same rate for women as for men. A cup of hot coffee cools at the same rate for women as for men. The speed of light is the same for both men and women. It is hard to think that Newton's laws and principle of universal gravitation, the laws of thermodynamics, or the principles of special relativity would have been any different had they been formulated by feminists. Perhaps Harding would concede this, and she would now say that it is only in the more "human" and social sciences such as anthropology, sociology, primatology, psychology, and so forth that adopting the feminist standpoint would make a significant difference.

Now it is certainly true that bias of various sorts has at times distorted science. Harding is quite right that the banner of scientific objectivity has often been unfurled to hide the ugliness of bigotry. Stephen Jay Gould's 1981 book *The Mismeasure of Man* is both amusing and horrifying when it recounts how nineteenth-century anthropologists pursued craniometry, the measurement of the size of human skulls. They simply assumed that a bigger skull would house a bigger brain and therefore indicate higher intelligence. They measured the cranial capacity of the skulls of many races—Europeans, Sub-Saharan Africans, Eskimos, Semites, Native Americans,

Australian Aborigines, and East Asians. Which group did these European researchers find to have the greatest cranial capacity and therefore the highest intellectual ability? You get one guess. German researchers even found that German skulls were more capacious than other European skulls. Other prejudices have distorted other sciences. Until the 1970s homosexuality was listed in psychiatry texts as a mental disorder. The silly things that male scientists have said about women could (and did) fill volumes. So, would these sciences have been made more objective had they adopted the feminist standpoint?

The answer depends, first, on whether Harding has shown that all science is inevitably and inextricably bound to political agendas and the promotion of non-epistemic values. If she has not, then perhaps the way to remove bias from science is not to bring in a new ideology, but to pursue the old-fashioned goal of a more impartial science. Second, we have to ask whether the feminist standpoint would itself introduce its own form of bias so that there will be no net gain in achieving a less "partial and distorted" science. Quite frankly, there are tenets of feminist doctrine that could bias science by placing an *a priori* ban on possible scientific results. For instance, perhaps the leading school of feminist thought today is called "gender feminism." Gender feminists argue that, while sex is a biological fact, gender is a social construct. That is, it is a natural fact that women bear children and men do not, but the various social roles that have traditionally been assigned to women and to men are, in their view, entirely products of culture. As gender feminists see it, the stereotypes about men and women's behavioral dispositions, such as that men, as a matter of biological fact, tend to be more physically aggressive and women more nurturing, are all false. In their view, in a restructured society, one engineered around feminist values, these supposedly "natural" behavioral differences would wash out.

But what if gender feminists are wrong on these points? What if there really are natural differences in the behavioral dispositions of the sexes? Of course, some women are more physically aggressive than some men, just as some women are taller than some men. But what if, just as men are, on average, naturally taller than women, they also, on average, are naturally more physically aggressive? Steven Pinker in his recent book *The Blank Slate* (2002) argues very cogently that there are innate, biological dispositional differences between the sexes. Pinker could be wrong; debates over these points are far from settled. But the point is that he could be right. There is no way we can know ahead of time; we have to carry out the research and see. If Pinker is right, that is if the natural facts are as he says, then gender feminists might be casting themselves in the role played by Pope Urban VIII when he proscribed Galileo's findings

Parsons: Copernican
Questions: A Concise
Invitation to the Philosophy
of Science

3. A Walk on the Wild Side:
Social Constructivism,
Postmodernism, Feminism,
and that Old–Time Religion

Text

© The McGraw–Hill
Companies, 2006

315

because they contradicted sacrosanct beliefs. Even if gender feminism turns out to be consistent with all empirical findings to date, we should continue to presume it true only so long as it continues to face all challenges. John Stuart Mill (himself a strong advocate of feminism) spoke what should have been the final words on this matter:

> There is the greatest difference between presuming an opinion to be true, because, with every opportunity for contesting it, it has not been refuted, and assuming its truth for the purpose of not permitting its refutation. Complete liberty of contradicting and disproving our opinion is the very condition which justifies us in assuming its truth for purposes of action; and on no other terms can a being with human faculties have any rational assurance of being right. (Mill, 1952, p. 276)

It is hard to avoid the impression that Harding would be most displeased if science had "complete liberty of contradicting and disproving" her version of feminism.

## IS SCIENCE GODLESS?

The science critics we have so far considered—social constructivists, postmodernists, and gender feminists—are representatives of the "academic left." Postmodernism, for instance, seems to have sprung from the failure of the French radical movement of the late 1960s. Yet it should come as no surprise that conservatives have also recently challenged the claimed objectivity of science, at least as it is now practiced. Science has traditionally clashed more often with conservative thinkers than left-wing ones. The most notorious conflicts occurred when science and religion clashed. Science and religion are not always opposed; sometimes they even cooperate in a symbiotic relationship. Yet conflicts are inevitable. Stephen Jay Gould, the author of *The Mismeasure of Man* mentioned above, argues that science and religion do not clash because they are what he calls "nonoverlapping magisteria." That is, science deals with matters of physical fact and theory while religion is the realm of value and spirit. But this is merely wishful thinking. There is no self-evident principle that relegates science and religion to different spheres. There is no *a priori* reason why religion cannot have something to say about the physical universe or why science cannot say something about value.

In fact, there are any number of ways that science and religion can clash. For instance, many religions teach that humans have an immortal soul, the seat of mind and consciousness, that will survive (and, according to some traditions, predates) its incarnation in a human body. Yet the flourishing field of neuroscience takes it for granted that mind and

Parsons: Copernican
Questions: A Concise
Invitation to the Philosophy
of Science

3. A Walk on the Wild Side:
Social Constructivism,
Postmodernism, Feminism,
and that Old–Time Religion

Text

© The McGraw–Hill
Companies, 2006

consciousness, those phenomena previously thought to be the province of the soul, are due entirely to the physical functions of neurons—brain cells. Of course, neuroscience has not, and may never, explain precisely how the firing of neurons creates consciousness. Nevertheless, the marvelously entertaining books of neurologist Oliver Sacks show in fascinating and sometimes disturbing detail just how intimately our deepest thoughts and feelings, indeed our whole conception of ourselves and our world, are related to brain function. Apparently, if you change your brain you change your *self*. Religion might also clash with the social and human sciences. It is a central tenet of Christian belief that humans are sinners and that sin is a matter of the conscious choice of morally responsible agents. Yet some psychological theories deny that humans have such freedom and interpret human behavior as caused by, for instance, conditioning (behaviorism) or subconscious motivations (psychoanalysis).

Of course, the most famous conflict between science and religion, one that occasionally erupts even in the present day, is the clash between conservative Christianity and evolutionary theory. As historian James Moore showed, it is false that Christian theologians consistently opposed Darwinian evolution from the beginning. As Moore indicates, many Christians were quickly reconciled to Darwinism and even embraced it enthusiastically. Today most Christian denominations officially accept evolution. Pope John Paul II stated that evolution is "more than just a theory," and that it is clearly the correct account of the origin of biological species. Still, many conservative Christians have simply never been able to accept evolution or square it with beliefs that are for them essential elements of Christian doctrine. Perhaps the main problem is that evolution contradicts a straightforward reading of the creation accounts in the Book of Genesis. For today's fundamentalists, like the Young Earth Creationists, this is undoubtedly the basis for much of their animus against evolution.

Not all opponents of evolution are fundamentalists. Phillip E. Johnson, a professor in the School of Law at the University of California at Berkeley, is perhaps the best-known current critic of Darwinism. Johnson is not a Young Earth Creationist. He is perfectly willing to admit that the earth is billions of years old, just as geologists and evolutionary biologists claim. Further, he is not committed to a view of Scripture as inerrant, so it is not the conflict of evolution with a literal reading of Genesis that bothers him. He does think that the evidence for evolution is shoddy, and he has written extensively trying to show that this is so. What really bothers him, though, is not evolution itself but what he sees as an even deeper problem with the reigning assumptions and practice of science. Why, he asks, if the evidence for evolution is so weak, is it so nearly universally accepted among scientists? His answer is that science has been adulterated

Parsons: Copernican
Questions: A Concise
Invitation to the Philosophy
of Science

3. A Walk on the Wild Side:
Social Constructivism,
Postmodernism, Feminism,
and that Old–Time Religion

Text

© The McGraw–Hill
Companies, 2006

317

by a philosophical dogma, the doctrine of metaphysical naturalism. Johnson explains metaphysical naturalism as follows:

> Naturalism assumes the entire realm of nature to be a closed system of material causes and effects, which cannot be influenced by anything from "outside." Naturalism does not explicitly deny the mere existence of God, but it does deny that a supernatural being could in any way influence natural events, such as evolution, or communicate with material creatures like ourselves. (Johnson, 1991, pp. 114–115)

In other words, metaphysical naturalism assumes that all natural things have only natural causes and therefore rejects out of hand any hypotheses postulating supernatural causes, like a divine Creator. It is this *philosophical* bias against the supernatural, says Johnson, not anything necessary for good science, that leads scientists to accept evolution and reject creationism:

> Creationists are disqualified from making a positive case, because science by definition is based upon naturalism. The rules of science also disqualify any purely negative argumentation designed to dilute the persuasiveness of evolution. Creationism is thus ruled out of court—and out of classrooms—before any consideration of evidence. (Johnson, 2001, p. 67)

So, Johnson's argument is that science has compromised its objectivity by ruling out supernatural hypotheses, like creationism, without a hearing while accepting naturalistic theories, like evolution, that have little going for them. How good is Johnson's case? This is not the place to enter into the evidence for evolution. Many good books have done that already. Also, this is not the place to rehash the whole creation/evolution debate. Many fine books, a few of which are listed below in the "Further Readings" section, have done that job admirably. Here we shall address just three questions: (1) Is philosophy ever relevant to the evaluation of scientific hypotheses? (2) Does Science assume metaphysical naturalism? (3) Are supernatural hypotheses like creationism dismissed by philosophical fiat and without a thorough empirical evaluation?

Well, why should there be any *philosophical* debate about *scientific* hypotheses? Why not just run every proposed hypothesis through a good empirical test? After all, isn't the whole point of scientific method supposed to be that we can test hypotheses rather than engage in long-winded philosophical debate? The simple fact of the matter is that far too many hypotheses can be thought up than can possibly be tested. The empirical evaluation of hypotheses is an exacting, time-consuming process that requires meticulous planning and frequently involves the use of very expensive equipment that is often available only on a very competitive

92    Chapter 3  *  *A Walk on the Wild Side*

basis. Astronomers sometimes have to wait months to get one night on one of the big telescopes, and if it turns out cloudy on their night to observe—too bad. Besides, scientists are very, very busy people. So, before scientists can even begin to consider a hypothesis for testing, it has to show considerable promise. Scientists get ideas all the time, the vast majority of them bad. Like the White Queen in *Through the Looking Glass,* scientists can often think of six impossible things before breakfast. How do we distinguish the hypotheses with promise, the ones that we actually will consider testing, from those that are throwaways?

Partly, scientists judge on the basis of track record. If a new hypothesis is just a variant of a kind that has been tried and has failed repeatedly, scientists are likely to give it short shrift. Now this may be unfair in many cases; some worthy hypotheses may be judged guilty by association. After all, *no* sort of hypothesis has a good track record until one of that sort actually does succeed. But nobody ever said science had to be completely fair, and there just does not seem to be any other way to proceed.

Philosophical considerations also inform our judgments about whether a hypothesis shows promise of test-worthiness. For instance, until well into the twentieth century, many professional biologists advocated *vitalism.* Vitalists held that life and living processes could not be completely explained in terms of the laws of chemistry and physics, so they postulated an additional "vital force" or animating "principle" that was supposed to permeate every tissue of living things. Vitalism was not a silly or obscurantist doctrine. Many of the leading figures in the history of the life sciences, including Pasteur, advocated some form of vitalism. However, vitalism was eventually abandoned in part because it lost repeatedly when placed head-to-head against mechanistic hypotheses. Another reason it was abandoned was that biologists came to see "vital force" as an explanatory dead end. Instead of explaining organic phenomena, invoking "vital force" just seemed to deepen the mystery.

The question of what constitutes a legitimate scientific explanation is a philosophical question, one pursued at considerable length by philosophers of science. Because this is such an important question in the philosophy of science, let's digress a bit to review briefly what some philosophers have said about it. It is widely agreed that one goal of science is to explain the observed features of the physical universe. Science therefore asks questions like these: Why are certain zones of the earth's crust particularly susceptible to earthquakes while others hardly ever have even a tremor? Why are galaxies arranged in clusters and superclusters rather than just spread randomly through space? Why are island faunas so unique, often displaying a range of adaptations not found in related

Parsons: Copernican
Questions: A Concise
Invitation to the Philosophy
of Science

3. A Walk on the Wild Side:
Social Constructivism,
Postmodernism, Feminism,
and that Old–Time Religion

Text

© The McGraw–Hill
Companies, 2006

319

Is Science Godless?    **93**

faunas of the nearest mainlands? Scientific explanations relieve our puzzlement about such questions by showing why these particular phenomena were to be expected.

The classic modern model of scientific explanation was articulated by philosophers Carl Hempel and Paul Oppenheim in 1948. Hempel later devoted much effort to refining and extending this model. The basic idea is that what sets scientific explanation apart from other ways of achieving elucidation or enlightenment is that scientific explanations have a distinct *form*. A scientific explanation has the form of an *argument* where a conclusion is drawn from a set of premises. The datum to be explained—what philosophers call the *explanandum*—is scientifically explained when it is correctly inferred from particular kinds of premises. For Hempel and Oppenheim, at least one premise needs to state a *natural law*. Another premise states *initial conditions,* i.e., an appropriate set of concrete physical circumstances. Propositions that state natural laws are called *nomological propositions* (from the Greek word "nomos" meaning "law"). A *Deductive Nomological* (DN) model of explanation is therefore one in which an explanandum is explained by deducing it from premises that state a natural law and a set of initial conditions. Because natural laws play a vital role in this model of explanation, it is called a "covering law" model.

According to Hempel and Oppenheim, many explanations in science have a DN form. Here is a simple example:

Natural law: When water freezes it expands with enormous force.
Initial conditions: The water in the pipes froze solid overnight.
Conclusion: The pipes burst.

Given that freezing water exerts an enormous expansive force—a force too great for household plumbing to contain—and given that the water in our pipes did freeze last night, we can *deduce* that our pipes burst. So, if we want to know why we have burst pipes, and a terrible plumber's bill to pay, we gain scientific understanding (but not much solace) when we know that freezing water expands and that the water in our pipes froze.

Many explanations in science fit the DN model and the allied *Inductive Nomological* (IN) model, which is much the same as the DN model, except that we infer the *probable* occurrence of the explanandum from a law and initial conditions. However, as various philosophers have pointed out, not all legitimate scientific explanations conform to the DN or IN models. Here is an example of one that does not:

Any unvaccinated person exposed to live influenza virus has a 20 percent to 40 percent chance of developing a case of the flu within 72 hours. Sam

**94**     Chapter 3 ● *A Walk on the Wild Side*

has had no flu shot this year and he sat for two hours in a movie theater next to Sarah, who was just coming down with an active case of the flu. Two days later Sam developed a case of the flu. Therefore, Sam got the flu because he was exposed to live influenza virus he got from Sarah.

Surely this is a legitimate explanation of why Sam got the flu, but it fits neither the DN nor the IN model. You cannot *deduce* that Sam will get the flu from the fact that he is unvaccinated and has been exposed to flu virus. It is not *certain* that Sam will get the flu; there is only a 20 percent to 40 percent chance. Also this explanation does not fit the IN model because it is not even *probable* that Sam will get the flu. If there is a 20 percent to 40 percent chance that Sam will get the flu, there is a 60 percent to 80 percent chance that he will not. So it is *probable* that Sam will *not* get the flu despite his exposure to the virus. Still, if Sam *does* get the flu, exposure to the virus is the explanation.

To deal with cases like this, philosophers developed the *Causal Statistical* (CS) model of scientific explanation. According to the CS model, we understand an event when we spell out the physical factors statistically relevant to the event and also specify the underlying causal processes that brought about the event. For instance we above explained why Sam came down with influenza by noting that he is unvaccinated and he came in contact with another person with an active case. To say that exposure to influenza is statistically relevant to Sam's getting the flu does not mean that such exposure makes it *likely* (i.e., more than 50 percent probable) that Sam will get the disease. It only means that such exposure makes it *more likely* that Sam will get the flu than if he had not been exposed. A 20 percent chance of the flu is greater than a 0 percent chance. We expand our explanation by specifying just how the influenza virus does its dirty work on the body. Viruses display a malign ingenuity in the way that they invade body cells and hijack the cell's genetic machinery to make more copies of themselves. Such knowledge about how viruses operate greatly expands our understanding of the facts about infection.

Other philosophers reject all such models of scientific explanation and recommend a pragmatic approach. According to these philosophers, all we can really say about a good explanation is that it answers our "why" questions about a given topic of concern by telling why *this* particular outcome was to be expected rather than one of the other members of that event's "contrast class." The "contrast class" consists of all of the other events that conceivably could have occurred in that situation but did not. For instance, a satisfactory scientific explanation of the dinosaurs' demise would tell us why the dinosaurs went extinct, but crocodilians sailed right through the K/T mass extinction and are with us today.

Is Science Godless?    **95**

Let's return from this (all too brief) review of what some philosophers have said about scientific explanation to the main question: Are philosophical considerations ever relevant to theory choice? In particular, might a philosophical consideration, like our ideas about what constitutes a good scientific explanation, reasonably guide us in deciding which hypotheses are promising candidates for further testing and which are nonstarters? It is important to note that concern about the nature of scientific explanation is not merely an armchair amusement for philosophers. As we saw in Chapter Two, Kuhn notes that scientists themselves often engage in vigorous debates over standards, like what should constitute a legitimate explanation for some range of natural phenomena. It seems therefore that philosophical considerations should sometimes guide us in choosing which hypotheses look promising enough to go to the trouble of testing. We cannot test every hypothesis that anyone proposes. If a hypothesis looks like it does not even offer us a good explanation, it is not unreasonable or unfair to pass it over, at least for the time being, in favor of something more promising.

Well what about supernatural hypotheses? Does philosophical bias prevent them from receiving due consideration? One complaint often made against hypotheses that invoke God's acts is that they do not explain things, but only hide our ignorance behind a theological fig leaf. For skeptics, saying "God did it" does not enhance our understanding of some strange phenomenon—a sudden, unexplained remission of metastatic cancer, for instance—but only drapes it in deeper mystery. Is this accusation fair? Do hypotheses that invoke God, or perhaps a more nebulous Creator, offer legitimate explanations, or are they only markers for our ignorance, placeholders for explanations we hope someday to get?

Defenders of supernatural hypotheses could strengthen their case if they could show that their hypotheses offer explanations that conform to one or more of the recognized models of scientific explanation. Let's consider whether there could be supernatural explanations that conform, for instance, to the DN or CS models. There do not seem to be any "laws of supernature" to serve as covering laws to explain particular events, so the DN model seems to be out. For instance, we just do not know the general circumstances in which God is likely to perform a miracle. We cannot articulate any general laws of the form "Every time God's people are in dire enough need, God performs a public miracle to deliver them." Putative beings like gods and ghosts are not constrained by natural law; their actions are unpredictable so it is hard to know what effects of those actions are to be expected. Whether supernatural hypotheses specify statistically relevant factors for the occurrence of events is a matter of debate among philosophers of religion. Some theistic philosophers argue that the existence of the universe, or of a particular kind of universe, is more likely if there is a God than if there is not. However, nobody can specify the particular causal processes whereby God is supposed to bring about his effects; after all, God's ways are proverbially mysterious. Nobody can be much more specific than to say that when God created something—birds, let's say—he just said "Let there be birds" and POOF! there were birds! Supernatural hypotheses are like the famous Sidney Harris cartoon showing two scientists standing before a chalkboard full of mathematical scribbles except in the middle where it says, "step two: A miracle occurs." One scientist comments dryly "I think you need to be a little more specific here in step two." This lack of specificity about causal mechanisms means that supernatural explanations do not conform to the CS model.

Supernatural explanations do not even meet our pragmatic explanatory needs very well. For instance, if we try to explain the sorts of anatomical homologies mentioned in the last chapter by saying that God created organisms according to a plan, this leaves all of our questions unanswered. Why this plan rather than one of the indefinitely many others that an all-powerful, all-knowing creator could have enacted? Why just this instance rather than one of an indefinitely large contrast-class?

Defenders of supernatural hypotheses will counter, correctly I think, that the models of scientific explanation so far developed do not necessarily exhaust all the legitimate possibilities. While philosophers of science may have identified *some* kinds of good scientific explanation, it is highly questionable whether they have identified *all* possible types. Therefore, the fact that supernatural explanations do not conform to any "model of scientific explanation" so far proposed does not mean that they cannot be legitimate scientific explanations. Fair enough, but surely the burden of proof is on the defenders of supernatural hypotheses. *Prima facie* such hypotheses do not seem to offer much elucidation. Again, if we say, for instance, that God created birds, what does that tell us? How did He do it? For what reason? Why birds? Why didn't He stick with the highly successful flying reptiles? Surely, any kind of acceptable scientific explanation should show why the explanandum—the existence of birds in this case—was to be expected. As philosophers Karel Lambert and Gordon G. Brittan, Jr. note (1987, p. 22), invocations of God's will, like appeal to signs of the Zodiac, just do not provide such information.

The upshot is that there *is* a philosophical motivation behind the scientific practice of giving short shrift to supernatural hypotheses, just as Johnson says. But until defenders of supernatural hypotheses can show

Parsers: Copernican
Questions: A Concise
Invitation to the Philosophy
of Science

3. A Walk on the Wild Side:
Social Constructivism,
Postmodernism, Feminism,
and that Old–Time Religion

Text

© The McGraw–Hill
Companies, 2006

323

that such hypotheses promise legitimate scientific explanations—and do not just disguise our ignorance—such practice is neither biased nor unfair. Please note that this does *not* mean that supernatural hypotheses cannot be true or that we cannot have very good reasons for thinking them true (more on this below). Maybe we will just have to admit that some things do not have a scientific explanation and are due to the mysterious acts of a Creator. Maybe on some topics, like the origin of life, say, scientists may someday come to the point where they should just throw up their hands and say that they will never explain some things and concede that there are ultimate mysteries, facts attributable only to the unfathomable and inscrutable actions of a Creator. But it is far from clear that that day is today.

Let's move to the second question raised by Johnson's critique: *Does science assume metaphysical naturalism?* This charge has been made many times, and the standard reply is that the naturalism science assumes is methodological, not metaphysical. The difference is this: Metaphysical naturalism is a doctrine about the nature of reality. It can take the strong line that only natural things are real or the weaker line that supernatural things might exist but they cannot causally interact with the natural world. Methodological naturalism does not offer opinions about the nature of ultimate reality; it merely requires that, as a matter of good scientific practice, we consider only naturalistic hypotheses. T. H. Huxley, Victorian scientist and man of letters, was very emphatic that metaphysical questions about the nature of ultimate reality were none of the business of science. Huxley said that you might as well inquire into the politics of extraterrestrials as to ask whether ultimate reality is material or spiritual. Yet he strongly advocated naturalism as a methodological requirement because he held that naturalistic explanations are comprehensible while supernatural explanations only hide mysteries behind a veil of theological obscurity. In a similar vein, contemporary philosopher Rob Pennock argues that science should be godless in the same sense that plumbing is godless. Good plumbing practice obviously does not involve grandiose metaphysical assumptions, but proceeds on the assumption that the cause of a problem is in the pipes. Pennock argues that the requirement that scientific hypotheses be testable entails that they involve only natural objects that follow predictable laws. As noted earlier, putative supernatural entities, like gods and ghosts, are not bound by natural law, and so are notoriously difficult to test.

Johnson does not buy these arguments and insists that methodological naturalism is only a dishonest front for metaphysical naturalism. I think we should concede that *in principle* good science could confirm supernatural hypotheses, however difficult they might be to test *in practice*. Nineteenth-century English scientist Francis Galton proposed a test for the efficacy of prayer. He noted that members of the royal family certainly were the beneficiaries of more prayers for their health than any other British family. He concluded that, if prayer works, the royal family should be healthier than other comparable families (he found that they were not healthier, by the way). Now a legitimate test of the efficacy of prayer is probably impossible to achieve in practice. How could Galton rule out that many disgruntled people may have been praying that God strike down the royal family? Still, this seems to be a practical difficulty, and not an indication that an experimental test of prayer is in principle impossible.

Interestingly, the Bible tells of an incident that would be about as good an experimental test of God's power as anyone could devise. I Kings, chapter 18, tells the story of Elijah and the priests of Baal. Elijah challenged the priests of Baal to a contest to see which god was real, Baal or the Lord, the God of Abraham, Isaac, and Israel. The priests of Baal built an altar and placed a sacrifice upon it. All day they cried for Baal to send fire to burn their sacrifice, but nothing happened. At the day's end Elijah erected an altar, placed a sacrifice on it, and had everything thoroughly soaked with water. He then called upon the Lord, and according to I Kings 18:38, "Then the fire of the Lord fell and consumed the burnt offering and the wood and the stones, and the dust, and licked up the water that was in the trench." Now this would certainly seem to be about as good an example of a crucial experiment as any scientist has ever devised. If it occurred today, the churches and synagogues would fill with former doubters. Of course, such things apparently do not happen today, but the point is, again, that there seems to be nothing *in principle* impossible about an experimental test of God's power.

So, is it simply a matter of ideological prejudice that supernatural hypotheses are rejected by science? No, for two reasons (besides the doubts raised earlier about supernatural "explanations"): First, though it is not a methodological *requirement* of science, naturalism has unquestionably proven a valuable *heuristic*. A "heuristic" is a presumption that serves as a guide for inquiry. An example of a heuristic principle that guides science is the principle of simplicity, the postulation that physical reality is ultimately simple, and that science should therefore seek simple theories. The idea that things will ultimately turn out to be simple is, of course, a speculation. Absolutely nothing guarantees that at bottom physical reality is simple. Yet no one can deny that the presumption that deep simplicity underlies the surface complexity of nature has been an extremely valuable heuristic guiding science.

Parsons: Copernican
Questions: A Concise
Invitation to the Philosophy
of Science

3. A Walk on the Wild Side:
Social Constructivism,
Postmodernism, Feminism,
and that Old–Time Religion

Text

© The McGraw–Hill
Companies, 2006

325

Similarly, naturalism has been a very successful heuristic principle. Unquestionably, much of the progress of science is due to the fact that it doggedly sought natural hypotheses and excluded those postulating gods, souls, angels, demons, ghosts, fate, magic, astrological influences, hexes, spells, good luck charms, and so forth. So long as a heuristic continues to deliver the goods, scientists are fully justified in sticking with it. Is there any indication that a naturalistic heuristic has served its purpose and now leads science in the wrong direction? For instance, does naturalism induce scientists to accept evolution despite a dearth of evidence? For decades, anti-evolutionists have charged that evolution is a "theory in crisis" and that Darwin is once again "on trial." They have insisted repeatedly that the evidence for evolution is so shoddy that the whole edifice of evolutionary science is about to come crashing down and that the only thing propping it up is naturalistic bias.

Let's pause for a second and consider just how strong a claim this is. A recent thorough electronic search of the professional, peer-reviewed scientific literature over the previous twelve-year period turned up over 100,000 articles with "evolution" as a key word and, by the way, practically none referring to concepts of supernatural design. So, if evolutionary theory has been "in crisis" and "on trial" for decades, this news has yet to reach the writers of the professional scientific literature. Evolutionary biology looks extremely spry for a field supposedly on its deathbed! Johnson and other anti-evolutionists have to attribute evolutionary biology's appearance of health and vigor to a massive intellectual fraud perpetrated on science by a cadre of ideologues. But no ideology, not even when backed by the power to burn dissenters at the stake, has ever held science down for long. Not even the enormous power and intellectual influence of the seventeenth-century Church could hide the bankruptcy of the old Ptolemaic system for long. So, it is just hard to believe that nothing but ideological obscurantism keeps scientists from recognizing the alleged weakness of evolutionary theory.

A second and more important reason for denying that negative attitudes towards supernatural hypotheses are due to bias is that Johnson's charge is simply false. The answer to the third of the questions we are addressing in this section is: No, creationism has not been dismissed by philosophical fiat. Dozens of books and hundreds of articles, many available on the Internet in the magnificent talk.origins archives, have subjected creationist claims to careful, extensive, point-by-point empirical critique. In *The Origin of Species* Darwin himself showed time and time again that natural selection better explains the natural facts than special creation. Therefore, the creationist hypotheses have not been rejected by philosophical fiat and without a fair and thorough hearing.

**100**     Chapter 3 • *A Walk on the Wild Side*

## CONCLUSION

In this chapter we have extensively examined critiques of scientific rationality and objectivity from both the left and the right. Our conclusion has to be that, though science is far from perfect, as any human enterprise must be, there is still something left of the Enlightenment ideal derided by Latour. There is a physical world "out there," and we can know some things about it. That is, we can say of the natural world, without qualification or apology, that some things really just *are* so, and are not artifacts of our percepts, concepts, or categories. Further, our observations of the physical world can be used to rigorously evaluate our theories, so that our theoretical beliefs are shaped and constrained by nature, and not merely by politics, rhetorical manipulation, or ideology. Disinterested knowledge really is possible, and is in fact achieved far more often than cynics suppose.

Yet even their harshest critics must admit that the social constructivist, postmodernist, and feminist science critics have performed a valuable service. These critics have certainly succeeded in disposing of what might be called the "passive spectator" stereotype of scientific knowledge. According to this stereotype, modern science began when the pioneers like Copernicus, Galileo, and Darwin stopped bowing to ancient authority and opened their eyes to the world around them. Once people started looking at *nature* rather than old books, scientific knowledge flowed into open scientific minds like water pouring into an empty bucket. Now, of course, this is a comic-book version of the history of science, and no serious scholar has ever thought that it really happened this way or that we gain scientific knowledge merely by the passive reception of information. Still, this has been a very influential stereotype. A powerful image can influence our thinking more than all the careful arguments of scholars. One of the indelible images of our intellectual culture is the picture of Galileo boldly scanning the heavens with his telescope, eager to discover whatever his eyes revealed to him, while his ecclesiastical oppressors, besotted with Scripture and Aristotle, refused even to look through the instrument. The founders of Britain's Royal Society, the preeminent British scientific body, were so impressed with this image of the scientist as the ideally objective and open-minded observer that they adopted as the Society's motto "*Nullius in Verba.*" This motto is hard to translate precisely, but it means that you should take nothing on authority. Instead, you should look and see for yourself.

Scientific discovery requires active engagement, however, not just passive seeing. Galileo didn't just look through the telescope and report what he saw; he interpreted, theorized, speculated, measured, analyzed, and

Conclusion  **101**

argued. Darwin did not just go to the Galapagos Islands, see some odd finches and tortoises, and then awaken to the truth of evolution in a flash of blindingly obvious insight (scientific discoveries are always "obvious" only in hindsight). Darwin's private notebooks, written as he struggled to define his ideas on evolution, reveal a complex process of questioning, argument, and counterargument, with tentative conclusions drawn and then repeatedly rejected or refined. Scientists do not just *absorb* a picture of the world; they *create* a picture and then do their best to see how accurate it is. Unavoidably, when we create our theories of the natural world, we must employ the only cognitive tools we have—the concepts, language, perspectives, interpretive and observational skills, and presumed background knowledge that we possess. Inevitably, multifarious biases lurking in our language and concepts will sometimes—all too often—slip unnoticed into our theories. Our only way of dealing with this problem is to continually refine and revise our ideas through ongoing interaction with the natural world and the effort to devise stricter methods, more rigorous tests, and more accurate measures. The work of Kuhn examined in the last chapter, and that of the radical science critics considered in this one, unquestionably succeeded in debunking the simplistic stereotype of the scientist as ideally objective, open minded, and a passive observer.

What we need then is a balanced view of science, one that rejects both the excessively cynical and the unrealistically idealized stereotypes of science. David Young, in his excellent book *The Discovery of Evolution*, strikes just the right note of balance in our interpretation of science; his words can serve as a coda for this chapter:

> The picture of the scientist as an objective spectator has died a natural death, thanks to the work of historians and philosophers of science. It is now clear that even simple observations are not imbibed passively from the external world but are made by a human mind already laden with ideas. The shaping of these ideas is a human activity carried out in a particular social context, with all the frailties and limitations that that implies. This has led some people to the other extreme, in which scientific knowledge is viewed as no more than the expression of a particular social group. On this view there are no such things as discoveries in science, only changes in fashion about how we choose to view the world. However, such a view cannot account for the fact that scientific understanding does not merely change but is progressive. . . . A sensible view of scientific theory must lie somewhere between these two extremes and embody elements of both. Certainly, scientific discovery does not involve a one-way flow of information from nature to a passive, open mind. It involves a creative interaction of mind and nature, in which scientists seek to construct an adequate picture from what they see of the world. (Young, 1992, pp. 219–220)

102    Chapter 3 • *A Walk on the Wild Side*

Young's view is neither novel nor especially profound. It lacks all of the edgy excitement of the radical science critiques. It only has one big advantage over those accounts: It is true.

## FURTHER READINGS FOR CHAPTER THREE

Paul de Kruif's *Microbe Hunters* (San Diego: Harcourt Brace & Company, 1926), is still in print eighty years after it was written. I remember being fascinated as a child reading an old dog-eared paperback copy. I am sure that it has inspired many readers to enter medicine or biomedical research. As I say in this chapter, de Kruif regards Pasteur and the other microbe hunters with unabashed hero worship and he treats the pursuit of science as the noblest and most selfless of activities. We now, of course, realize that these views are naïve. Ambrose Bierce once defined a saint as "a dead sinner, revised and edited," and no doubt well-meaning admirers like de Kruif have likewise redacted the stories of the "saints" of science. Historians of science perform a valuable service when present the story "warts and all." However, "warts and all" does not mean "nothing but warts." In my view, undercutting one myth, the myth of the saintly scientist grappling with the demons of disease, should not lead to the creation of more pernicious stereotypes, such as the image of the scientist as cynical self-promoter, rampant ideologue, or stooge of vested interests.

Upon reading a draft of this chapter, one referee said that I had introduced Bruno Latour as the "villain" who insulted the memory of France's national hero of science, Pasteur. No. I present Latour as a radical revisionist, a characterization I have no reason to think he would repudiate. In fact, Latour boasts of the deflationary intention of his work. In a letter to the editor of the (now, sadly, defunct) magazine *The Sciences* (vol. 35, no. 2, p. 7, 1995), Latour compares his work in science studies to the work of Darwin in biology: "Those of us who pursue science studies are the Darwins of science, showing how the exquisite beauty of facts, theories, instruments and machines can be accounted for without ever resorting to teleological principles or arguments by design." I see no other way to read this passage than as a statement of Latour's intent to replace traditional representations of science as motivated by *reasons* with a reductionistic sociological analysis. And that is how I have presented him in this chapter.

There is a lot to be said for the slogan "it is more important that an opinion be interesting than true." Some errors are uninteresting because they are due to silly mistakes in reasoning; others are interesting because they involve deep confusions in our concepts or language. Bruno Latour's errors are *never* dull. When he is wrong, you learn a lot about science and

Parsons: Copernican
Questions: A Concise
Invitation to the Philosophy
of Science

3. A Walk on the Wild Side:
Social Constructivism,
Postmodernism, Feminism,
and that Old–Time Religion

Text

© The McGraw–Hill
Companies, 2006

329

Further Readings for Chapter Three    **103**

how it operates in society even as you try to pinpoint his errors and sort out what is really behind his conclusions. Latour made his big splash with *Laboratory Life: The Construction of Scientific Facts* (Princeton: Princeton University Press, 1979; reprinted with new postscript and index in 1986). This book, co-written with Steve Woolgar, was one of the founding documents of the whole "science studies" movement. It is rather technical in places, and the prose is often muddy. Still, the aim of going into a laboratory as an anthropologist, to observe scientists in their native habitat as one would the Yanomamo or the Inuit was a brilliant idea and makes for fascinating reading.

Latour examines Pasteur and his influence in *The Pasteurization of France* (Cambridge: Harvard University Press, 1988), translated by Alan Sheridan and John Law. Latour's most ambitious and comprehensive work is *Science in Action: How to Follow Scientists and Engineers through Society* (Cambridge: Harvard University Press, 1987). Latour's thought took an interesting turn in 1993 with the publication of *We Have Never Been Modern* (Cambridge: Harvard University Press), translated by Catherine Porter. Here Latour claims to abandon social constructivism and aims to explore a middle course between constructivism, the view that scientific facts are cultural artifacts, and the view of scientists that such objects are objective truths about nature. Latour defines what he calls "quasi-objects" that are neither wholly natural nor wholly constructed. Unfortunately, just what he means by a "quasi-object" is not made entirely clear.

Steve Woolgar develops his views in confrontational style in *Science: The Very Idea* (London: Tavistock Publications, 1988). One very well-known scientist and writer who, at least sometimes, seemed to endorse social constructivism was Stephen Jay Gould. His book *The Mismeasure of Man* (New York: W. W. Norton, 1981) is often cited by social constructivists, postmodernists, and feminists, as proof of how bias and bigotry shape science. Matt Cartmill's perceptive but acerbic characterization of Latour's social constructivism is found in his review of *Mystery of Mysteries: Is Evolution a Social Construct?* by Michael Ruse. This review appeared in *Reports of the National Center for Science Education* 19, no. 5 (1999), 49–50. The story of the wrongheaded dinosaur episode is found in Chapter One of my book *Drawing Out Leviathan* (Bloomington, Ind.: Indiana University Press, 2001). Michele Marsonet's very interesting discussion of the way that philosophy can slide into "linguistic idealism" is found in his *Science, Reality, and Language* (Albany, N.Y.: State University of New York Press, 1995). John Searle's discussion of the "default settings" of the human mind are found in his book *Mind, Language, and Society* (New York: Basic Books, 1998).

As I say, the roots of postmodernism can be traced at least back to Nietzsche. Nietzsche is an exciting but challenging thinker. His writings often have a declamatory or oracular character, which puts some readers off. Also, he is very easy to misread. Sometimes he sounds like an anti-Semite, a misogynist, or a proto-fascist, though his defenders insist that he was none of these things. Because of some of the difficulties with reading Nietzsche, it might be good to start by reading a reliable introduction to his thought. A good, succinct, and readable account is *On Nietzsche*, by Eric Steinhart (Belmont, Calif.: Wadsworth, 2000).

An essential document for understanding postmodernism is Lyotard's manifesto, *The Postmodern Condition: A Report on Knowledge* (Manchester: Manchester University Press, 1979), translated by Geoff Bennington and Brian Massumi. Richard Rorty's *Philosophy and the Mirror of Nature* (Princeton: Princeton University Press, 1979), introduced many characteristic postmodernist theses to English-speaking philosophers. Rorty's work attracted quite a bit of notoriety because he had previously been regarded as one of the really tough-minded philosophers of the analytical tradition, and it seemed to many of his contemporaries that he was simply abandoning philosophy. A fun and very accessible introduction to postmodernism is Glen Ward's *Postmodernism* (NTC/Contemporary Publishing, 1997). Postmodernism is largely a development of recent literary theory, and a perceptive critique of postmodernism by an expert on such theory is *The Illusions of Postmodernism* by Terry Eagleton (Oxford: Blackwell Publishers, 1996).

The two works I selected to represent postmodernist commentary on science were Donna Haraway's *Primate Visions: Gender, Race, and Nature in the World of Modern Science* (New York: Routledge, 1989) and W. J. T. Mitchell's *The Last Dinosaur Book: The Life and Times of a Cultural Icon* (Chicago: University of Chicago Press, 1998). What makes these books particularly interesting is that they deal with primatology and dinosaur paleontology, which are branches of science that are easier for most people to relate to than, say, particle physics. When scientists encounter Haraway's and Mitchell's books, they often are nonplussed or outraged. Matt Cartmill's trenchant review of *Primate Visions*, published in the *International Journal of Primatology* 12, no. 1 (1991), must surely express the exasperation many primatologists would feel toward Haraway's book. I coauthored an essay with geologist Peter Copeland, "Toward a Postmodernist Paleontology?" in *Academic Questions* 17, no. 2 (spring 2004) that examines and criticizes Mitchell's claims in detail. Alan Sokal's *faux*-postmodernist essay, "Transgressing the Boundaries: Towards a Transformative Hermeneutics of Quantum Gravity," is most conveniently found in *The Sokal Hoax: The Sham That Shook the Academy* (Lincoln, Neb.: University of Nebraska Press, 2000), edited by the editors of the magazine *Lingua*

Further Readings for Chapter Three     **105**

*Franca*. This volume is a lot of fun, with fierce polemics and much outraged harrumphing on both sides.

A good place to start with the feminist philosophy of science is the entry "Feminist Accounts of Science" by Kathleen Okruhlik, in *A Companion to the Philosophy of Science*, edited by W. H. Newton-Smith (Oxford: Blackwell Publishers, 2000). Okruhlik provides an authoritative overview of the diverse views of feminist philosophers of science. As I state in both Prefaces, Sandra Harding appears in this chapter not as a "typical" representative of feminist philosophy of science (though I do not consider her too atypical either) but as a controversial figure whose opinions are bound to excite discussion. If Harding has piqued your interest in feminist philosophy of science, you should probably next read Elizabeth Fox Keller's *Reflections on Gender and Science* (New Haven: Yale University Press, 1985), and Helen Longino's *Science as Social Knowledge: Values and Objectivity in Scientific Inquiry* (Princeton: Princeton University Press, 1990). The Harding quote in this section comes from her *Whose Science? Whose Knowledge? Thinking From Women's Lives* (Ithaca, N.Y.: Cornell University Press, 1991). For convenience, I quoted Harding from the selection "Feminist Standpoint Epistemology and Strong Objectivity" from the book *The Science Wars* (bibliographical details below).

For critiques of the feminist philosophy of science, see Cassandra Pinnick, "Feminist Epistemology: Implications for the Philosophy of Science," in the journal *Philosophy of Science* 61 (1994): 646–657; Janet Radcliffe Richards's "Why Feminist Epistemology Isn't," and Noretta Koertge's "Feminist Epistemology: Stalking an Un-Dead Horse." Richards's and Koertge's essays are found on pages 385–412 and 413–419, respectively, in Paul Gross, Norman Levitt, and Martin Lewis, eds., *The Flight From Science and Reason* (New York: New York Academy of Sciences, 1996). A book-length critique of feminist epistemology and philosophy of science is Ellen R. Klein's *Feminism Under Fire* (Amherst, N.Y.: Prometheus Books, 1996). Steven Pinker's provocative discussion of gender differences is found in his *The Blank Slate: The Modern Denial of Human Nature* (New York: Viking, 2002). The quote from John Stuart Mill is from his classic *On Liberty*, in *Great Books of the Western World*, Robert Maynard Hutchins, editor-in-chief (Chicago: Encyclopedia Brittanica, Inc., 1952).

The debates over social constructivist, postmodernist, and feminist accounts of science reached the boiling point in the mid-1990s as scientists began to fire back at what they perceived as attacks on the aims, methods, and values of science by critics of the "academic left." The "science wars" really erupted with the 1994 publication of Paul Gross and Norman Levitt's splendidly pugnacious *Higher Superstition: The Academic Left and its*

**106**    Chapter 3  •  *A Walk on the Wild Side*

*Quarrels with Science* (Baltimore: Johns Hopkins University Press). The academic left responded in equally bellicose fashion in the collection of essays *Science Wars,* edited by Andrew Ross (Durham, N.C.: Duke University Press, 1996). Alan Sokal, of the Sokal hoax, and his collaborator Jean Bricmont stated their case in *Fashionable Nonsense: Postmodern Intellectuals' Abuse of Science* (New York: Picador USA, 1998). A good collection of critiques of the left-wing science critique is *A House Built on Sand: Exposing Postmodernist Myths about Science,* edited by Noretta Koertge (Oxford: Oxford University Press, 1998). By 2000, the rhetorical temperature of the science wars had cooled a bit and books appeared that were less polemical in tone. A clear and insightful survey of the main issues debated in the science wars in the context of the recent history of the philosophy of science is James Robert Brown's *Who Rules in Science: An Opinionated Guide to the Wars* (Cambridge: Harvard University Press, 2001). I offer an introduction to some of the main writings and debates in the anthology *The Science Wars: Debating Scientific Knowledge and Technology,* edited by Keith M. Parsons (Amherst, N.Y.: Prometheus Books, 2003).

Stephen Jay Gould's views on the relation between science and religion are found in his book *Rock of Ages: Science and Religion in the Fullness of Life* (New York: Ballantine Publishing, 1999). A solid, thorough overview of the relations between science and religion is John Hedley Brooke's *Science and Religion: Some Historical Perspectives* (Cambridge: Cambridge University Press, 1991). A detailed yet quite readable examination of the theological response to Darwinism in Britain and America is James R. Moore's *The Post-Darwinian Controversies: A Study of the Protestant Struggle to Come to Terms with Darwin in Great Britain and America, 1870–1900* (Cambridge: Cambridge University Press, 1979).

The recent controversy over "intelligent design," actually a continuation of the controversy over creationism of the 1980s, was kicked off by the publication of Phillip E. Johnson's *Darwin On Trial* (Washington, D.C.: Regnery Gateway, 1991). A history and overview of the intelligent design movement written by a sympathizer is Thomas Woodward's *Doubts about Darwin: A History of Intelligent Design* (Grand Rapids, Mich.: Baker Books, 2003). An anthology of writings by advocates of intelligent design theory with responses by critics is *Intelligent Design Creationism and its Critics: Philosophical, Theological, and Scientific Perspectives* (Cambridge: MIT Press, 2001, ed. by Rob Pennock), which includes the essay by Johnson quoted in this chapter, "Evolution as Dogma: The Establishment of Naturalism."

The volume of literature on evolution is simply stupendous in its quantity (and highly variable in its quality). Here I shall simply recommend one book that seems to me the best presentation of evolutionary

Parsons: Copernican
Questions: A Concise
Invitation to the Philosophy
of Science

3. A Walk on the Wild Side:
Social Constructivism,
Postmodernism, Feminism,
and that Old–Time Religion

Text

© The McGraw–Hill
Companies, 2006

333

Further Readings for Chapter Three    **107**

theory for the nonspecialist, Colin Patterson's *Evolution,* second edition (make sure you get the second edition, it is much better than the first) (Ithaca, N.Y.: Comstock Publishing, 1999). Patterson's treatment is crystal clear, and, while it presents the evidence for evolution cogently, it is very undogmatic in tone. Really to understand Darwinism, you need to see it presented in the context of its historical development. A superbly written, insightful, and beautifully illustrated history of evolution is David Young's *The Discovery of Evolution* (Cambridge: Cambridge University Press, 1992). Perhaps the best nontechnical statement of the intelligent design position is still the Johnson book mentioned above. I think that for most readers the best critique of Johnson's view and the claims of intelligent design creationism is Robert T. Pennock's *Tower of Babel: The Evidence Against the New Creationism* (Cambridge: MIT Press, 1999).

One very good introduction to the topic of scientific explanation is the chapter "Scientific Explanation" by Wesley C. Salmon in Salmon, et al., *Introduction to the Philosophy of Science* (Englewood Cliffs, N.J.: Prentice-Hall, 1992). Salmon, one of the top philosophers of science of the twentieth century, made many seminal contributions to our understanding of scientific explanation. He was also a gifted expositor who could make difficult ideas very clear for beginners. Another very clear and helpful overview of the topic of explanation is in *An Introduction to the Philosophy of Science,* third edition, by Karel Lambert and Gordon G. Brittan, Jr. (Atascadero, Cal.: Ridgeview Publishing Company, 1987).

T. H. Huxley's comments on methodological naturalism are found in his essay "On the Physical Basis of Life," in *Selected Works of Thomas H. Huxley* (New York: D. Appleton, no date), 130–165. Huxley's prodigious learning, wit, and trenchant style are as enjoyable now as they must have been discomfiting for his nineteenth-century opponents. "Darwin's bulldog" still has considerable bite. For full details on the search of scientific literature that turned up 100,000 articles with "evolution" as a key word, see Staver, J. R., "Evolution and Intelligent Design." *The Science Teacher* 70, no. 8 (2003): 32–35.

# Glossary of Philosophical Terms

Donald C. Abel

Donald C. Abel was born in 1948 in Pomeroy, Washington. He attended Gonzaga University and received his bachelor's degree in philosophy in 1971. After completing his master's degree in philosophy at Tulane University in 1973, he taught for two years at Gonzaga. In 1975 he was awarded a licentiate in philosophy from St. Michael's Institute in Spokane, Washington. Abel then pursued graduate studies in theology at Loyola University of Chicago, earning a master of divinity degree in 1979. He enrolled in the doctoral program in philosophy at Northwestern University and completed his degree in 1983. After working for a year as an editor at the Great Books Foundation, Abel accepted a position as Assistant Professor of Philosophy at St. Norbert College in De Pere, Wisconsin. He was promoted to Associate Professor in 1991 and became Professor of Philosophy in 2000. At St. Norbert College, he has received two awards for excellence in teaching and an award for outstanding scholarship.

Abel is the author of *Freud on Instinct and Morality* (1989) and of three McGraw-Hill textbooks: *Theories of Human Nature: Classical and Contemporary Readings* (1992), *Fifty Readings in Philosophy* (1994; 3rd ed., 2008), and *Fifty Readings Plus: An Introduction to Philosophy* (2005). He is coauthor (with Samuel Enoch Stumpf) of the fourth edition of the McGraw-Hill textbook *Elements of Philosophy: An Introduction* (2002). Abel also edits *Discourses*, McGraw-Hill's electronic database of philosophy readings from which this "Glossary of Philosophical Terms" is taken.

This glossary is intended to help students read philosophical texts by giving brief definitions of some of the terms commonly used in philosophical writing. If a word in a definition is italicized, the word is defined in its own glossary entry.

▼

**accident**  a property not essential for a *substance* to be the kind of thing it is

**act utilitarianism**  *see utilitarianism*

**ad hominem**  [Latin, "to the person"]  directed not against an opponent's contention, but against the opponent himself or herself

**aesthetics**  (also spelled *esthetics*)  the study of the nature of beauty and art and of the experience of beauty and art

**a fortiori**  [Latin, "from the stronger (argument)"]  with all the more reason

**agnostic**  someone who claims that God's existence is unknown, and perhaps unknowable

**analogy**  a comparison based on the similarity between things

**analytic statement**  a statement in which the predicate is contained in the subject (contrasted with *synthetic statement*)

**analytic(al) philosophy**  a method of philosophical inquiry that seeks to analyze concepts, statements, theories, and so on, into their constituent elements

**a posteriori**  [Latin, "from what comes later"]  dependent on experience (contrasted with *a priori*)

**a priori**  [Latin, "from what comes earlier"]  independent of experience; deduced from abstract principles (contrasted with *a posteriori*)

**argument**  in *logic*, a set of statements in which one or more statements (the *premises*) are used to establish a further statement (the *conclusion*)

**begging the question**  the *fallacy* of assuming what one is attempting to prove; also called *petitio principii*

**behaviorism**  the doctrine that human behavior can be explained and predicted by environment and genetics, without reference to mental states

**Brahman**  in Hinduism, the ultimate reality, the ground of all being

**categorical syllogism**  a *syllogism* consisting of three categorical statements (statements that affirm or deny a relation between two classes [categories] of things), in which the *premises* connect two classes of things by means of a third class

**cogent argument**  an *inductive argument* that is *strong* and has all true *premises* (contrasted with *noncogent argument*)

**compatibilism**  see *determinism*

**conclusion**  in *logic*, the statement in an *argument* that is intended to be established by the *premises*

**consequentialism**  the ethical doctrine that the morality of an action is determined by its consequences (contrasted with *deontology* and *virtue ethics*)

**Continental philosophy**  philosophical views developed in Continental Europe from about the beginning of the twentieth century, especially *existentialism* and *phenomenology*

**contingent**  capable of being otherwise, or of not occurring at all; not necessary

**cosmological argument**  an *argument* for the existence of God based on some obvious and pervasive feature of the universe (contrasted with *ontological argument*)

**cosmology**  the study of the origin, nature, and structure of the universe

**cultural relativism**   the doctrine that all moral values derive entirely from individual cultural codes, and there are no objective, independently correct moral values

**Cynics**   a school of ancient Greek *philosophy* that held the ideal of self-sufficiency through the mastery of one's desires and needs

**deductive argument**   an *argument* that claims to lead from the *premises* to the *conclusion* in a necessary way (contrasted with *inductive argument*)

**deontology**   the ethical doctrine that the morality of an action is determined by its intrinsic quality (contrasted with *consequentialism* and *virtue ethics*)

**determinism**   the doctrine that all events are determined by preceding causes and that we can never act otherwise than we do (contrasted with *indeterminism* and with *libertarianism*). *Hard determinism* accepts determinism and denies the existence of free will and moral responsibility; *soft determinism* maintains that, although determinism is true, actions determined by certain kinds of internal causes are free and that we are morally responsible for these actions. (Soft determinism is also called *compatibilism* because it maintains the compatibility of determinism with free will and moral responsibility.)

**dialectical method**   a process in which one person tries to help another reach greater understanding of a topic by asking a series of questions (also called the *Socratic method*)

**disjunction**   *logic,* a sentence that combines ("disjoins") two propositions ("disjuncts") with "or" and states that at least one of the two propositions is true

**disjunctive syllogism**   a *syllogism* whose *premises* are a disjunctive (either-or) statement and a statement that affirms or denies one part of the disjunctive statement

**dualism**   in the philosophy of human nature, the theory that human beings are composed of two fundamentally different kinds of reality—body and mind (soul, self)

**efficient cause**   the agent that brings something into being or imparts change (contrasted with *final cause*)

**egoism**   see *ethical egoism* and *psychological egoism*

**élan vital**   [French] vital force

**emotivism**   the doctrine that ethical judgments are not statements that are true or false, but simply expressions of emotions or attempts to arouse emotion in others

**empiricism**   the doctrine that knowledge is attained primarily through sense experience (contrasted with *rationalism*)

**Enlightenment**  an eighteenth-century philosophical movement that had great confidence in the power of reason to understand the universe and improve the human condition

**Epicureanism**  a school of ancient philosophy that held that pleasure is the only *intrinsic good*

**epiphenomenalism**  the doctrine that mental events are *phenomena* caused by bodily events and have no causal power (mental events are called *epi*phenomena because they are viewed as secondary phenomena caused by and accompanying the primary phenomena of bodily events)

**epistemic**  relating to knowledge

**epistemology**  the study of the nature and grounds of knowledge

**equivocal**  having two or more meanings and likely to mislead (contrasted with *univocal*)

**equivocation**  the use of a word or phrase in different senses, which makes an apparently correct *argument* actually incorrect

**essence**  the basic nature of a thing, necessary for it to be what it is

**esthetics**  see *aesthetics*

**ethical egoism**  the doctrine that to be moral means to pursue one's own self-interest; contrasted with *psychological egoism*

**ethical hedonism**  the doctrine that all pleasure, and only pleasure, is an *intrinsic good,* and that all other goods are only *instrumental goods,* as means to pleasure (contrasted with *psychological hedonism*)

**ethics**  the branch of *philosophy* that studies right conduct and character; includes *normative ethics* and *metaethics*

**excluded middle, principle (law) of**  the principle that, with regard to a particular proposition, either it or its negation must be true; also called *tertium non datur* (Latin, "a third [possibility] is not given")

**existentialism**  a school of *philosophy* that holds that human beings create their own nature by their free choices

**fallacy**  an *argument* with an incorrect *inference*

**final cause**  that for the sake of which something exists or is produced or done (contrasted with *efficient cause*)

**foundationalism**  the doctrine that knowledge consists of basic beliefs known immediately, and of facts inferred from these beliefs

**functionalism**  the doctrine that mental states can be defined by the role they play (their function) in an organism

**genus**   (plural *genera*) a broad class or kind, composed of *species*

**hard determinism**   see *determinism*

**hedonism**   see *ethical hedonism* and *psychological hedonism*

**homunculus**   (plural *homunculi*)  miniature human beings postulated to exist inside human beings, as a way to explain psychological processes

**hypothetical syllogism**   a *syllogism* whose *premises* are a hypothetical (if-then) statement and a statement that affirms or denies one part of the hypothetical statement

**idealism**   the theory that only mental entities are real (contrasted with *materialism*)

**ignoratio elenchi**   [Latin, "ignorance of refutation"]  the *fallacy* of trying to establish or refute a claim by proposing an *argument* that is beside the point

**indeterminism**   the doctrine that some events are not determined by causes (contrasted with *determinism*)

**indexical**   having a reference dependent on the circumstance in which an expression is uttered

**induction**   the *inference* of a general conclusion from particular cases

**inductive argument**   an *argument* that claims to lead from the *premises* to the *conclusion* in a probable way (contrasted with *deductive argument*)

**inference**   the mental process of moving from the *premises* of an *argument* to the *conclusion*

**instrumental good**   something that is desired as a means (an instrument, a tool) to something else (contrasted with *intrinsic good*)

**intentionality**   the property that a mental state has of pointing to something, of being about something

**interactionism**   the doctrine that the mind and body causally interact

**intrinsic good**   something that is good in itself, desired for its own sake (contrasted with *instrumental good*)

**intuitionism**   in *ethics,* the doctrine that rightness and wrongness of certain actions can be known immediately, without a reasoning process

**invalid argument**   a *deductive argument* in which the *conclusion* does not follow necessarily from the *premises* (contrasted with *valid argument*)

**is-ought problem**   the problem of how one can derive statements of value ("ought" statements) from statements of fact ("is" statements)

**jus ad bellum**   [Latin "the right to go to war"]  the part of *just war theory* that specifies the conditions required to morally justify the act of going to war

**jus in bello**  [Latin "right conduct within war"]  the part of *just war theory* that specifies the necessary conditions for morally justifiable conduct during war

**just war theory**  the doctrine that initiating a war and performing certain kinds of acts during war are morally justified if certain conditions are met

**lex talionis**  [Latin, "law of retaliation"]  the law that retribution should be equivalent to the offense

**libertarianism**  the doctrine that human beings have free will and that either some human actions not determined by preceding causes, or that some human actions are not determined by any cause except the person as a whole (contrasted with *determinism*)

**logic**  the branch of *philosophy* that systematically studies correct and incorrect *inferences*

**materialism**  the theory that only material entities are real (contrasted with *idealism*)

**maya**  in Hinduism, the sense-world of phenomena as an illusion created by *Brahman*

**mechanism**  the doctrine that living things can be explained completely by physics and chemistry

**metaethics**  the study of the meaning, nature, and justification of ethical terms, concepts, and judgments (contrasted with *normative ethics*)

**metaphysics**  the branch of *philosophy* that studies the nature and kinds of reality; also called *ontology*

**middle term**  in *logic*, that which connects two elements and allows one to make an inference about the relation of those elements

**mind-body problem**  the problem of explaining how the mind (soul, self) and body are related and can interact, if they are two fundamentally different kinds of reality

**modern philosophy**  the period of Western philosophy from approximately the seventeenth through the nineteenth centuries

**monism**  in *metaphysics*, the doctrine that there is only one kind of ultimate reality (contrasted with *pluralism*)

**moral argument**  in the *philosophy of religion*, an argument that the nature or experience of morality proves that God exists

**moral certainty**  a very high degree of probability, but not absolute certainty

**naturalism**  the view that nature is all that exists, and that nothing supernatural exists

**naturalistic fallacy** the alleged mistake of identifying ethical goodness with a "natural" object

**natural law** a set of moral directives claimed to be derived from the nature of the universe in general, or from human nature in particular

**natural theology** the study of truths about God that can be known by reflecting on nature (contrasted with *revealed theology*)

**neopositivism** a revised, twentieth-century version of *positivism*

**nominalism** the doctrine that only individual entities are real, and that no realties correspond to general concepts or terms

**nomological dangler** an entity that does not fit in with the accepted laws of science

**noncogent argument** an *inductive argument* that is *weak* and/or has one or more false *premises* (contrasted with *cogent argument*)

**non sequitur** [Latin, "it does not follow"] an inference that does not follow from its premise(s)

**normative ethics** the study of the norms (standards, criteria) for right conduct and character (contrasted with *metaethics*)

**noumenon** (plural *noumena*) a thing as it exists in itself, independently of any mind apprehending it (contrasted with *phenomenon*)

**occasionalism** the doctrine that mental and bodily events do not causally affect each other, but that on the occasion of a mental event God produces a corresponding bodily effect, and vice versa

**Ockham's razor** (*Occam's razor*) the principle that entities are not to be multiplied beyond necessity

**ontological argument** the *argument* that the very concept or definition of God implies that God exists (contrasted with *cosmological argument*)

**ontology** synonym for *metaphysics*

**performative** relating to an expression that, by its utterance, brings about what it says

**petitio principii** [Latin, "assuming a principle"] the *fallacy* of assuming what one is attempting to prove; also called *begging the question*

**phenomenology** the study of how things appear to and are experienced by a knowing subject

**phenomenon** (plural *phenomena*) the appearance or manifestation of a thing to a knowing subject (contrasted with *noumenon*)

**philosophy**   the search for wisdom regarding fundamental questions about the universe and about human existence

**philosophy of religion**   the philosophical study of religious belief

**physicalism**   the doctrine that all mental states are ultimately physical in nature

**pluralism**   in *metaphysics,* the doctrine that there two or more kinds of ultimate reality (contrasted with *monism*)

**positivism**   the doctrine that the only source of genuine knowledge is empirical science

**post hoc ergo propter hoc**   [Latin, "after this, therefore because of this"] the *fallacy* of assuming that one thing is caused by another because it occurs after it

**postmodernism**   a set of reactions against the suppositions of *modern philosophy,* especially the supposition that objective, certain knowledge is possible

**pragmatism**   the doctrine that the function of thought is to guide action and that the meaning of concepts and the truth of ideas lie in their practical usefulness

**preestablished harmony**   the doctrine that things in the universe affect each other not directly but only indirectly, in the sense that God took the action of each thing into account when constructing the universe

**premise**   in *logic,* a statement in an *argument* used to establish a *conclusion*

**prima facie**   [Latin, "at first glance"] on first appearance; a *prima facie right* or *prima facie obligation* is a right or obligation that holds unless overridden by another, stronger right or obligation

**primary qualities**   physical qualities inherent in objects, such as three-dimensionality, shape, size, and motion (contrasted with *secondary qualities*)

**prime matter**   matter devoid of all forms

**non contradiction, principle (law) of**   the principle that a thing cannot both be and not be at the same time and in the same respect

**problem of evil**   in the philosophy of religion, the problem of how an all-good and all-powerful God can allow evil to exist in the world

**psychological egoism**   the doctrine every human action is motivated ultimately by self-interest (contrasted with *ethical egoism*)

**psychological hedonism**   the doctrine that every human action is motivated ultimately by the desire for pleasure, and that things other than pleasure are desired simply as means to pleasure (contrasted with *ethical hedonism*)

**psychophysical parallelism**  the theory that every event in the mind occurs simultaneously with an event in the body, and vice versa, but that there is no causal interaction between mind and body

**quale**  (plural *qualia*) [Latin, "something of such a kind"]  a qualitative property of conscious experience, such as the experience of red

**quietism**  the attitude of being passive, of not getting involved

**real definition**  a definition that states the essential properties of a thing

**rationalism**  the doctrine that knowledge is attained primarily through the mind (innate ideas, intuition, relations among ideas, logical inference, and so on) (contrasted with *empiricism*)

**realism**  in *metaphysics*, the doctrine that objects of perception or knowledge exist independently of the mind

**reductio ad absurdum**  [Latin, "a leading back to the absurd"]  the refutation of a proposition by showing that it logically leads to an absurd conclusion

**reductionism**  the doctrine that one kind of thing can be "reduced to" (explained fully in terms of) another kind of thing—for example, that the mind can be explained fully in terms of the brain

**relativism**  the doctrine that truth and knowledge in a particular area are relative to (conditioned by) the knower. One form of relativism is *cultural relativism.*

**revealed theology**  the study of truths about God made known through divine revelation (contrasted with *natural theology*)

**rule utilitarianism**  see *utilitarianism*

**scholasticism**  a medieval approach to *philosophy* that emphasized commentaries on classic texts

**secondary qualities**  powers that physical objects have of producing in us, under certain conditions, sensory experiences such as color, taste, and smell (contrasted with *primary qualities*)

**semantics**  the study of the meaning of symbols, especially the meaning of words

**skepticism**  the doctrine that we cannot attain certainty in knowledge

**slippery slope**  in *logic,* an *argument* claming that if a particular event occurs, another and less desirable event will occur, followed by a third and even less desirable event, and so on, culminating in a thoroughly undesirable state of affairs

**social contract**  a hypothetical or actual voluntary agreement that people make to form a political society

**Socratic method**   see *dialectical method*

**soft determinism**   see *determinism*

**sophism**   a plausible but incorrect *argument* intended to deceive

**Sophists**   a class of teachers in ancient Greece who emphasized rhetoric as a means to successful living

**sound argument**   a *deductive argument* that is *valid* and has all true *premises* (contrasted with *unsound argument*)

**species**   (plural *species*) a class or kind that is a part of a *genus*

**state of nature**   the condition of human life before the formation of political society

**Stoicism**   a school of ancient *philosophy* that held that inner tranquillity is achieved by accordance with nature

**straw man**   a position that is unfairly interpreted so it can be easily refuted

**strong argument**   an *inductive argument* in which the *conclusion* follows probably from the *premises*, whether or not the premises are true (contrasted with *weak argument*)

**substance**   something that can exist by itself and possesses *accidents*

**supererogation**   doing more than required by duty or obligation

**supervenient property**   a property that occurs as a result of some other property (or properties) but cannot be reduced to it (or them)

**syllogism**   a *deductive argument* consisting of two *premises* and a *conclusion*

**synthetic statement**   a statement in which the predicate adds something to the subject (contrasted with *analytic statement*)

**tautology**   a statement that is necessarily true because of the meaning of the words

**tertium non datur**   [Latin, "a third (possibility) is not given"] the principle that, with regard to a particular proposition, either it or its negation must be true; also called the *principle (law) of the excluded middle*

**theodicy**   a defense of God as all-good and all-powerful, despite the existence of evil in the world

**teleological argument**   an *argument* that God must exist because things in nature act for a goal, or because the universe as a whole shows design

**teleology**   the study of the goals or purposes of things; the doctrine that things can be explained in terms of their goals or purposes

**token**   a member of category; an instance of a type

**underdetermined**  able to be accounted for by a principle or theory other than the one proposed

**universal**  a reality corresponding to a general concept or term

**univocal**  having only one meaning (contrasted with *equivocal*)

**unsound argument**  a *deductive argument* that is *invalid* and/or has one or more false *premises* (contrasted with *sound argument*)

**utilitarianism**  the ethical doctrine that one should always act in a way that maximizes "utility," which is understood as the greatest good for the greatest number. According to *act utilitarianism*, one should perform the *act* that maximizes utility in a particular situation; according to *rule utilitarianism*, one should follow the rule that, when generally followed, maximizes utility—even if following the rule in a particular situation does not maximize utility. Utilitarianism is a form of *consequentialism*, since it specifies utility as the consequence that determines the morality of an action.

**valid argument**  a *deductive argument* in which the *conclusion* follows necessarily from the *premises*, whether or not the premise are true (contrasted with *invalid argument*)

**virtue ethics**  the ethical doctrine that the virtue of the agent is the primary factor in morality (contrasted with *consequentialism* and with *deontology*)

**vitalism**  the doctrine that living things possess a nonmaterial life-force

**voluntarism**  the doctrine that reason is subordinate to the will

**weak argument**  an *inductive argument* in which the *conclusion* does not follow probably from the *premises* (contrasted with *strong argument*)